'*The Clash of Fundamentalisms* is well worth read[...] the harshest critics of fundamentalism are ofter[...] fundamentalism.' **John Gray,** *Independent*

'Ali writes lucidly, interweaving his political history with passages from the literature of many Muslim countries, making *The Clash of Fundamentalisms* a compelling point of departure for further study of the culture and politics of Islam.' *Village Voice*

'. . . the current antiwar movement would benefit from his historical perspective, ideological clarity, and humour.' *San Francisco Bay Guardian*

'Ali's own writing is lucid, not at all dogmatic, consistently humorous and rational, and in both style and content demonstrates an alternative to the texts of the twin fundamentalisms.' *Scotsman*

'. . . readers . . . will find here much important material that is not easily available elsewhere.' **Hugh Montefiore,** *Church Times*

The Clash of Fundamentalisms

By the same author

The Clash of Fundamentalisms

Crusades, Jihads and Modernity

TARIQ ALI

VERSO

London • New York

First published by Verso 2002
© Tariq Ali 2002
Paperback edition first published by Verso 2003
© Tariq Ali 2003

1 3 5 7 9 10 8 6 4 2

Verso
UK: 6 Meard Street, London W1F 0EG
USA: 180 Varick Street, New York NY 10014–4606
www.versobooks.com

Verso is the imprint of New Left Books

ISBN 1–85984–457–X

British Library Cataloguing in Publication Data
A catalogue record for this book is
available from the British Library

Library of Congress Cataloging-in-Publication Data
A catalog record for this book is
available from the Library of Congress

Typeset in Bembo by M Rules
Printed in the UK by Biddles Ltd,
in the USA by R. R. Donnelley & Sons
and in Australia by Griffin Press

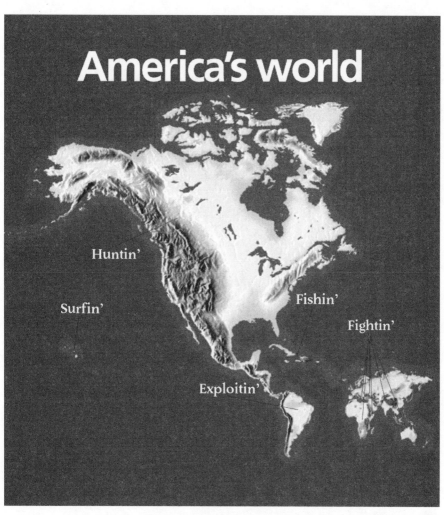

America's world

Huntin'

Surfin'

Fishin'

Fightin'

Exploitin'

For
Tahira

Contents

Acknowledgements

For the last fifteen years while working on my novels – 'the Islam Quintet' – I've been thinking of mullahs and heretics and the bulging vein of dissent and eroticism in the history of Islam. This book was going to be titled 'Mullahs and Heretics', but the first half of the title, without my permission, decided to create mayhem in New York and Washington on 11 September 2001. I decided that a slightly different book was needed. It was no longer sufficient to discuss the petrified memory of Islamic fundamentalists. An important question had been raised in public by the US President, George W. Bush, even though his own answer was slightly unconvincing. At a press conference on 12 October 2001, the leader of 273 million American people stated: 'How do I respond when I see that in some Islamic countries there is vitriolic hatred for America? I'll tell you how I respond: I'm amazed. I just can't believe it because I know how good we are.'

This is a fundamental belief shared by a large number of US citizens. Nor is it unusual. Powerful empires in previous centuries have never understood the wrath of their subjects. Why should the American Empire be any different? This book is an attempt to explain why much of the world doesn't see the Empire as 'good'. In the clash between a religous fundamentalism – itself the product of modernity – and an imperial fundamentalism determined to 'discipline the world', it is necessary to oppose both and create a space in the world of Islam and the West in which freedom of thought and imagination can be defended without fear of persecution or death.

While this book was still being written, two extracts appeared in the *London Review of Books*, whose redoubtable deputy editor Jean McNicol will not be pleased at my re-inserting the 'pencil of creation' which she had so carefully withdrawn from the 'Story of Kashmir'. A shorter piece on Iraq apppeared as an editorial in the *New Left Review.*

My thanks to Professor Tarif Khalidi at Cambridge for reading and commenting on a section on early Islamic history and to Mehdi Kia of the *Iran Bulletin* for doing the same on the chapter on Iran. Neither of them should be held responsible for my assertions.

At Verso thanks are due to Jane Hindle, Tim Clark, Steve Cox, Fiona Price, Gavin Everall, Niels Hooper and Peter Hinton for ensuring a swift production.

Tariq Ali
January 2003

Introduction to the Paperback Edition

For the person sitting in darkness somewhere in the United States

The world only goes forward because of those who oppose it.
Goethe

Since this book was first published, the consequences of 11 September 2001 have remained visible on several fronts. My argument that the most dangerous 'fundamentalism' today – the 'mother of all fundamentalisms' is American imperialism – has been amply vindicated over the last eighteen months. What is obvious is that the leaders of the United States wish to be judged by their choice of enemies rather than the actual state of the world. Psychologically, the American Empire has constructed a new enemy: Islamic terrorism. Its practitioners are evil, the threat is global and, for that reason, bombs have to be dropped wherever and whenever necessary. Politically, the United States decided early on to use the tragedy as a moral lever to re-map the world. Militarily, its bases now cover every continent. There is a US military presence in 120 of the 189 member states of the United Nations. Domestically, the Bush administration covered up the deteriorating situation of the US economy with the so-called security threat. A series of special measures were enacted, whose principal object was to ensure obedience to the dictates of the CBR (Cheney–Bush–Rumsfeld) White House. CBR sought and obtained extensive new powers to make war abroad while detaining and deporting suspects, mainly Arabs and South Asians, at will.

THE CLASH OF FUNDAMENTALISMS

The Tweedledum–Tweedledee character of official politics was further highlighted by the failure of the Democrats to mount even the most limited opposition to these measures. Instead, the craven rhetoric deployed by the former First Lady, Hillary Rodham Clinton (her husband exiled to the Convent of Repentance) and the former vice-presidential nominee, Jo Lieberman, was aimed at outflanking CBR from the Right.★ All this, assisted by the pusillanimity of a neutered media, unleashed a frenzy of reaction in the country at large. Dissent was labelled as 'anti-patriotic' and 'patriots' in the academy were encouraged to spy on and report students who expressed anti-patriotic views. This in turn generated a modest opposition, which began to grow as people realized the extent to which CBR had manipulated the events of 11 September to impose a traditional far-right Republican agenda on the whole United States.

Meanwhile, preparations for an all-out war against and the occupation of an independent Arab state, Iraq, appear to have reached the final stage without any real opposition in the Senate or the House of Representatives. Some 150,000 troops are in a state of readiness in the countries surrounding Iraq. The Pentagon is boasting that this will be the 'greatest precision-bombing aerial assault in history.' State Department sponsored Iraqi exiles speak openly of an acceptable casualty rate: 250,000. And there is no danger of any US politician or military commander being charged with war crimes, since the Empire situates itself above international law. Simultaneously military operations in Afghanistan are costing a billion dollars each month – compared to the $25 million a month the US claims it's spending on humanitarian aid, which is either feeding local corruption or being used to pay the maintenance costs of foreign aid workers. And armoured terminators drive or fly past the hundreds of thousands of homeless peasants trying to survive the winter. The media circus has long departed and their plight is of no concern to those who once eagerly supported this war.

In this brave new world of infinite war it is hardly a surprise that the Pentagon budget will increase by $38 billion to almost $400 billion in 2003.

★ Al Gore, the former vice president, was the only senior Democrat to warn against a war in Iraq, and the growing economic crisis, but this was not in the script. He was forced to withdraw from the presidential contest. Why? Because big money was not forthcoming. His liberalism could not be cashed in a marketplace dominated by friends of Israel desperate for a war in Iraq.

The increase alone is practically the entire budget of the second-biggest military spender, China. Despite a great deal of unease within the American and European politico-military establishments and the outright opposition of a majority of citizens in most parts of the world, the war is, barring unforeseen circumstances, likely to go ahead. None of the Articles embodied in the Charter of the United Nations can justify this war, but legal niceties have rarely bothered the post-Cold War Security Council, which has rarely stood up against the demands and needs of the United States.

Why is the current regime in the United States so determined to wage this war? There are three major considerations. The first is that Iraq, a rich oil producer, remains outside the control of the United States. The second is the size of Iraq's army – it is now the only force in the region that could threaten Greater Israel. And thirdly there is the domestic agenda. To wean the pro-Zionist Jews away from the Democrats is an important tactical goal and the Christian fundamentalists of the Republican Party make no secret of their unflinching support for every Israeli atrocity. After all, the Old Testament decrees that the Land of Israel belongs to the Jews.

The months that followed the first anniversary of 11 September were dominated by the dynamic of two interrelated developments: preparation for war on Iraq and the deterioration of the economy. The interaction of these two will decide the shape of the global conjuncture over the next few years. The great thinker-president and his hard-core advisers appear to have broken decisively from the Clinton cant of the 1990s: American supremacy plus allied support plus permanent deregulation equals global governance accompanied by a flatulent Third Way rhetoric. This formula appears to have been ditched. Leaving aside the moral question as to why an unjust war would become just if backed by the UN Security Council, it is perfectly possible for the United States to secure such support to invade Iraq. The French and Russians will be bribed and the Chinese offered some minor concessions on Taiwan to secure their vote or an abstention. But Cheney and Rumsfeld clearly regard these methods as abhorrent. They know perfectly well that Anglo-American bombing raids of Iraq over the last fifteen years have bypassed the Security Council with impunity. They are the leaders of the world's only Empire and in the unlikely case of a Security Council veto they will behave accordingly.

Ever since the US Supreme Court sanctioned CBR's election victory, the control of the world's oil seems to have absorbed the whole energy of the American state. This is the principal reason for the war against Iraq. All the talk of 'weapons of mass destruction' consists of fairy tales designed to frighten the children/citizens at home and in Western Europe. Few in Europe believe that Iraq poses a threat to any other country. The 1980s was the last period during which it used chemical weapons against Iran and its own Kurdish population and those weapons had been supplied by the United States. Ronald Reagan had despatched a special envoy to Baghdad to signal the approval of the White House, a Mr Donald Rumsfeld, currently in charge of the Pentagon.

And while many US apologists in the European press fervently deny that this is a war over oil, rather than one which will 'bring democracy', their counterparts in the United States suffer from no such delusions. Here is the unabashed Thomas Friedman, the US media's top running-dog, refusing to draw a complete veil over reality:

> Is the war that the Bush team is preparing to launch in Iraq really a war for oil? My short answer is yes. Any war we launch in Iraq will certainly be – in part – about oil. To deny that is laughable. . . . I say this possible Iraq war is partly about oil because it is impossible to explain the Bush team's behaviour otherwise. Why are they going after Saddam Hussein with the 82nd Airborne and North Korea with diplomatic kid gloves – when North Korea already has nuclear weapons, the missiles to deliver them, a record of selling dangerous weapons to anyone with cash, 100,000 US troops in its missile range and a leader who is even more cruel to his people than Saddam?★

Does this mean that Mr Friedman is opposed to such a war? Abandon the thought: 'I have no problem with a war for oil – if we accompany it with a real program for energy conservation.' Was this particular column aimed at drawing the German Greens into a war against Iraq? If so, the inducement was unnecessary. Few of their debased leaders require promises of 'energy conservation'. They are willing and happy to be part of any bloody circus as long as 'humanitarian' promises are made in advance.

★ Thomas L. Friedman, 'A War for Oil?', New York Times, 5 January 2003.

In reality Friedman did not need to stray as far as East Asia to discover a rogue state that is currently far more dangerous than Iraq. There is a perfectly good example of one in the Middle East and not so far from Iraq. This is a country that regularly invades neighbouring states, defies UN Security Council Resolutions, occupies territories that it was not legally permitted to steal, treats the inhabitants of these territories as if they were *Untermensch* and possesses an arsenal of nuclear and chemical weapons. Israel, however, is the great untouchable of American politics. After 11 September, both Congress and the Senate agreed resolutions giving the Israeli regime a blank cheque approving all its future actions in advance, a prize never awarded to their own presidents. The result of all this is a tame US media which barely reports the daily sufferings of the Palestinians. There is more critical coverage of Israeli actions in the Israeli press than in the United States.

Nor is it the case that the Arab regimes are spared the rod of criticism in their own countries. It is not easy for the Saudi monarchy or the Egyptian president to publicly support a war against Iraq. They, like Syria and the Israeli protectorate of Jordan, will do nothing to stop it, but there is much nervousness in the Arab world: street and palace do not want a new oil war. In Cairo and Abu Dhabi, the two Arab capitals I have visited since 11 September, I met nobody in favour of a pre-emptive strike against Saddam Hussein on the grounds that he might, at some point in the future, authorise the production of nuclear weapons. The whole Arab world sees this as a classic display of imperial double-standards. They know that the only country which possesses both nuclear and chemical weapons is Israel. Arab public opinion has not been so united for decades. And a cable television station, al-Jazeera ('the Peninsula'), has played a crucial part in both promoting and symbolising this unity. It has raised mass consciousness in the region by providing at the same time a ruthless analysis of what is wrong with the Arab world.

Unity was the recurring theme of the nationalist period of Arab political history. First there was Nasser and his dream of a united Arab republic. Then defeat in war. Then the laments of exiled poets – Nizar Qabbani from Syria, Mahmoud Darwish from Palestine and Muthaffar al-Nawab from Iraq. The Egyptian diva Um Kalthoum sang their poetry and was revered. Then darkness. The 1991 Gulf War demoralised and atomised the Arab world. Secular dissenters continued to meet in the cafés of Damascus, Baghdad, Beirut and Cairo, but could speak only in whispers. Elsewhere, mosques became the organising centres for a confessional resistance to the New Order and the Great Satan that underpinned it.

The state media networks continued to broadcast propaganda of the crudest kind; criticism of government was unheard of. Then, in 1996, al-Jazeera arrived, a TV news channel that defies taboos and prohibitions. Arab viewers abandoned the state networks overnight and al-Jazeera's newsreaders and talk-show hosts became instant celebrities.

Nothing like this had been witnessed since the early 1960s, when nationalist radio stations in Cairo, Baghdad and Damascus issued daily incitements to listeners to topple every crowned head in the region. The Jordanian king was nearly overthrown and the Saudi monarchy seriously destabilised. In both countries Western aid helped to crush the nationalist revolts. Al-Jazeera has no such ambitions: the men running the channel are only too aware that a crowned head, the eccentric emir of Qatar, provides the funds and the headquarters for their operation. The emir has also allowed the US to construct the largest military base in the region, which boasts a recently completed 13,000-foot runway to handle heavy bombers. Iraq will no doubt be attacked from this base while on al-Jazeera commentators denounce US aggression. Or will they?

The idea of a semi-independent Arab TV network was first suggested by BBC World Service journalists and supported by the Foreign Office. A deal was signed with Orbit Radio and Television Service to provide a news programme in Arabic for Orbit's Middle East channel. But Orbit was Saudi-owned, and its financiers were unwilling to allow news bulletins critical of the Saudi kingdom. The project collapsed in April 1996 after footage of a public execution was broadcast. The BBC retired hurt and the Arab journalists who had been made redundant began to search for a new home. They were lucky. Their quest coincided with a change of rulers in the tiny state of Qatar.

In 1995, his son, Hamad bin Khalifa al-Thani, who promised to modernise the statelet, deposed the old emir, a traditionalist. Starting with a dramatic gesture, he abolished the Ministry of Information. When informed of the collapse of the BBC venture, he offered the journalists a headquarters in Doha and $140 million to restart operations. Sheikh Hamad's father and grandfather had together owned 452 cars, including ones hand-built for them. A TV station must have seemed cheap by comparison, and has given the sheikhdom more visibility and prestige than it has ever had. Encouraged by the response to his action, Hamad allowed women to vote and to stand as candidates against men in municipal elections in 1999. This was a shot across the Saudi bows and was recognised as such.

Virtually none of the journalists who came to work for the new channel was a local. The Syrian-born Faisal al-Kasim, al-Jazeera's most controversial host and now one of the most respected journalists in the Arab world, studied drama at Hull and spent a decade as the anchor of the BBC's Arabic Service. His show, 'The Opposite Direction', features political debates and confrontations conducted with an intensity rarely seen on Western networks. When I met him in Abu Dhabi he had just finished an interview with the local paper and was fending off other journalists and well-wishers. I asked whether the complaints about his show had started to drop away: 'They never stop,' he replied. 'People can't believe that I choose the guests and the subjects. No authority has ever tried to influence or censor me and I have much more freedom than I ever did at the BBC.'

In the early days, the Qatari government received at least one official complaint about the channel every day from fellow Arab governments – five hundred in the first year alone. Gaddafi withdrew his ambassador from Qatar after the station broadcast an interview with a Libyan opposition leader; Iraq complained when the channel revealed the amount of money that had been spent on Saddam Hussein's birthday celebrations; Tunisia was angry at having been accused of human rights violations; Iranian newspapers resented 'slurs' against Ayatollah Khomeini; Algeria cut off the electricity in several cities to prevent its citizens from watching a programme that accused its army of complicity in several massacres; Arafat objected to Hamas leaders being interviewed; and Hamas was angered by the appearance of Israeli politicians and generals on 'The Opposite Direction'. In 2003, an al-Jazeera correspondent in Gaza was arrested by the Palestinian Authority for speaking out of turn.

The Saudi and Egyptian governments were enraged at criticisms made by dissidents on al-Jazeera. As loyal allies, both countries have had a relatively good press in the West. Before 11 September it required the death of a Westerner in Saudi Arabia to focus attention on the kingdom, but the furore never lasted long. Over the last decade, the Saudis have spent hundreds of millions of pounds to keep Western and Arab media empires and their employees on side, and al-Jazeera's broadsides were viewed as treachery. Riyadh and Cairo put massive pressure on Qatar to muzzle the station, but the emir ignored the protests and his government denied that the channel was the instrument of Qatari foreign policy.

During its early years, al-Jazeera was warmly welcomed in Washington and Jerusalem. Thomas Friedman celebrated the birth of the station with a bucketful of praise: it marked, he said, the dawn of Arab freedom. Ehud Ya'ari was similarly warm two years ago in the *Jerusalem Report*: 'Out of a modest, low-rise prefab, five minutes' drive from the Emir's diwan, the tiny Sheikhdom of Qatar is now producing a commodity much in demand in the Arab world: freedom.' The channel's 'powerful video signals', he continued, 'are gradually changing the cultural and political order in the Middle East.'

September 11 put a stop to these eulogies, especially after al-Jazeera broadcast interviews with Osama bin Laden and his Egyptian deputy, al-Zawahiri. The bin Laden interviews were banned on Western television on the spurious grounds that they might contain coded instructions for future terrorist hits. In fact, it was because bin Laden's soft features undermined the media's portrayal of him as evil incarnate.

Qatar now came under very heavy pressure to do something about al-Jazeera. Maureen Quinn, the US ambassador, delivered a strongly worded complaint to the Foreign Minister. It had little impact. In October, Colin Powell was sent to browbeat the emir, who once again defended the freedom of the press and stressed that the state could not interfere with what he described as a 'private commercial operation'. US officials who met al-Jazeera executives were heard politely and told that the channel would be delighted to interview the American president or his nominees: Condoleezza Rice, Tony Blair and Colin Powell were allowed unlimited time to explain their points of view. To say that the effect of these broadcasts on Arab public opinion was negligible would be an exaggeration.

When the bombing of Afghanistan began, al-Jazeera was the only TV network sending out regular reports. And so began its dazzling ascent. Its footage was eagerly sought, bought, carefully edited and shown on CNN, BBC and every major European network. Then the building in Kabul it was using as a temporary studio was bombed, just as a BBC journalist using its facilities had begun to broadcast a live report. He hit the floor and we witnessed the 'accidental bombing' live on our TV screens. When NATO forces targeted a Belgrade TV station in 1999, Clinton and Blair admitted the bombing was deliberate, and justified it on the grounds that 'deliberate misinformation' was being broadcast. Qatar could hardly be categorised as an enemy and so the spin doctors were far more careful when it came to explaining the bombing in Kabul: the building was targeted, they claimed, because of 'reports' that it had housed al-Qaida suspects, and they hadn't known that it was al-Jazeera's base.

It is on the second front of the 'war against terror', however, that al-Jazeera's coverage has made the most significant impact. After Israeli tanks entered Nablus in one of their many incursions since 11 September, the channel broadcast a story about the following incident (the description here comes from LAW, a Palestinian human rights organisation): Khaled Sif (41), who is married and has four children, received a call on his cellular phone. In order to get a better signal he went to the balcony. The moment he stood at the balcony, Israeli forces shot him in the head and killed him. After he heard the shot, Muhammad Faroniya, who is married and has six children, walked to the balcony. Israeli forces opened fire and also shot Muhammad Faroniya, wounding him in his chest and abdomen. Mahmoud Faroniya, Muhammad's brother, tried to save his brother, but Israeli forces pointed their guns at him and he was prevented from doing so. Muhammad bled to death. According to eyewitnesses, Israeli forces deliberately left Muhammad Faroniya bleeding for ninety minutes.

The daily coverage on al-Jazeera of stories such as this one stands in contrast to what is shown in Europe, let alone the United States. CNN established its reputation during the Gulf War through the work of its correspondent Peter Arnett, who remained in Baghdad and whose reports of civilian casualties and the bombing of non-military targets enraged the US, with the result that Western governments are now much more careful to control access to information during times of conflict. They also try hard to stop anyone else covering the stories they are trying to suppress.

Having failed to curb al-Jazeera's influence, however, the US is now going to try to mimic its success. With a war in Iraq seemingly imminent there are plans to launch a satellite channel in Arabic funded by the US Information Service, to which can be added the expertise of CNN and BBC World. The Israelis have already launched their own version, with little effect. The notion that the Arabs are brainwashed and all that is needed to set them right is regular doses of Bush and Blair is to ignore every reality of the region. But the plot is far advanced.

'What will they name their channel?' I asked Faisal al-Kasim. 'The Empire?'

'No,' he said, 'they have a name for it already. Al-Haqiqat.'

That translates neatly into Russian as Pravda.

There is however a new possibility. Once CBR succeeds in occupying Iraq, there will be no need for Pravda. With a few adjustments, the harsh Voice of Baghdad will become the sweet Voice of America.

There is no support for this war anywhere in the Arab world. A near-universal view is that if waged and won, far from being seen as deterrence, it would greatly facilitate the growth of mass support for terrorist groups. Many Arab intellectuals see Israel as the biblical ass whose jaw has been borrowed by an American Samson to destroy the real and imagined enemies of the Empire. There is also a popular perception that the opening of a 'third front' in the infinite war could have far more serious consequences than the shenanigans in Afghanistan, which have already destabilised South Asia and Saudi Arabia. The consequences of invading an oil-rich Arab state to create a puppet regime are not quantifiable.

What is the balance sheet of the 'war against terror'? With the help of its Pakistani creators, the Taliban regime was overthrown without a serious struggle, though approximately three thousand innocent Afghan men, women and children perished under the bombs. For the West, these lives meant nothing compared to those of the US citizens who died in New York and Washington. No memorials honouring innocent victims will be built in Kabul. The torture and mass execution of prisoners of war leaves many liberal supporters of 'humanitarian wars' unmoved. However, despite all this, the central aim of the military operation, which was the capture ('dead or alive') of Osama bin Laden and his confederates and the physical destruction of al-Qaida, has still not been accomplished. On 16 June 2002, the *New York Times* reported: 'Classified investigations of the Qaida threat now underway at the FBI and CIA have concluded that the war in Afghanistan failed to diminish the threat to the United States, the officials said. Instead the war might have complicated counter terrorism efforts by dispersing potential attackers across a wider geographic area.'

Nor has the imperialist occupation of Afghanistan led to stability, peace or prosperity in the region. The character of the Afghan government is symbolised by the fact that the US-backed leader, Hamid Karzai, asked and received a bodyguard consisting exclusively of US soldiers. He did not feel safe guarded by Afghans belonging to his own tribe. The lack of trust is mutual. The factions of the Northern Alliance who rule outside Kabul dislike Karzai and would despatch him overnight if they could do so without incurring retaliatory bombing raids. To preserve this regime the United States will have to maintain a permanent military presence. In other words democracy and human and social rights are as remote as they have been for a very long time in Afghanistan.

The 'wider geographical area' includes neighbouring Pakistan. Washington's closest ally is the country's newest military dictator. On 19 September 2001, General Pervaiz Musharraf went on TV to inform the people of Pakistan that their country would be standing – or rather flying – shoulder to shoulder with the United States in its bombardment of Afghanistan. Visibly pale, blinking and sweating, he looked like a man who had just signed his own death warrant; indeed since then there have been two attempts on his life. Moreover, in October 2002 the Islamists were elected to office in the two Pakistani provinces bordering Afghanistan.★

While the 'war against terror' has destabilised South Asia, it has buttressed Israel still further. If the United States had been serious in its oft-stated desire to stop the flow of recruits to organisations like al-Qaida, it would have concentrated on ending the occupation of Palestine. Ariel Sharon has been supported by Bush, Cheney and Rumsfeld in his attempt to obliterate the political identity of the Palestinians – what a dissident Israeli historian, Baruch Kimmerling, has referred to as 'politicide'. The blank cheque given to Israel by the US Senate and the House of Representatives is without precedent in recent history. The result has been spectacular. Since September 2001 over 100,000 Palestinian refugees have fled to Jordan. Sharon does not even try and conceal the fact that his aim is a major ethnic cleansing ('transfer') of the Palestinians from the West Bank. Gaza will be transformed into a modern equivalent of an Indian reservation. This he is pursuing with direct physical force and by making everyday life unbearable for the Palestinians living in the

---

★ I have added a new chapter, 'The Colour Khaki', to explain the impact of this on Pakistani politics and its domination by the military. See pp. 253–278.

Occupied Territories. Even if these plans succeed, the notion that they will help defeat 'terrorism' is a sick joke. The brutal punishment being inflicted on the Palestinians for refusing to accept Israeli suzerainty can be seen every day by the entire Arab world on al-Jazeera television. Until now the Arabs have watched and suffered in silence, but this passivity is deceptive. There is growing anger and signs of unrest in every capital, and there have been large demonstrations in Saudi Arabia and Egypt. The region could erupt if the 'war against terror' is extended to Iraq.

And then there is Colonel Putin's very own 'war against terror' in Chechnya. Here is a textbook case of a small nation being denied rights granted to former members of the Soviet Union. If Kyrgistan, the Ukraine, Belarus, Georgia, Armenia and Azerbaijan have the right to become independent market-states, why not Chechnya? Partly because of oil and partly because of Great-Russian chauvinism, deployed by a weak and corrupt layer of politicians to maintain their grip on the country. The destruction of Chechnya is much worse than anything that happened in Kosovo before or after NATO's war against Yugoslavia. The Chechen capital, Grozny, home to both Chechens and Russians, has been razed to the ground. Schools, hospitals, libraries and homes are now shells. Civilian casualties number 15,000 at least, if not double that figure. Desperate Chechen nationalists drawing attention to their cause by acts of terror are shot dead after chemical weapons have been used to disable them. Many Russian hostages were killed by the use of chemical weapons deployed by their own government to 'protect' them from the terrorists. And in this upside-down, amoral world, Putin receives public support from big Bush and little Blair. Shoulder-to-shoulder in the 'war against terror'.

In the wake of 11 September, the United States won near-universal support from states and governments and Western intellectuals when it went to war in Afghanistan. This unanimity, dented by disagreements on Palestine, is now confronting serious problems as the time for a new war against Iraq approaches. Here, unlike Bosnia, Kosovo and Afghanistan, the West is divided. Apart from Blair and Berlusconi, few European leaders are keen on the project. They are unlikely to hinder the United States and some will end up backing the adventure, but they are also aware that there is a mass antiwar movement in Europe, larger in Italy and Britain than elsewhere, but with a potential to spread throughout the continent.

★

What of those intellectuals, former critics of imperialism, who were trapped by the debris of 11 September? Many have now become its most vociferous loyalists. I am not, in this instance, referring to the *belligerati* — Salman Rushdie, Martin Amis and friends — ever-present in the liberal press on both sides of the Atlantic. They might well shift again. (Rushdie's decision to pose for the cover of a French magazine draped in the Stars and Stripes could be a temporary aberration. His new-found love for the Empire might turn out to be as short-lived as was his conversion to Islam. It shows no signs of doing so, but one can always hope . . .)

No, what concerns me more is another layer: the men and women who were once intensely involved in left-wing activities. It has been a short march for some of them: from the outer fringes of radical politics to the antechambers of the State Department. Like many converts, they display an aggressive self-confidence. Having honed their polemical and ideological skills within the left, they now deploy them against their old friends. This is why they have become the useful idiots of the Empire. They will be used and dumped. A few still dream of becoming the Somali, Pakistani, Iraqi or Iranian equivalents of the Afghan puppet, Hamid Karzai. They, too, might be disappointed. The queue is long and transcontinental transplants are expensive. Operations can go wrong. And, more importantly, only tried and tested agents can be put in power. Most former Marxists/Maoists/Trotskyists do not yet pass muster. To do so they have to rewrite their entire past and admit that they were wrong in ever backing the old enemies of the Empire in Cuba, Vietnam, Angola, Indonesia, Afghanistan, the Arab East, etc. They have, in other words, to pass the David Horowitz test. Horowitz, the son of old communists and a biographer of the late Isaac Deutscher, underwent the most amazing self-cleansing in post-Seventies America. Today he is a leading polemicist of the right, constantly denouncing soft liberals as a bridge to the more sinister figures of the left.

Compared to him, Christopher Hitchens must still appear as a marginal and slightly frivolous figure, though his current sidekick Kanaan Makiya would certainly pass the Horowitz test. Unlike Hitchens, who was strongly opposed to the 1990 Gulf War, Makiya, an Anglo-Iraqi favourite of the Richard Perle wing of the State Department, chose that very same year to defect. He is, at least, consistent. For he was in favour of a Japanese-style US occupation of Iraq even then and was shocked that Bush *père* refused the role of Emancipator and acted in what were then regarded as vital US interests by keeping Saddam in power. If he was burnt by that betrayal, he shows few signs of it now as he is paraded on transatlantic TV talk shows and news programmes as the voice of Iraq. I have a feeling that even this time his ambitions may not be realised. He has become too eager. Given an outing in London's liberal daily, the *Guardian*, as 'Iraq's most eminent dissident thinker', Makiya declared: 'September 11 set a whole new standard as to what could be achieved, and if you're in the terrorism business you're going to start thinking big, and you're going to need allies. And if you need allies in the terrorism business, you're going to ask Iraq.'

Far from being an eminent thought, this is a total fabrication of which most self-respecting intelligence officers on either side of the Atlantic would be ashamed. But Makiya has become a reckless operator. So keen is he to fly alongside the men of the 82nd Airborne that his capacity to spin extraordinary spirals of assertion, one above the other, based on no empirical facts whatsoever, knows no bounds. Not a single US intelligence agency has managed to prove any Iraqi links with 11 September. Attempts by Tony Blair to force British intelligence teams to prepare a dossier proving these links backfired badly. Perhaps they should have consulted 'Iraq's most eminent thinker'. It is because none of these links existed that CBR, in order to justify a war, moved on to other issues such as the possession of 'dangerous weapons'.

Hitchens started off with a thoughtful piece on 13 September 2001 in which he stated that the 'analytical moment' had to be 'indefinitely postponed,' but nonetheless linked the hits to the past policies of the United States and criticised Bush for confusing an act of terrorism with an act of war. He soon moved on to denounce those who made similar but much sharper criticisms, and began to talk of the supposed 'fascist sympathies of the soft left' – Noam Chomsky, Harold Pinter, Gore Vidal, Susan Sontag, Edward Said, et al. In more recent television appearances he sounds more like a saloon-bar bore than the fine, critical mind which blew away the halos surrounding Kissinger, Clinton and Mother Teresa.

Sounding more and more like the pompous neo-conservatives he once derided, he has hitched himself to the bandwagon of the Pentagon's most-favoured Iraqi exile and the darling of US oil interests, Ahmed Chalabi. On behalf of the Iraqi National Congress, this old rogue received between $60 and $70 million dollars from the CIA in the early 1990s. The INC was subsequently accused by the State Department of an inability to account for the money and of using too much of it to keep the INC leaders travelling and living in the style to which they had become accustomed. Arnaud de Borchgrave, a veteran commentator not known for his radical views, has written of how Chalabi defrauded his own Jordanian bank:

> No one is more upset at the idea of Chalabi becoming Washington's man in Baghdad than Jordanian leaders – past and present. He was sentenced April 9, 1992, to 22 years hard labour by a Jordanian state security court on 31 charges of embezzlement, theft, misuse of depositor funds, and speculation with the Jordanian dinar. The court also handed down harsh sentences and fines to 16 others, including several brothers and close relatives who were members of the board of Chalabi's Petra Bank, or owners of affiliated companies.
>
> Chalabi, a one-time favourite of King Hussein's royal court, had already skipped across the border to Syria, hidden in the trunk of a royal palace car. Chalabi says former Crown Prince Hassan drove him to the border. Both the driver and the woman friend who organized the getaway deny this. . . .
>
> What was undeniable was that Chalabi's Petra Bank, Jordan's third largest, had gone belly up and some $300 million in depositors' accounts had suddenly vanished. . . .
>
> In the 12 years between when Chalabi founded the bank and its crash, this scion of a wealthy and powerful Iraqi Shiite family developed a reputation for contacts at the highest level. When the free-market value of the dinar plunged in 1988, it was common knowledge in Amman that the Petra Bank was one of the most active purchasers of dollars. Yet when Central Bank Governor Mohammed Said Nabulsi sought to enforce a requirement on banks to deposit 30 percent of their foreign exchange holdings with the Central Bank as part of his efforts to prop up the currency, Petra was unable to comply.★

Should any of this disqualify him to run Occupied Iraq? On the contrary. The sleaze-bag favoured by Hitchens and chums is, in fact, well suited to the position of the most eminent political leader of the new Iraqi market-state. Chalabi has already promised two 'reforms' after the 'liberation of Iraq' and his installation (so he believes) as its leader: Iraqi oil will be privatised and handed over to US companies and within three months he will recognise Israel. At least this old crook has no illusions regarding the real war aims of his masters.

★ Arnaud de Borchgrave, 'Commentary', *Washington Times*, 29 November 2002.

What unites the New Empire loyalists is an underlying belief that, despite certain flaws, the military and economic power of the United States represents the only emancipatory project and, for that reason, it has to be supported against all those who challenge its power. A few prefer Clinton-as-Caesar to Bush, but they recognise this as a trivial self-indulgence. Deep down they know the Empire always stands above its leaders.

What they forget is that empires always act in their own self-interests. The British empire cleverly exploited the anti-slavery campaigns to colonise Africa, just as Washington uses the humanitarian hand-wringing of NGOs and the *bien pensants* to fight its new wars today. European continental pieties are however beginning to irritate Cheney and Rumsfeld. They laugh in Washington when they hear European politicians talk of revitalising the United Nations.

Imperial power is sustained by the creation of satrapies that accept its economic priorities and strategic control. Neo-liberal economics, imposed by the IMF mullahs, have reduced countries in every continent to penury and brought their populations to the edge of despair. The social democracy that appeared as an attractive option during the Cold War no longer exists. The powerlessness of democratic parliaments and the politicians who inhabit them to change anything has discredited democracy. Crony capitalism can survive without it.

At a time when much of the world – Latin America and South Korea being the most striking examples – is beginning to tire of being 'emancipated' by the United States, so many liberals have been numbed into silence. It is not so much the re-writing of history as ignoring its very presence. This is something I have not been able to do. Even as a teenager I was greedy for history, and found it in the oddest places.

A curious experience disturbed my first few visits to the United States: I was plagued by visions. Unlike those seen by Joan of Arc mine were ghostly, not divine. One image remained persistent. I would look down from the window-seat of the plane on the vast open spaces and imagine thousands of Native Americans engaged in the business of everyday life. Mostly they were on horseback, hunting or being hunted. Sometimes I imagined them arguing with each other in village assemblies on how best to respond to the white conquerors.

The first time this happened was in the late winter of 1969. I was flying from New York to Minneapolis. Below me lay a carpet of thick, layered snow, punctured irregularly by trees that resembled scaffolds. Suddenly I saw a chaotic procession of dark-skinned men, women and children, their bodies covered with fur and buffalo hide, being driven along by uniformed soldiers as if to a cattle pen. I looked away and returned to the unread novel lying on my lap. As I became more familiar with the United States, these images began to fade and soon, they disappeared forever. The memories remain vivid, but I no longer see them on my travels.

Why had these visions occupied my mind at all? I fear for the most banal of reasons. It was the cumulative impact of all the westerns I had watched during my misspent youth in Lahore. This was during the Fifties. A changing of the imperial guard had taken place. The Union Jack had gone home. Post-colonial Pakistan had become a recipient of commodities stamped with the Stars and Stripes. These arrived in the shape of both soft and hard power: Hollywood, Elvis Presley, Coca-Cola as well as military hardware.

We wanted desperately to be modern (and in my case simultaneously anti-imperialist) and so the soft power was avidly consumed. Digesting it was another matter. I was upset by the sight of so many 'red Indians' being regularly murdered in cold blood on the screen of the Regal and Plaza cinemas in downtown Lahore. They were not our 'baddies' and even though it was counter-historical, I always wanted them to win. Those images haunted me. In the short term they stimulated an obsessive interest in Native American history. I would look up the names of the tribes in various encyclopaedias; scour second-hand bookshops and libraries for anything that was available. I thought about them a great deal. Sometime later I read that the Sioux words for Black Mountain was 'paha sapa'. In Punjabi, my mother tongue, mountain is 'pahar' and black is 'siah'. Close enough. How had these words crossed the Siberian ice-bridge all those years ago? Could they be Indians after all? The western raised questions that Hollywood could never answer.

Those distant thoughts concerning the first inhabitants of the Americas had remained hidden in the memory cellar and erupted the first time I actually visited the USA. What did they teach one, those endless afternoons spent watching the cinematic reconstruction of a violent past, a history of an ever-expanding frontier? Whichever side you supported, one fact was unchallengeable. The hegemony achieved by the settler-republic over its native inhabitants was the result of pure coercion. Consent was neither sought nor desired.

Protestant fundamentalism had fuelled the migratory urges of the first settlers and this ideology combined with superior technology and skills was the foundation stone of the new colonies: 'Thus God made way for his people, by removing the heathen.' In 1637, the zealots set fire to the Pequod settlement in Connecticut. Four hundred members of this tribe were burned alive as they sought to escape. A colonist wrote: 'It was a fearful sight to see them frying in the fire . . . and horrible was the stink and scent thereof; but the victory seemed a sweet sacrifice, and they gave the praise therof to God.'

Their mission was not to 'civilize' the heathen. That was a Catholic weakness deployed by the Spaniards and Portuguese who took the southern half of the continent, but provided the whole with a European name: America (after a Florentine explorer, Amerigo Vespucci, who had sailed with a Spanish expedition to Venezuela in 1499 and later with the Portuguese down the coast of what became Brazil). They, too, killed natives in large numbers, but there were some 57 million of them and labour was in short supply. Some had to be converted. After this cleansing process, inter-marriages multiplied. The Protestants who stayed in the northern hemisphere were puritans. Well-versed in the Old Testament, they argued in favour of a literal interpretation. They genuinely believed that extermination was the simplest and the kindest solution. It was God's will. The confidence and righteousness that has marked America's imperial adventures was present from the beginning.

Two hundred years after the Pequod massacre, some of the country's finest – poets, writers, and intellectuals – were reciting from the same hymnbook. Listen to the great judicial mind of Oliver Wendell Holmes, pontificating on civilized values and speaking of the natives as a 'red-crayon sketch of humanity laid on the canvas before the colours of real manhood were ready. . . . Irreclaimable, Sir, – irreclaimable! A provisional race, Sir, – nothing more . . . passing away according to the programme.'

This is Walt Whitman writing in patriotic mode, excited, like many other citizens of the 'athletic democracy', by the expanding frontier of the dynamic new Republic.

What has Mexico, inefficient Mexico – with her superstition, her burlesque upon freedom, her actual tyranny by the few over the many – what has she to do with the great mission of peopling the new world with a noble race? Be it ours to achieve that mission. . . . For our part, we look upon the increase of territory and power, not as the doubter looks, but with the faith which the Christian has in God's mystery.

Melville, too – the greatest of American novelists – was tempted by the programme, but like his friend Hawthorne, could not stomach the atrocities. Like Whitman, he celebrated the Mexican War, but a fevered patriotism often collided with more decent instincts that sought to protect and defend the rights of the 'primitives'. This insoluble contradiction is at work throughout *Moby Dick*, first published in 1815. The ship that goes in search of the white whale is named 'the Pequod'. The tribe of Massachusetts Indians has almost been exterminated. Melville will immortalize its name. And in the concluding pages of his great novel we read of the American eagle – 'the bird of heaven with archangelic shrieks' going down with the damned ship. Both the *Pequod* and the eagle lie buried in Melville's ocean. The whale took Ahab

There was no peace, even after the bloodletting of the Civil War: a Wagnerian epic destined to be part myth, part tragedy. The aged Whitman was filled with gloom and despair. How would it all end? But the two states would be welded together by a common destiny. Their unity sealed with the blood of Indians and the conquest of the Philippines. Not all the wounds of the Civil War would be forgotten, but global piracy was a healing elixir, although not to everybody's taste.

It was well after the internal Empire had been consolidated that President Monroe enunciated a doctrine that declared its intention to control and dominate the Latin American backyard, a hegemonic process that fascinated German theorists during the Third Reich. Carl Schmitt, in particular, much admired the Monroe doctrine and drew water from the same well to justify the Nazi Order in Europe – the *Grossraum* or 'large space'.

The model of what needs to be done by dissenters was established in the last year of the nineteenth century. Over a hundred years ago, Mark Twain, shocked by the chauvinist reaction to the Boxer Rebellion in China and the US occupation of the Philippines, sounded the tocsin. Imperialism was the problem. It had to be opposed. The result was a mammoth gathering in Chicago in 1899 to found the American Anti-Imperialist League, whose membership had grown within two years to half a million. Its founder members, among them Twain and T.W. Higginson, who had commanded the first black regiment created during the Civil War, were pitched in battle against L.E. Wright, the second Governor-General of the Philippines, who had once fought for the Confederacy and needed no training in how to treat the Filipinos.

The magazines and pamphlets of the League contained contributions from some of America's most gifted writers and thinkers. These included Henry and William James, W.E.B. DuBois, Charles Elliot Norton, William Dean Howells and Frederick Douglass, Jr. They wrote essays and short stories and poems and stood shoulder-to-shoulder with Twain to oppose imperial wars. In November 1916, on the eve of US entry in the First World War, *Harper's Monthly*, which was then, as now, an outlet for sane voices inside the asylum, published a scathing essay by Twain. The 'loud little handful' of whom Twain wrote are still with us:

> The loud little handful – as usual – will shout for the war. The pulpit will – warily and cautiously – object – at first; the great, big dull bulk of the nation will rub its sleepy eyes and try to make out why there should be a war, and will say, earnestly and indignantly, 'It is unjust and dishonourable, and there is no necessity for it.'
>
> Then the handful will shout louder. A few fair men on the other side will argue and reason against the war with speech and pen, and at first will have a hearing and be applauded; but it will not last long; those others will outshout them, and presently the anti-war audience will thin out and lose popularity.
>
> Before long you will see this curious thing: the speakers stoned from the platform, and free speech strangled by hordes of furious men who in their secret hearts are still at one with those stoned speakers – as earlier – but do not dare to say so. And now the whole nation – pulpit and all – will take up the war-cry, and shout itself hoarse, and mob any honest man who ventures to open his mouth; and presently such mouths will cease to open.
>
> Next the statesmen will invent cheap lies, putting the blame upon the nation that is attacked, and every man will be glad of those conscience-soothing falsities, and will diligently study them, and refuse to examine any refutations of them; and thus he will by and by convince himself that the war is just, and will thank God for the better sleep he enjoys after this process of grotesque self-deception.★

★ Quoted in *Mark Twain: Social Critic* by Philip S. Foner, New York 1958.

Prologue

The honour of great peoples, is to be valued for the beneficience, and the aydes they give to peoples of inferiour rank, or not at all. And the violences, oppressions, and injuries they do, are not extenuated, but aggravated by the greatness of the peoples, because they have least need to commit them. The consequences of this partiality toward the great, proceed in this manner. Impunity means Insolence; Insolence, Hatred; and Hatred an Endeavour to pull down all oppressing and contumelious greatnesse.

Thomas Hobbes, *Leviathan*, 1651

Tragedies are always discussed as if they took place in a void, but actually each tragedy is conditioned by its setting, local and global. The events of 11 September 2001 are no exception. There exists no exact, incontrovertible evidence about who ordered the hits on New York and Washington or when the plan was first mooted. This book is not primarily concerned with what happened on that day. A torrent of images and descriptions has made these the most visible, the most global and the best-reported acts of violence of the last fifty years.

I want to write of the setting, of the history that preceded these events, of a world that is treated virtually as a forbidden subject in an increasingly parochial culture that celebrates the virtues of ignorance, promotes a cult of stupidity and extols the present as a process without an alternative, implying that we all live in a consumerist paradise. A world in which disappointment breeds apathy and, for that reason, escapist fantasies of every sort are encouraged from above. The growing crisis in Argentina, a symbol of the dead-end that market-fundamentalism had reached, came to a head on 5 September 2001. It was ignored. A multi-class uprising followed. Four presidents fell within the space of a fortnight.

The complacency of this world was severely shaken by the events of 11 September. What took place – a carefully planned terrorist assault on the symbols of US military and economic power – was a breach in the security of the North American mainland, an event neither feared nor imagined by those who devise war-games for the Pentagon. The psychological blow was unprecedented. The subjects of *the* Empire had struck back.

I want to ask why so many people in non-Islamic parts of the world were unmoved by what took place and why so many celebrated, in the chilling phrase of Osama bin Laden, an 'America struck by almighty Allah in its vital organs'. In the Nicaraguan capital, Managua, people hugged each other in silence. In Porto Alegre, in the deep south of Brazil, a large concert hall packed with young people erupted in anger when a visiting Black jazz musician from New York insisted on beginning his performance with a rendering of 'God Bless America'. The kids replied with chants of 'Osama, Osama!' The concert was cancelled. There were celebrations on the streets in Bolivia. From Argentina the Mothers who had been demonstrating for years to discover how and when the local military had 'disappeared' their children refused to join the officially orchestrated mourning. In Greece the government suppressed the publication of opinion polls that showed a large majority actually in favour of the hits, and football crowds refused to observe the two-minute silence.

In Beijing the news came too late in the night for anything more than a few celebratory fireworks, but in the week that followed the reaction became clearer. While the Politburo dithered for over twenty-four hours, Hsinhua, the official Chinese news agency, put out a short video of the 11 September footage complete with Hollywood music so that the moment could be relished at leisure. A second video mixed images of the events with footage from *King Kong* and other disaster movies. Beijing students interviewed by the *New Yorker* spoke openly of their delight. Some of them reminded the shocked journalist of the lack of response in the West when NATO planes had bombed the Chinese embassy in Belgrade. Only six Chinese had been killed compared to the three thousand in New York, but the students insisted that for them the six were as important as the three thousand.

The necessity to explain these reactions does not mean justifying the atrocity of 11 September. It is an attempt to move beyond the simplistic argument that 'they hate us, because they're jealous of our freedoms and our wealth'. This is simply not the case.

We have to understand the despair, but also the lethal exaltation, that drives people to sacrifice their own lives. If Western politicians remain ignorant of the causes and carry on as before, there will be repetitions. Moral outrage has some therapeutic value, but as a political strategy it is useless. Lightly disguised wars of revenge waged in the heat of the moment are not much better. To fight tyranny and oppression by using tyrannical and oppressive means, to combat a single-minded and ruthless fanaticism by becoming equally fanatical and ruthless, will not further the cause of justice or bring about a meaningful democracy. It can only prolong the cycle of violence.

Capitalism has created a single market, but without erasing the distinctions between the two worlds that face each other across a divide that first appeared in the eighteenth and became institutionalised in the nineteenth century. Most of the twentieth century witnessed several attempts to transcend this division through a process of revolutions, wars of national liberation and a combination of both, but in the end capitalism proved to be more cunning and more resilient. Its triumph has left the first of these worlds as the main repository of wealth and the principal wielder of uncontrolled military power. The second world, with Cuba the only exception, is governed by elites that either serve or seek to mimic the first. This closure of politics and economics produces fatal consequences. A disempowered people is constantly reminded of its own weakness. In the West a common response is to sink into the routines that dominate everyday life. Elsewhere in the world people become flustered, feel more and more helpless and nervous. Anger, frustration and despair multiply. They can no longer rely on the state for help. The laws favour the rich. So the more desperate amongst them, in search of a more meaningful existence or simply to break the monotony, begin to live by their own laws. Willing recruits will never be in short supply. The propaganda of the deed – the homage paid by the weak to the strong – will endure. It is the response of atomised individuals to a world that no longer listens, to politicians who have become interchangeable, to corporations one-eyed in the search for profits and global media networks owned by the self-same corporations and locked into a relationship of mutual dependence with the politicians. This is the existential misery that breeds insecurity and fosters deadly hatreds. If the damage is not repaired, sporadic outbursts of violence will continue and intensify.

Acts of violence depend neither on the will of an individual leader, however charismatic, nor on the structure of a single organisation, the existence of one country or the fanaticism of a sinister religion, its believers fuelled by the visions of a glorious afterlife. The violence, unfortunately, is systemic. It assumes varied forms in different parts of the globe. Nor is it the case that the bulk of this violence is directed against the United States. Religious fanatics of all hues often brutalise co-religionists whose purity is suspect or who are not as vigorous in their search for God and, as a result, are more critical of superstitions or empty and meaningless rituals.

There is a universal truth that pundit and politician need to acknowledge: slaves and peasants do not always obey their masters. Time and time again, in the upheavals that have marked the world since the days of the Roman empire, a given combination of events has yielded a totally unexpected eruption. Why should it be any different in the twenty-first century?

I want to write about Islam, its founding myths, its origins, its history, its culture, its riches, its divisions. Why has it not undergone a Reformation? How did it become so petrified? Should Koranic interpretations be the exclusive prerogative of religious scholars? And what do Islamist politics represent today? What processes led to the ascendancy of this current in the world of Islam? Can the trend be reversed or transcended? These are some of the issues explored in the hope that they will encourage further discussion and debate within and without the House of Islam.

To avoid all possible misunderstandings, a brief confession is in order. Religious beliefs have played no part in my own life. From the age of five or six I was an agnostic. At twelve I became a staunch atheist and, like many of the friends I grew up with, have remained one ever since. But I was brought up in that culture and it has enriched my life. It is perfectly possible to be part of a culture without being a believer.

The historian Isaac Deutscher used to refer to himself as a non-Jewish Jew, identifying himself with a long tradition of intellectual scepticism, symbolised by Spinoza, Freud and Marx. I have thought a great deal about this and have, on occasion, described myself as a non-Muslim Muslim, but the appellation doesn't quite fit. It has an awkward ring to it. This is not to suggest that the House of Islam lacks its secular intellectuals and artists. The last century alone produced Nazim Hikmet, Faiz Ahmed Faiz, Abdelrehman Munif, Mahmud Darwish, Fazil Iskander, Naguib Mahfouz, Nizar Qabbani, Pramoeda Ananta Toer, Djibril Diop Mambety amongst many others. But these are poets, novelists, film-makers. They have no equivalents in the social sciences. Critiques of religion are always implicit. Intellectual life has become stunted, making Islam itself a static and backward-looking religion.

I was born a Muslim. A maternal uncle, who always believed (wrongly) that Islam was the main source of moral strength for the impoverished peasants on our family's feudal estates, muttered the sacred invocation in my right ear. The year was 1943. The venue was Lahore, then under British imperial rule. It was a cosmopolitan city: Muslims constituted a majority, with Sikhs a close second and the Hindus not far behind. Mosques, temples and gurdwaras dominated the skyline in the old city. A tragedy was about to take place, but nobody was aware of the fact. It came four years later in the shape of a monsoon with red rain.

I was not quite four that August, when the old British empire finally departed and India was partitioned. A religious state, Pakistan was conceded to the Muslims of India, even though most of them were either indifferent to or had no idea of what it would mean. Pakistan literally means 'the land of the pure', something that became the cause of much mirth throughout the country, especially for the refugees who had come voluntarily. Personally, I have no childhood memories of Partition. None. The confessional cleansing which marked that year throughout northern and eastern India as the great sub-continent was divided along religious lines did not affect my childhood. Lahore changed completely. Many Sikhs and Hindus were massacred by their neighbours. The survivors fled to India. Muslims in North Indian cities suffered the same fate. Partitions are often like this, regardless of religion, though its presence brings an added fervour.

Later, many years later, my father's old wet-nurse, an extremely sweet and gentle but deeply religious woman, who had supervised my childhood as well, would recall how she had taken me out on to the streets of Lahore to greet Mohammed Ali Jinnah, the founder of Pakistan. She had bought me a little green and white crescent replica of the emblem of the new state and insisted that I had waved it enthusiastically and chanted 'Pakistan Zindabad' (Long Live Pakistan). If so it was not an experience that I ever had occasion to repeat. I have always been allergic to religious nationalism or its post-modern avatar, religious multiculturalism.

In 1947, we had lived on the Race Course Road in a 'protected' part of the city, the section which the British used to refer to as the 'civil lines'. It was isolated from the dense, overcrowded old walled city that had been con-structed around the Fort long before the last of the Great Mughals, Aurangzeb, had built the Badshahi (Royal) mosque. Some of the oldest Hindu temples were also situated in the old city, and it was here too that the ashes of the great Sikh ruler, Maharaja Ranjit Singh, were interred. Slowly, as is the way with cities, an extension was built and attached to the old. A ring of suburbs spread. Special quarters were constructed for railway work-ers close to the new railway stations. Around them grew engineering workshops and then came the shopping arcades and the High Courts and Government House, beyond which lay civil lines with their neat bungalows and large lawns. This Lahore was the centre of administration of the old province of the Punjab, which the British used to call 'our sword-arm' or 'our Prussia'.

The old city was always much more exciting, with its narrow streets and lanes and its bazaars which specialised in different commodities and wares, including food. It had remained virtually unchanged since medieval times and often, as children, we used to imagine the procession of elephants that brought the Mughal emperor to his palace-Fort and how the local shop-keepers vied with each other to ensure that this or that product was preferred above the rest in the evening when the emperor sampled the city's delights.

This, one felt, was the real Lahore. It was here in 1947 that the killings were at their most intense. We were far away from the maddened crowds. Sometimes the screams of victims could be heard by those who lived on the edge of the 'civil lines', and many stories circulated of how bloodstained Sikh men and women were given shelter by good Muslims. But I never heard screams or saw blood, and as for the stories, they all came later.

Nobody in my family was killed. We were not going anywhere. We were not destined to form part of the stream of refugees which flowed in both directions. We were the lucky ones. We had always belonged to what was now the Land of the Pure. We were spared the traumas, tragedies and the unbounded anxieties which afflicted millions of Sikhs, Muslims and Hindus in those terrible times.

Few politicians on either side foresaw the outcome. Jawaharlal Nehru's romantic nationalism portrayed independence as a long-delayed 'tryst with destiny', but even he never imagined that the tryst would drown in blood. Mohammed Ali Jinnah, the founder of Pakistan, genuinely believed that the new state would be a smaller version of secular India, with only one difference. Here Muslims would be the largest community and Sikhs and Hindus a loyal minority. He actually believed it would still be possible for him to spend time each year in his large Bombay mansion.

Jinnah was shaken by the orgy of barbarism, though Gandhi alone paid the price. For defending the rights of innocent Muslims in the post-Partition India, he, the most religious of nationalist leaders, who had insisted on using Hindu imagery to appeal to the peasants, was assassinated by Nathuram Godse, a Hindu fanatic. That past is corroding the present and rotting the future. The political heirs of the hanged Godse have shoved aside the children of Nehru and Gandhi. Today they exercise power in New Delhi. Politics is being enveloped by the poisonous fog of the religious world. History, unlike the poets of the subcontinent, is not usually prone to sentiment.

I loved Lahore. By the time I was at secondary school we had moved from Race Course Road to our own apartments in a large block which my paternal grandfather had built for his five children. These were on Nicholson Road, but very close to the tiny streets and shops of Qila Gujjar Singh, an old Sikh-dominated locality, constructed around a small Sikh fortress. The street names were unchanged. Not that I ever asked myself what had happened to all the Sikhs. My early childhood was dominated by kite-flying and playing cricket with street urchins. It wasn't till much later that I even discovered that Basant, the festival of kites, when the Lahore sky is filled with different colours and shapes as old rivals seek to tangle with and cut down each other's kites, was the millennium-old product of Hindu mythology. For us what was decisive was not the origins of the kite-battles but the quality of string to be purchased. In the old city there were experts in the art of preparing special string for the kites. The string was coated with a mixture of finely crushed glass and glue and then left to dry overnight. I was too busy making sure I had enough money to buy the best-quality string in the market to worry much about history.

Awareness came slowly. My family came from the northern extremities of the Punjab, just south of Peshawar and the Khyber Pass, close to the ancient city of Taxila. They were an old landed family belonging to the Khattar tribe, and like others in their position had been forced to take sides in the struggles for power in north India. In his memoirs, the emperor Jahangir complained of their rudeness, boorishness, arrogance and, more important, their obstinate refusal to pay the tribute owed him. The description rings true. Often the family had divided on the question of who governed the Punjab, with a family faction backing each side. This ensured that whoever was in power, the family estates would remain safe. Whether this was collective feudal cunning or the result of blood and property feuds, I have no way of knowing. Perhaps it was a mixture of both. What is certainly true is that in the 1840s the rivalry between two brothers – Sardar Karam Khan and Sardar Fateh Khan – led to the first of them (my great-great grandfather) being murdered by his younger sibling.

The two men had gone on a hunting expedition, but an ambush had been carefully prepared. Karam Khan's horse returned to the family home with blood on the saddle. The body was found a few hours later. As news of the murder spread, a neighbouring landlord, fearful that Karam Khan's heirs might be next on the list, gave shelter to the widow and her five sons. He also organised the revenge killing of Fateh Khan. A week later, the sons of Karam Khan were taken into care by General Abbott and provided with British protection. The eldest of them, Sardar Mohammed Hayat Khan (my maternal great-grandfather), remained loyal to the new rulers. He took his own complement of tribal cavalry and fought shoulder-to-shoulder with the British in the Second Afghan War. I will not be writing too much about him in this book.

The other wing of the family, the heirs of Cain, referred to contemptuously in family folklore as the 'lesser khans', had earlier sided with the Sikhs against the British and been defeated. Mohammed Hayat Khan, now the head of the family, ensured that this defeat was suitably commemorated. A grateful colonial authority legalised his division of the spoils. Success went to his head. Till then family custom had dictated that the owners of the land did not flaunt their wealth, but lived modestly. Mohammed Hayat's brother Gulab Khan wanted to continue this tradition, but was overruled. A large two-storied manor house was constructed in the heart of the old village of Wah, a house that could be seen by peasants for many miles. My father once told me of meeting an old peasant woman who described Mohammed Hayat as 'big-headed, big-cocked and a show-off', which always struck my father as a serious understatement.

India could only be ruled with the consent of the indigenous chiefs and rulers. The Mughal emperors had learnt this lesson very quickly. Akbar had even attempted to create a new religion synthesising Hinduism and Islam. Even the more religious-minded Aurangzeb did not attempt any wholesale Islamisation of his army. Some of his ablest generals were Hindu chiefs.

The British, when confronted with the nightmare of actually governing India, realised that without serious alliances they would not last too long despite their superior technology. The raj was maintained by a very tiny British presence.

My grandfather, Sikandar Hyat Khan, the leader of the Unionist Party (a united front of Muslim, Hindu and Sikh landlords), was elected prime minister of the Punjab in 1937, one of the two regions where the Congress Party of Gandhi and Nehru had not made any inroads. He was a staunch believer in a federal India with proper safeguards for all minorities. He died of a heart-attack in December 1942, aged forty-nine, but during his last year in office he had signed a pact with Jinnah, the aim of which was to prevent the Muslim League from arousing crude religious emotions. If he had lived he would have made every possible effort to stop the partition of the Punjab. But would he have succeeded?

In fact even Jinnah, as late as June 1946, was prepared to consider a federal solution as proposed by the Cabinet Mission sent to India by the Labour government. It was the Congress Party which made that particular solution impossible. This failure meant that exactly one year before Partition, Hindu–Muslim riots began in eastern India. During four days in August 1946, nearly 5,000 people were killed and three times that number wounded in Bengal. The mood in the Punjab became edgy. Fear overcame rationality.

In April 1947 my mother, an active member of the Communist Party, and heavily pregnant with my sister, found herself alone at home. Suddenly a loud knock shook the front door. She rushed to open it and was overcome by anxiety. In front of her stood a giant Sikh. He saw the concern on her face and understood. All he wanted to know was the location of a particular house on the same road. My mother gave him the directions. He thanked her warmly and left. She was overpowered by shame. How could she, of all people, have reacted in that fashion? Lahore had, for many centuries, been a truly multi-cultural and cosmopolitan city. Now its citizens were overcome by madness.

Jinnah conceived of Pakistan as an amalgamation of an undivided Punjab, an undivided Bengal, plus Sind, Baluchistan and the North-West Frontier Province. This prescription would have yielded a Punjab 40 per cent Hindu and Sikh and a Bengal 49 per cent Hindu. It was a utopian solution. Once confessional passions had been aroused and neighbours were massacring each other (as in Bosnia fifty years later) it was difficult to keep the two provinces united.

'I do not care how little you give me,' Jinnah is reported as saying in March 1947 to the last viceroy, Lord Mountbatten, 'as long as you give it to me completely.'

The price of separation was high. Two million dead. Eleven million refugees. Saadat Hasan Manto, one of the most gifted Urdu writers of the subcontinent, wrote a four-page masterpiece entitled 'Toba Tek Singh', set in the lunatic asylum in Lahore at the time of Partition. When whole cities are being ethnically cleansed, how can the asylums escape? The Hindu and Sikh lunatics are told that they will be transferred to institutions in India. The inmates rebel. They hug each other and weep. They have to be forced on to the trucks waiting to transport them to India. One of them, a Sikh, is so overcome by rage that when the border is reached, he refuses to move and dies on the demarcation line which divides the new Pakistan from old India. When the real world is overcome by insanity normality only exists in the asylum. The lunatics have a better understanding of the crime that is being perpetrated than the politicians who agreed to it.

A year later, in 1948, a different but comparable process was to transform the Arab world. Another confessional state, Israel, was brought into being. Once again the particularist defeated the universal. In the case of both Pakistan and Israel, the founding fathers were far removed from confessional politics. Mohammed Ali Jinnah was a known agnostic who broke most of the taboos of his religion. Ben-Gurion and Moshe Dayan were self-proclaimed atheists. Yet religion was used as a central motif in the creation of these two states against the wishes of fundamentalists. The Jamaat-e-Islami and its Jewish counterparts opposed the formation of these states. The former rapidly adjusted its position. The latter has remained hostile and often shown a far greater sympathy for the dispossessed Palestinians than its secular counterparts.

The scale of deaths in Palestine was not the same as in South Asia, but the aggressive and ruthless brutality utilised to drive the Palestinians out of their villages and off their lands created a wound that could never heal. Despite the horrors of Partition, none of the refugees were left stateless or homeless. They were accommodated in India or Pakistan, and in many cases received a degree of compensation for lost property.

The Palestinians expelled by the Zionist settlers became people without a state, destined to spend their lives in exile or in the debilitating conditions of refugee camps. None of this had much impact in Pakistan till the triumph of Gamal Abdel Nasser in Egypt. It was when Israel joined Britain and France to invade Egypt in 1956 that I first registered what this new state in the Middle East meant for the region. Till then memories of the Judeocide had led one to ignore or underplay the plight of the Palestinians.

I became aware of the scale of the catastrophe for the first time while visiting the Palestinian camps in Jordan and Syria in 1967, a few weeks after the Six Day War. I was deeply affected by the wounds inflicted on Palestinian children, the conditions in which the refugees were compelled to live and the stories that poured out of the mothers, sisters and wives. None of the women with whom I spoke at the camps was veiled and only a few had covered their heads. It was then that I thought seriously for the first time of the dual tragedy that had taken place. The sufferings of European Jewry, from the pogroms in Tsarist Russia to the slaughterhouses of Auschwitz and Treblinka, were the responsibility of bourgeois civilisation. The Palestinian Arabs were being made to pay for these crimes, while the West was arming Israel and paying it 'conscience money'.

Decades later I was recording a conversation with Edward Said in New York. We agreed that 1917 had been the year that defined the twentieth century. For me the formative event was the Russian Revolution, for him the Balfour Declaration. The collapse of the first and the triumph of the second were somehow also linked to what took place in New York and Washington on 11 September 2001.

PART I

Mullahs and Heretics

Vast and powerful Empires are founded on a religion. This is because dominion can only be secured by victory, and victory goes to the side which shows most solidarity and unity of purpose. Now men's hearts are united and co-ordinated, with the help of God, by participation in a common religion . . .

Ibn Khaldun (1332–1406), *The Muqaddimah*

To dream that you are sodomising a young man you do not know is a sign of victory over one's enemies . . . if, however, you dream that you are making love to a woman when, in reality, you are having a sexual relationship with a man, your request to this man will be fulfilled even though you have been humiliated by him in the past . . . To dream of having sex with an animal is a sign of prosperity and long life . . .

Ibn Sirin (634–704), *The Interpretation of Dreams*

1

An atheist childhood

I never really believed in God. Not even for a week, not even between the ages of six and ten, when I was an agnostic. This unbelief was instinctive. I was sure there was nothing else out there except space. It could have been my lack of imagination. During the sweet, jasmine-scented summer nights, long before mosques were allowed to use loud-speakers, it was enough to savour the silence, look upwards at the exquisitely lit sky, count the shooting stars and fall asleep. The early morning call of the muezzin was like a pleasant-sounding alarm clock.

There were many advantages in being an unbeliever. Threatened with divine sanctions by family retainers, relations or cousins – 'If you do this Allah will be angry' or 'If you don't do that Allah will punish you' – I was unmoved. Let him do his worst, I used to tell myself, but he never did, and I think it was this passivity on his part that strengthened my belief in his non-existence. An early case of scepticism as the spare rib of vulgar empiricism.

My parents, too, were non-believers. So were most of their close friends. Religion played a tiny part in our Lahore household. There were others, of course, who professed the faith, but even they did so sheepishly and without a fuss. In the second half of the last century a large proportion of educated Muslims had embraced modernity. They realised that organised religion was an anachronism. Old habits persisted, nonetheless: the would-be virtuous made their ablutions and sloped off sheepishly to Friday prayers. Sometimes they fasted for a few days each year, usually just before the new moon was sighted, marking the end of Ramadan. I doubt whether more than a quarter of the population in the cities fasted for a whole month. Café life continued unabated. Many more claimed that they had fasted so as to take advantage of the free food doled out at the end of each fasting day by the mosques or the kitchens of the wealthy. In the countryside the figure was slightly lower, since outdoor work was difficult without sustenance, and especially without water when Ramadan coincided with the summer months. Eid, however, was celebrated by all.

One day, I think in the autumn of 1956, when I was twelve, I was eavesdropping on an after-dinner conversation at home – children, like servants, were regarded as both deaf and invisible. This worked in our favour, since we amassed a great deal of information not intended for innocent ears. On this occasion my sister, assorted cousins and I had been asked nicely to occupy ourselves elsewhere. From an adjoining room, we began to giggle as we heard a particularly raucous, wooden-headed aunt and a bony uncle berating my parents in loud whispers: 'We know what you're like . . . we know you're unbelievers, but these children should be given a chance . . . They must be taught their religion.'

My giggles were premature. A few months later a tutor was hired to teach me the Koran and Islamic history. 'You live here,' said my father. 'You should study the texts. You should know our history. Later you may do as you wish. Even if you reject everything, it's always better to know what it is that one is rejecting.'

Sensible enough advice, but regarded by me at the time as hypocritical and a betrayal. How often in our house had I heard talk of superstitious idiots, often relatives, who hated a Satan they never knew and worshipped a God they didn't have the brains to doubt? Now I was being forced to study religion. I strongly resented the imposition and was determined to sabotage the process.

It didn't occur to me at the time that my father's decision might have had something to do with an episode from his own life. Perhaps he recalled the religious experience he was compelled to undergo at a similar age. In 1928, aged twelve, he had accompanied his mother and his old wet-nurse (my grandmother's most trusted and senior maid) on the pilgrimage to perform the *hajj* ceremony. Women, then as now, could only visit Mecca if accompanied by a male over twelve years old. The older men flatly refused. My father, as the youngest male in the family, was not given a choice in the matter. His oldest brother, the most religious member of the family, never let my father forget the pilgrimage. His letters addressed to my father always used to arrive with the prefix *al-Haj* (the Pilgrim) attached to his name, a cause for much merriment at teatime.

Decades later, when the pores of the Saudi elite were sweating petrodollars, my father would remember the poverty he had witnessed in the Hijaz and recall the woeful tales recounted by numerous non-Arab pilgrims who had been robbed on the road to Mecca. In the days before oil, the annual pilgrimage had been one of the main sources of income for the locals. Often they would augment their meagre earnings with well-organised raids on pilgrims' lodgings. The ceremony itself requires the pilgrim to come clothed in a simple white sheet and nothing else: all valuables have to be left behind. Local gangs were especially adept at stealing watches and gold. Soon the more experienced pilgrims realised that the 'pure souls' of Mecca weren't worth a damn. They began to take precautions and a war of wits ensued. Perhaps one day an Iranian film-maker will present us with an Eastern *hommage* to Buñuel.

The trip to the Holy Land had little impact on my father. Or perhaps it did, because several years later he became an orthodox communist and remained one for the rest of his life. Moscow became his Mecca. Perhaps he thought that immersing me in religion at a young age might also result in a similar transformation. I like to think that this was his real motive, rather than pandering to the more dim-witted members of our family, whose company he rarely sought and whose presence was always irksome. He always found it strange that these healthy young men and women could expend so much energy on trivia and did so unselfconsciously for the rest of their lives.

In later years, I came to admire my father for breaking away from what he would refer to as 'the emptiness of the feudal world'.[1] He had done so by

---

1 Empty the feudal world may have been on several levels, but it always knew how to defend its class interests. My father's membership of the Communist Party of India did not ruffle as many feathers as he had imagined. He was approached by his father and cousins and offered a safe seat – safe in the sense that it, like several others in the region was controlled by our family – in the 1946 elections to the Punjab Legislative Assembly, which was to determine the make-up of the Constituent Assembly after the birth of Pakistan in 1947. My father took the offer to the Politburo

developing an interest in political theory and a political party that made him sensitive to and aware of the realities underlying both, an option that is non-existent in the Islamic world today.

Since I did not read Arabic, the Koran could only be learnt by rote. This did strike my father as marginally distasteful, but his proposed solution enhanced the torture. He suggested that before I embark on a course of Koranic studies, I should learn the divine language. I refused point-blank, justifying my philistinism by the fact that it *was* the divine language. This is something I have long regretted, but never remedied.

My tutor, Nizam Din, arrived on the appointed day and work commenced. Thanks to his heroic efforts, I can still recite the opening lines from the Koran in the divine language: *Alif, lam, mim* and then the crucial sentence . . . *This book is not to be doubted.* Nizam Din, to my great delight, was not deeply religious himself. From his late teens to his late twenties, he had sprouted a beard. In 1940 he went into top gear, shaved off his beard, deserted religion for the anti-imperialist cause and became a devotee of left-wing politics. Like many others he had served a spell in a colonial prison and been further radicalised. But he never forgot the Koran. As late as December 2000, he would say that truth was a very powerful concept in it, but had never been translated into practical life because the mullahs had destroyed Islam.

At an early stage Nizam Din realised that I was bored with learning Koranic verses, with the result that he did not even attempt to teach me Islamic history. A pity. He might have had an unusual interpretation or perhaps, what is more likely, he knew very little of the real history himself.

The allotted hour was usually spent discussing history: the nationalist struggle against British imperialism, the origins of terrorism in Bengal and the Punjab, the heroism of the Sikh terrorist Bhagat Singh, who had thrown a bomb in the Punjab Legislative Assembly to protest against repressive legislation and the massacre of Jallianwala Bagh (Amritsar) in 1919. Once

---

of the CPI. The comrades thought long and hard. They were tempted by the thought of gaining easy representation, but finally decided to reject the offer as unprincipled. The person chosen to contest the seat for the CPI was a veteran working-class militant, Fazal Elahi Qurban, who picked up a few hundred votes as a result of some intensive canvassing by my parents. The actual victor was some obscure relation whose name I cannot recall.

imprisoned, he had refused to plead for mercy. In prison, he renounced terrorism as a tactic and moved close to a traditional Marxism. He was tried in secret and executed by the British in the Central Jail in Lahore, a fifteen-minute walk from where Nizam Din was telling me the story. 'If he had lived,' Nizam Din used to say, 'he would have become a leader the British really feared. And look at us now. Just because he was a Sikh, we have not even marked his martyrdom with a monument.'

He spoke of good times when all the villages in what was now Pakistan had been inhabited by Hindus and Sikhs and of their coexistence. Many of his non-Muslim friends had left for India. We would often discuss the politicians and the never-ending political crisis in Pakistan.

'They are pygmies,' Nizam Din would tell me in a slightly raised, high-pitched voice. 'Do you understand what I'm saying, Tariqji? Pygmies! Look at India. Observe the difference. Gandhi was a giant. Jawaharlal Nehru is a giant.' Over the years, I learnt far more about history, politics and everyday life from Nizam Din than I ever did at school. Much of it was a foundational knowledge, useful to this day. But his failure to interest me in religion had been noted.

A young maternal uncle, who had grown a beard at an early age and sought refuge in religion, volunteered to take on the task. His weekly unannounced visits to our house when I had just returned from school irritated me greatly. We would pace the garden while, in unctuous tones, he related a version of Islamic history which, like him, was unconvincing and dull. It comprised tales of endless heroism, with the Prophet raised to the stature of a divinity, and a punitive Allah. As he droned on, I would watch the paper kites flying and tangling with each other in the afternoon sky, mentally replay a lost game of marbles, or look forward to the first cricket match Pakistan was due to play against the West Indies. Anything but religion. After a few weeks he too gave up, announcing that the unbeliever's gene in me was too strong to dislodge. Secretly the sly viper nourished the hope that something of what he had taught would stay. He was wrong. Nothing remained.

During the summer months when the heat in the plains became unbearable and the schools closed down for over two months, we would flee to the Himalayan foothills, to Nathiagali, then a tiny and isolated hill-resort perched on the ridge of a thick pine forest and overlooked by the Himalayan peaks. Nature dwarfed all else. Here I would make friends with Pashtun boys and girls from the Frontier towns of Peshawar and Mardan. Even the children from Lahore whom I rarely saw in the winter months became summer friends.

Friendships indeed became intense. The atmosphere in the mountains was relaxed, social restrictions virtually non-existent. I acquired a taste for total freedom. We all had our favourite hiding places, which included mysterious cemeteries with English names. It always moved me that death had caught them so young. There was a deserted wooden Gothic church, which had been charred by lightning. It had one of the best views of the valley below and was occasionally used as a trysting place.

And then the burnt houses. How were they burned? I would ask the locals. Back would come a casual reply. 'They belonged to Hindus and Sikhs. Our fathers and uncles burnt them.' But why? 'So they could never come back, of course.' But why? 'Because we were now Pakistan. Their home was India.' But why, I persisted, when they had lived here for centuries, just like your families, spoken the same language, despite the different gods? The only reply was a sheepish grin and a shrugging of shoulders. It was strange to think that Hindus and Sikhs had been here, had been killed in the villages below. In these idyllic surroundings, the killings and burnings seemed strangely abstract to our young minds. We knew, but could not fully understand, and therefore did not dwell on these awful events till much later. The friends from Peshawar would speak of Hindu and Sikh Pashtuns who had migrated to India. In the tribal areas – the no-man's-land between Afghanistan and Pakistan – quite a few Hindus stayed on and were protected by the tribal codes. The same was true in Afghanistan itself (till the mujahidin and the Taliban arrived).

One of my favourite spots in Nathiagali was a space that lay between two giant oaks. From here one could watch the sun set on Nanga Parbat (number three in the pecking order after Everest and K2). The snow covering the peak would turn orange, then crimson. The cold nights could be even more dramatic. The sky and its offspring appeared much lower here than in the plains. When the full moon shone on the snow-covered peak of Nanga Parbat it bathed the entire valley in its light. Here we would breathe the air from China, look in the direction of Kashmir and marvel at the moon. Given all this, why would one need a multi-layered heaven that lay beyond, let alone the crucial seventh layer that belonged to us alone – the Islamic paradise? It must have been different in the desert.

These sights filled one's head with romantic fantasies, not religion. During the day our gang, male and female, would climb mountains, try and provoke the wild monkeys into a war of pine cones that we hurled at them. The locals always warned us against throwing stones at them. There was the legend of a British colonial officer of the nineteenth century, who had shot a monkey dead. One day, while he was out for a walk, the monkeys had ambushed and stoned him to death. The death had been real enough, but it was difficult to believe in the legend of the killer monkey. The women of this region were both attractive and unveiled, and it was much more likely that the Englishman had molested one of them and been punished somewhat severely by her male relatives. But this was always denied vigorously by the *paharis* (people of the mountains). 'You think we could kill a White man and survive?' It remained an unsolved mystery to be discussed the following summer.

We would return to our homes exhausted and ready for lunch. In the afternoons there was tennis and more walks and bridge and, yes, teenage romances. At night cheetahs and leopards prowled the forests in search of prey. What had religion to do with any of this?

One day, to my horror, my mother informed me that a local mullah from a neighbouring mountain village had been hired to make sure I completed the Koran. She had pre-empted all my objections. He would explain what each verse meant. This was torture. My summer was about to be wrecked. I moaned. I groaned. I protested, pleaded and tantrumed. To no avail. My friends were sympathetic but powerless. Most of them had undergone the same ritual.

Mullahs, especially the rural variety, were objects of ridicule, widely regarded as dishonest, hypocritical and lazy. It was widely believed that they had grown beards and chosen this path not because they were imbued with spiritual fervour, but in order to earn a crust. Unless attached to a mosque, they depended on voluntary contributions, tuition fees for teaching the Koran and free meals. The jokes that circulated at their expense, however, concerned their sexual appetites; in particular, a penchant for boys below a certain age. The fictional mullah of story-tellers or puppet-masters who travelled from village to village was a greedy and lustful arch-villain who used religion to pursue his desires and ambitions. He humiliated and cheated the poor peasant, while toadying to the local landlord or potentates. In all these tales virtue and purity became a natural cover for vice.

On the dreaded day, the mullah arrived and ate a hearty lunch. He was introduced to me by our old family retainer, Khuda Baksh (God Bless), who had served in my grandfather's household and often accompanied us to the mountains. Because of his status and age, he enjoyed a familiarity denied to other servants. God Bless was bearded, a staunch believer in the primacy of Islam; he said his prayers and fasted regularly but was deeply hostile to the mullahs, whom he regarded as pilferers, perverts and parasites. Nonetheless, he could not restrain a smile as the mullah, a man of medium height, in his late fifties, exchanged greetings with me. The sky was cloudless and the snow-capped peaks of the Himalayas clearly visible. We took our seats around a garden table placed to catch the warming sun. The afternoon chorus was in full flow. I breathed a delicious scent of sun-roasted pine needles and wild strawberries.

When the bearded man began to speak I noticed he was nearly toothless. The rhymed verse at once lost its magic. The few false teeth he had wobbled. I began to wonder if it would happen, and then it did: he became so excited with fake emotion that his false teeth dropped out on to the table. He smiled, picked them up and put them back in his mouth. At first I managed to restrain myself, but then I heard a suppressed giggle from the veranda and made the mistake of turning round. God Bless had stationed himself behind the large rhododendron to eavesdrop on the lesson and was choking with silent laughter. At this point I excused myself and rushed indoors. Thus ended the first lesson.

The following week God Bless, approaching his sixtieth birthday, dared me to ask the mullah a question before the lesson began. I did. 'Have your false teeth been supplied by the local butcher?' I inquired with an innocent expression, in an ultra-polite voice. The mullah asked me to leave: he wished to see my mother alone. A few minutes later he, too, left, never to return. Later that day he was sent an envelope full of money to pay for my insolence. God Bless and I celebrated his departure in the bazaar café with a delicious brew of mountain tea and home-made biscuits.

The attempt was never repeated. Henceforth my only religious duty was to substitute for my father once a year and accompany the male servants of our household to Eid prayers at the mosque, a painless enough task.

Some years later, when I came to Britain to study, the first group of people I met were hard-core rationalists. I might have missed the Humanist

Group's stall at the Fresher's Fair had it not been for a young spotty Irishman, dressed in a faded maroon corduroy jacket, with a mop of untidy dark brown hair, standing on a table and in a melodious, slightly breathless voice shouting: 'Down with God!' When he saw me staring, he smiled and added 'and Allah' to the refrain. I joined on the spot and was immediately roped into becoming the Humanist rep at my college. Some time afterwards when I asked how he had known I was of Muslim origin rather than a Hindu or a Zoroastrian, he replied that his chant only affected Muslims and Catholics. Hindus, Sikhs, Jews and Protestants ignored him completely.

It wasn't only as a consequence of my new Humanist duties that my knowledge of Islamic history remained slender (though I noticed that those who studied it diligently and were awarded university degrees did not appear to know much more than I did). As the years progressed, Pakistan regressed. Islamiat – the study of Islam – was made compulsory in the late Seventies, and still the children gained only a very limited knowledge, a tiny sprinkling of history on a very large portion of fairy-tales and mythology.

My interest in Islam lay dormant till the Third Oil War (also known as the Gulf War) in 1990. The Second Oil War in 1967 had seen Israel, backed by the West, inflict a severe defeat on the combined might of Arab nationalism, from which it never really recovered. The 1990 war was accompanied by a wave of crude anti-Arab propaganda. The level of ignorance displayed by most pundits and politicians was distressing. I began to ask myself questions which, till then, had barely seemed relevant.

Why had Islam not undergone a Reformation? Why had the Ottoman empire been left untouched by the Enlightenment? A reply necessitated long hours in the library. I began to study Islamic history quite obsessively, and later travelled to the regions where it had been made, concentrating on its clashes with Western Christendom. My study and travels, which helped greatly in writing the first three novels of my planned Quintet, are not yet over.[2]

---

2 It was travelling to Spain that inspired me to start writing the series of historical novels known as the 'Islam Quintet'. *Shadows of the Pomegranate Tree*, *The Book of Saladin* and *The Stone Woman* are completed. On 5 September 2001, I had begun to write *The Night of the Golden Butterfly*. It was proceeding well when one of the characters disrupted history. My punishment and his, when I return to that book, will be to remove him altogether. The banality of keeping him in would be unbearable.

2

The origins of Islam

Judaism, Christianity and Islam all began as versions of what we would today call political movements. The politics and culture of the period necessitated the creation of credible belief-systems to resist imperial oppression, to unite a disparate people or both. If we look at early Islam in this light, its history poses few mysteries. Its Prophet appears as a visionary political leader, its triumphs as a vindication of his action programme. The philosopher Bertrand Russell once compared early Islam to Bolshevism, arguing that both were 'practical, social, unspiritual, concerned to win the empire of the world'. By contrast he painted Christianity as 'personal' and 'contemplative'. Whether this view is applicable to the religion's primitive period is arguable, but it is quite untenable as a description of Constantine. Once Christianity had became the religion of an empire and embarked on its own conquests, its development followed a familiar pattern. By the sixteenth century, for instance, the language used by the victims of the Spanish Inquisition was frighteningly similar to that of the Stalinist show-trials of the 1930s.

Nonetheless Russell had intuitively grasped that the first two decades of Islam had a distinctly Jacobin feel. I think this is true. Sections of the Koran remind one of the vigour of the founding manifesto of a new political organisation. At times the tone towards its Jewish and Christian rivals becomes ultra-factional. It is this aspect of Islam that makes the history of its rapid growth genuinely interesting.[3]

---

3 The growing academic discourse on whether the new religion was born in the Hijaz or Palestine

Where to begin? The possibilities are limitless, but I will short-circuit the traditional beginnings and start in AD 629. It is Year 8 of the new Muslim calendar, even though it has yet to come into being. Twenty armed horse-men are on their way to the sanctuary of the popular Meccan goddess, Manat. The men and their leader have been dispatched by the Prophet to destroy the statue of the goddess of Fortune. For eight years Muhammad tolerated an uneasy coexistence between the pagan male god Allah and his three daughters: al-Lat, al-Uzza and Manat. While al-Uzza (the morning star – Venus) was the goddess most worshipped by the Quraish, the tribe to which Muhammad belonged, it was Manat (Fate) who was popular in the region as a whole, idolised by three key Meccan tribes, which Muhammad was desperately trying to win over to the new religion. Local politics deter-mined the eight-year truce.

By Year 8, however, three important military victories against rival pagan and Jewish forces had been won. The battle of Badr had seen Muhammad tri-umph against the Meccan tribes despite the small size of his own army. The tribes had been impressed by the muscularity of the new religion. Further ide-ological compromise must have been deemed unnecessary. And so it transpired that one late afternoon as twilight approached and shadows began to embrace the desert, the Prophet's emissary arrived with his twenty horsemen to enforce the new monotheism.

Manat's sanctuary at Qudayd was situated on the road between Mecca and Medina. The keeper saw the horsemen approach, but remained silent as they dismounted. No greetings were exchanged. Their demeanour indicated that they had not come to honour Manat or to leave a token offering. The keeper did not stand in their way. According to Islamic tra-dition as the commander of the group went towards the beautifully carved

---

or elsewhere is essentially of archaeological interest. Over the last thirty years the scholarship of John Wansbrough and Patricia Crone has transformed the study of Islamic history. Both of them have exposed the early biographies of Muhammad as works of 'pious imagination' and argued that the Islamic identity, the centrality of Mecca and the Koran emerged many years *after* his death. Believing Muslims would, no doubt, find this deeply shocking, but these researches strengthen the case for advancing a secular view of Islamic history. The fact is it happened, its growth was phenomenal, it trav-elled to every continent, it replaced two great empires in its vicinity and reached the Atlantic coast soon afterwards. At it height three Muslim empires dominated large parts of the globe: the Ottomans with Istanbul as their capital, the Safavids of Persia and the Mughal dynasty that ruled India.

statue of Manat, a naked black woman arose out of nowhere. The keeper called out to her: 'Come, O Manat, show the anger of which you are capable!' Manat began to pull out her hair and beat her breasts in despair. All the while she cursed her tormentors. Sa'ad beat her to death. Then and only then did his twenty companions join him. Together they approached the statue and began to hack away at it till it was completely destroyed. Al-Lat and al-Uzza were dealt with in similar fashion and on the same day. Did Allah weep? Did Allah protest? Legend failed to record any dissent on his part.

Some months before this event, Muhammad had received a revelation that he recited as part of the Quran:

> Have you thought on al-Lat and al-Uzza
> And on Manat, the third other?
> Those are the swans exalted;
> Their intercession is expected;
> Their likes are not neglected.

After the sanctuaries of the three goddesses had been destroyed, the last three lines were deleted and the new verse read as follows:

> Have you thought on al-Lat and al-Uzza
> And on Manat, the third other?
> Are you to have the sons, and He the daughters?
> This is indeed an unfair distinction!
> They are but names which you and your fathers have invented;
> Allah has vested no authority in them;
> The unbelievers follow but vain conjectures and the whims of their soul, although the guidance of Allah has long since come to them. (53.7–11)

The public explanation for the shift – Satan had spirited in the earlier verses, subsequently abrogated by Allah – must have been unconvincing at the time. The episode of the 'satanic verses' led to much convoluted apologetics by theologians and Islamic historians alike. The reality was more straightforward. A seventh-century prophet could not become a true spiritual leader of a tribal community without excercising political leadership and, in the Peninsula, mastering the basics of horsemanship, swordplay and military strategy. It was the Prophet-as-politician who understood the necessity of delaying the final breach with polytheism till he and his companions were less isolated. In tactical terms it made sense not to alienate the worshippers of the three female goddesses prematurely. Hence the hesitations and ambiguities that marked the first decade of the new faith.

Once the decision to declare a strict monotheism was taken, no concessions were permitted. Six hundred years earlier, the Christian Church had been forced into a permanent compromise with its pagan forebears and had accordingly readjusted its mythology. Its new followers were given a woman to worship, and not just any woman, but one who had conceived a child with God. Though it was a virgin birth, and far removed from the sexual adventures of Zeus, the failure to push through a total break with paganism had been noted.

Muhammad, too, could have picked all or any one of Allah's daughters to form part of the new constellation. This might have made it easier to attract new recruits, but here factional considerations acted as a restraint. A new religious party had to demarcate itself forcefully from its main monotheistic rival, while simultaneously marginalising the temptations on offer from contemporary paganism. The oneness of a patriarchal Allah appeared as the most attractive option, essential not only to demonstrate the weakness of Christianity, but also to break definitively with the dominant cultural practices of the Peninsula Arabs, a conscious obliteration of all links with polyandry and a matrilinear past. Muhammad himself had been the third and youngest husband of his first wife Khadija. Since divorce was widespread and women had the right to discard a husband, it is assumed that Khadija had divorced one husband and lost another, but the evidence is sketchy on all counts and after the triumph of Muhammad the subject was not widely broached. Khadija died three years before the birth of the Islamic calendar.

The influence of these early traditions should not be underestimated. What the later historians of Islam, following Muhammad's lead, referred to as the *jahiliyya* (the time of Ignorance) was much more fun than the monotheisms on offer. For the pre-Islamic tribes, the past was the preserve of their poets, who served also as part-time historians, skilfully blending myth and fact in odes designed to heighten tribal egoisms. The future was considered irrelevant. It was the present that was all-important. Remarkably similar to a strain within the Epicureans of antiquity, the Arabs of the *jahiliyya*, as their poetry indicates, lived life to the full:

Roast flesh, the glow of fiery wine
To speed on camel fleet and sure
As thy soul lists to urge her on
Through all the hollow's breadth and length;
White women statue-like that trail
Rich robes of price with golden hem,
Wealth, easy lot, no dread of ill
To hear the lute's complaining string –
These are Life's joys. For man is set
The prey of Time, and Time is change.[4]

The Koran countered this view with the following revelation:

They say: 'There is this life and no other. We die and live;
Nothing but Time destroys us.' Surely of this they have no
Knowledge. They are merely guessing.
And when Our revelations are recited to them in all their
Clarity, their only argument is: 'If what you say is true,
Bring back to us our fathers.'
Say: 'It is Allah who gives you life and then He causes you to die . . .' (45.246)

The tribal humanism of the pre-Islamic period had many attractive features, but it was incapable of theorising its practice or using it to unite the tribes, let alone raising it to the level of a universal philosophy of existence. One reason for this was the profusion of gods and goddesses. These were nothing more than supernatural versions of the human, but belief in them perpetuated tribal divisions and disputes, often caused by commercial rivalries. The world of those days was dominated by merchant caravans. The principal discourse concerned terms of trade. Civil conflicts were common.

Muhammad fully understood this world. He belonged to the Quraish, an Arab tribe that prided itself on its genealogy and claimed descent from Ishmael. Before his marriage he had worked as one of Khadija's trusted employees on a merchant caravan. He travelled all over the region, coming into contact with Christians and Jews and Magians and pagans of every

---

4 C.J. Lyall, *Translations of Ancient Arabian Poetry*, London 1930.

stripe. We can only assume that the journeys provided him with many insights and considerably broadened his mind. Whether or not Mecca itself was at this time the centre of a trade route is currently a hot debate within the academy, but even if it wasn't the centre, there were still Meccan traders, and they must have had to deal with two giant neighbours: the Christians of the Byzantine empire and the fire-worshipping Zoroastrians of Persia. To be successful traders in both milieux meant belonging to neither. True, there were several Jewish clans in the region, but Judaism's self-definition as the religion of the 'chosen' excluded it as a serious alternative. It has never been a proselytising faith. It was this closed character that had produced a reform movement in the shape of Christianity, and it was unlikely to attract pagan Arabs even if recruitment possibilities had existed.

Muhammad's spiritual drive was partially fuelled by socio-economic passions, by the desire to strengthen the commercial standing of the Arabs and the need to impose a set of common rules.[5] His vision encompassed a tribal confederation united by common goals and loyal to a single faith which, of necessity, must be both new and universal. Islam became the cement utilised by Muhammad to unite the Arab tribes and, from the beginning, it regarded commerce as the only noble occupation.

The new religion was typified by a mindset simultaneously nomadic and urban. The peasants who worked the land were regarded as servile and inferior beings. A telling *hadith* quotes the Prophet's words on sighting a ploughshare: 'That never enters the house of the faithful without degradation entering at the same time.' Even if the tradition was invented it reflected the reality of the period.

Certainly the new rules being devised made observance in the countryside virtually impossible. Praying five times each day, for example, played an

---

5 Some of these are contained in the Koran, which for a Holy Book can be remarkably practical, on one level. Thus the second chapter (2.282): *Believers, when you contract a debt for a fixed period, put it in writing. Let a scribe write it down for you with fairness; no scribe should refuse to write as God has taught him. Therefore let him write; and let the debtor dictate, fearing God his Lord and not diminishing the sum he owes* . . . Or later in the chapter headed 'Women' (4.10–12): *A male shall inherit twice as much as a female. If there be more than two girls, they shall have two-thirds of the inheritance; but if there be one only, she shall inherit the half. Parents shall inherit a sixth each, if the deceased have a child; but if he leave no child and his parents be his heirs, his mother shall have a third* . . .

3

The empire of the world

The military successes of the first Muslim armies were remarkable on every front. The speed of their advance startled the Mediterranean world. The contrast with early Christianity could not have been more pronounced. Within twenty years of Muhammad's death in 632, his followers had laid the foundations of the first Islamic empire in the regions of the Fertile Crescent. This base was then used to spur the growth of Islam throughout the region. Impressed by these successes, whole tribes embraced the new religion. Mosques sprouted in the desert. The army expanded accordingly. The swift triumphs of this army were seen as a sign that Allah was both omnipotent and on the side of the Believers.

A combination of factors explains these remarkable victories. By AD 628 the Persian and Byzantine empires had been at war for almost a century: a titanic conflict that had enfeebled both sides, alienated the subject populations and created an opening for new conquerors. Syria and Egypt were part of the Byzantine empire. Iraq was ruled by Sasanid Persia. All three now fell to the might and fervour of a unified tribal force.

The Arab triumphs against the highly skilled and experienced war-machines of two empires are not explicable by force of numbers or a sophisticated military strategy. The ability of the Muslim generals to skilfully manoeuvre their camel cavalry and to alternate it with an effective guerrilla-style infantry undoubtedly confused an enemy which had, till then, been used to hit-and-run nomadic raids and had not confronted fluidity on this scale, but on its own this would not have inflicted defeats. A decisive element was the active sympathy shown for the new invaders by a sizeable section of the local people. Most remained passive, waiting to see which side would triumph, but no longer prepared to fight for or aid the old empires.

The fervour of the unified Arab tribes cannot be explained simply by the appeal of the new religion or promises of pleasures in Paradise. It was the comforts of this world that motivated the tens of thousands who flocked to fight under the command of Khalid ibn al-Walid and took part in the conquest of Damascus. The ninth-century weaver-poet Abu Tammam referred to this in a verse:

> No, not for Paradise didst thou the nomad life forsake:
> Rather, I believe, it was thy yearning after bread and dates.

A view strongly endorsed by Ahmad al-Baladhuri, a distinguished Arab historian from the same century whose account of the Arab conquests is generally accepted as authoritative. He cites Rustum, the defeated Persian general who defended his country against the Arab assault, saying to an Arab envoy: 'I have learnt that ye were forced to what ye are doing by nothing but the narrow means of livelihood and by poverty.'

In 638, soon after the Muslim armies took Jerusalem, the caliph Umar visited the city to enforce the terms of peace. Sophronius, the patriarch of Jerusalem, who greeted him was taken aback by the ordinariness of the Muslim and the lack of pomp. Umar, like other Muslim leaders of the period, was modestly dressed. Dust of the journey marked his clothes. His beard was untrimmed. The poverty of his appearance surprised the patriarch. The chronicles record that he turned to a servant and said in Greek: 'Truly this is the abomination of desolation spoken of by Daniel the Prophet as standing in the holy place.'

The 'abomination of desolation' did not rest long in Jerusalem. The strategic victories against the Byzantines and the Persians had been accomplished so easily that the Believers became extremely confident and filled with a sense of their own destiny. After all, they were the people whose leader had received the last and definitive message of God. The conquest of Persia had overthrown a dynasty that had ruled for twelve centuries. The Arabs inherited its wealth and culture. This was the first time they had sighted the yellow metal known as gold. Baladhuri writes of an Arab soldier who sold a young woman of high birth he had inherited as war booty for a mere bagatelle: 1,000 dirhams. When asked to explain his stupidity, he replied that he 'never thought there was a number above ten hundred'.

The German tribes who took Rome had preserved their power by insisting on social privileges, but had succumbed completely to a superior culture, and later accepted Christianity. The Arabs who conquered Persia also found themselves presiding over a network of alien social and cultural practices. They too preserved their monopoly of power by confining military service to themselves and temporarily restricting intermarriage. Bewitched they might have been by the wonders of Persia, but they were never tempted to abandon their identity, language or the new faith. It was Muhammad's vision of a universal religion as the precursor of a universal state that had captured the imagination and furthered the material interests of the tribes. Not for them the temptation of becoming a ruling elite of a Christian or Persian empire and abandoning Arabic for Greek or Persian.

This did not imply a refusal to adapt or learn from the civilisations they had overpowered. Rather it was the cultural synthesis resulting from the Arab conquest of Syria and Persia that seeded the new Islamic civilisation, quickly absorbing the refined arts, literature and philosophy of Hellenistic culture into a common heritage. It was the multi-ethnic make-up and the populist and egalitarian propaganda of the Abbasid faction within Islam that enabled it to defeat the narrow nationalism of the Umayyads, even though the last remaining prince of the latter escaped to al-Andalus and founded a rival caliphate in Cordoba, which rivalled Baghdad as a cosmopolitan centre.

The development of medicine, a discipline in which Muslims later excelled, provides an interesting example of how knowledge travelled, intermingled and matured during the First Millennium. Two centuries before Islam, the city of Gondeshapur in southwestern Persia (now Khuzestan) acquired the reputation of a safe haven and became a refuge for dissident intellectuals and freethinkers, facing repression in their own cities. The Nestorians of Edessa had fled here in 489 when their school was sealed. Forty years later the emperor Justinian decreed that the school of Neoplatonic philosophers in Athens be closed. Its students and teachers, too, made the long trek to Gondeshapur. News of this city of learning spread to neighbouring civilisations. Scholars from India and according to some, even China, arrived to participate in the lively discussions with Greeks, Jews, Arabs, Christians and Syrians. While these ranged over a wide variety of subjects, it was the philosophy of medicine that attracted the most followers.

The theoretical instructions in medicine were supplemented by practice in a *bimaristan* (hospital), making the citizens of Gondeshapur the most cared-for in the world. The first Arab who earned the title of physician, Harith bin Kalada, was later admitted to the court of the Persian ruler, Chosroes Anushirwan, and a conversation between the two men was recorded by scribes. According to this the physician advised the ruler to eschew overeating and undiluted wine, drink much water each day, avoid sex while drunk and baths after meals. He is reputed to have pioneered enemas to deal with chronic constipation.

Medical dynasties were well established by 638, when the Arab armies took the city. This was followed by Arabs being trained at the medical schools and then moving elsewhere in the growing Muslim empire. Treatises and documents, too, began to flow. Ibn Sina and al-Razi, the two great Muslim philosopher physicians, were only too well aware that the origins of their medical knowledge lay in a small town in Persia.

While the seeds from Edessa and Athens had developed into giant trees of medical knowledge in Gondeshapur, Umar's successors had not idled on the military front. They fanned out from Egypt to North Africa. A base was established and consolidated in the southern Tunisian city of al-Qayrawan. Carthage became a Muslim city. The Arab governor of Ifriqiya, Musa bin Nusayr, established the first contacts with continental Europe. As he eyed the land across the water, he received promises of support and much encouragement from Count Julian, the exarch of Septem (Ceuta). Musa's leading lieutenant, Tarik bin Ziyad, a young Berber recruit, assembled an army of 7,000 men and with the aid of Count Julian's boats led them to the shores of Europe, near the rock which has ever since borne his name, Jabal Tarik.[6] It was April 711. Less than a hundred years had passed since the death of Muhammad. Once again the Muslim armies were aided by the unpopularity of the ruling Visigoth elite. In July of that same year, King Roderic was

---

6 The corrupted version survives today as Gibraltar. Count Julian's role has been a matter of great controversy in Spanish historiography. The Spanish novelist Juan Goytisolo, however, regards Julian as the model of an honourable Spaniard in the novel that bears his name.

defeated by Tarik's army. The local population flocked to the banners of the invaders who had rid them of an oppressive ruler. By autumn, Cordoba and Toledo had both fallen. As it became obvious that Tarik was determined to take the Peninsula, an envious Governor Musa bin Nusayr left Morocco with 10,000 men to join his victorious subordinate in Toledo.

Together the two armies marched northeastwards and took Saragossa. Most of Spain was now under their control, largely because of the population's stubborn refusal to defend the old regime. The two Muslim leaders were planning to cross the Pyrenees and from there embark on the long march through France to take Paris. So they dreamed, but their Andalusian adventure had been a local initiative.

Instead of obtaining permission from the caliph in Damascus, they had merely informed him of their progress. Angered by this cavalier attitude to authority, the Commander of the Faithful dispatched messengers to summon the conquerors of Spain to the capital. Instead of honouring the two men, he made sure the rest of their lives were spent in disgrace. They never saw Europe again. Lesser men came forward to carry on the struggle, but the impetus had been lost.

The forward march of the Islamic revolution was soon halted. At the battle of Poitiers in October 732, Charles Martel's forces commemorated the end of the first Muslim century by inflicting a sobering defeat on the soldiers of the Prophet: naval bases remained in the south of France – at Nice and Marseille, for example – but, for now, Islam was confined to the Iberian Peninsula. A century later the Arabs took Sicily, threatening the heel of the mainland, but were kept at bay. Palermo became a city of a hundred mosques, but Rome survived a Muslim raid and remained sacrosanct. To this day xenophobic northern Italians refer to the Sicilians as 'Arabs', a sobriquet not intended as the compliment it once was in al-Andalus.

When in 958 Sancho the Fat left his cold and windy castle in the northern kingdom of Navarre, desperate to find a cure for obesity, he went south to Cordoba, the capital of the western caliphate. This was not the dusty provincial town of today, described by Lorca's gypsy as 'distant and alone'. Caliph Abderrahman III had made the city the major centre of culture in Europe. Its closest rival lay not in Europe but in distant Mesopotamia, where another caliph from another dynasty presided over Baghdad. Both were renowned for their schools and libraries, musicians and poets, physicians and astronomers, mullahs and heretics and, yes, taverns and dancing-girls.

Cordoba had the edge in dissent. The fact that Islamic hegemony was not forcibly imposed had led to genuine debates between the three religions, producing an Andalusian synthesis from which native Islam benefited a great deal. The city became notorious for its dissenters and sceptics. In Baghdad they would speak, half in admiration, half in fear, of the 'Andalusian heresy'. The Andalusian passion for experimentation can also be seen in some of its architecture.

The interior of the Great Mosque in Cordoba is awesome. The impression of infinite space, the forest of pillars could only have been created by architects who understood the city and had participated in the intellectual ferment that thrived within its walls. Inevitably one thinks of what the space must have been like before it was violated by the construction of a Catholic altar, an organ, baroque images, chubby cherubim, heavy wood-carvings and oppressive wrought-iron. I screamed inwardly to protest against this imposition which, in a literal sense, darkens the interiors and prevents the flow of light. What had the Cordobans felt when it was first constructed to celebrate the victory of one faith over another? Perhaps they did not have time to reflect on the horror. Their own lives, too, had been transformed. Many had converted to Christianity in order to remain in the city. Others preferred exile and took ship for Morocco. The fate of the mosque must have been low in their list of priorities, and many converted Muslims, watched by the spies of the Inquisition, tended to avoid their old haunts. But after the cathedral was built, they must have prayed there to show their loyalty. Did they too scream inwardly on first sighting the monstrosity? I like to think they did for aesthetic, if not religious, reasons.

When he visited Cordoba in 1526, Charles I of Spain rebuked his priests: 'You have built what can be seen anywhere and destroyed what is unique.' The remark was generous enough, but Charles had not realised that the only reason the mosque had been preserved was because of the church that now lay inside.

The construction of the church violates the sense of infinite space, disrupting the oasis of stone palms with their red and white keystones. It is a dam stopping the flow of visitors from one side to the other. Over the years, I've seen virtually all the great mosques of the Muslim world, visited many churches and admired synagogues in some very unusual settings. None has affected me more than the mosque in Cordoba. Is it simply an act of solidarity against its rape by a repellent cathedral? I don't think so. There is something magical about this mosque: its geography, its refusal to be enclosed, its link with a real world. All this is embedded in its construction. And there is, of course, the history. Perhaps it is the history that moves me, but I resist this explanation. The answer surely lies in the architecture.

The architects who built the mosque had done so with great care, but they must have imbibed the atmosphere of the city. What they created would represent a culture that is the opposite of one that crammed its space with graven images. The mosque is an absolute void. In Cordoba the luxuriant details heighten the void. All paths lead to emptiness. Reality is affirmed through its negation. In this specially created void only the Word exists, but in Cordoba (and, of course, not only there) the mosque was constructed as a political and public space, not simply for the word of God.

The space in Cordoba, however, often echoed with debates where harsh and sceptical words were exchanged on both sides as the Koran was discussed and analysed. The philosopher poet Ibn Hazm would sit amid the sacred columns and chastise those Believers who refused to demonstrate the truth of ideas through argument. They would shout back at him that the use of the dialectic was forbidden. 'Who has forbidden it?' Ibn Hazm would ask in return, implying that the forbidder and only he was the enemy of the true faith. The attempt to reconcile reason and divine truth became an Andalusian speciality to be treated with great suspicion in Baghdad and Cairo.

It would take hundreds of years before the Reconquest could obliterate this culture and create a 'pure' European identity. The fall of Granada in 1492 marked the completion of this process. The first of Europe's attempted final solutions was inaugurated by the ethnic cleansing of Muslims and Jews from the Iberian Peninsula.[7] This is not to imply that a perfect world was destroyed from without. There were no perfect worlds. The Andalusian

---

7 One outcome of this cleansing was, in fact, the breakdown of personal hygiene. Because baths were associated with Islam and regarded as breeding-grounds of sensuality, the Catholic leaders of Spain ordered their destruction. Since many Muslims were forced to convert or be expelled, the spies of the Inquisition kept a sharp watch to see if the converts were still having baths or making their ablutions.

entity had been weakened by civil wars within Islam. A hardline Berber fundamentalism, reminiscent of Wahhabi puritanism of later centuries, had
physically destroyed palaces and buildings and killed Christians, Jews and
Muslims at various times in accord with its particular vision of Islam. All this
shows is that there is no such thing as a monolithic faith. Opposing currents
have existed within all three religions. There were, however, periods in
Islamic Spain which can be described as a 'golden age', and it is this golden
age that remains within us whatever our particular origins may be.

Islam had always prospered through contact with other traditions. Its
origins lay in close contact with Judaism and Christianity. Its earliest defenders utilised methods of exposition first developed by the cosmopolitan
philosophers in the old schools of Alexandria. The interrelationship between
the Neoplatonists and the Sufi tradition was both direct and subconscious.
It is not common knowledge that after the demise of classical civilisation,
the Islamic renaissance of the early Middle Ages preserved and refined the
thought of the ancient Greeks, producing work in the practical arts and sciences which, a few centuries later, served as an intellectual bridge to the
European Renaissance and ideas that would dominate the modern West.
The mix produced by the commingling of cultures during the Cordoba
caliphate and the Arab occupation of Sicily left marks on the histories and
geographies of both Islam and Europe. The road from Ancient Greece to
Western Europe made a long detour through the world of Islam. 'Indeed,'
writes M. I. Finley, a distinguished historian of the ancient world, 'were it
not for the disunity and clashes which had already developed within Islam,
it is possible that neither the Eastern Empire nor the Western would have
survived at all.'

4

Jerusalem, Jerusalem

How would Christianity respond to the phenomenal successes of its upstart rival? The advancing Arab armies had become the most dynamic force in the struggle for the Mediterranean world and beyond. By the end of the First Millennium, the Islamic world stretched from Central Asia to the Atlantic coast. Its political unity had been disrupted soon after the bloody victory of the Abbasids. Three centres of power emerged: Baghdad, Cordoba and Cairo, each had its own caliph. Soon after the death of its Founder-Prophet, Islam had divided into two major factions, the Sunni majority and a Shia minority. The Sunnis ruled in al-Andalus, parts of the Maghreb, Iran, Iraq and the regions beyond the Oxus. The Fatimid caliph in Cairo belonged to the Shia tradition, and claimed a spurious descent from the fourth caliph Ali and his wife Fatima, the daughter of the Prophet: hence the name of the dynasty. The first four Fatimid caliphs had ruled parts of North Africa and lived in the Maghreb till a Fatimid expeditionary force under the command of the legendary Berber general Jawhar captured Egypt in AD 969.

The traditions in each of these regions were different. Furthermore, each had its own material interests and needs, which determined its policy of alliances and coexistence with the non-Islamic world. Religion had played a major part in building the new empire, but its rapid growth had created the conditions for its own dismemberment. Baghdad had lacked the military strength and the bureaucracy needed to administer an empire of that size. Sectarian schisms had played their part. The notion of a monolithic and all-powerful Islamic civilisation had ceased to have meaning at the beginning of the tenth century and probably earlier. It would soon be put to the test.

Western Christendom was preparing to unleash the First Crusade – to capture the Holy Land, but also to loot as much wealth as available and bring it back to Europe – on a complacent Muslim world riven by civil conflicts. A thirty-year war between the Sunni and Shia factions had debilitated both sides. Key rulers, politicians and military leaders in both camps had died in the years immediately preceding the Crusade. 'This year', wrote the historian Ibn Taghribirdi in 1094, 'is called the year of the death of caliphs and commanders.' The deaths sparked off wars for the succession in both Sunni and Shia camps. This new round of internecine warfare further weakened the Arab world. Two years later, the Franj struck. Their brutal determination shook the divided world of Islam. It rapidly crumbled.

In 1099, after a forty-day siege, the Crusaders took Jerusalem. The scale of the massacre traumatised the entire region. The killing lasted two whole days, at the end of which most of the Muslim population – men, women and children – had been killed. The Jews had fought side by side with the Muslims to defend the city, but the entry of the Crusaders created a sense of panic. In remembrance of past ritual, the Elders instructed the entire Jewish population to gather in the synagogue and in its surrounds to offer a collective prayer. It was a fatal mistake. The Crusaders surrounded the perimeter of the synagogue, set fire to the building and made sure that every single Jew was burnt to death. A thick greasy cloud of triumphant vulgarity was to cast a long shadow over the entire region for another century. Exactly nine hundred years after these atrocities – among the worst crimes committed by religious fundamentalism – the Pope apologised for the Crusades.

News of the massacres in Jerusalem spread slowly through the Muslim world. The caliph al-Mustazhir was relaxing in his palace when the venerable *qadi* Abu Sa'ad al-Harawi, his head clean-shaven in mourning, arrived in Baghdad and, brushing the guards aside, burst into the royal quarters. He had left Damascus three weeks ago, and travel in the blistering heat of the desert sun had not improved his humour. The scene he observed in the palace did not please him. His tirade was recorded by Arab chroniclers:

> How dare you slumber in the shade of complacent safety, leading lives as frivolous as garden flowers, while your brothers in Syria have no dwelling place save the saddles of camels and the bellies of vultures? Blood has been spilled! Beautiful

young girls have been shamed . . . Shall the valorous Arabs resign themselves to insult and the valiant Persians accept dishonour . . . Never have the Muslims been so humiliated. Never have their lands been so savagely devastated . . .

The chroniclers describe how grown men began to wail and weep, especially when he described the fate of Palestine and the fall of Jerusalem. The speech affected everyone present, but al-Harawi was unmoved by the display of emotion:

'Man's meanest weapon is to shed tears when rapiers stir the coals of war.'

Over the next century, the Crusaders settled in the region and many Muslim potentates, imagining that the Franj were there to stay, began to collaborate with them commercially and militarily. The softness of the civilisation they had attacked began to have some impact on the Crusaders. A few of their leaders broke with Christian fundamentalism and made peace with their neighbours. But a majority continued to terrorise their Muslim and Jewish subjects and reports of their violence circulated.

In 1171, an unassuming Kurdish warrior, Salah al-Din (Saladin), ended the Fatimid regime in Cairo and was acclaimed Sultan of Egypt. A few months later, on the death of his much-venerated patron Nur al-Din, the young Kurd marched to Damascus with his army. He was given the freedom of the city and became its sultan. City after city accepted his suzerainty. The caliph trembled in fear. He knew that Baghdad, too, would fall under the spell of the young conqueror. He might come here and take the caliph under his wing. Saladin was aware of how he was regarded by the nobility. He knew that the Syrian aristocracy resented his Kurdishness and 'low upbringing'. It was best not to provoke them and others like them at a time when maximum unity was necessary. For that reason he never went near Baghdad and was always deferential to the caliph.

The unity of Egypt and Syria, symbolised by prayers offered in the name of the same caliph in the mosques of Cairo and Damascus, laid the basis for a concerted assault against the Crusaders. Patiently, the Kurdish leader embarked on an undertaking that had till then proved impossible and had eluded his predecessors: the creation of a unified Muslim army to liberate Jerusalem. Contrary to common belief the concept of jihad as 'holy war' had a limited pedigree. After the early victories of Islam it had been quietly dropped as a mobilising slogan. It was the barbaric zealotry of the First

Crusade that sustained Saladin in uniting his own side behind the colours of Islam.

'Regard the Franj,' he exhorted his soldiers. 'Behold with what obstinacy they fight for their religion, while we, the Muslims, show no enthusiasm for waging holy war.' The prestige of the Franks was such that Muslims used their name to refer to all West Europeans.

Saladin's long march finally ended in victory. Jerusalem was taken in 1187 and once again made an open city. The Jews were provided with state subsidies to rebuild their synagogues. The churches were left untouched. No revenge killings were permitted. Like Caliph Umar five hundred years before him, Saladin proclaimed the freedom of the city for worshippers of all faiths. But his failure to take Tyre was to prove a costly tactical error. Pope Urban dispatched the Third Crusade to take back the Holy City and Tyre became their vital base of operations. Their leader, Richard Plantagenet, reoccupied Acre, executing prisoners and drowning its inhabitants in blood, but Jerusalem survived. It could not be retaken. For the next seven hundred years the city, with the exception of one short-lived and inconsequential Crusader occupation, remained under Muslim rule. During this period no blood soiled its pavements.

The twentieth century was to mark a new turning point: the successful British-backed Zionist struggle to create an exclusively Jewish state destabilised Jerusalem once again. Forced removal of populations and more bloodshed has been the outcome. At the time of writing, the status of Jerusalem remains disputed, its population divided, and the place of Reason once again usurped by military might.

The Crusades left a deep mark on European and Arab consciousness. In July 1920 the French general Henri Gouraud took charge of Damascus. Syria had been allocated to France in the division of spoils following the First World War which led to the total collapse of the Ottoman empire. One of his first acts as he entered the city was to visit Saladin's tomb near the Grand Mosque. Here he shocked the entire Arab world by his vulgarity as he stood to attention and declaimed: 'Saladin, we have returned. My presence here consecrates the Cross over the Crescent.'

A more comical replay of the Crusades was enacted in the French embassy during the Lebanese civil war of the 1980s. One day a group of local Christian notables arrived unannounced and demanded to see the ambassador. On being granted an interview, the oldest notable explained in perfect French that they were all direct descendants of Frankish knights who had first come to this benighted region in the twelfth century. As the story of their families unfolded, the ambassador appeared sympathetic. An indulgent smile lit his face. This was not the first time that echoes of the past had reverberated in his office. The notables exploded their bombshell. Since their forebears had been Frenchmen, they had come to demand French passports for themselves and their families so that they could return to their country of origin. At this point His Excellency's demeanour underwent a change.

'Messieurs,' he is reported to have said, 'at the time of which you speak, the French Republic was not in existence. For that reason I have to reject your request and conclude our meeting.'

5

Ottomanism

The Crusades had disrupted a world already in slow decline. Saladin's victories had halted the process temporarily, but the internal structures of the caliphate were damaged beyond repair and new invasions were on the way. A Mongol army led by Hulagu Khan laid siege to Baghdad in 1258. The Mongol leader called on the caliph to surrender, promising that if he did so the city would be spared. Foolish and vain till the last, the caliph refused. The Mongol armies carried out their threat, sacked the city and executed the last Abbasid caliph. The caliphate made an inglorious exit. A whole culture perished as libraries were put to the torch. The Mongols often showed their resentment of a more advanced civilisation by destroying its treasury of knowledge. Baghdad was never to regain its pre-eminence as the capital of Islamic civilisation.

Elsewhere in the region power diversified as regional potentates recovered their dominion, but the centre of Islam was moving in the direction of the Bosphorus. By the middle of the fifteenth century Islam had spread across three continents. The pincer movement of military force and trade was not the result of some great master-plan, but its effect was the same.

Muslim armies had began to enter India via Afghanistan and the Indus during the eighth and ninth centuries, while the populations on the southern coast of the subcontinent were simultaneously coming under the sway of Arab traders. Mass conversions began to take place. Disaffection with local religions and the simplicity of Islam must have played an equal part in this process. Muhammad's combination of a monotheist universalism and the equality of all believers before God was an attractive formula to those burdened with caste systems and religious hierarchies.

In the centuries that followed, the same pattern was followed at the conflu-ence of the three major land trade-routes in the region of Xinjiang in northwest China, while Muslim merchant fleets reached the Indonesian archipelago and southern China as well as the western and eastern coasts of Africa. By the four-teenth century, Islam's centre of gravity was moving in the direction of the Bosphorus. Rome had been saved. Constantinople fell. On four previous occasions the armies of the caliphate from Damascus and Baghdad had laid siege to the capital of Eastern Christianity. On each occasion the city had survived. From 1300 onwards, the frontier emirate of Anatolia had been expanding slowly as it steadily ate into Byzantine territory. In 1453, old dreams were realised and the ancient city of Byzantium, later Constantinople, now acquired a new name: Istanbul. And a new ruler: Mehmet II, whose forebear, Uthman, had founded the dynasty that bore his name over a hundred years before.

On the eve of the total collapse of Islamic civilisation in the Iberian peninsula, the Ottoman dynasty inaugurated its reign by opening a new Islamic front in southeastern Europe. Within the next century, the Ottomans took Hungary, swallowed the Balkans, nibbled away at parts of the Ukraine and Poland and threatened Vienna. The Spanish Catholics feared and Andalusian Muslims hoped that the victorious Ottomans might dispatch their navy to Andalusian seaports and relieve their co-religionists, but a continental jihad was not part of the Ottoman plans any more than it had been of Saladin's, though on one occasion at the height of the Crusades, Saladin had visited the Mediterranean shore and confided to an adviser that the only way to defeat the Franj plague decisively might be to conquer and civilise their homelands. Jerusalem had sufficed for him. Constantinople satisfied Mehmet II.

Throughout the fifteenth and sixteenth centuries, a majority of Muslims lived under the rule of the Ottoman, Safavid (Persia) and Mughal (India) empires. The sultan in Istanbul was recognised as the caliph by the major-ity of Muslims and became the caretaker of the holy cities of Mecca and Medina. Istanbul became the new centre of this world. The overwhelming majority of Arabs became the subjects of the sultan. While Arabic remained the divine language, Turkish became the court vernacular, used by the ruling family and administrative and military elites throughout the empire, even though most of the religious, scientific, literary and legal vocabulary was lifted wholesale from Persian and Arabic. The original Turkish contribution was poetry, statecraft and architecture.

The Ottoman state, which lasted five hundred years, was a remarkable enterprise on many levels. It was a multi-religious state with the rights of Christians and Jews recognised and protected. Many of the Jews expelled from Spain and Portugal were granted refuge in the Ottoman lands and, strange irony, that is how a large number returned to the Arab world, settling not just in Istanbul, but serving the empire in Baghdad, Cairo and Damascus.

Jews were not the only privileged refugees. German, French and Czech Protestants fleeing Catholic revenge-squads during the wars of the Reformation were also given protection by the Ottoman sultans. In the latter case there was an additional political motive. The Ottoman state closely followed developments in the rest of Europe and vigorously defended its interests via a set of diplomatic, trade and cultural alliances with some of the major European powers. The Pope, however, was not regarded as a neutral observer and revolts against Catholicism were viewed kindly by the Porte.

The Ottoman sultan in turn became a major figure in European folklore, often demonised and vulgarised, but himself always aware of his place in geography and history, as evidenced in this modest letter of introduction by Suleiman the Magnificent, who reigned from 1520 to 1566, to the French king:

> I who am the Sultan of Sultans, the sovereign of sovereigns, the dispenser of crowns to the monarchs on the face of the earth, the shadow of God on earth, the Sultan and sovereign lord of the White Sea and of the Black Sea, of Rumelia and of Anatolia, of Karamania, of the land of Rum, of Zulkadria, of Diyarbekir, of Kurdistan, of Aizerbaijan, of Persia, of Damascus, of Aleppo, of Cairo, of Mecca, of Medina, of Jerusalem, of all Arabia, of Yemen and of many other lands which my noble forefathers and my glorious ancestors (may Allah light up their tombs!) conquered by the force of their arms and which my August Majesty has made subject to my flaming sword and my victorious blade, I, Sultan Suleiman Khan, son of Sultan Selim, son of Sultan Bayezid: To thee, who art Francis, King of the land of France.

The tolerance shown to Jews and Protestants was rarely, if ever, extended to heretics within Islam. The mullahs of the empire ensured that in all such cases punishment was brutal and swift. 'Remember Martin Luther,' the *kadi* warned the sultan. The Reformation could be supported because it served to divide Christianity, but the very idea of a Muslim Luther was unacceptable. From the viewpoint of a majority of Muslims, however, the Ottomans had preserved the heritage of their religion, extended its frontiers, and in the Arab East created a new universalist synthesis: an Ottoman Arab culture that united the entire region via a state bureaucracy that presided over a common administration and financial system. Even where the Ottoman bureaucrats usurped power, as in the case of the Albanian-born Muhammad Ali in Egypt, the basic structures of the state remained unchanged.

But what was this state? And given its flaws, how did it manage to delay its disintegration for so long? Three basic features marked the Ottoman and, to varying degrees, other Muslim empires of the period: the absence of private property in the countryside, where the cultivator did not own and the owner (i.e. the state) did not cultivate; the existence of a powerful non-hereditary bureaucratic elite in the centres of administration; and a professional trained army with a slave component. The first civil service academies in Europe were created by the Ottomans. They had abolished the traditional tribal aristocracy, forbidden the ownership of landed estates and, in this fashion, preserved themselves as the only dynasty in the empire and as the only repository of semi-divine power. This was the theory, and though in practice many skilful bureaucrats found ways to circumvent the rules, the basic structure was never challenged. In combating dynastic threats, the Ottomans created a civil service cadre recruited from the whole empire. The *devshirme* system forced Christian families in the Balkans and elsewhere to part with a son, who became the property of the Ottoman state. He was sheltered, fed and educated till old enough to train in the academy as a soldier or a bureaucrat. Thus Circassians, Albanians, Slavs, Greeks, Armenians and even Italians often rose to occupy the highest offices of the empire.[8]

Traditional Islamo-nomadic hostility to the ploughshare undoubtedly determined the urban bias of the dynasties who ruled large tracts of the world, but how far was it also the cause of the absence of landed property within the Muslim domain? Was this simply the result of local conditions? History would suggest otherwise. Despite the current vogue for micro-narratives and national specificities, the fact remains that in very different

---

8 One such figure inspired Ivo Andric's anti-Ottoman masterpiece, *The Bridge on the Drina*. An example of Greek integration into the Ottoman empire is provided by the epic figure of Khaireddin Barbarossa, the admiral of Greek origin, who conquered Algeria for the Ottomans. Stories of his exploits inspired versions of Red Beard the Pirate.

local conditions, the caliphates in Cordoba, Baghdad, Cairo and Istanbul, and later the Mughal empire in India, did not favour the creation of a landed gentry or peasant-ownership or village communities. Either would have aided capital-formation, which might later have led to industrialisation.

Someone in search of a micro-narrative could discover the richness of the agricultural techniques employed by the Arabs in Spain to prove that working on the land was not taboo. But the Spanish example is generally confined to the land surrounding the towns, where cultivation was intense and carried out by the townsfolk. Land in the countryside was rented from the state by middlemen who then hired peasants to work on it. Some of the middlemen did become wealthy, but they lived in the towns and that is where the surplus was spent. A rigidly dynastic political structure, dependent on a turbulent military caste, combined with the social subordination of the countryside could not sustain the political and economic challenge posed by Western Europe.

The main reason that the Ottomans staggered on till the First World War is that none of the three vultures eyeing the prey – the British empire, Tsarist Russia and the Austro-Habsburgs – could agree on a division of the spoils. The only solution appeared to be to keep the empire on its knees. The prolonged death-agony encouraged an insecure Turkish nationalism, the epilogue of what had once been a model multinational empire. The worst atrocities took place during the First World War, when hundreds of thousands of Armenians were slaughtered and their properties confiscated, but the process had begun much earlier.[9]

The end had already been visible since the middle of the nineteenth century. Radical nationalist impulses had begun to develop in the heart and the periphery of the Ottoman lands as early as the eighteenth century. Modernist Turkish officers, influenced by the French Revolution and Comte, began to plot against the regime in Istanbul, while an altogether more retrograde influence was at work in the Arab peninsula, inflamed by the teachings of a puritanical preacher named Ibn Wahhab.

---

9 The Turkish novelist Yashar Kemal depicts the social decay and the anarchy of this threatening world in several novels. Perry Anderson's *Passages from Antiquity to Feudalism* and *Lineages of the Absolutist State* remain among the most insightful explanations of the reasons for the rise of capitalism in Western Europe and not in the Muslim lands.

6

The joys of heresy

Islam expressly forbids a clergy. All Believers are the same before Allah. No hierarchy is permitted in the mosques and, technically, any Muslim can be invited to address the faithful after Friday prayers. How Islam would have developed if it had been compelled to spend the first hundred years in the wilderness is an interesting abstraction, but it was never faced with this choice. Instead its leaders rapidly found themselves at the head of large empires, with the result that a great deal of improvisation had to take place. The authorised version of the Koran was published many years after the death of Muhammad, its accuracy guaranteed by the third caliph Uthman, and it was accepted as the authentic version, though modern 'infidel' scholars such as Patricia Crone have found 'no hard evidence for the existence of the Koran in any form before the last decade of the seventh century . . .'

Regardless of the date, Koranic prescriptions, while quite detailed on certain subjects, did not suffice to provide a complete code of social and political conduct needed to assert Islamic hegemony in the conquered lands. And so the *hadith* (traditions) came into existence, consisting of what the Prophet or his Companions or wife had said at a particular time and date to X or Y, who had then passed it on to Q or Z, who had informed the author, who in turn wrote down the 'tradition'. Christianity had undergone a similar experience, but restricted it to four gospels, making sure that the contradictory versions of performed miracles or other episodes were either edited out or reduced to a bare minimum.

This wonderful game of Arabian whispers that began in the peninsula and moved to Damascus could not be restricted to four or even five slim volumes. Mercifully the Prophet, in an admirable self-denying ordinance, had repudiated any ability to perform miracles. He was simply a messenger bringing the revealed word to a wider audience. This exempted the new religion from producing accounts of miracles, but some chroniclers could not resist competing with Christianity, though their products were even less convincing. A pity, since the striking imagination of the Arabs might well have created a remarkable literature in this field, leaving Moses, Jesus and the rest far behind. Muhammad's early biogaphers did associate him with miracles, but these could not compete with those of Moses or Jesus.

The need to create traditions resulted in the birth of a new craft, which provided employment to hundreds of scholars and scribes throughout the seventh and eighth centuries, even though most of them were intellectually ill-equipped for the purpose. It led to ferocious arguments regarding the authenticity of particular traditions. It led to rival factions within Islam recruiting scholars to aid their cause. Later the Sufi mystics published their own traditions in which they stressed what they wanted to hear. 'No monkery in Islam' sounded authentic enough, but did the Prophet really say: 'Pray five times a day, but tie your camel first'? If he did, what was the implication? Was he hinting that some Believers might utilise the time of prayer to steal another Believer's camel? Or to prevent the camel from being stolen by an Unbeliever? Or was it purely a safety precaution designed to prevent the camel from following its owner and polluting the mosque? Or what? The war of traditions still goes on, raising the basic question whether any of them are authentic. Specialists have been debating this for over a thousand years, but no consensus is ever reached, nor is one possible, though over the centuries Islamic scholars have reduced the number of acceptable traditions and named the most reliable authors.

The point, however, is not their authenticity but the ideological role they played in Islamic societies. Sunni traditions challenge the Shia 'heresy'. The origins of Shi'ism lie in a disputed succession. After Muhammad's death in 632, his Companions decided to elect a successor. They chose Abu-Bakr and, after his death, Umar to lead them. Muhammad's son-in-law, Ali, probably resented this, but did not protest. It was the election of the third caliph Uthman that provoked Ali's anger. Uthman, from the Umayya clan, represented the tribal aristocracy of Mecca. His victory annoyed the loyalist old guard. They would have preferred Ali. If the new caliph had been younger and more vigorous he might have managed to effect a reconciliation, but Uthman was in his seventies, an old man in a hurry. He appointed close relatives and clan-members to key positions in the newly conquered provinces. In 656 he was murdered by Ali's supporters, following which Ali was anointed as the new caliph.

This resulted in Islam's first civil war. Two old Companions of Muhammad, Talha and al-Zubair, called on troops loyal to Uthman to rebel. They were joined by Aisha, the Prophet's feisty young widow. Battle was joined near Basra, and Aisha, mounted on a camel, exhorted her troops to defeat the 'usurper'. In what is known as the 'Battle of the Camel', it was Ali's army that triumphed. Talha and al-Zubair died in the battle. Aisha was taken prisoner and returned to Medina, where she was placed under virtual house-arrest.

Subsequently Ali was outmanoeuvred in another battle by his Umayyad opponents. His decision to accept arbitration and defeat annoyed hardliners within his own faction, and it was one of them who assassinated Ali outside a mosque in Kufa in 660. His opponent, a brilliant Umayyad general, Muawiya, was recognised as caliph, but Ali's sons refused to accept his authority and were defeated and killed in the battle of Karbala by Muawiya's son Yazid. This defeat led to a permanent schism within Islam. Henceforth the *Shia't* (Faction) of Ali was to create its own states and dynasties, of which medieval Persia and contemporary Iran are the most striking examples.

The Shia developed their own traditions, some of which are extremely offensive regarding Aisha and the Umayyads. The aim was to discredit her, since she had actually led an armed rebellion against the legally chosen Caliph Ali. The latter's followers alleged that the weak-kneed Caliph Uthman, who organised the first authorised version of the Book, removed whole verses from it because they favoured his factional rivals, the supporters of Ali. One of the traditions attributed to Aisha claims that in its oral phase the Koran, in a moving homage to the Old Testament, recommended 'stoning till dead' as the price for adultery, whereas Uthman's published version suggests that a good flogging is punishment enough.

It would have been surprising if this highly-charged atmosphere of actual and intellectual civil wars – tradition versus counter-tradition, differing schools of interpretation, disputes on the authenticity of the Koran itself – had failed to yield a fine harvest of sceptics and heretics. These emerged in due course. What is remarkable is how, during the first twelve centuries of

Islam, so many of them were tolerated for so long. Those who challenged the Koran were usually captured and executed, like the ninth-century Yemeni heretic who invented a set of traditions described at the time as both blasphemous and impugning the moral standing of the Prophet. Tragically, the fiction and its author were both destroyed.

But many poets, philosophers and heretics expanded the frontiers of debate and dissent in the search for knowledge and thus enriched Islamic civilisation. The mullahs' protests often went unheard by the rulers, an indication that at the time Islam was a growing and self-confident religion. The Andalusian philosophers usually debated within the confines of Islam, though the twelfth-century Cordoban Ibn Rushd (1126–98) occasionally crossed the permitted frontiers. Known to the Latin world as Averroes, he was the son and grandson of *kadis* – the supreme judge of a Muslim city – and a grandfather had served as the imam of the Great Mosque of Cordoba. Ibn Rushd himself had been the *kadi* in both Seville and Cordoba, though even he had to flee the latter city during a wave of clerical reaction when his books were burnt and he was banned from entering the Great Mosque.

The clashes with orthodoxy sharpened his mind, but also put him on his guard. When the enlightened Sultan Abu Yusuf questioned him about the nature of the sky, the astronomer-philosopher did not initially offer a reply. The prince insisted: 'Is it a substance which has existed from all eternity or did it have a beginning?' Only when the ruler indicated his awareness of the works of ancient philosophers did Ibn Rushd respond by explaining why rationalist methods were superior to religious dogma. The philosopher was only too aware that to confess oneself a semi-materialist could lead to sudden death, but he had decided to trust his ruler, who encouraged his researches. When the sultan indicated that he found some of Aristotle's work obscure and wished it to be explained in clear and concise language, Ibn Rushd obliged with a set of books. The *Commentaries* attracted the attention of Christian and Jewish theologians. Most of his work in Arabic was lost or destroyed and exists only in fragments. What survived did so in Latin and was studied a great deal during the Renaissance, but even that constituted a tiny proportion of his corpus. The *Commentaries* served a dual function: they were an attempt to systematise Aristotle's vast body of work and to introduce rationalism and anti-mysticism to a new audience, but also to move beyond it and promote rational thought as a virtue in itself.

Two centuries earlier, a Persian scholar, Ibn Sina (980–1037), born near Bukhara, had laid the basis for a study of logic, science, philosophy, politics and medicine. He was critical of Aristotle's *Logic*, regarding it as too remote from everyday life and therefore inapplicable. His skills as a physician led his employees, the native rulers of Khurasan and Isfahan, to seek his advice on political matters. Here, like Machiavelli after him, he gave advice that annoyed some of his patrons. This meant that he often had to leave the city of his employment in a hurry. In these periods he disappeared from public life, earning his living as a physician. His *Kanun fi'l-tibb* (Medical Canon) was a summary of existing medical knowledge together with his own theories and cures developed through many hours of regular clinical practice. This became the major textbook in medicine throughout the medical schools of the Islamic world and sections of it are still used in contemporary Iran. His *Kitab al-Insaf* (Book of Impartial Judgement), which dealt with 28,000 different philosophical questions, was lost when Isfahan was sacked during his lifetime. He had lodged his only copy at the local library.

It was his philosophical ideas contained in other works, and transmitted through fragments, which engaged with metaphysical questions of substance and being, existence and essence. In subsequent centuries these were to reach Western Europe, where 'Avicenna' was hotly debated. He questioned the resurrection of the body, but not the soul (probably a concession to Islamic orthodoxy). This was one reason why two decrees in 1210 and 1215 banned his works from being studied in the Sorbonne. Fifteen years later, a more clement pope, Gregory IX, lifted the restriction.

Ibn Hazm, Ibn Sina and Ibn Rushd typified certain trends of semi-official thought during the first five hundred years of Islam. The last two, in particular, chafed at the restrictions of religious orthodoxy but, like Galileo after them, chose to live and continue their researches in preference to martyrdom. There were others, far more outspoken, who challenged the entire edifice of Islam.

The ninth-century Baghdad heretic Ibn Rawandi wrote several books that questioned the basic principles of the Big Three: the monotheistic religions and their favoured god-in-the-sky. In this he went far beyond the Mu'tazilite sect to which he had once belonged. The Mu'tazilites believed that it was possible to combine rationalism and belief in one god. Some of them rejected the Revelation and insisted that the Koran was a created and not a revealed book. Others strongly criticised the quality of its composition, its lack of eloquence and the 'impurity' of its language. They insisted that Reason alone dictated obligation to God. Their more extreme followers denounced the Prophet for impiety and having too many wives.

They utilised rationalist arguments to explain the world, combining fragments of Greek philosophy with speculations based on their own studies and observations. The Koran was seen as extraneous to this project. Mu'tazilite thinkers developed theories to explain the physical world: bodies were conceptualised as agglomerations of atoms; a distinction was drawn between substance and accident; all phenomena could be explained through the inherence of atoms that constituted bodies. They speculated endlessly to try and understand location and movement in the universe. Was the Earth immobile? If so, why? What was the nature of fire? Was there a void in the heart of the universe?

Remarkably, in the first half of the ninth century this sect acquired state power for thirty years. Three successive caliphs from al-Mamun onwards forced state officials, theologians and *kadis* to accept that the Koran was confected by humans and was not a revealed text. The caliphs ordered that some of the theologians who refused to break with Koranic orthodoxy be flogged in public. This was not an endearing demonstration of the power of Reason and the period soon came to an end. The Mu'tazilites scurried away to other parts of the Islamic world, but aware of the inherent dangers in their philosophy, they became more cautious.

It is difficult not to speculate on what might have happened had they remained in power. If their ideas had developed further it seems obvious they might have ended up questioning the very existence of God. A comparison with the Islamic thinkers of the twentieth century, whose works are taught in the more serious religious schools and seminaries in Cairo and Qom, reveals that the thinkers of the ninth century were more advanced on every level. The poverty of contemporary Islamic thought contrasts with the riches of the ninth and tenth centuries. Yet the imams who teach by rote in the hole-in-the-wall mosque-schools in the cities of Western Europe and North America would probably find it too difficult even to acknowledge the existence of the Mu'tazilites. This shrunken perspective is one of the tragedies of 'modern' Islam.

In the enriched intellectual atmosphere of the mid-ninth century the emergence of a critical voice like Ibn Rawandi's is unsurprising. His meditations on the nature of prophets, prophecies and miracles, including

Muhammad, were scathing. He argued that religious dogmas were always inferior to reason because it was only through reason that one could attain integrity and moral stature. The ferocity of his assault first surprised then united Islamic and Jewish theologians, who denounced him mercilessly. Ibn Rawandi responded by demonstrating that miracles were simply the hocus-pocus of magicians. Far from exempting his own religion from these strictures, he included the Revelation that produced the Koran as patently fake. For him the Koran was neither revealed nor an original piece of work. Far from being a literary masterpiece, it was repetitive and unconvincing. He had started life as a Believer, but ended up as an atheist. His path must have been a hard and lonely one. None of his original work survives. What is known of him and his writings is almost exclusively through the texts of Muslim and Jewish critics who devoted tomes to refuting his heresies.

There is an exception: Abu al-Ala al-Ma'ari (973–1058), the poet-philosopher from Aleppo. Blinded by smallpox at the age of four, he used the disability to develop a prodigious memory. His knowledge of the world and his awareness of the capacity human beings possess to inflict untold damage on each other made him sceptical, pessimistic and, unusually for a Muslim, fonder of the animal kingdom than its human counterpart. The world consisted of 'either enlightened knaves or religious fools'. Two years at the Academy in Baghdad failed to quell his doubts. He began to compose quatrains, four-line rhyming stanzas, later adopted by his Persian admirer Omar al-Khayyam. Whereas Khayyam's verses were luscious and his scepticism expressed in more oblique language, al-Ma'ari tended towards a political asceticism, frontally critical of religion:

> What is religion? A maid kept close that no eye may view her;
> The price of her dowry baffles the wooer.
> Of all the doctrine that I have heard
> My heart has never accepted a single word.

His views on prophecy echoed those of Ibn Rawandi:

> The Prophets, too, among us come to teach,
> Are one with those who from the pulpit preach:
> They pray, they slay, they pass away, and yet
> Our ills remain as pebbles on the beach.

That he knew Ibn Rawandi's texts was made obvious in his own epic rhymed prose poem, *Risalat al-Ghufran* (Treatise on Forgiveness), set in Paradise and Hell, and which, according to the Spanish scholar Asin Palacios, inspired Dante's *Divine Comedy*. In the *Risalat*, al-Ma'ari has Ibn Rawandi addressing God thus: 'Thou didst apportion the means of livelihood to Thy creatures like a drunk revealing his churlishness. Had a man made such a division, we would have said to him: "You swindler! Let this teach you a lesson."'

The expression of al-Ma'ari's shocked response is an obvious pretence designed as a shield: 'If these two couplets stood erect, they would be taller in sin than the Egyptian pyramids in size.'

While careful to exempt God from any blame, he had expressed similar sentiments himself:

> And where the Prince commanded, now the shriek
> Of wind is flying through the court of state:
> 'Here,' it proclaims, 'there dwelt a potentate
> Who could not hear the sobbing of the weak.'

His most controversial work, *Al-Fusul wa al-Ghayat* (Paragraphs and Periods), worried his admirers greatly, for this was a parody of the Koran and they feared for his life. Nothing happened. The poet, whose affinity with animals made him a vegetarian, died in his eighty-fifth year. Since he was opposed to procreation, his work was his only legacy to the world, but did he have an aversion to sex as well? His poetry is strictly non-sensual, which is rare for that time.

The poets of Baghdad, Abu Nuwas in particular, were notorious for their sexuality and delighted in the more outrageous verses being repeated and sung in court and tavern alike. Many of the stories contained in the *Thousand and One Nights* (Abu Nuwas makes an appearance in some of them) are set in this period.

In Cordoba, Wallada bint-al-Mustakfi, an exact contemporary of al-Ma'ari, wrote a set of audacious poems to her lover, which she had embroidered on the sleeves of her robe and flaunted in public:

> Must separation mean we have no way to meet?
> Ay! Lovers all moan about their troubles.

For me it is a winter, not a trysting time,
Crouching over the hot coals of desire . . .

Wallada's literary salon became one of the most celebrated meeting places for the literati: poets and philosophers, men and women came here to listen to recitations of erotic and love poetry, most of which was never published. There were often heated debates on non-literary matters, including the analysis of dreams.

Dreams played an important role in pre-Islamic Arab culture and interpreters were highly sought after. Islam did not forbid this custom. After all the first revelation had appeared to Muhammad in a dream 'with the clarity of the dawn light'. Ibn Sirin, the first major Muslim analyst, was born a few years after the death of the Prophet. His compendium *The Interpretation of Dreams* was published some years after his death in 704 and also contains anecdotes about his life and practice. The book does not rate a mention in Freud's index, which indicates that the Viennese master was probably unaware of its existence.

Ibn Sirin's explanation of dreams is startlingly original and remarkably frank. It provides the reader with a rare picture of the social mores and sexual practices of first-century Islam. Homosexuality, incest, bestiality, transvestism appear with surprising frequency in the dreams decoded. Nothing appears to surprise him and, with the exception of erotic dreams that become wet and are the 'work of Satan', he had an explanation for everything. At times he came suspiciously close to the mark, as recounted in the following anecdote:

A man went to Ibn Sirin and said: 'I had a strange dream, and I am ashamed to tell you.' Ibn Sirin asked him to write it down. The man then wrote: 'I have been absent from my house for three months and saw myself return to my house in the dream. I found my wife asleep and two rams were fighting with their horns above her private parts, one of them having bloodied his adversary. Since that dream I have avoided my wife and do not know what to think despite the love I bear her.' Ibn Sirin replied: 'Do not avoid her any more. The dream suggests a free and pure woman. When she learnt of your imminent return, she wanted to shave her private parts and, in her haste, she cut herself with a pair of scissors . . . you have only to go to your wife and verify this.' The man returned to his wife and tried to touch her, but she rebuffed him saying: 'Don't come near me until you can tell

me why you have avoided me since your return.' He told her of his dream and Ibn
Sirin's interpretation. 'He spoke the truth,' she stated, taking her husband's hand
and placing it on the cotton over the wound.

Seven hundred years after the death of Ibn Sirin, the Tunisian writer Ibn
Muhammad al-Nafzawi wrote *The Perfumed Garden*, a collection of erotic
stories, poems, medical advice and comments on the meaning of dreams. Its
denunciation by clerics as the mindless and sex-obsessed work of a maniac
who 'died in the gutter' indicated that this was a much more subversive
volume than a first reading would suggest. And Edward Said's criticism of
the Orientalist misreading of this book as 'a seductive degradation of knowledge' was totally justified.

The Perfumed Garden is a multi-layered work. It is, among other things, a
biting critique of religious hypocrisy, which is as relevant now as it was
when first composed in the fifteenth century. For instance, the opening
short story is an account of the roguish false prophet Musaylima and his
seduction of Sajah, a self-proclaimed prophetess from the tribe of Tamim.
Both are genuine historical figures. Musaylima, the leader of the important
Hanifah tribe of Eastern Arabia, claimed to have also conversed with Allah
and accordingly suggested a division of power in the peninsula. Muhammad
rejected the impertinence and his followers denounced Musaylima as a false
prophet. Sajah likewise was a leader of the Tamim, influenced by Christian
ideas which she mixed with paganism. She and Musaylima united to fight
the successors of the Prophet. Both were defeated. Musaylima was killed in
battle and Sajah returned to her tribe and became a Muslim. Yet early
Muslim historians, including the normally restrained al-Tabari, chose to
treat their political alliance as a sexual union. In al-Nafzawi's version the two
meet, sexually distract each other and Musaylima, unable to contain himself
any longer, makes a bawdy suggestion:

> The bedroom's prepared, pray let us go through,
> Lie down on your back, I'll show something to you,
> Take it bending or squatting, on your hands and your knees,
> Take two-thirds or all of it, whatever would please!

The book is addressed to a vizier, but its entire tone and style suggests that
it was written to be recited in the squares and markets of the city and taken

abroad by travelling storytellers. Even an Arab audience that knew the bare outlines of the story would have gasped at the audacity of the third line. What Musaylima is proposing to Sajah is that they make love in the positions that correspond exactly to the ritual prayer of Islam. The author's knowledge that they were unbelievers did not make his lines less subversive.

While not a feminist work, *The Perfumed Garden* does reveal an understanding of female sexuality. Lesbianism is accepted and men are constantly advised to be unselfish in their quest for pleasure. It is in his search for aphrodisiacs that al-Nafzawi disappoints:

> Cook chick-peas and onions together thoroughly and sprinkle with a little powdered pelleter [a bitter-sweet root found in the Maghreb] and ginger. Eat a satisfying amount of this and you will find that sexual pleasure becomes wonderfully intense.

Not true.

Women versus eternal masculinity

The reality of women in Islam is a prefabricated destiny. Here the Koran is unambiguous. The chapter entitled 'Women' recognises the importance of the female sex and, for that reason, deems it essential to impose a set of severe social and political restrictions that determine their private and public conduct. While some sections of the text are open to a more generous inter-pretation, the foundational verse leaves no room for doubt:

> Men have authority over women because Allah has made the one superior to the other, and because they spend their wealth to maintain them. Good women are obedient. They guard their unseen parts because Allah has guarded them. As for those from whom you fear disobedience, admonish them, forsake them in beds apart, and beat them. Then, if they obey you, take no further action against them. Surely Allah is all-knowing and wise. (4.34)

Several chapters later, Allah's limitless generosity recognises the exclusive needs of the Prophet in this department and thoughtfully provides him with a blank cheque:

> Prophet, We have made lawful for you the wives to whom you have granted dowries and the slave-girls whom Allah has given you as booty; the daughters of your paternal and maternal uncles and of your paternal and maternal aunts who fled with you; and any believing women who gives herself to the Prophet and whom the Prophet wishes to take in marriage. This privilege is yours alone, being granted to no other believer. (33.50)

Muhammad reported this revelation to his wife Aisha. She was a woman of great intelligence and always displayed a keen interest in politics and state-craft. On a previous occasion she had asked him to explain why Allah assumed that all Believers were male. This unexpected question resulted in an immediate gender-shift. All future Revelations were addressed to both men and women. Informed of the latest pronouncement from the sky, her sarcastic response, as revealed in a *hadith* was characteristic: 'Verily, thy Lord hastens to do thy pleasures.'

A *hadith* collected by Bokhari (vol. iv, p. 91) quotes Muhammad as saying, on the occasion of his night-trip for the heavenly summit, that he had 'noticed that hell was populated above all by women', and he confessed in the same vein according to a different *hadith* that 'If it had been given to me to order someone to be submissive to someone other than Allah, I would certainly have ordered women to be submissive to their husbands, so great are a husband's rights over his wife.' Since most of these traditions are invented, what matters here is not whether these words were actually spoken by the Prophet, but the fact that they are believed to have been spoken and so are part of Islamic culture.

Traditions such as these reveal that early Islam, which is endlessly exalted by Islamic fundamentalists today, was incapable of imposing a universal oppression on women. It was resisted from above and below. In the crucially important verbal and military clashes with the pagan tribes, women played an important role on both sides. In 625, during the battle of Uhud, in which the Muslims suffered a heavy defeat, the pagan wife of an important Meccan chief, Hind bint Utbah, exhorted her troops thus:

> We reject the reprobate!
> His Allah we repudiate!
> His religion we loathe and hate!

Umar, a leading lieutenant of the Prophet and a future caliph, responded with a revealing riposte:

> May Allah curse Hind
> Distinguished among Hinds
> For her large clitoris,
> And may he curse her husband with her!

During Muhammad's lifetime and for many decades after his death, women fought alongside men, despite their supposed inferiority. They also fought to preserve their independence. Sukaina, the granddaughter of the fourth caliph, Ali, the inspirer of Shi'ite Islam, was once asked to explain her liberated appearance and her gaiety, compared with the austere and solemn demeanour of her sister. She is said to have replied that she had been named after her pre-Islamic great-grandmother, while her sister bore the name of their Muslim grandmother.

Islam sought to repress the political and sexual anarchy that characterised the *jahiliyya*. Muhammad's genius lay in the political rather than the spiritual realm. The latter, as the exchanges with Aisha suggest, usually served an instrumentalist function. He needed a state to promote his creed. His bodies of armed men and women were the first, most primitive appearance of the new state. To be effective, however, the new order had to be sacral. In the face of rival paganisms and monotheisms, Reason must be exiled. Though this could/can never be admitted by Believers, the fact remains that in terms of creating a new system, the code of conduct was more important than belief. The latter was necessary to impose the conduct, but once that had been achieved, the new identity would become strong enough to resist all rival attractions. In a world without nations or nationalisms, the Islamic identity came close to being a universal 'nationality'. If some sections of the Koran read like a factional document to differentiate itself from Judaism and Christianity, others are composed of detailed social, economic and sexual prescriptions, essential for the new state.

Over the centuries, as Islam expanded and created empires or communities that stretched from the Atlantic to the coastland of China, its institutions and customs became woven into a seamless fabric that was the Muslim identity. The continuity provided a sense of security. Dissent was not uncommon, but after the First Millennium it rarely crossed the frontiers of the existing politico-religious cosmos. There was no better world.

The collapse of the Ottoman empire shattered this complacency. The shards could never be remoulded. In the face of modernity, often brought to the Islamic world via the bayonet and the Gatling gun, the traditionalists settled into an easy collaboration with the colonial power. Unlike Napoleon in Egypt, the nineteenth- and twentieth-century representatives of the latter were not interested in extending the values of the Enlightenment. The works of Rousseau, Voltaire, Montesquieu, Paine, Fourier, Feuerbach or Marx were not part of the colonial curriculum. Privileged access was permitted to those who could secure a European education, but their numbers were limited. It suited both sides to preserve the 'cultural' continuity of Islam. The rigid statutes that safeguarded the inequality of women were zealously preserved, out of reach to old colonialism and *nouveau* capitalism alike. The family became the great untouchable: the innermost asylum of Muslim identity, portrayed with critical sensitivity in the novels of Naguib Mahfouz. Preserving this aspect of Muslim identity became the great fundamentalist battle-cry against the depredations of imperialism. Sayyid Kutb and Ruhollah Khomeini both denounced the freedoms enjoyed by Western women as false. Better a woman protected by the Islamic state than a random sex-object, viewed as such by any passerby.

What this reflected was a masculine fear of women, an anxiety that regarded the strength of women's desire as untameable, dangerous and thus requiring repression through strict codes of conduct, whose violation led to brutal punishments. This was a pronounced feature of early Islam, exemplified in a tradition attributed to the caliph Ali: 'Almighty Allah created sexual desire in ten parts; then he gave nine parts to women and one to men.' This oversexing of women was in sharp contrast to Christian piety, with its emphasis on sexual abstinence and matrimony, which the Pauline tradition grudgingly accepted as a necessary prerequisite to procreation. The origins of this attitude lay in pagan Arab society, where women played a central role in commerce, tribal politics and sex.

Polyandry, as I suggested above, had not been uncommon. Islam both inherited and inverted this tradition. It is this that explains the contradictions. On the one hand Islam is almost Reichian in its preoccupation with sex. Life is bathed in sexuality. The sexual *is* sacral. A healthy sex life for both men and women is essential to realise communal harmony. Muhammad stresses the importance of love-play and 'tasting each other's honey'. But men alone, through the new laws, will determine and control the social and legal space in which copulation is permitted. A deregulation of sexual pleasure was no longer permitted. A woman could take the most daring initiatives in bed, but not in society as a whole. In contrast to the puritanical patriarchy of Christianity, this was a patriarchy that flourished on hedonism. In *The Thousand and One Nights,* the ending is always careful to

satisfy the most orthodox believer, but even in other sections of the story
Eros and Allah mingle happily, as in Shahrazad's homage to the orgasm:

> Glory to Allah who did not create
> A more enchanting spectacle than that of two happy lovers.
> Drunk with voluptuous delights
> They lie on their couch
> Their arms entwined
> Their hands clasped
> Their hearts beating in tune.[10]

The Islamic *paradiso* was the magical culmination of all carnal pleasure, but
the patriarchal bias was preserved, even after death. Heaven in this case is a
much sharper reflection of the life led on Earth by the wealthy. Old men are
rewarded: their beards removed, they're provided with a wardrobe of seventy
costumes, each of which changes colour seventy times an hour. They are
made more and more beautiful with each passing day till age itself disappears.
Each is permitted seventy houris in addition to the wives the Chosen One
had on Earth, which must make for an interesting combination. And how is
this newly revitalised hunky male going to survive the arduous pleasures
afforded him? Patience, reader. Allah has thought of everything. It has been
decreed that love will be made in Heaven as on Earth, but with one small difference. Heaven is the site for the infinite orgasm. Each climax is extended
and its minimum duration is twenty-four years. What about old women? Do
the same privileges extend to them? Perish the thought or perish yourself!

As the Muslim conquests proceeded the patriarchal codes became more
and more stringent. The new identity had to be harshly protected against
older and more relaxed traditions. The economic rights of women became
meaningless as they were denied public space to negotiate these rights.[11]

---

10 *The Thousand and One Nights*, 'The Tale of Young Nur and the Warrior Girl', vol. 3.

11 For example, in contemporary Saudi Arabia some 40 per cent of private wealth is held by
women, including about 50 per cent of real estate in the city of Jiddah, but the women who own this
wealth cannot leave the country without the written permission of a male relative or drive a car or
appear unveiled in public. However, when they travel abroad they can use their wealth as they choose,
wear what they want and behave as they please. A contradiction, surely, whose explosion cannot be
delayed for too much longer, despite the protection afforded to the kingdom by US imperialism.

They were barred from the presence of all men except their husbands and close relatives. It was forbidden (*haram*) to enter the quarters to which they were confined in town house and palace alike. Later, temporary cloth partitions appeared in the hovels of the urban poor, to prevent the sighting of women by male visitors. For materialist reasons, much of the Islamic countryside managed to avoid segregation. In fact it was the birth of late twentieth-century fundamentalism that imposed this in parts of the Islamic world, of which Afghanistan was to become the best-known example.

How did women deal with these restrictions? Within the private sphere they completely subverted them. The evidence for this is present in numerous accounts, as well as in the literature that emerged from the different cultures which had embraced Islam. Muslim women in the cities devised elaborate methods to transcend their spatial and social confinement. In Senegal they were never fond of the veil; in Bengal they covered their heads but not their stomachs; in Java they displayed both. Everywhere they led secret lives, usually undiscovered by husbands or male relatives. Not that the latter were innocent when it came to engaging in forbidden acts.

Islam's strictures on homosexuality are almost pathological. It is unnatural because it violates the antithetical harmony that characterises heterosexuality. The effeminate man and the boyish woman are both denounced as deviants in revolt against the laws of God. In this respect, at least, the three monotheisms are in agreement. According to the *hadith*, Allah is angered by four deviations: 'Men who dress themselves as women and women who dress themselves as men, those who sleep with animals and those men who sleep with men.' Male homosexuality evokes the toughest punishment: torture and death. By contrast, lesbianism, necrophilia, masturbation and bestiality are treated indulgently: a strong reprimand and a warning.

Given the Islamic view of sodomy as the lowest of the low, the mother of all perversions, the father of all depravities and punishable with death (as Khomeini demonstrated in Iran after the Revolution), one might have assumed that this particular form of sex would have become marginalised within Islamic culture. In fact it was/is a common practice among both men and women in the Islamic world, where it has been greatly encouraged by the restrictions commonly imposed there on male–female relations. Even though these vary from country to country, the segregation of the sexes forms part of the daily routines of everyday life. To underline the theoretical joys of heterosexuality, while imposing severe legal restrictions on its practice, pushes people who might not otherwise have ventured there in homosexual directions. The result is an official society bathed in sexual repression and hypocrisy. Below the surface it is always the hour of the furnace.

The first Muslim philosopher to give serious thought to the structural defects of Islam in relation to women was Ibn Rushd, from Cordoba, whom we have met before. Often denounced as a *zindiq* (heretic), Ibn Rushd never retreated on the woman question. His open thinking pre-dated the invention of Europe, and therefore did not come *from* but, in time, would go *to* the Europe that was created by the Renaissance. Ibn Rushd argued that five hundred years of segregation had reduced the status of women to that of vegetables:

> In these (our) states, however, the ability of women is not known, because they are merely used for procreation. They are therefore placed at the service of their husbands and relegated to the business of procreation, child-rearing and breast-feeding. But this denies them their (other) activities. Because women in these states are considered unfit for any of the human virtues, they often tend to resemble plants. One of the reasons for the poverty of these states is that they are a burden to the men.[12]

Six more centuries would pass before the question was taken up again. The new champion of women's rights was a young Egyptian, Rifaat al-Tahtawi (1801–73). He grew up in the Egypt of Muhammad Ali, an Ottoman officer who became semi-independent and wanted to modernise the country. The student mission he dispatched to France included Al-Tahtawi, and here the young scholar learnt French, studied the philosophers of the Enlightenment and observed the freedom enjoyed by French women. On his return he published two books on the condition of women in Egypt. Like Ibn Rushd before him, he demanded that Muslim women be allowed social, economic and political equality with men. He condemned the *haram* as a prison that needed to be destroyed, and argued that child-marriage should be banned, and education provided to all women. Over

---

12 E.I.J. Rosenthal, quoted in *Political Thought in Medieval Islam*, Cambridge 1958, p. 190.

half a century later Tahtawi's baton was picked up by the Egyptian judge Qassem Amine, whose books *The Liberation of Women* (1899) and *The New Woman* (1901) became the founding texts of Arab feminism. Nationalism was still a few decades away, and it was still possible to emulate European progress without compromising the local position of Islam.

The twentieth century saw the birth and growth of movements for women's rights in the Arab world as well as South Asia. These dovetailed with the growing anti-colonialist campaigns and later both nationalist and socialist versions of anti-imperialism. The women's movements were uneven. During the early phase they demanded equal political rights without challenging the religious codes that governed family laws.

Later, in the post-colonial phase, women were granted social equality as well as the right to vote, but with the exception of Kemalist Turkey and Tunisia, the *shari'a*, Islamic law, was not challenged. Women had demanded the right to learn, work and vote. The first two were granted in Egypt, Iraq and Syria, but since these were one-party states the vote for men and women was of no significance. Even though women had fought for freedom alongside the men, once independence was achieved their demands for the reform of the civil codes governing family structures were totally ignored. Preserving these retrograde measures seemed to become the central pillar of Islamic identity in the post-colonial period. Pakistan and Bangladesh were to elect women prime ministers, but they were still subject to laws that regarded them as inferior citizens.

By the end of the twentieth century, with the defeat of secular, modernist and socialist impulses on a global scale, a wave of religious fundamentalism swept the world. Some of the rights won by women were under threat in the United States, Poland, Russia and the former East Germany. The victory of the clerics in Iran, the defeat of the left in Afghanistan, the continued existence of the Wahhabi regime in Saudi Arabia, the rise of hardline fundamentalist groups in Egypt and Algeria, the postmodernist defence of relativism appeared to have buried the hopes of women once again. In a global epoch it can seem as if the defence of one's identity is the only difference left. But whose identity is being defended, and in whose interest?

Many leading feminists in the Muslim world, who once courageously confronted mullah and military dictator alike, have bent in the face of the fundamentalist storm. We are sometimes told that arranged marriages and the veil are superior to Western marriages and adultery, as if all marriages in the Muslim world were arranged and adultery unknown. If Ottoman rule was more acceptable because of religious and cultural affinities, then why did the Arabs unite with the infidel against the Ottomans?

History may yet surprise us. A new wave of struggles might well arise in the clerical dictatorships of Iran and Saudi Arabia. Experience remains the best teacher.

PART II

One Hundred Years of Servitude

'By God, Your Excellency, we were as happy as we could be before those devils came along,' said Miteb. 'But from the first day they came to our village, life has been camel piss. Every day it gets worse.'

The emir answered him sharply. 'Listen, Ibn Hathal, I am speaking to you and all others, and let him who is present convey it to him who is absent. We have only one medicine for trouble-makers: that.'

He pointed to the sword hanging against the wall and shook his finger in warning. 'What do you say, Ibn Hathal?'

Miteb al-Hathal laughed briefly as if wanting to show he was not finished yet. A heavy silence echoed through the room.

'Hah . . . so what do you say, Ibn Hathal?'

'You are the government, you have the soldiers and the guns, and you'll get what you want, maybe even tomorrow. After the Christians fetch the gold for you from under the ground you'll be even stronger. But you know, Your Excellency, that the Americans aren't doing it for God.'

Abdelrahman Munif (1933–), *Cities of Salt*

8

A spring memory

April 1969. Lahore. A beautiful spring day, and not only because the jacarandas are in bloom. A Washington-backed military dictatorship has been toppled by students and workers after a struggle lasting five months.[13] The people achieved this on their own, without the help of any foreign power. Both Washington and Beijing tried but failed to keep the Field Marshal, Ayub Khan, in power. The student–worker demands – democracy and socialism – won the support of millions. The religious fundamentalists were totally marginalised.

After speaking at meetings in different parts of the country, I was back in Lahore to lecture the 'National Thinkers Forum' on the Soviet invasion of Czechoslovakia, to speak against the tanks that had crushed 'socialism with a human face' because it promised democracy. The hall was packed mainly with students, but also with pro-Moscow communists and vocal, though ageing, supporters of Chairman Mao. At the time I was actively engaged as a militant of the Trotskyist Fourth International, whose views were not widely circulated in South Asia. An attempt had been made to set the tone for the meeting. A hack versifier had been rented by the Maoists to compose a few lines celebrating the murder of Trotsky. While the audience was bemused, I ignored the provocation.

My critique of the Soviet invasion was well received. I had contrasted the

---

13 I have written at length about the resistance and the victory in *Pakistan: Military Rule or People's Power?*, London and New York 1970.

Czech students favourably with the Red Guards of the Cultural Revolution. Many of the students present instinctively solidarised with their counterparts in Prague. The pro-Moscow crowd was thoughtful, asked a few questions, but mainly remained silent. The Maoists embarked on a crazed polemical assault. They denounced my analysis and branded me as an agent of Western imperialism for suggesting that bureaucratic socialism was approaching its demise, that invading Prague might be one of the last nails in its coffin and that socialism could only be strengthened by democratisation. They condemned the Soviet 'social-imperialists', but insisted that Alexander Dubcek, the popular Czech communist leader, was also a revisionist and a 'capitalist-roader'. An ugly debate ensued, at the end of which a white-bearded veteran took the floor.

'Look at us,' he reprimanded the meeting. 'Our children have won us a big victory. They have overthrown a dictator and all we can do is fight each other.' Then in more pleading tones: 'Listen. The left in Pakistan is divided enough as it is.' He turned to the pro-Moscow stalwarts: 'Here, we have our Sunnis.' He glared at the Maoists: 'Here, we have our Shia.' Then he looked in my direction and smiled. 'And now this young firebrand wants us to embrace Wahhabism. Please, dear friend, have pity on us.'

As the meeting erupted in laughter, it was difficult not to sympathise with the approach of the old man. At the time I had only a vague idea of Wahhabism, let alone its founder. It was ultra-puritanical, it was the state religion of the Saudi kingdom, and the Saudis patronised the local Jamaat-e-Islami, a small but well-funded fundamentalist organisation. That was the extent of my knowledge. Later I would discover that the Wahhabis accepted the authority of Muhammad, while disapproving of the excessive veneration. They were hostile to the worship of saints and relics, but accepted the authority of the first four caliphs – the Righteous Ones. After that, in their eyes, Islam had begun to degenerate.[14]

---

14 The analogy with Trotskyists is not completely far-fetched. They too recognised the authority of Lenin, disliked the excessive worship and the display of his body, and only recognised the decisions of the first four Congresses of the Communist International. After that the deformation began, leading later to a complete degeneration.

9

The roots of Wahhabism

From the sixteenth century onwards, the Arab peninsula and the Fertile Crescent had been under the suzerainty of the Ottoman empire. Cairo, Baghdad, Jerusalem and Damascus became Ottoman–Arab towns, governed by a bureaucracy appointed by Istanbul. Even though Mecca and Medina were under the direct protection of the caliph on the Bosphorus, the peninsula's primitive tribal structure and its geographical isolation – the overland trade routes had long disappeared and been replaced by merchant fleets – reduced its economic and strategic attraction. It was neglected and never fully incorporated in the empire. The tribes both resented and exploited this lack of control.

They were still dependent on trade, but commerce was now largely confined to local needs. Old caravan routes were still in use, but mainly by pilgrims on their way to the Holy Cities. The necessity to feed the pilgrims and provide them with lodgings helped but did not fully sustain the local economy. Some of the tribes organised protection rackets. As long as money changed pouches, the safety of the pilgrims could be guaranteed. But this money was limited. Intertribal rivalries grew apace.

This was the context in which the birth of a new revivalist sect heralded change in the region. Its inspirer was Muhammad Ibn Abdul Wahhab (1703–92), the son of a local theologian, born in the small and relatively prosperous oasis-town of Uyayna. Muhammad's father, Abdul Wahhab defended an ultra-orthodox eighth-century interpretation of Muslim law. Tired of tending date palms and grazing cattle, his young son began to preach locally, calling for a return to the 'pure beliefs' of olden times. He opposed the worship of the Prophet Muhammad, condemned Muslims who prayed at the shrines of holy men, criticised the custom of marking graves, stressed the 'unity of one God', and denounced all non-Sunni and even some Sunni groups (including the Sultan-Caliph in Istanbul) as heretics and hypocrites. All this provided a politico-religious justification for an ultra-sectarian jihad against other Muslims, especially the Shia 'heretics' and including the Ottoman empire.

These views were hardly original. Puritanism in Islam always had its defenders. On their own, Ibn Wahhab's views would have been harmless. It was his social prescriptions – a belief in Islamic punishment beatings, an insistence on the stoning to death of adulterers, the amputation of thieves and public execution of criminals – that created real problems in 1740. Religious leaders in the region objected strongly when he began to practise what he preached. Annoyed by this nonsense and fearing a popular revolt, the emir of Uyayna asked the preacher to leave the city.

For the next four years, Ibn Wahhab travelled throughout the region and visited Basra and Damascus to gain first-hand experience of the laxity and looseness that the Ottomans had brought to Islam. He was not disappointed. Everywhere he travelled he noticed deviations from the true faith. He also found like-minded clerics who encouraged him in his beliefs. Ibn Wahhab now became even more determined to restore Islam to its primitive purity. This constant harking back to a 'pure' or golden age was sheer fantasy, but it served a function. It is not possible to create a revivalist movement without a purist reconstruction of whatever belief or religion is involved.

'Fanatics have their dreams,' wrote John Keats, 'wherewith they weave a paradise for a sect.' The English Romantic poet was referring to the Puritan religious sects that arose before, during and after the English Revolution of the seventeenth century, but the words could apply just as well to the desert preacher who made his way back to build his movement in the area he knew best. In 1744 Ibn Wahhab arrived in Deraiya, another petty oasis city-state in the province of Nejd. The soil was fertile and the people poor. The city was known for its orchards and date plantations and for its notorious bandit-emir, Muhammad Ibn Saud, who was delighted to receive a preacher expelled by a rival potentate. He understood at once that Ibn Wahhab's teachings might further his own military ambitions. The two men were made for each other.

Ibn Wahhab provided theological justification for almost everything Ibn Saud wanted to achieve: a permanent jihad that involved looting other Muslim settlements and cities, ignoring the caliph, imposing a tough discipline on his own people and, ultimately, asserting his own rule over neighbouring tribes in an attempt to unite the Peninsula. After lengthy discussions, the emir and the preacher agreed to a *mithaq*, a binding agreement, that would be honoured by their successors in eternity. The two clauses inserted by Ibn Saud indicated what he had in mind. Spiritual fervour in the service of political ambition, but not *vice versa*.

Ibn Saud had realised immediately that the preacher's charisma was infectious. Determined to monopolise both the man and his teachings, he demanded a blanket pledge: under no circumstances should Ibn Wahhab ever offer his spiritual allegiance and services to any other emir in the region. Incredibly, for a man of religion who defended the universality of Islam with a crazed vigour, Ibn Wahhab consented to abide by this restriction. The second demand of the emir was downright cynical. However bad it might appear, the preacher must never thwart his ruler from exacting necessary tributes from his subjects. On this point, too, Muhammad Ibn Wahhab accommodated his new patron, reassuring him that soon these tributes would be unnecessary since 'Allah promises more material benefits in the shape of *ghanima* [loot] from the unbelievers.'[15]

This covenant was sealed by a marriage. Ibn Wahhab's daughter became one of Ibn Saud's wives. Thus was laid the basis for a political and confessional intimacy that would shape the politics of the peninsula. This combination of religious fanaticism, military ruthlessness, political villainy and the press-ganging of women to cement alliances was the foundation stone of the dynasty that rules Saudi Arabia today.

By 1792, the Saudi-Wahhabi forces had overcome the resistance of neighbouring rulers and subjugated the cities of Riyadh, Kharj and Qasim. The new power began to sweep victoriously in all directions. The failure of rival tribes to unite and resist the Wahhabis allowed Ibn Saud's successors to

---

15 Ibn Wahhab's father and brother both rejected the new dogma. His brother Soleiman systematically refuted the Wahhabi interpretation, pointing out that the early leaders of Islam had never denounced other Muslims as purveyors of polytheism and unbelief.

threaten the holy cities of Islam. In 1801 they raided Karbala, the holiest city of the Shia, killed five thousand of its inhabitants, looted individual homes and shrines and returned home in triumph. In 1802 they occupied Taif and massacred its population. The following year they took Mecca and instructed the *sharif* of Mecca to destroy the domed tombs of the Prophet and the caliphs. This was done, and it was only after the Ottomans defeated the Wahhabis that they were rebuilt. Wahhabi doctrine rejected ostentatious gravestones.[16]

How long would Istanbul tolerate the Wahhabi rebellion? Its largest military base was in Egypt, but its hegemony here had always been unstable. The traditional elite of the Lower Nile posed an unending challenge, and while attempts to divide the Circassian and Bosniac factions from each other were often successful, Istanbul could never relax. As long as the dues were regularly paid into the coffers of the empire, the sultan ignored the threat. He was now also constrained by the new developments in Western Europe. Capitalism was beginning to thrive. The age of modern imperialism had begun. New conquerors of the world were on their way. Possibly the most remarkable enterprise in the history of mercantile capitalism was preparing to move eastwards.

The East India Company had been established in 1600. Just over a hundred years later an Iberian traveller, Don Manoel Gonzales, left us with a description of the first headquarters of globalisation:

> On the south side of Leadenhall Street also, and a little to the eastward of Leadenhall, stands the East India House, lately magnificently built, with a stone front to the street; but the front, being very narrow, does not make an appearance answerable to the grandeur of the house within, which stands upon a great deal of ground, the offices and storehouses admirably well contrived, and the public hall and committee room scarce inferior to anything of the like nature in the City.

The astronomical profit margins on East India goods caused Adam Smith to pen a trenchant passage in *The Wealth of Nations*, where he noted that the

---

16 The reason for this was egalitarian. All Muslims are supposed to be equal before Allah in life and death.

monopoly of this Company was paid for by the people who bought the merchandise, but they were also paying 'for all the extraordinary waste which the fraud and abuse, inseparable from the management of the affairs of so great a company, must necessarily have occasioned'.

As long as the English and Dutch states granted semi-sovereign powers (i.e. the right to maintain their own armies) to a group of merchants, the 'fraud and abuse' would be transplanted to India, where no Asian traders enjoyed similar privileges, any more than did the merchants of the Ottoman empire. As armed trading proceeded apace, the Company expanded outwards from its Calcutta base. After the battle of Plassey in 1757, it took the whole of Bengal. Within a few years the nominal Mughal emperor at the Fort in Delhi had became a pensioner of the Company, whose forces had rapidly spread westwards from Bengal. The Dutch had already occupied parts of Ceylon and the islands of the Indonesian archipelago.

Napoleon's conquest of Egypt in 1798 was designed as the first step to reverse his main enemy Britain's advances in India. Once the conquest was consolidated, the French planned to move eastwards and link up with the anti-British Muslim rulers of Mysore, but it was not to be. After a stalemated campaign in Syria, Napoleon returned to France, leaving behind two generals. One was assassinated the following year, while his colleague converted to Islam and became Abdallah (Allah's Slave) Menou. In 1801 a British force intervened to back the Ottomans. After a three-year occupation, the French withdrew from Egypt. The new empires of Europe were still in their infancy, but already the more far-sighted Ottoman functionaries could visualise the collapse of their whole world.

One such person was Muhammad Ali, a young officer of mixed parentage: his father was an Albanian officer in the Ottoman army who had married a Macedonian woman. He had arrived in Egypt with the Ottoman army in 1801 as the commander of an Albanian battalion ready to fight the French. He heard of how, after an uprising in Cairo, the French had circumvented the warring elites, promoted the local clerics to the status of representatives of the people, consulted them on numerous occasions and, generally, adopted a more benevolent attitude towards the populace than the Ottomans. More importantly, the emissaries of the French Revolution had plunged a dagger through the heart of a hated tax system that impoverished the countryside.

The tax-collectors of the Ottoman empire were the most unpopular wing of the state bureaucracy. Appointed to levy taxes from peasants who worked the land, they behaved like rural despots, treating the peasants as serfs while living in great splendour themselves. This system of state control ensured that taxes were paid regularly to the Treasury of the empire. Nothing else mattered. Soon after his arrival, Napoleon enacted the law of 16 September 1798: this established the price of land, recognised the peasant's right to own and inherit the land on which he worked, and established records of landownership. Ottoman and Mughal structures were comparable, but the contrast with the land policies the British were preparing to introduce in Bengal could not have been more pronounced. Paris favoured the peasant, London created the landlord.

Muhammad Ali had also noted that the French withdrawal had only been made possible because of the Ottoman alliance with the British. And so he began to plan and plot a *coup d'état*. He established close links with the two leading clerics who had collaborated with the French and bided his time. After some years of skilful manoeuvring, Muhammad Ali seized power in 1804. The sultan reluctantly appointed him the *wali* of Egypt. Without effecting a formal break with his superiors in Istanbul, he had became the de facto sovereign ruler of Egypt. When required, he defended Ottoman interests by curbing the depredations of the Hijaz tribes. In return, a grateful, if sulky, Istanbul usually left him alone.

It was Muhammad Ali's soldiers who defeated the Wahhabis in 1811, retook Mecca and Medina and drove them out of the Hijaz. In 1818 his son, Ibrahim Pasha, crushed the Saud–Wahhabi forces in their home-base of Nejd and destroyed their capital, Deraiya. Ottoman control was re-established and, even though the Wahhabis took back the Nejd, they would have to ally with the powerful British empire to wage a jihad against the 'hypocritical' Muslims of the caliphate a hundred years later before they once again established themselves as a regional power. Another and even more powerful imperial state would later entrust them with the entire peninsula. Wahhabism in its purest form – an unalloyed mixture of confessional rigidity and political opportunism – had become an instrument of the infidel.

10

The kingdom of corruption

An impatient European imperialism revelled in the spectacle of a declining Ottoman empire. Britain, Germany and Russia were scrambling neck and neck for the spoils. France had already taken Algeria from the Ottomans in 1830. Greece had exploited the decay to gain its independence. Russia's eyes were fixed on the Balkans. Britain already dominated Egypt and its agents were roaming the deserts of the Arabian peninsula in search of other allies. In Western Europe itself, the stumbling peace that had existed since the end of the Napoleonic wars was about to be shattered. Inter-imperialist rivalry was its cause. The war was triggered by an assassination in Sarajevo, but behind it lay the contest between Austria and Russia for the Balkans. Germany backed its Austrian cousins. Britain and France backed Russia.

The Ottoman sultan could have stayed neutral, but decided to join the Austro-German alliance. In retrospect his choice seems foolish, but at the time the Porte saw it as an adroit move to revive its fortunes. No empire likes to believe that its decline may be terminal. Neither the Ottomans nor the Hohenzollerns regarded the United States as a world power. Nor could they or anyone else have foreseen the sudden collapse of Tsarism in Russia and the subsequent victory of Lenin and the Bolsheviks. The latter event played a big part in persuading the United States to enter the First World War. Since Germany was perceived as the only European power who had the potential to threaten their interests, the United States backed Britain and France – though not for a while.

Defeat in the 1914–18 conflict sealed the fate of the Austro-Hungarian empire and the Istanbul caliphate. Over the centuries they had often clashed. United at last against a new enemy, they went down together. Their dominions were assigned a new future by the Conference of Victors in Versailles in 1919, when the liberal imperialism of Woodrow Wilson promised self-determination to every nation. Coupled with Bolshevik calls for rebellion in the colonies, this had the effect of drawing oppressed populations into world history. An unknown Indo-Chinese, Ho Chi Minh, managed to plead for his country's independence at the gathering in Versailles, but Britain had vetoed the attendance of delegates representing the Egyptian government. This refusal led to a popular uprising. It was defeated, but its leader Saad Zaghlul (c. 1850–1927) created the Wafd – the first real nationalist party of the Arab world.

The men at Versailles agreed that the former Ottoman Arab states should be given a formal independence, but under the tutelage or 'mandate' of imperialist states, not unlike Bosnia, Kosovo and Afghanistan today. The League of Nations was there to make sure that the victors mutually guaranteed each other's war booty. The collapse of Germany, Austria and Russia had left two imperialisms intact. They had already agreed a deal, making 'national' frontiers items of barter. Britain was 'mandated' to run Iraq and Palestine and watch over Egypt, while France was awarded Syria and the Lebanon as a consolation prize. Thus Britain gained a chunk of the Mashreq (East), while France retained the Maghreb, with the addition of Syria.

The collapse of the caliphate and the empire led directly to an explosion of nationalism. Rebellions erupted in Iraq and Syria, and though they were crushed by the imperialist powers, they created a smouldering resentment throughout the Arab world. The peoples of the new puppet states could see that, compared with new countries like Yugoslavia, Bulgaria, Romania and Czechoslovakia, the independence granted them was a sham. Then there was the Russian Revolution. It had turned the world upside down and proclaimed a Communist International dedicated to a universal revolution. Its radical anti-imperialist appeals addressed to the 'peasants of Mesopotamia, Syria, Arabia and Persia' had reached intellectuals in Cairo, Baghdad and Damascus as well as Kabul, Delhi and Djakarta. Would it and could it ever grip the people it addressed: the Muslim masses and the toilers of the East? A supremely self-confident Britain and France proceeded as if nothing much had happened in Europe. They underestimated both the effective rise of the United States and the Russian Revolution.

Already in 1917 the Balfour Declaration pledged the British empire to 'view with favour' the establishment of 'a Jewish national home' in Palestine, provided it did not affect the rights of the other inhabitants. Using this as a pretext, the British annexed Palestine. The small state of Trans-Jordan was carved out of Eastern Palestine and given nominal independence. The rest of Palestine was kept under direct rule so that the British could facilitate 'a Jewish national home'. The Zionist organisations in Europe had won a tremendous victory. A trickle of Jewish immigration to Palestine began soon afterwards.

The British and the French differed on the structures of their semi-colonies. Republican imperialism refused to tolerate the presence of Emir Feisal in Syria and asked him to leave Damascus. The British made him king of Iraq. His brother Abdullah was provided with a throne in Trans-Jordan. Both men were the sons of the *sharif* Hussein of Mecca, the Guardian of the Holy Cities, the chief of the clan of Hashem and directly descended from the Prophet. Hussein declared himself the king of Hijaz, assuming that the British would recognise the *fait accompli*, but he was an incompetent ruler and after a couple of years the British transferred their support to a more reliable and brutal client, Emir Abdal Aziz Ibn Saud from the Nejd, whose forebear had signed the compact with Ibn Wahhab almost two centuries before. Ibn Saud had no need for a preacher. Times had changed. The cursed Ottomans had gone forever. Their place was being taken by the English. Ibn Saud had realised this a long time ago. He had been guided all along by his great admirer, the Arabist and British agent H. St John Philby, who encouraged him to follow the lead of the Prophet and unite the disparate tribes of the peninsula.

Balfour and Philby. Loved by a few, hated by many. The two names symbolise imperial decisions with deadly consequences. Balfour paved the way for a Jewish settler-state in Palestine. Philby sponsored the creation of a tribal kleptocracy in the Arabian peninsula. Balfour has yet to find a muse, but the creative intelligence of the Saudi novelist Abdelrahman Munif has given us a penetrating portrait of Philby. Munif's genius lies in concentrating the intellectual and the popular in characters who are neither. His own strength derives from his ability to rise above all local prejudices. He is the patriarch of the writing tribe. His *Cities of Salt* trilogy depicts the transformation of Eastern Arabia from ancient Bedouin homeland to a hybrid oil state. In the absence of a proper and comprehensive history of the peninsula, Munif's trilogy inspires and clarifies without ever descending to nihilism. It is his acute psychological insights that explain his enormous popularity in the Arab world, and for writing these novels he has been deprived of his Saudi nationality and exiled. This is a writer who will never become 'official', never write to please, never drape himself in any country's flag.

In *Cities of Salt*, the opening novel of the series, Munif tells the story of the desert Bedouin who inhabit Wadi al-Uyoun. For centuries, caravans have quickened their pace to reach its good water and sweet, relaxing breezes. And then in the early 1930s modernity arrives in the shape of three Americans who turn up and make camp by the brook. They represent an oil company, but it is said they are friends of the Emir and have come to look for more water. 'Just be patient and you will all be rich,' their Arab translator tells the locals. The desert people are taken aback by the behaviour of the Americans: they stride around shouting, collecting unthinkable things in bags and boxes, writing obsessively late into the night. They take no notice of the people or their astonishment. One of them even lies down virtually naked outside the tent with his eyes shut, ignoring the children who are watching him. The women refuse to go to the brook any more.

Surprise is replaced by uneasiness, followed by fear and apprehension. The young bloods talk of killing the infidels, but the elders of the village forbid such talk. They are the guests of the Emir. Later the elders, too, are split. Miteb al-Hathal is against the Americans from the start. Ibn Rashed argues that they will come anyway and make everyone rich, so why not cooperate from the start? He becomes a different man when he is with the Americans, forgetting the incisive, proverb-laden speech of the Bedouin, rubbing his hands together in gestures of servility, overdoing everything and laughing like a hyena. 'It's the only way they can understand us,' he explains to Miteb. Reading the description one is reminded of Egyptian presidents Anwar Sadat and Hosni Mubarak in the company of US presidents and Israeli leaders.

The Americans go away, only to return with many more people and machines, and one morning the people are aroused by the sound of thunder. Bulldozers are attacking the orchards 'like ravenous wolves, tearing up the trees, piling them on heaps', and the people are left 'like windblown scarecrows made of rags and palm branches'. Wadi al-Uyoun is no more. Its place has been taken by an American encampment surrounded by barbed wire. The water is pumped back into the hole, as if to quench the thirst of the ghastly hordes of screaming *djinn* who are burning in the fires below.

Miteb al-Hathal gallops off into the desert to become a legend of the resistance, and the story moves with his son Fawaz to the coastal town of Harran: from a mixed community to a male one. The novel suddenly expands, like a river merging with the sea, and the story becomes one of globalisation: the countless millions of people made to travel centuries in a few brief, chaotic years, and not even in economy class but in the cargo hold of modern capitalism.

Ibn Rashed has now become the flustered, bullying, recruiting-officer for the American oil company. The Bedouin workers, dressed in tight oil company overalls, are confused and exhausted amid the roar of tractors. They carry wooden planks and steel girders with so much fear and misgiving that they are constantly falling down, dropping things and making every possible mistake. The wrath of the supervising Americans is incomprehensible to them.

One night, in Munif's most extraordinary description, a great ship arrives off the coast, covered in lights and blaring out music. The weather is sultry. Its deck is crowded with men and women, bare except for a small piece of coloured cloth, hugging and pressing against each other, laughing and shouting. The Arab workers sit watching on the beach, silent, panting, confused and bitter, both aroused and denied. They watch in silence as the foreigners pile off the boat and into the houses built by the Arabs, but from which they are excluded.

Variations of Night and Day, the concluding novel of the trilogy, is set in an earlier period, when the British rather than the American empire rules over the region. These are different times, and the Englishman has learnt to speak Arabic, the purest version, first spoken in the desert to which he has been dispatched. This fictional account of the wars waged by Ibn Saud to win the peninsula is far more real than any history. Sultan Khureybit and Hamilton are the imagined versions of Ibn Saud and Philby.

During the sultan's official council meetings, the Englishman, aware that most of those present neither like nor trust him, is monosyllabic but, writes Munif:

Hamilton was a different person at night, when their councils stretched on till late.

'. . . And you know, Your Majesty, that his Britannic Majesty's Government must consider conditions in the region, and local reaction. While the government offers you its unreserved support, as is made clear by their aid, and by my presence here among you as well, you may not actually provoke others, or turn them into Britain's enemies. Thus the government privately and tacitly agrees to take measures to eliminate your rivals; all we need to do is find a covert and acceptable means.'

Hamilton pronounced these words belatedly, and after doing some careful checking. The sultan, who had been waiting for this consent, wasted no time.

With every step the sultan grew more inclined to listen to what Hamilton said: 'If it is possible to annex this region peacefully, by enriching the tribes and sheikhs, that would be preferable to annexing it by force. If we can do that secretly, or noiselessly, that would be preferable to doing it openly, or by stirring up others.'

Month after month, year after year, they were not two persons, but Siamese twins, one body with two heads. While they did part late at night, the whole daytime and early evening sufficed them to talk about everything: How Britain thought and how people of the desert thought. What Britain wanted, now and in the future, and what the sultan wanted . . .

The peninsula refused to be taken noiselessly. Cash handouts were not sufficient to buy the two big rivals to the al-Saud clan. They had to be disposed of militarily. The British supplied the weapons. Ibn Saud's warriors used them to good effect. After he had conquered the city of Hail and defeated the powerful emirs of the Rashidi clan, Ibn Saud declared himself the sultan of Nejd. The whole of Central Arabia was now under his control. As his forebears had done in the past, the new sultan force-married wives of his defeated rivals.

The treatment of Muhammad Ibn Talal, the former emir of Hail, provided an image of the future Saudi Arabia. Ibn Talal was promised his freedom if he came to Riyadh. When he arrived he was imprisoned for two years and then put under house arrest. When restrictions were lifted, he was followed everywhere by fifty men. One of the great oral poets of Central Arabia, Al Oni, was a loyalist of the deposed emir, but Ibn Talal was not allowed to meet him. Ibn Saud feared that the poet would compose a poem in favour of his rival, which might raise a storm as it swept through the desert. The poet and the fallen prince met in secret, but were caught. The poet was blinded in prison and kept in such bad conditions that he died. Ibn Talal was assassinated.

The conquered cities went into an economic and spiritual decline. Fearing the Wahhabi dictatorship, many citizens fled to Iraq, Syria and the Yemen. But the search for oil was to transform everything and everyone in the region. The United States was determined not to permit Britain a monopoly of the riches underneath the sand. US oil prospectors arrived in the early 1930s and established contact with Ibn Saud, who agreed to grant them a concession. The price was low. In 1933 Standard Oil paid gold worth £50,000. The United States government, fearful of competition from Britain, merged Standard Oil with Esso, Texaco and Mobil to form the Arabian American Oil Company (ARAMCO). In 1938 the production of oil began.

Later, during the Second World War, the link was strengthened and the newly-established USAF base in Dhahran was deemed crucial to 'the defense of the United States'. The Saudi monarch was paid millions of dollars to aid 'development' in the kingdom. The regime was recognised to be a confessional despotism, but this unattractive quality was compensated for by the massive oil reserves that it commanded. Saudi Arabia was to become an important bulwark against communism and secular nationalism in the Arab world. Unsurprisingly, the United States safeguarded its own economic and imperial interests and chose to ignore what took place within the borders of the kingdom.

11

Zionism, the First Oil War, resistance

The end of the Second World War inaugurated a new process of decolonisation. The old empires had been weakened by the conflict. German imperialism had been defeated, but not by France and Britain. It was the epic Soviet resistance, symbolised by the battles of Kursk and Stalingrad, that had broken the spine of the Wehrmacht. Economic and military aid provided by the United States had also played a decisive part. The US had emerged as the strongest economic power in the world, but it was nervous of the prestige and military strength acquired by the Soviet Union. Even while the Second World War was being fought, the Cold War that was to succeed it had already begun. The United States, the Soviet Union and Britain had agreed to divide Europe into spheres of influence. Germany would be partitioned. Stalin would get Eastern Europe and in return would curb the communist resistance in France, Italy and Greece, which countries were to be the responsibility of Anglo-American imperialism. As for the rest of the world, and especially Asia, there was no agreement. The United States had nuked Japan and occupied the country, but elsewhere there was turmoil.

This was the context in which the United States, fearful of revolutions, insisted on a rapid decolonisation by Britain and France. In 1947 the British withdrew from India. The defeat of Japan had led to renewed revolutionary struggles in Indo-China, Malaya and Indonesia. On the Chinese mainland, the communist armies were inflicting defeat after defeat on the Nationalists, and in 1949 Mao Zedong would take Beijing and declare the formation of the People's Republic.

In 1948 the United Nations ended the British mandate in Palestine and agreed to the formation of the state of Israel. This event had little impact elsewhere. The newly independent Muslim states of Pakistan and Indonesia were immersed in concerns of their own. Iran was indifferent. In the Arab world, however, it was impossible to remain detached. The occupation of Palestine by Zionist settlers from Europe affected everyone. An Egyptian, Iraqi, Saudi, Syrian was not affected in the same way as a Palestinian Arab, but everyone felt the sense of loss. What till then had been a common culture for Muslim, Christian and Jewish Arabs had now suffered a serious fracture, a profound rupture that was to become known as *al-nakba*, the disaster. The Zionist victory had challenged Arab modernity, and some writers asked whether the continuity of the Arab presence in history had been destroyed for ever.

In Europe, where left and liberal anti-imperialists had welcomed the independence of India and the victories in China, the question of Israel caused a great deal of bitterness and disagreement. The Judeocide was, understandably, the central reason for supporting the creation of a Jewish homeland, but the communist parties in Europe and elsewhere (India, for instance) were also falling in line behind Stalin's decision to back and arm the new state. It was argued that given the social character of most of the regimes in the Middle East, socialist Israel would become a beacon of progressive values. Few, if any, asked questions as to how this state had been conceived and brought into being. Outside the Arab world and for some even within that world, the Palestinians became the discarded offspring of history.

The new Muslim state of Pakistan was closely aligned to the West and, apart from not recognising Israel, its leaders rarely mentioned Palestine or its uprooted people, nor did most of the media. The ignorance affected us all. 1956 was to change all that. The combined English–French–Israeli invasion of Egypt woke us up. The government of Pakistan backed the West, but the university students took to the streets and marched through all the schools, including mine. The Irish Brothers agreed to close it down and permitted us to join a mass demonstration on the streets of Lahore whose slogans were against our own stooge government. The Egyptian leader, Gamal Abdel Nasser, became our hero. He had stood up to the imperialists, he had told Britain that he was determined to nationalise the Suez Canal and if the former owners didn't like it they could choke in their own rage. Instead they tried to choke Nasser and failed, largely because Washington was horrified by their unilateralism. Nasser survived and we went back to school. That was the first time I thought about Israel. The newspapers had denounced it as a Western creation, a permanent dagger in the heart of the Arab world. It seemed accurate enough, but there my thinking stopped.

It was only when I came to Britain in the Sixties that I began to understand the scale of the disaster that had taken place in 1948. Those who educated me were mostly socialists, Marxists, anarcho-libertarians of Jewish origin. Ygael Gluckstein (who practised revolutionary socialist politics and wrote under the name of Tony Cliff) described himself as a Palestinian who had left Israel, unable to tolerate the anti-Arab discrimination that was embedded in the structures of the new state and at every level. He was particularly scathing of the Zionist labour movement for collaborating and justifying anti-Arab racism. 'You know why the West needs Israel?' he would ask, and insist on replying himself. 'Oil. Oil. Oil. Do you understand?' I did. Definition, repetition, lucidity were deployed to engage and clarify the politics of the Middle East.

Akiva Orr, born in Berlin in 1931, had fought in the 1948 war and never lost the appearance of a battle-hardened veteran. I was glad he was on our side. He had long abandoned Israeli patriotism, but he had been an insider and he knew a great deal. He lived in Britain for many years, returning to Israel in 1990. He lives near Jerusalem, close to several Palestinian friends. We speak on the phone sometimes and e-mail each other. His anger has become more intense. He knows well the jaundiced eyes of the tribal-minded exclusionists who masquerade as left-Zionists. He has been battling against their ideas for almost half a century, and they know that his passion and mastery of Israeli history make him a formidable opponent.

Jabra Nicola was a Palestinian of Christian origin, who lived in Haifa but spent the last years of his life in exile. He was a strong believer in a binational Palestinian state, where all citizens would have the same rights and which would one day form part of a federation of Arab socialist republics. He brooked no dissent from this position. There were *no* intermediate solutions, except for time-servers and opportunists. Nationalism was the problem, not the solution. Could we not see what Jewish nationalism had done to Palestine? The answer was not to reply in kind with the nationalism of the oppressed, but to transcend it altogether. It sounded grand and utopian. I was easily convinced.

I met him for the last time in the late 1970s. His son had rung and said his father wanted to see me urgently. It was raining when I reached Hammersmith Hospital in West London. The old Palestinian lay dying in a geriatric ward, surrounded by fellow patients watching TV soaps. Since most of them were partially deaf, the cacophony made conversation difficult. He grabbed my hand and held it firmly. His strength startled me. 'I want to die,' he said in an embittered tone. 'I can't do anything more.' And then he let go of me and made a gesture with his right hand, indicating the contempt he felt for the world. Who could blame him? He hated being in this hospital. I thought of the orange groves, the blue skies and the Mediterranean that he had left behind. He must have been thinking the same. I held his hand tight, told him he was still needed, a new generation would have to be educated just as he had once prepared us, but he shook his head angrily and turned his face away. He was not a sentimental man and I think he was annoyed with me for pretending that he could live on. He died a few weeks later. We buried him in a London cemetery. Another Palestinian burial far away from home.

All of them had told different stories relating to three dissimilar experiences, but the overarching narrative that informed each version was the same. Zionism – a secular Jewish nationalism – was the creation of atheist Jews who felt that European antisemitism had made individual assimilation impossible. Jews could assimilate only as an organised group and should create their own nation-state. Theodor Herzl (1860–1904), the founding father of the new creed, was open-minded as to where the new state should be sited. He was prepared to consider Argentina, Mauritius, Uganda or anywhere else. His more extreme followers, however, were insistent that a Jewish state could only exist in the Zion of the Old Testament: hence Zionism. According to biblical mythology this meant the area known as Palestine, and which had been populated by Arabs for over a thousand years. Herzl capitulated to the fantasy and the Zionists, a tiny minority within European Jewry, began to raise money to settle Jews in Palestine. All sorts of promises were made and untruths manufactured to lure potential migrants. One of the fairy tales circulated was that the land was uninhabited.

Some years before the birth of the Zionist project the Franco-Jewish

Baron Edmund de Rothschild had, with the permission of the Ottoman sultan, funded a few Jewish settlements in Palestine. In 1891, six years before Herzl founded the Zionist organisation, after a lengthy visit to the Rothschild settlements, the Jewish thinker Asher Ginzburg (1856–1927) wrote 'Truth from Palestine', a remarkably prescient text. In this he predicted that a continuation of the settlements could only lead to conflict with the Palestinians and warned against the crude and racist stereotypes of Arabs circulating within Jewish communities in Europe. The real importance of the article lies in its demolition of a Zionist fundamentalist myth: Palestine as 'a land without people' designed for Jews, 'people without a land'. In Ginzburg's words:

> We are used to believe abroad that Palestine nowadays is entirely desolate, a desert without vegetation, and that anyone desiring to buy land there can come and buy to his heart's content. This is really not the case. Throughout the land it is hard to find arable land that is not cultivated. Only sandy areas or rocky mountains which are suitable only for planting trees, and this too after much labour and great expense, are not cultivated because the Arabs are unwilling to work hard in the present for the sake of a distant future. Therefore not every day can one find good land for sale. Neither the peasants nor the big landlords will easily sell good and unblemished land . . . We are used to believe abroad that Arabs are savages from the desert, ignorant like animals, who neither see nor understand what happens around them. This is a great mistake. The Arab, like all Semites, has a sharp mind and is very cunning . . .
>
> The Arabs, particularly those who live in the towns, see and understand our aims and activities in Palestine. They pretend not to know because they see no threat to their future in what we do and they try to exploit us too . . . The peasants rejoice when a Jewish colony is established because they get good wages for their labour there and enrich themselves each year. The big landowners are glad too because we pay for sandy and stony soil a high price they never dreamt about in the past. However should a time come when the life of our people in Palestine will develop to such an extent as to push out, to a small or large extent, the indigenous population of the country, then not easily will they give up their place.

Elsewhere in the text Ginzburg explains how the envisaged state cannot be regarded as Jewish if it becomes an admirer of 'physical power'. For him the diaspora had preserved itself through 'spiritual power'. What was being discussed in relation to Palestine could be no different from a traditional colonial operation:

So that the state of the Jews will finally be a state like that of the Germans, or French, only inhabited by Jews. A small example of this process exists already now in Palestine. History teaches that during Herod's kingdom Israel was indeed the 'State of the Jews' but the Jewish culture was rejected and persecuted . . . Such a state of the Jews will be mortal poison to our people and will grind its spirit in the dust . . . This small state . . . will survive only by diplomatic intrigues and by constant servility to the powers that happen to be dominant . . .

Thus it will really be, much more than now, 'a small, miserable, people', a spiritual slave to whoever happens to be dominant . . . Isn't it preferable for 'an ancient people, which has been a light unto nations', to disappear from history rather than reach such a final goal?[17]

Ginzburg realised that if a Jewish 'cultural presence' was replaced by a political state it would inevitably lead to conflict with the local inhabitants, and that is exactly what happened.

The cynicism of the atheist pioneers of the Zionist state and the willing brutality they deployed to aid the colonial British state in crushing the first Palestinian *intifada* (1936–9) was a sign of the future. The Palestinian uprising was a protest against Jewish colonisation, which they would have stopped long before if the British had not been present. The eruption of popular anger was crushed by 25,000 British troops and Zionist auxiliaries helped by the bomber squadrons of the Royal Air Force. The counter-insurgency mounted by the British empire was the largest of its kind till the Malayan campaign after the Second World War. At the height of the colonial offensive against the Palestinians, Winston Churchill gave evidence to the Peel Commission of Inquiry in 1937 and justified the action on grounds of the racial superiority of the Jews, which he further stressed by an ill-chosen image:

---

17 I am grateful to Akiva Orr for drawing my attention to this text, which he translated from the Hebrew for his own book, *Israel: Politics, Myths and Identity Crises,* London 1994. Orr points out that Ginzburg, who favoured a cultural and not a political presence in Palestine, was a distinguished secular thinker and mentor to many, including Israel's first president, Chaim Weizmann, and bemoans the fact that his ideas have been marginalised and his work is virtually unknown in Israel today. The translated quotations are from the Hebrew edition of the *Collected Works of Ahad-Ha'am,* Jerusalem 1950. Ahad-Ha'am ('One of the People') was the pseudonym used by Ginzburg.

> I do not agree that the dog in the manger has the final right to the manger, even though he may have lain there for a very long time. I do not admit that right. I do not admit, for instance, that a great wrong has been done to the Red Indians of America, or the black people of Australia. I do not admit that a wrong has been done to these people by the fact that a stronger race, a higher grade race, a more worldly-wise race, to put it that way, has come in and taken their place.

This was the time-worn defence of imperial buccaneers. Not surprisingly, Churchill drew no parallel with the events taking place at the time in Nazi Germany, where another 'higher-grade race' was seeking to assert its superiority. The Palestinian insurrection was finally defeated just as war was about to erupt in Europe. Grateful for their support in crushing the Arabs, the British promised the Zionists their own state, but only after the war. Simultaneously, to appease the Palestinians, they promised to restrict Jewish immigration. This created tensions with the Irgun, the right-wing segment of the Zionists, who unleashed a terror campaign against the British. The Zionist left under Ben Gurion's leadership backed Churchill, and Haganah volunteers helped to track and round up Irgun suspects. The intra-Jewish civil war ended with the Second World War. The two factions now combined against the British.

In 1947 the British returned their mandate to the United Nations. This august body, with on-the-spot guidance from the United States and the backing of the Soviet Union, agreed to the partition of Palestine. The plan was rejected by the Arab states and irritated Britain, which felt it had lost part of its empire too suddenly. The British now used their influence in Iraq, Egypt and Trans-Jordan and encouraged these states to send in their armies to frustrate the plan. London hoped that in the resulting chaos it would be asked to resume control of the region and orchestrate an orderly transition to independence. Armed by the Czech government on Moscow's instructions, the Israeli army surprised the British and defeated the Arab legions.

The Israeli leader Ben-Gurion literally bought off the Jordanian King Abdullah by offering him money and half of the Palestinian territory (the West Bank) that had been allocated by the UN for the Palestinians. The remaining half was ingested by Israel. The Hashemite ruler, placed on his throne by the British, direct descendant of the Prophet Muhammad and son of the guardian of Mecca and Medina, accepted this sordid deal. He demanded a cash payment, informing the Israeli emissary that 'one who wants to get drunk should not count the glasses', meaning that in return for half of Palestine and his neutrality, the Israelis should not be too strict when weighing the pieces of silver. The Palestinians had been lavishly betrayed. An unholy trinity of British imperialism, the UN Security Council and an Arab king had sold them to the Zionists, who expanded their country without fear of reprimand from the Big Powers. The deal between Abdullah and the Zionists had flouted the UN plan, but the Security Council did not act to reverse the process.

From the moment of its foundation, the Zionist leaders of Israel were determined to depopulate the country. They wanted a home that matched the myth they had fostered in Europe of a 'land without a people'. The Palestinians were now a non-people. Those who could not be driven out were treated like *Untermenschen*. Many Jews obliterated these unsavoury episodes from the collective memory-bank of Israel. With the destruction of Palestinian villages and the expulsion of whole communities, most of the citizens of the new state retreated into a realm of make-believe. Cocooned from the rest of the Arab world, they believed that Palestinian stories could never be verified, or the statistics of displacement checked. And for almost a decade they succeeded in covering up the crimes that had been committed by them or in their name.

The story recounted by Yael Oren Kahn, born in Israel in 1953, is not uncommon. One can only hope that those who shared this experience will write about it as lucidly and honestly as she has done. The daughter of German refugees who had escaped to Britain in 1937 and later to Palestine, she grew up in a world where the diaspora Jews were constantly attacked for their inability to resist the fascist slaughter and were compared unfavourably with the young Zionist braves who had created the new state. And this was a world where Palestinians were invisible:

As a very young child I remember sitting on my dad's shoulders when we walked in magical gardens and orchards. I ran along the rows of prickly pear cacti. I imagined paradise would be like this. Yet, the scattered ruins disturbed me. I did not understand why they were deserted. Who would abandon such a paradise? The name of the place was Basheet. I asked my father and got no answer. When this paradise was destroyed and replaced with new houses and a new name, Aseret, my questions vanished with it. I befriended the Israelis who moved in and forgot the ghosts of the past. That is, until many years later, when I met the former inhabitants of Basheet in the Rafah Refugee Camp on the Gaza Strip. By then I knew that Kfar Mordechai, my childhood home, was built on the land of Basheet, but I no longer lived there.

Looking at the refugee shacks embarrassed me. I thought of the new villas that had been built on their land and felt the bitter pain of helplessness. One woman, who originally came from Yibnee, a town near Basheet, saw how distressed I was and comforted me. She had so much compassion. I then found out that she had lost a husband on an Israeli building site and a son to Israeli bullets.[18]

Ben-Gurion's greed and brutality left a scar on the future. Had he stayed within the borders demarcated by the UN then, regardless of the basic injustice, Israeli leaders and their supporters in the diaspora could have argued with some justification that they had accepted the UN decision and would defend their borders against any invader. Instead they did exactly the opposite. They colluded with Abdullah to steal more territory than had been granted by the UN, and they began to carry out the ethnic cleansing they had decided on many years ago. It had always been part of the Zionist project. In 1895 Herzl wrote in his diary: 'We shall try to spirit the penniless population across the border by procuring employment for it in the transit countries, while denying it any employment in our country . . . Both the process of expropriation and the removal of the poor must be carried out discreetly and circumspectly.'

In 1938 Ben-Gurion defended the concept of 'compulsory transfer' to the Jewish Agency Executive and argued: 'I favour partition of the country because when we become a strong power after the establishment of the state, we will abolish partition and spread throughout all of Palestine.'

It was this that made the Zionist position morally and politically untenable. In furtherance of his dreams, Ben-Gurion had hoped to sign a separate peace treaty with Abdullah and thus effect what he hoped might be the rapid and final solution of the Palestinian problem. Instead, a young Palestinian shot Abdullah dead outside the al-Aqsa mosque in Jerusalem in 1951 and temporarily disrupted the Ben-Gurion plan. Rarely in the Arab

---

18 *Secrets and Lies: A Journey to the Truth,* unpublished memoir by Yael Oren Kahn.

world has the assassination of a local potentate been greeted with such open expressions of joy.

The repercussions of Palestine continued to cause ferment. A year after Abdullah was dispatched, a group of nationalist-minded colonels, majors and captains, grouped in a clandestine organisation of Free Officers in the Egyptian army, toppled their corpulent monarch, bringing to an end the dynasty of Muhammad Ali. King Farouk, delighted that his life had been spared, left without a fuss for the French Riviera.

Soon after the Second World War, the British General Allenby had declared: 'The English can evacuate Egypt with an easy mind: in effect they have created a class of large landowners on whom Great Britain can rely to assure her policy in Egypt.' But the briefer duration of the British presence in Egypt made it difficult to successfully transplant the Indian colonial model on the banks of the Nile. Memories of Muhammad Ali's brand of enlightened Ottomanism had not been obliterated. The progeny of the rural rich had been given a privileged position inside the Egyptian army, but in 1936 the astute liberal-nationalist minister for defence, using British-imposed military conditions as a pretext, insisted on the creation of a national army. He ended restrictions on the recruitment of officers and invited cadets from urban middle-class and petty-bourgeois backgrounds to enter the military academy. This gradually changed the character and social base of the officer corps. The new recruits were influenced by ideologies emanating from the city mileu: nationalism, Islamism, socialism. The cadet intake of 1938–40 provided the bulk of the cadres of the Free Officers.

Nor did the 1952 seizure of power by the Free Officers come as a thunderbolt from a cloudless sky. Throughout the years 1949–51, the large estates, including the royal family's, were hit by a wave of peasant rebellions. On a number of occasions, the peasants attacked private guards and police barracks with an array of modern weaponry that could only have been supplied by sympathisers in the army. It was the communist organisations that linked the peasant militants on the estates to the centres of industry and, to a lesser extent, the barracks. From 1944–48, the Egyptian communists had succeeded in building strong trade unions and creating united-front committees in the countryside which brought in students and teachers to work with peasant activists.

The Free Officers were aware, but not part of all these developments. The coup they carried out was seen by some as the first step towards a social revolution in the country. The overthrow of the monarchy excited the population and triggered off a series of popular struggles that exceeded the aims of even the most radical army officers. On 13 August 1952 a strike by workers in British-owned factories was brutally repressed by the new regime. A military tribunal put the two principal working-class leaders on trial, found them guilty and sentenced them to death. The next day the two men were hanged. A month later the more radical members of the governing Revolutionary Command Council regime, keen to avoid a peasant insurrection and simultaneously to break the political power of the landed gentry, announced a limited land reform. This restricted land ownership to a maximum of 300 *feddans* (120 hectares) and pledged that the state would distribute all the land it had expropriated to landless peasants within the next five years. The landlords shrieked in anguish, hurling pro-private property verses from the Koran at the regime, but with nil effect. The reform had the desired effect, but a decade later it was noted that only 10 per cent of the land had been distributed to 2 million peasants. A pathetic result.

There were, at the time, two main currents of thought in the country. The influence of the Egyptian communists on peasants, workers and important sections of the intelligentsia made the nationalists nervous. The repression of the communists by the preceding regime had enhanced their prestige throughout the country. Bereft of a coherent ideology which they could deploy against the left, the Free Officers approached the Muslim Brotherhood with whom some of them had already established contact.

The Muslim Brotherhood (Jamiat al-Ikhwan Muslimun) had an interesting genealogy. It was a revivalist movement similar to those that arose in India after the collapse of the Istanbul caliphate in 1924. Kemal Pasha's bold decision to get rid of an outmoded institution that had failed to reform itself and the religion divided the house of Islam. The modernisers were pleased, but conservative theologians and traditional believers, who delighted in flaunting their identity by wearing the *fez,* now felt orphaned.

One of these was Hasan al-Banna (1906–49), a discontented Egyptian schoolteacher from Ismailia. He had been extremely upset by the secular constitution that had been adopted by Egypt in 1923, and the abolition of the caliphate a year later was an unacceptable epilogue. It decided him against modernity and its evils. When he looked at the state of the Islamic world he was impressed by the Wahhabi conquest of the Arabian peninsula and could see no reason why this triumph should not be repeated elsewhere. In 1928 he founded the Muslim Brotherhood to propagate moral and political reforms through education and propaganda. The character of the new organisation was clear from its founding manifesto. It suggested a return to the politics of the seventh century: 'God is our purpose, the Prophet our leader, the Koran our constitution, Jihad our way and dying for God's cause our supreme objective.' In order to challenge and defeat rival orthodoxies, pagan and monotheistic, the Prophet of Islam needed to create a new socio-economic-political system. Much of this had to be worked out literally 'on the hoof' as the Muslim cavalry conquered new territories. The speed of the expansion necessitated an amalgamation of creed and state, book and sword, as well as the creation of new laws that could serve as a complete code for everyday life. Christianity had to wait for Constantine before it could stop turning the other cheek. Islam never confronted a philosophical dilemma of this nature.

The practice of early Islam had already been abandoned in favour of a much more relaxed regime during most of the eighth and ninth centuries. To argue for its revival in the face of the challenges posed by modernity and the twentieth century was courageous, but it also announced a retreat from the existing world and its problems. The Muslim Brotherhood was, from the start, much softer in its reaction to the enemy without than it was to the 'hypocrites', 'renegades' and 'apostates' who existed within Islam.

The first decade of its existence was taken up with recruitment of cadres and propaganda. This was directed largely against modernisers and communists in Egypt. In 1936, the leaders of hard-core nationalist groups and the Islamists grouped in the Green Shirts of the Young Egypt party had been received as fraternal delegates to the Nazi Congress in Nuremberg. During the war when Field Marshal Rommel's army was in El Alamein, about 70 kilometres west of Alexandria, mass demonstrations erupted against the food shortages that the people believed had been caused deliberately by the British. The main chant of the crowds was not designed to improve the morale of British soldiers: *Ila'l-amam ya Rommel!* (Forward Rommel!). If the German and Italian armies had defeated the British and entered Alexandria there is little doubt they would have been welcomed as 'liberators' by the nationalist crowd. But not, it should be stressed, by the Muslim Brotherhood or the communists.

Hasan al-Banna kept the Muslim Brotherhood aloof from these activities. Even though the Brotherhood was behaving more and more like a clandestine political party – an underground armed wing had been organised – it insisted on presenting itself as a social movement. It saw the Egyptian communist party as its principal enemy and, after the war, collaborated with the British to weaken the effective anti-imperialist coalition led by left-nationalists and communists. The Muslim Brotherhood hurled its cadres into battle against the Egyptian left and excoriated the popular movement in the name of Islam. Its apologists still try to cover up the fact that Hasan al-Banna was in regular contact during this period with Brigadier Clayton of British Military Intelligence, who was serving as the 'Oriental counsellor' at the British embassy in Cairo.[19]

From 1945 to 1948 the Brotherhood unleashed a carefully planned campaign of terror, which involved assassinations of nationalist and left-wing leaders, the bombing of theatres and, after the birth of Israel, the repeated dynamiting of Jewish businesses. In September 1948 they hit Haret el-Yahud (the Jewish quarter) itself, killing two dozen people and injuring three times that number. The aim was to force the government to declare a state of emergency and suspend the constitution, which they assumed would weaken the forces of radical secularism in society. The Brotherhood's decision to dispatch the general in command of the police did lead to severe curbs on civil liberties, but the government was also forced to act against the organisation responsible for the killing. Three weeks after he outlawed the Brotherhood, Prime Minister Nuqrashi Pasha was shot dead by a Brother. 'When words are banned,' explained their leader, 'hands make their move.' Three months later, on 12 February 1949, opposing hands made their move and the 'Supreme Guide' was put out of action: in a carefully planned extra-judicial killing, Hasan al-Banna was executed by a government agent.

---

19 Details of the Muslim Brotherhood's collaboration with British imperialism and a careful analysis of their pronouncements during this period are contained in *The Moslem Brotherhood in the Balance*, Cairo 1945. The book had already disappeared from public libraries by the early 1960s.

The reason for the Islamist jihad against secular nationalists and Marxists is self-evident. The very presence of such groups in a Muslim country, let alone their ability to win popular support, was perceived as a dagger pointing at the heart of the Muslim Brotherhood. Why? Because the enemy were materialists. What Hasan al-Banna, the Brothers and their numerous successors today can never accept is materialism: not as a school of thought or a doctrine in the narrow sense of the word, nor even as a chance occurrence, but as an undeniable reality. Something that cannot be altered regardless of who rules the state. The materialism of all living creatures – animals, Wall Street bankers, politicians, priests, nuns, mullahs and rabbis – is fuelled by the same subconscious instincts. Thinking people search for truth in matter because they are aware that there is nowhere else for them to search.

Egypt's last free general election, held in January 1950, had returned a liberal nationalist majority with the Wafd as the leading party, but the British military occupation created a sharp divide within the nationalists. When the new prime minister informed the nation that he was on the verge of reopening negotiations with Britain and signing 'a treaty of friendship, trade and navigation' with the United States, the country erupted. There were forty-nine strikes in 1950 alone and mass demonstrations in every city. The mood was clear. The British had to go. In vain did the Egyptian foreign minister plead with the British to understand that their continuing presence in the country had created a situation where the people could no longer distinguish 'between patriotism and communist propaganda'.

The most radical Labour government in British history behaved with an imperial arrogance that drew murmurs of admiration from its Conservative predecessors. It refused to withdraw from Egypt unless the elected government agreed to join a Washington-sponsored alliance. Fearing a revolutionary explosion the government rejected the US proposal to participate in an Arab extension of NATO (other members were to include the USA, Great Britain, France and Turkey). This announcement in the Chamber of Deputies led to joyful rallies in all the cities. In Ismailia, British troops opened fire on demonstrators.

Within weeks of this episode, student–worker–peasant committees had formed guerrilla detachments and headed in the direction of the Suez Canal zone. Not all of them belonged to the nationalists or the left. Units set up by the Muslim Brotherhood and the ultra-nationalist Young Egypt took part in the action. Who would lead the struggle? The secular nationalists and the left or the religious nationalists and the right? Sections of the Egyptian army trained volunteers from both sides in the use of weapons and the rules of combat. It was when the peasants were mobilised in large numbers that the battles became more intense, and on a number of occasions the British forces had to withdraw.

The Labour government now faced a mutiny in its military ranks. The troops airlifted from Mauritius made it clear that if they were ordered to open fire on the Egyptian people, they would refuse. Several hundred were arrested. Those soldiers who did fight were demoralised and even *The Times* was constrained to remark in its leader of 26 December 1951 that: 'The nerves of British soldiers are subjected to a harsh ordeal. They wonder what interest there can be in retaining a military base that has lost all its usefulness because of an opposing national feeling . . .'

Six hundred volunteers from every city had died during this struggle. The Wafd government knew that if it did not act it might be swept from power by a popular upheaval. It therefore recalled its ambassador from London; announced that any citizen collaborating with foreign troops would be dealt with severely; bowed to the demand that every citizen be allowed to bear arms; threatened a total break with Britain and sent out feelers to Moscow; and publicly discussed the creation of an anti-imperialist front in the Arab world. Even the right-wing press demanded a British withdrawal. The Labour government in London refused to budge.

On 25 January 1952 the Egyptian police in Ismailia fought against British tanks and artillery and the whole country assumed that the Egyptian army would soon enter the fray. The next day a general strike brought the entire country to a halt. Students and workers marched to the town centre and were addressed by the prime minister, who pledged an immediate break with Attlee's Britain and a treaty with the Soviet Union. Messages arrived pledging solidarity from Moscow and Beijing, but also from Belgrade, Jakarta and New Delhi.

Over-estimating the threat from the left, the monarchists and their advisers in British intelligence decided to provoke a civil war. The Islamists were unleashed. The Muslim Brotherhood and its allies set Cairo's business district on fire. Later they began firing on lovers in dark alleyways and people coming out of Cairo's numerous bars. The government panicked and declared a state of siege. Next day it was dismissed by the king. Thousands of the volunteers who had fought against the British and the leftists were arrested. The fire in Cairo had served its purpose. When asked to explain what the Muslim Brotherhood stood for, its leaders replied: '. . . a *salafiyya* [traditionalist] message, a Sunni way, a Sufi truth, a political organisation, an athletic group, an economic enterprise and a social idea.'

Six months later the Free Officers took the country. Of the eighteen principal majors and colonels involved in carrying through the 'military revolution', four were members of the Muslim Brotherhood (Sadat, Amer, Hussein, Mehanna), three were Marxists (Khaled Mohiedin, Rifaat, Saddik) and the rest were nationalists. Nasser's own formation was eclectic. He had started with the Wafd, moved on to the Muslim Brotherhood and ended as a sympathiser of the left. What defined most of these officer-intellectuals was an urban petty-bourgeois/middle-class background. They read a great deal, debated with each other and held study-classes for like-minded officers.[20] As professor of history at the Military Academy, Gamal Abdel Nasser had a direct influence on the new recruits. Here he would lecture the cadets on the early military victories of the Arabs, and the light that radiated from the science and civilisation of early Islam at a time when Europe slumbered in semi-darkness. He would tell them how, as the Renaissance dawned, Islam handed over its inheritance to the Western Europeans, while it sank into a torpor and atrophied. Past glories were fine, but would not return. Now one had to think creatively of how to reawaken the national consciousness of the Arab world, move it forward and modernise. This long march necessitated a knowledge of science and the latest ideas.

Soon after the Free Officers' victory of 1952, their leader, Muhammad Naguib, the only general involved in the takeover, was removed and Nasser became the effective ruler of Egypt. This was achieved by isolating the

---

20 This characteristic of the Egyptian, Syrian and Iraqi armies in the Fifties and Sixties was in marked contrast to the colonial military formations painstakingly constructed in South Asia and parts of Africa. The colonial presence in the Arab world was relatively brief and, with the exception of the Bedouins trained to perfection by Glubb 'Pasha' in Trans-Jordan, the British and the French could not create reliable enforcers in Egypt, Syria, Iraq or even Saudi Arabia. In Syria and Iraq, in particular, the young cadets who became officers were influenced by anti-imperialist ideologies of different kinds.

secular left and concluding a de facto alliance with the Muslim Brotherhood. One of the arguments deployed against the left was its refusal to back the 1948 war against Israel. Arab communists, following Moscow's lead, had accepted the right of Israel to exist on the grounds of national self-determination. Many of them had been interned or imprisoned as a result. As Israel embarked on a land-grab in collaboration with Abdullah of Trans-Jordan, the view of the Egyptian left changed completely. Now they saw Israel as an imperialist transplant, but they were never forgiven. Muslim Brotherhood propaganda constantly referred to this 'betrayal of the communists'.

The Egyptian communists had always been a fractious bunch. Three rival groups had existed since the Twenties, but the infighting had annoyed Moscow so much that in 1930 it disaffiliated them from membership of the Communist International (Comintern). They were readmitted the following year after promising to behave, but Moscow appointed the new leadership. In March 1932 the Moscow-appointed Egyptian communists, in line with Comintern ultraleftism of the period, published a draft programme, full of colour and invective, but short on 'a concrete analysis of the concrete situation'. It described Egypt as a large British cotton plantation worked by slave labour, with the landlords and the monarch playing the role of slave-drivers and middlemen. The Wafd represented 'bourgeois-landlord-counter-revolutionary-national-reformism'.

Two months later, the Comintern's official weekly, *Inprekorr*, commenting on the surreal nature of the Egyptian document, denied its own responsibility and insisted on a more sinister explanation: '. . . as a result of the temporary weakness of the labour movement in Egypt, police *provocateurs* and petty-bourgeois adventurers succeeded in disorganising the activity of the Egyptian CP, detaching it from the workers, and alienating it from the revolutionary mass struggle.'

Both master and pupil came to their senses a decade later, but one constant remained: the influence of Egypt's communists in the mass movement always outweighed their actual strength. The actual membership of the party never exceeded 2,500. Its confessional opponents in the Muslim Brotherhood had at least 250,000 members. Even if one accepts that this figure included both hardened cadres and sympathisers, the difference is striking. True, the importance of the communists lay in their links to the state machines in Moscow and Beijing, but their weakness on the ground partially explains the ease with which Nasser, soon after he took power, could push them aside in favour of joint manoeuvres with the Muslim Brotherhood. In retrospect it is the restraint of the latter that is remarkable. They did not use the streets to make a bid for power; they collaborated willingly with the Free Officers, at least till February 1954; their Supreme Guide, Sayyid Kutb, turned down an offer to become the minister for education.

Having demonstrated to the divided Cold War world that he was not a communist sympathiser, Nasser then turned against the Muslim Brotherhood. It was the Islamists who provoked the dispute by insisting that the new Egypt be governed in accordance with the *shari'a* and that all secular laws should be subordinated to it. The officers who had, till now, happily utilised Islamist rhetoric, and had enhanced the prestige of the ancient Sunni university of al-Azhar by endowing it with more money, balked at the demand. Their response was typical. The Muslim Brotherhood was banned. Seven months later, on 23 October 1954, a Brotherhood assassin attempted a revenge killing. Nasser eluded the bullet. The would-be killer and five accomplices were arrested, tried and executed. Several thousand members of the organisation were imprisoned. It was alleged that the Brotherhood was once again colluding with the British to remove a leader hostile to imperialist interests.

This turn of events pushed the regime and the left closer to each other, though once again Nasser and his colleagues preferred to integrate radical intellectuals within their own structures of power. Rival organisations were not to be tolerated. All these developments took place in a highly charged international context. The new regime was no more prepared than its predecessor to enter into a security alliance with the West. The mood was one of 'positive neutralism' in the Cold War, a line of argument developed by the Indian prime minister, Jawaharlal Nehru, who visited Egypt frequently during 1952–6 and gave public support to Nasser's campaign against the continuing British occupation of the Suez Canal zone.

At the Bandung Conference of newly independent Afro-Asian states in 1955, Nasser was impressed by the support he received from China and India and shocked by the servile pro-Western politicians who represented Pakistan, the Philippines and Thailand. On his way home he made stopovers in New Delhi, Karachi and Kabul. Once again he was impressed by Nehru. A few months later he had his first meeting with the Yugoslav leader, Josip Broz Tito, who reinforced Nehru's arguments. Tito and Nehru convinced Nasser to remain outside the Cold War blocs while simultaneously pressuring the British to withdraw from Egypt in perpetuity.

The Egyptian leadership saw that the world of Islam was totally divided. In 1956, most of the governments in the Muslim world were stooges of Washington and London: Turkey, Pakistan, Iran, Saudi Arabia, Jordan and Iraq. Syria was a semi-stooge. Only Indonesia and Egypt were prepared to chart an independent course, and both would be punished severely for their defiance.

Egypt's first punishment had already been prepared. For several months the Egyptian government had been negotiating a deal with the United States and the International Bank for Reconstruction and Development (IBRD) for financing the High Dam on the Nile at Aswan. This had finally been agreed and the offer was on the table. Suddenly, Washington withdrew its offer. It was annoyed by what it regarded as Nasser's posturing on the world stage. The *New York Times* claimed that loyal allies Pakistan, Iran and Turkey had argued vociferously against the 'biggest single US aid project' being granted to a country that was 'not only neutral but occasionally actively anti-Western'. The three stooges felt they had better claims to the funds that had been allocated.

The US secretary of state, John Foster Dulles, had informed Egypt of the decision on 19 July 1956. Nasser's fury reflected the popular mood. On 26 July 1956 the Egyptian president, speaking in Alexandria, denounced the Anglo-American blackmail: 'Let the imperialists choke in their rage,' he warned and went on to inform a rapturous crowd that Egypt had decided to nationalise the Suez Canal. The revenues would finance the Dam and Egypt would regain its sovereignty over its economy and its territory. Nasser's speech was designed as a gauntlet to hit the dilapidated British empire smack in the face and in full public view. Overnight Nasser became the hero of the Arab and anti-colonial world. Divisions appeared in every army in the region. Crowned heads feared the worst, pro-Western politicians observed the popular response and began to tremble. How would the West respond? The British prime minister, Sir Anthony Eden, denounced the Egyptian leader as 'that Hitler on the Nile'. Nasser knew the British well. He was aware that their first instinct would be gunboat diplomacy. He knew, too, that Israel would be used by the West. He sent a message to the Israeli prime minister, Moshe Sharett, offering a comprehensive peace settlement, provided Israel stayed out of the coming conflict. Sharett was not unsympathetic, but Ben-Gurion smelt blood. The offer was contemptuously rejected.[21]

Without obtaining permission from Washington, the Conservative British prime minister, Anthony Eden, his Socialist French confederate, Guy Mollet, and their willing Zionist camp-follower, Ben-Gurion, planned to invade and occupy Egypt. On 29 October the Israeli army attacked the Sinai peninsula. Two days later an Anglo-French expeditionary force para-chuted into the Suez Canal zone. This action was verbally supported by Turkey, Iran and Pakistan.[22]

As the Egyptian army crumbled, the Soviet Union sent an ultimatum to the three occupying powers. The very next day the military action was halted. The following week US President Eisenhower publicly attacked the three countries who had dared to carry out this action behind Washington's back and stated: 'We cannot and will not forgive armed aggression.' On 22 December, British and French troops evacuated Port Said.

Nasser had lost the battle, but won the war. His New Year gift to Egyptians was the nationalisation of all foreign banks, insurance companies and commercial agencies owned by foreign enterprises. The Polish econo-mist Oscar Lange had visited Cairo two years before the Suez War and convinced the military leaders that economic planning would benefit the country and the majority of the population. The aftermath of the Suez inva-sion offered a dual opportunity: to punish the NATO powers – Britain, France and Turkey – by sequestering their enterprises and simultaneously to create the basis for economic planning. The streets were jubilant. Cairo recalled the words of its poet Ahmed Shawqi: 'The morning of hope wipes out the darkness of despair, now is the long-awaited daybreak.'

---

21 Maurice Orbach, the left-wing Labour MP from Willesden in northwest London, who took the message from Cairo to Tel Aviv, was severely criticised for his courage by local Zionists. For a detailed account see Avi Shlaim, *The Iron Wall*, London 2000, pp. 118–30.

22 The British Labour Party, mercifully in opposition, refused to back the war, dividing British public opinion and enlarging the space for dissenting voices in the media and elsewhere.

The thinking behind the First Oil War was clearcut. Britain and France wanted to destroy the nationalist alternative offered by Nasserite Egypt to protect their interests elsewhere in the region. Britain feared the loss of Iraq. France was worried by the birth of a nationalist movement in Algeria. The Zionist regime in Israel wanted to weaken Egypt and prevent the spread of radical nationalist ideas. The repercussions of the debacle had the opposite effect.

In February 1958 a union between Egypt and Syria – the United Arab Republic (UAR) – came into existence. This was the merger that, in the twelfth century, had enabled Saladin to unite the Arabs and take back Jerusalem. The historical memory of the Arab world goes very deep, and the news stirred many an Arab heart. The Yemen and the Lebanon expressed interest in becoming part of a wider federation. But the West was preparing an alternative. The Jordanian monarchy, which then, as now, functioned as an extension of the Foreign Office or the State Department, immediately called for an alliance between the Hashemite rulers of Jordan and Iraq and the Wahhabites of Saudi Arabia. In Riyadh, the Wahhabis were extremely worried by the turn of events. The king was persuaded to hand over power to emir Feisal, the crown prince, seen as a member of the al-Saud dynasty who, if circumstances compelled, could broker a deal with Nasser.

In Cairo and Damascus they talked of a new future, a transformed landscape, if only a major oil-producing country would become part of the UAR. Such a combination would polarise the peninsula and create strong foundations for a unified Arab nation, whose oil wealth would be used to service the needs of the Arab people. This was the dream, a desire that seemed utopian, and yet it came close to being fulfilled, sooner than anyone had realised.

In July 1958 a nationalist revolution toppled the monarchy in Iraq. The Hashemite King Feisal and his hated uncle were executed. Joyful crowds took over the streets in Baghdad to celebrate the seizure of power by Abdel Kerim Kassem and a group of radical nationalist officers. The West and its allies were stunned. Their regional security arrangement known as the Baghdad Pact died with the monarchy. A Cairo–Damascus–Baghdad axis now became a real possibility. Political agitators based in the radio stations of the three capitals began to incite the Jordanian population to open rebellion. The message was popular: Rise and overthrow your monarchy, which took money from the Zionists and betrayed Palestine. It is now a shameless pawn of Western imperialism and must be toppled.

Jordan survived largely through behind-the-scenes interventions by the Western powers, but its population was angry and embittered. Few friends of the monarchy doubted that if free elections had ever been permitted, the nationalists would have swept to power. But the lack of accountability was not just a characteristic of the pro-Western monarchies. The military Bonapartism which had come to power with massive popular support in Egypt and Iraq had pushed through badly-needed economic and social reforms, which benefited the poor. On the political level, however, their model was that of a rigid one-party state.

The justification was threefold. First, the ideologues of the regimes argued that bourgeois democracy was a farce since money determined everything, and that given the strategic importance of the Middle East, imperialist money would constantly be deployed to exploit any openings on offer in their countries. Second, they pointed at the examples of China and Yugoslavia to show that a different state structure was possible and served the genuine needs of the people much better than even India. Third, the West had created the system of shahs, sultans and emirs after the First World War and buttressed them further once oil had been discovered in the countries over which they ruled. Where local democracy emerged and attempted to challenge the West as had happened in Iran in 1952, the British and the Americans had discarded the popular moderate nationalist Mossadegh and brought back the shah who had fled the country. The West's supposed affection for democracy was thus purely instrumental and decorative, since a majority of their client states in every continent bar Europe were squalid, corrupt and brutal dictatorships, which preserved the wealth of the oligarchies.

Not all these arguments were weak, but what they ignored was the actual needs of the Arab people, especially in conditions where a United Arab Republic was under permanent discussion. Nasser's popularity throughout the Arab world as an anti-imperialist leader was not in doubt. His portraits were displayed in Palestinian refugee camps, in private homes in the Hijaz, in the casbahs of the Maghreb and everywhere else in the Arab world. But this acceptance did not mean that everything he did inside Egypt or Syria or everything he demanded from the new Iraqi regime had the same degree of support. Against the West, he would have won a massive majority in any plebiscite. At home this majority would have been much smaller, and in Syria and Iraq, despite the support for him, it is unlikely that he would have won an election without an alliance with other progressive parties.

Nasser's own political party, the Arab Socialist Union, was devised as a populist 'third way', a halfway house between capitalism and socialism that spoke not for one particular class but in the interests of the 'whole people'. The only way to determine whether the people accepted these views was by permitting them the right to elect a parliament of their choice. The repression directed against the Brotherhood and the left, the strict control of the mass media, the semi-regimentation of the intelligentsia, implied an insecurity on the part of the regime, which did not augur well for a wider union of Arab states. In Syria and Iraq there were other organisations with popular support and anti-imperialist credentials: the Ba'ath (Resurrection) Socialist Party and the communists. Even if these had agreed to merge with the Arab Socialist Union, differences would have remained. But no such agreement could be reached.

In Egypt itself the government came close to being destabilised by the Muslim Brotherhood. Three times they tried to kill Nasser in 1964. The regime's response was ferocious: mass arrests, followed by the execution of Sayyid Kutb and other leaders in 1965. Kutb was highly respected even in non-religious circles for his refusal to compromise, his honesty and integrity, his austere lifestyle. Believers also respected his intellect, and his last book, *Milestones,* completed in prison, became a bestseller after his death. This slim volume, a summary of Kutb's ideas, is studied by believers to this day, widely used as a manual for educating Islamic cadres, and is one of the honoured texts of Islamic Jihad and similar groups spawned by the Brotherhood elsewhere in the Muslim world. From a materialist viewpoint the book is repetitive, banal, uninspiring and intellectually offensive. Yet it has had a massive impact on two generations of Muslims, and that alone necessitates an engagement with its ideas.

Kutb's basic arguments can be summarised as follows. First, the only Muslims worthy of emulation are the first generation of Islam, because they were pure in mind and spirit. In three successive paragraphs there are several references to 'clear springs' as the only places where Muslims 'quench their thirst'. The clear spring is the Koran. Kutb insists throughout his book that the Koran and it alone can be the source of knowledge and the guide to daily life. He quotes a *hadith* of Aisha, the Prophet's youngest bride, who on being asked to define the character of her late husband, replied: 'His character was the Koran.'[23] He points out that while Greek, Roman and Persian cultures abounded in the world, the 'unique generation' ignored all else and relied on the Word of the Koran. For the influence of these cultures had created the *jahiliyya* (ignorance), and in order to break from it they had to study the Koran and nothing else.

Second, if Muhammad had been an Arab nationalist he could have united the tribes behind crudely nationalist motifs and driven out the occupying Roman and Persian powers, but instead he preferred to do so in the name of Allah as a universal God who could easily accept Persians, Romans, Africans and anyone else in the new community that Muhammad was creating in his name provided they swore allegiance to Allah and his Prophet.

Third, Muhammad could have easily started a social movement based on the have-nots, defeated the rich and redistributed their wealth to the poor. Once this had been done the poor would have rallied to the banner of Allah without any persuasion but, Kutb informs the reader, Allah did not lead the Prophet down this road either, because he preferred a Third Way: 'He knew that true social justice can come to a society only after all affairs have been submitted to the laws of God and society as a whole is willing to accept the just division of wealth prescribed by Him . . .'

The degeneration of Islam began with the second generation, who abandoned the purity of Islam and began to drink from the polluted streams of other civilisations and traditions. From this it follows that only a return to the true faith can save Islam from a total disaster.

Let us leave to one side the synthetic character of the Koran itself and its debt to the Old Testament. Kutb was engaged in a life-and-death political struggle. As a thinly veiled polemic against Nasser's vision of a pan-Arab universe and the communists, *Milestones* served its function, but as a political alternative its message was both contradictory and bleak. It favoured a return to early Islam as visualised in the Koran. In order to achieve this goal

---

23 There is, of course, more than one way to interpret this remark. Aisha's precocity has never been doubted and her comment, if it was ever made, could just as well imply, with the Mu'tazilites, that the Book was not revealed.

a two-stage jihad was crucial: 'This movement uses the methods of preaching and persuasion for reforming ideas and beliefs; and it uses physical power and the jihad for abolishing the organisations and authorities of the *jahili* system which prevents people from reforming their ideas and beliefs but forces them to obey their erroneous ways and make them serve human lords instead of Almighty Allah.' For Kutb the jihad is coercion and persuasion in one. The book, as a fundamentalist text, prefers to cast a veil over awkward possibilities. What if the majority of the people do not wish to live like the early generation or accept Koranic law as their code of conduct? What if all attempts at persuasion fail? The implication is clear. They will have to be coerced. Kutb's votaries in Islamic Jihad, who united with Osama bin Laden's levy of Wahhabi Arabs to form al-Qaida, believe that the 'Emirate of Afghanistan' was the only model of true Islam. The Taliban regime as an image of both past and future.

Would Kutb have agreed with this assessment? It is difficult to know. But his death and the phase of repression could only be a temporary solution for the regime. Nasser was supremely self-confident. Having dealt religious extremism a sharp blow he now began to devise a strategy to defeat his rivals on the left. The Egyptian communists had by the mid-Sixties been either integrated in the official structures or demoralised beyond repair. The main threat to Nasserite hegemony came from the supporters of the Ba'ath.

Given that different factions of the Ba'ath Party have ruled Syria and Iraq for almost half a century, a study of its origins is not a purely academic exercise. The party was the brainchild of Michel Aflaq (1910–89), a left-leaning Arab nationalist intellectual of Greek Orthodox Christian origin, who was born into a nationalist household in Damascus in 1910. Both his parents were politically engaged. His father had been imprisoned by the Ottomans and their French successors. Michel Aflaq was educated at the Sorbonne, fell in love with Paris, founded an Arab Students Union and discovered Marx. On his return to Syria in 1932 he worked closely with the local communists and wrote for their magazine. Like many others he assumed that the French Communist Party favoured the independence of French colonies, but this illusion was broken in 1936 when the Popular Front government left the colonial structure intact, and the Syrian communists accepted this as an accomplished fact. Many years later he told an interviewer:

During this period I admired the hardness of the Communists' struggle against the French. I used to admire the toughness of the young men in the Communist Party. After 1936 and the assumption of power in France by the Léon Blum Front government, I became disenchanted and felt betrayed.[24]

He now decided that the local communists were loyal, not to an idea, but to the foreign policy interests of the Soviet state, and for that reason would be unreliable allies in any protracted struggle. This experience pushed Aflaq, his close comrade Salah Bitar and other young idealistic Arab nationalists away from any internationalist perspective. They were shocked by the 'imperialist nature' of European socialism and communism. For them the key question was how to achieve freedom and independence for their countries. Everything else was subordinated to that goal.

It was during the Second World War that Aflaq developed the theory which motivated his followers: there was one Arab nation, one Arab people, and they required one Arab republic. This unity derived from history. Islam and its Prophet had united the Arabs as never before, and this historical experience was now the property of all Arabs, not just the Muslims. Nation and nationality became the main focus of his work in the early period. This, coupled with his total disillusionment with the pro-colonial European left, led him to view the Second World War through a strictly nationalist prism. A defeat for the British and French empires would be good for the Arab cause.[25] Nationalists, as exemplified by the Alexandrian crowd, hoped that Rommel might make their task easier.

The Ba'ath was founded exactly one year after Rommel's 1942 defeat in El Alamein. After Syrian independence in 1947, it began to work closely with non-communist socialists and its influence grew throughout the Arab world.

---

24 Kamel S. Abu Jabar, *The Arab Ba'ath Socialist Party*, New York, 1966.

25 Further east, the nationalist leaders of the Indian National Congress had come to a similar view and launched a movement of civil disobedience against British power in August 1942, at the height of the Second World War.

I was given a potted history of Aflaq and his theories by the Raja of Mahmudabad over lunch one day during the late Fifties in Lahore. The Raja had helped to fund Jinnah's Muslim League, but was thoroughly disillusioned. He had left Pakistan and lived in the Middle East, where he had met Aflaq, and now thought a version of the Ba'ath was needed in Pakistan. Bhutto's People's Party was the closest Pakistan came to that, but a big difference was the non-political tradition of the Pakistan Army.

Underground parties were established in Jordan and Iraq, cells operated in the Hijaz and the Yemen. Syria and the Lebanon alone permitted legal, functioning parties for varying periods. It was Syria that first repressed the party and arrested Aflaq, who served four spells in prison in 1949–54. In Paris he had been impressed by the toughness of French communists. In Syria he impressed this need for 'toughness' on the new recruits, most of whom were students.

Throughout Aflaq's tenure – 1943–65 – as the secretary-general of the Ba'ath, he made sure the party was seen as a Pan-Arab organisation and dominated its policies and its organisation. He shunned the attributes of power, preferring his job in the party. It was Aflaq who had been the moving force behind the Egypt–Syria merger in 1958, but the mutual antipathy between him and Nasser proved too strong. Both men were modernising, anti-imperialist nationalists with the elements of an anti-capitalist programme. Both shared a passion for ideas, but whereas Aflaq was essentially a party insider, Nasser was a public leader and one whose name had become a symbol of anti-imperialism. It irked him to deal with Aflaq as if he were an equal. This explains why the Syrian ideologue was prepared to share power. Nasser, however, preferred a monopoly. And it was the high-handedness of Abdel Hakim Amer, the Egyptian pro-consul in Damascus, that brought the union to an end.

But underlying these divisions was a material reality of more recent vintage. Since the defeat and collapse of the Ottoman empire after World War One, the new states encouraged by the imperialist powers had developed a sub-nationalist existence of their own, based on a combination of modernity and local/regional histories and traditions. The Ottomans had united the Arab East from without, but had not established the structures that could do so from within and, as we have seen, Egypt enjoyed a semi-independence after Napoleon's brief occupation. Subsequently, nationalist ideology proved too weak a vessel to contain regional rivalries. This was the case even where the imperialist-imposed divisions were most awkward geographically, as in Syria and the Lebanon.

The peninsula was another story altogether. Ignored by the Ottoman empire for most of its existence, tribal divisions had created multiple sovereignties in the region. Even though the British-backed al-Sauds had finally taken the peninsula, it had been the discovery of oil, the creation of the US oil giant ARAMCO and the giant USAF base in Dhahran that preserved the unity of Saudi Arabia and made it a bastion of Arab reaction. Imperialism, oil and, after 1948, Israel were the three factors that gave a tremendous boost to Arab nationalism. The existence of the Soviet Union provided it with a pillar to which it could cling in moments of difficulty. If the Zionist state had not existed it is likely that Arab nationalism would have disappeared with the withdrawal of Britain and France from the region and been replaced with each country defending its national interests.

The rivalry between Egypt and the Ba'athists in Syria and Iraq weakened all three states. The final blow to Arab nationalism was being prepared in Tel Aviv.

12

Marginal notes on the chapter of defeats

The 1948 *nakba* had left the Palestinians leaderless and dispersed. Their lives, in every sense of the word, were under the strict control of the Arab states. It took fifteen years for the Arab League to agree on the establishment of the Palestinian Liberation Organisation (PLO), but what this meant was the formation of Palestinian units integrated in the armies of Syria, Iraq, Jordan and Egypt. In the Arab capitals a new breed of Palestinians in exile began to develop a new consciousness, radicalised by the events of 1956 and the polarisation that followed. These were young men and women, the infants and toddlers of 1948, who had no direct memory of the ethnic cleansing. They had been brought up on stories of the disaster and developed a collective memory all the more potent for not having the direct experience of defeat.

Like the rest of the Arab world they divided into nationalists and Marxists, though unlike that world the religious currents were infinitesimal. This was the period in which the Fatah (Victory) group emerged, flanked on its left by the Popular Front for the Liberation of Palestine (PFLP) and, later, the Popular Democratic Front for the Liberation of Palestine (PDFLP). The difference between the groups was strategic: Fatah favoured direct and independent actions by Palestinian guerrilla units against Israel; its rivals argued that Palestine could not be won without a series of socialist revolutions in the Arab countries.

In 1965 the Fatah guerrillas, backed by the Syrian Ba'ath, began to carry out actions inside Israel. The Zionist leaders decided on an offensive response. The economic and military aid (including chemical weapons) they had received from the United States and West Germany had helped them to construct the most powerful air force in the region. The size of the population had grown, and with it the army. The Israeli High Command was confident that it could conquer the rest of Palestine without putting the existence of Israel at risk. Syria, Egypt and Jordan signed a military agreement pledging to defend each other's territory.

On 5 June 1967 the Israelis attacked Egypt and destroyed its entire air force. Within six days Israeli armour had captured Jerusalem and the West Bank from Jordan, occupied the Golan Heights in southern Syria and taken the Sinai as far as the Suez Canal in Egypt. It was a comprehensive defeat, a second *nakba*, and with more far-reaching consequences.

Jerusalem had fallen. Some of the holiest Christian and Muslim sites were now under Jewish control. Israel's military abilities had a powerful impact on the Pentagon and the State Department. The Zionist entity had turned out to be a much more stable and powerful relay in the region than they had visualised. US–Israeli relations underwent a dramatic shift. Israel became the most dependable ally of the United States in the region, and this reality was sanctified by a massive turn towards Israel on the part of the Jewish population in the United States.

And the Palestinians? The Israeli occupation meant that the last bastions of Palestine – Jerusalem, Gaza and the West Bank – were now under direct rule from Tel Aviv. Having won a quick victory, the Israeli regime could have suggested a solution that entailed an independent Palestine, but they were drunk with success. The shell-shocked Arab states reacted by refusing to recognise the occupation. Large numbers of Palestinians fled to hastily constructed refugee camps in Jordan and Syria.

The 1967 war destroyed Nasserism as a popular anti-imperialist force in the Middle East. How would Egypt react? On 9 June 1967, as the scale of the disaster became visible to the entire Arab world, Muslim Brotherhood-inspired gangs were heading in the direction of the Soviet embassy. They blamed Moscow for the disaster. Burning its embassy was seen as a prelude to the restoration. Members of the old ruling elites did not waste time. They were ensconced in plots with senior officers from the army. Two years earlier the Indonesian military had orchestrated events to defeat the left. The world's largest communist party in a non-communist country had been wiped out. A million people had died. This event had been greeted with delight by the Islamists and the local agencies of the United States throughout the third world. In Cairo, the Brotherhood dreamt of revenge. Now was the time to topple the Pharaoh and kill his supporters. More traditional rightist groups wanted to reverse 'fifteen years of socialism'. They knew the West would back them with money to make oil 'safe' once again, to take Egypt back and then punish Syria and Iraq till they returned to the fold.

On that same Black Friday, a weeping Nasser addressed the Egyptian people on television in a resignation speech relayed throughout the Arab world. He appeared a broken man, but he did not search for scapegoats and accepted complete responsibility for the debacle. His enemies rejoiced and began to prepare for change, but they had assumed that a defeated people would not rise again.

What followed was unprecedented, and not just in the Arab world. The Egyptian historian Anwar Abdel-Malik's lyrical description of how the Arab streets responded to Nasser's resignation retains its power:

> After a few moments of hesitation the whole country swung into action: the streets of Cairo were flooded with more than two and a half million; the whole population of Tantah, the centre of the Delta, was marching on the capital; the same in Port Said, where, however, the people were recalled in a desperate move not to empty the city; from every city, town and village, from Alexandria to Aswan, from the Western desert to Suez, a whole nation marched. And its slogans could not be misunderstood: *'No imperialism! No dollar!'*; *'No leader, but Gamal.'* Ever since the May 1967 crisis, the people of Cairo and Alexandria had instinctively taken up the 1919 revolution's popular battle hymn – *Biladi, biladi, fidaki dami!* (My Fatherland, O fatherland, Yours is my Blood!) – and now it exploded like a thunderstorm and a shield, broke through intrigues and conspiracies and found its way to the national broadcasting station, asserting Egypt's nationhood and national resolve . . .
>
> Gone were the days of passivity. Gone was the feeling of not-belonging. Gone was the lack of identification between a people and its fatherland.[26]

Nasser was not allowed to resign, but he knew that this war marked a turning point. As a military historian he realised the scale of the defeat. As a politician he understood that something had to change in the Arab world.

---

26 Anwar Abdel-Malik, *Egypt: Military Society*, New York, 1968.

Three years later he was dead. His funeral was attended by millions, who half-realised that they were not saying farewell to Nasser alone, but to his dream of Arab unity.

The Soviet Union resupplied the Egyptian army and air force. Nasser's successor, Anwar al-Sadat, surprised Israel in 1973 by pushing it back and neutralising its air force. Israel recovered, but a point had been registered and the United States and the Soviet Union imposed a stalemate. Each Big Power determined not to let its side be defeated. The Arabs were helped also by a rare unity and the temporary use of the oil embargo.

But it was not simply a question of more advanced weaponry sold by the Big Powers. There was a more fundamental problem, internal to the Arabs. This was the message of the great Syrian poet Nizar Qabbani, whose poems were recited in bazaar and salon alike. In his 1956 poems, Qabbani had celebrated the heroism of the ordinary soldier. Despite the military defeat that Egypt had suffered, the political mood was one of optimism. A decade later the landscape had altered.

Immediately after the 1967 war, Qabbani composed twenty verses entitled *Hawamish 'ala Daftar al-Naksah* (Footnotes to the Book of Setback). He lashed the entire Arab leadership, sparing neither sultan nor colonel. Political interventions by poets are not rare in cultures that punish dissent, but rarely has a single poem had such an explosive impact. Verse 17, in particular, outraged the scribes of the state and the secret police in every Arab capital, but was recited and sung throughout the Arab world.

Denounced by critics from both right and left, the poet remained unrepentant. He knew that he was not alone. He expressed the despair of millions, without succumbing to it. He knew that despair creates passivity or a mindless violence. Hope, always present in his political poems, is a creative and active emotion. Qabbani's images of hope are always potent and youthful, addressed to future generations. He writes:

1
Friends,
The old word is dead.
The old books are dead.
Our speech with holes like worn-out shoes is dead.
Dead is the mind that led to defeat.

2
Our poetry has gone sour.
Women's hair, nights, curtains and sofas
Have gone sour.
Everything has gone sour.

3
My grieved country,
In a flash
You changed me from a poet who wrote love poems
To a poet who writes with a knife.

4
What we feel is beyond words:
We should be ashamed of our poems.

5
Stirred by Oriental bombast,
By boastful swaggering that never killed a fly,
By the fiddle and the drum,
We went to war
And lost.

6
Our shouting is louder than our actions,
Our swords are taller than us,
This is our tragedy.

7
In short
We wear the cape of civilisation
But our souls live in the stone age.

8
You don't win a war
With a reed and a flute.

9
Our impatience
Cost us fifty thousand new tents.

10
Don't curse heaven
If it abandons you,

Don't curse circumstances.
God gives victory to whom He wishes.
God is not a blacksmith to beat swords.

11
It's painful to listen to the news in the morning.
It's painful to listen to the barking of dogs.

12
Our enemies did not cross our borders
They crept through our weaknesses like ants.

13
Five thousand years
Growing beards
In our caves.
Our currency is unknown,
Our eyes are a haven for flies.
Friends,
Smash the doors,
Wash your brains,
Wash your clothes.
Friends,
Read a book,
Write a book,
Grow words, pomegranates and grapes,
Sail to the country of fog and snow.
Nobody knows you exist in caves.
People take you for a breed of mongrels.

14
We are a thick-skinned people
With empty souls.
We spend our days practising witchcraft,
Playing chess and sleeping.
Are we the 'Nation by which God blessed mankind'?

15
Our desert oil could have become
Daggers of flame and fire.
We're a disgrace to our noble ancestors:
We let our oil flow through the toes of whores.

16

We run wildly through the streets
Dragging people with ropes,
Smashing windows and locks.
We praise like frogs,
Swear like frogs,
Turn midgets into heroes,
And heroes into scum:
We never stop and think.
In mosques
We crouch idly,
Write poems,
Proverbs,
Beg God for victory
Over our enemy.

17

If I knew I'd come to no harm,
And could see the Sultan,
This is what I would say:
'Sultan,
Your wild dogs have torn my clothes
Your spies hound me
Their eyes hound me
Their noses hound me
Their feet hound me
They hound me like Fate
Interrogate my wife
And take down the name of my friends.
Sultan,
When I came close to your walls
And talked about my pains,
Your soldiers beat me with their boots,
Forced me to eat my shoes.
Sultan,
You lost two wars.
Sultan,
Half of our people are without tongues,
What's the use of a people without tongues?
Half of our people

Are trapped like ants and rats
Between walls.'
If I knew I'd come to no harm
I'd tell him:
'You lost two wars
You lost touch with children.'

18
If we hadn't buried our unity
If we hadn't ripped its young body with bayonets
If it had stayed in our eyes
The dogs wouldn't have savaged our flesh.

19
We want an angry generation
To plough the sky
To blow up history
To blow up our thoughts.
We want a new generation
That does not forgive mistakes
That does not bend.
We want a generation of giants.

20
Arab children,
Corn ears of the future,
You will break our chains.
Kill the opium in our heads,
Kill the illusions.
Arab children,
Don't read about our suffocated generation,
We are a hopeless case.
We are as worthless as a water-melon rind.
Don't read about us,
Don't ape us,
Don't accept us,
Don't accept our ideas,
We are a nation of crooks and jugglers.
Arab children,
Spring rain,
Corn ears of the future,

You are the generation
That will overcome defeat.[27]

The poem created a storm throughout the Arab world. The Egyptian government, as if to prove Qabbani's point, banned all his books, including the poetry sung by Umm Kulthum. He was banned from entering the country. A few of the more sycophantic courtiers actually demanded that Qabbani be tried *in absentia*. Some months later the poet appealed directly to Nasser. All the restrictions were lifted, bringing the affair to an end.

But the poet had touched a nerve. I first heard of him in July 1967, when I visited Amman, Beirut and Damascus as part of a five-man delegation from the Bertrand Russell Peace Foundation. Earlier that year I had been in North Vietnam on behalf of the Russell/Sartre War Crimes Tribunal. It was while the Tribunal was in session in Stockholm that news of a likely war in the Middle East reached us.

After the six-day blitzkrieg in June, I was told to prepare for a trip to the Middle East. We were to visit, inspect and report on the conditions in the Palestinian camps. We left for Amman on a Sunday in the month of August. I remember buying a copy of *Observer* at the airport and reading that the Marxist historian Isaac Deutscher had died the previous day in Rome. I had last met him in Stockholm where he was one of the judges at the War Crimes Tribunal and had given me a really hard time for a stray remark in which I had let slip that the intensive and indiscriminate bombing of North Vietnam by the United States revealed a degree of racism. Deutscher asked me whether they would bomb any differently in Europe in order to crush a revolution. I replied that they would be more circumspect. He lambasted me. This was as I was giving my testimony. Afterwards he took me aside to root out the nationalist deviation he had spotted in my evidence. Now he was dead. His fierce intelligence would not be deployed to analyse the 1967 war. I felt pretty desolate as I boarded the flight for Amman.

Arriving in the capital of a Jordan truncated by the war, it was hardly surprising that Qabbani's poem was still the subject of heated debates. The

---

27 Nizar Qabbani, 'Footnotes to the Book of Setback', in *Modern Poetry of the Arab World*, London 1986, translated and edited by Adbullah al-Udhari.

Palestinians we met could recite several stanzas, much to the embarrassment of the officials who accompanied us. It was the same story in Damascus and Beirut, with this difference: in the Syrian capital I was told of the poem by Mowaffak Allaf from the foreign ministry, who claimed friendship with the poet. The most radical wing of the Ba'ath was in power and Syrian government ministers would remark that Qabbani had described the Egyptian scene extremely well.

It was the camps in Jordan that gave me my first lesson in Palestinian history. I had seen victims of war on a big scale in Vietnam that year, but they were in their own country, cared for by their own doctors, and people throughout the world were sending medical aid and other forms of help. In the camps too, I saw and photographed children who had suffered napalm burns, but this was a stateless people ignored by the Arab world and left to rot.

In the West few politicians knew or cared. Riddled with guilt for the Judeocide of the Second World War, they turned a blind eye to Israeli atrocities.

At the Civil Hospital in Damascus I saw further evidence of chemical weapons. Several patients had been burnt by napalm. We were told of the disappeared doctors, of how the Israelis had captured five doctors in a medical tent on the front and shot them dead. I interviewed Muhammad al-Mustafa, a seventeen-year-old shepherd from Kuneitra, who described how they were tending their flock when Israeli soldiers stopped them. His twelve-year old cousin had got frightened and run. He was shot in the back. Muhammad, too, was hit by a bullet. He pleaded for medical help, but was left lying there while his two younger brothers were taken away. The stories were endless.

Nor did the Syrian prime minister, Dr Youssif Zouyyain, manage to cheer me up even though he said everything that one wanted to hear in those days. He was a doctor of medicine and had worked in hospitals in Wales and Scotland during his training. The afternoon we met he told me that Syria would soon become the Cuba of the Middle East; the days of the Saudi monarchy were numbered; the Ba'athist revolution would be developed further till capitalism was completely eliminated. 'I can reassure you,' he said. 'You needn't worry. The Arab people will not emigrate to Yemen and live in tents. We will resist this invasion and in the end victory will be ours. Against the occupiers we must wage a people's war learning from the Chinese resistance against Japan. We can't compete with them or their backers in Washington and London as far as weapons are concerned. This war can only be won by the people, not by more expensive weapons. It will be a protracted struggle . . .' Within the next few months the 'ultra-radicals' in the Syrian government had been toppled after a not-so-protracted struggle by moderates backed by the authority of Aflaq.

In Beirut I had my first meetings with Palestinian intellectuals, and useful lessons in history followed in the garden of the old house of Walid Khalidi. Many of them were in a state of shock, stunned by the defeat, barely able to articulate their view of the future. There were others, whom I met in restaurants and cafés. They were much more hard-headed. They argued in favour of fighting on their own, not depending on the sultans and the colonels, learning from the examples of others. And then the inevitable question. Have you heard of Qabbani's latest poem?

On returning to London, I went to condole with Isaac Deutscher's widow, Tamara, and heard from her that some weeks before his death he had given a lengthy interview on the Six Day War to the *New Left Review*. Both the Deutschers had lost the bulk of their families during the Judeocide. Deutscher rarely permitted emotion to override reason. Nonetheless a sympathy for Israel as a state of refuge, if not a state that created refugees, was only natural. I didn't expect too much from the interview. I was wrong. He referred to the Israelis as the 'Prussians of the Middle East' and issued a chilling and prescient warning:

> The Germans have summed up their own experience in the bitter phrase: *'Man kann sich totsiegen!'* 'You can rush victoriously into your grave.' This is what the Israelis have been doing. In the conquered territories and in Israel there are now nearly a million and five hundred thousand Arabs, well over 40 per cent of the total population. Will the Israelis expel this mass of Arabs in order to hold 'securely' the conquered lands? This would create a new refugee problem, more dangerous and larger than the old one. . . . Yes, this victory is worse for Israel than a defeat. Far from giving Israel a higher degree of security, it has rendered it much more insecure.[28]

---

28 Rereading the Deutscher interview (*New Left Review* I, 44, July–August 1967) after thirty-four

As Isaac Deutscher predicted, the Israeli victory in 1967 solved nothing. The Palestinians refused to become a disappeared people. A new generation began a new struggle for national self-determination, the last of a series of liberation wars that began in the early years of the twentieth century. Israel is the only remaining colonial power – of the nineteenth–twentieth-century model – in the world today. This is now becoming accepted by a courageous minority of Israeli intellectuals. Baruch Kimmerling, a professor of sociology at Hebrew University, recently published a homage to Emile Zola, 'I accuse', in the 1 February 2002 edition of the Hebrew weekly Kol Ha'Ir. It is a savage indictment of the Israeli military leadership of the sort that never appears in the Western media:

> I accuse Ariel Sharon of creating a process in which he will not only intensify the reciprocal bloodshed, but is liable to instigate a regional war and partial or nearly complete ethnic cleansing of the Arabs in the 'Land of Israel'. I accuse every Labor Party minister in this government of cooperating for implementation the right wing's extremist, fascist 'vision' for Israel. I accuse the Palestinian leadership, and primarily Yasir Arafat, of shortsightedness so extreme that it has become a collaborator in Sharon's plans. If there is a second *naqba*, this leadership too will be among the causes. I accuse the military leadership, spurred by the national leadership, of inciting public opinion, under a cloak of supposed military professionalism, against the Palestinians. Never before in Israel have so many generals in uniform, former generals, and past members of the military intelligence, sometimes disguised as 'academics,' taken part in public brainwashing. When the judicial committee of inquiry is established to investigate the 2002 catastrophe, they too will have to be investigated alongside the civilian criminals.
>
> The late philosopher Yeshayahu Leibovitz was right – the occupation has ruined every good part and destroyed the moral infrastructure upon which Israeli society exists. Let's stop this march of fools and build society anew, clean of militarism and oppression and exploitation of other people, if not worse . . . And I accuse myself of knowing all of this, yet crying little and keeping quiet too often . . .

The story of Palestine remains unfinished.

---

years, one is struck again by its clarity and courage. Both Isaac and his wife Tamara had lost virtually all their relatives in the Judeocide. It did not make them Zionists. For that reason, and in the hope of encouraging a new readership, I have included it as an appendix to this book. See pp. 394–412.

13

The anti-imperialism of fools

The post-1973 stalemate continued for another four years. Jimmy Carter, the new Democratic president in the White House, was reported to favour pressuring both sides in the Middle East to reach an agreement on Palestine. Before he could make a move, the Egyptian regime startled the world by a unilateral decision to make a separate peace with Israel: in November 1977 President Sadat flew to Jerusalem, publicly embraced the Israeli prime minister, Menachem Begin, and signed a peace treaty. The Israelis vacated the occupied territory belonging to Egypt, the two countries exchanged ambassadors and it appeared, if only for a moment, that the spectacle would be enough to solve remaining problems with the same ease. Reports on Egyptian TV and radio were coated in obedient lies. Israel made it clear then and later that it would neither cease nor suspend its policy of building Jewish settlements in the conquered territories.

Sadat's démarche had a dual purpose. The *infitah* (open door), as the process was named, marked the official break with the main tenets of the Nasserist past. In foreign policy, it signalled the end of neutrality, military dependence and re-entry into the Western sphere.

The domestic consequences of the *infitah* on the country's social geography were just as startling. The massive public sector had provided the majority of Egypt's people with some protection in terms of food, housing, health and education. This may not have been adequate, but it was better than what they were about to experience. Wealth differentials, throughout the Nasserite period, had remained relatively low. It was the corruption and political repression that were greatly resented. They were the main cause of alienation from the old regime.

Sadat decided to privatise the country, without liberalising its political structures. In other words the commodity was beyond criticism. The Egyptian left grumbled in private, but was too weak and demoralised to protest. Secular liberals decided to back the new orientation in the belief that it would bring democracy in its wake. Nothing of the sort took place. The privatisations and the openings to foreign capital led to a severe class polarisation which found no reflection in the political structures of the post-Nasser state. Under the previous regime too, politics had been strictly controlled, but the well-delineated factions within the Arab Socialist Union were responsive to different social layers of the population. Now even that was gone. The only possible opposition would be clandestine.

The organisation with an accumulated reservoir of experience in underground activities was the Muslim Brotherhood and its more radical offshoots. They had infiltrated the army and now decided to carry out a spectacular and public action to demonstrate their hostility to the regime. On 6 October 1981, four years after the *infitah*, the Egyptian president was taking the salute at a military march-past when four soldiers lowered their weapons and sprayed the VIP podium with machine-gun fire, killing Sadat and wounding several members of the entourage. The elite mourned. The nation remained indifferent. The contrast with Nasser's funeral could not have been more pronounced.

The assassins were captured, tried and executed. Live ammunition was henceforth banned from ceremonial occasions, and not just in Egypt. But the internal and external conditions that had produced a sharp revival of Islamist activity remained unchanged. Sadat was replaced by Mubarak, who soon made concessions to the religious extremists in the social and cultural sphere in return for retaining his moth-eaten dictatorship. This strengthened them and helped to expand their social base of support. The event that had inspired the renewed outburst of politico-religious fervour, however, lay outside the Arab world.

The symbolic battle-lines had been drawn in 1971, when a vain, over-confident monarch, blinded by the praise of sycophants at home and abroad, unaware of his isolation from the people, decided to mimic Cecil B. De Mille. He wanted a birthday party to honour the Great Cyrus and 2,500 years of 'Iranian kingship'. Like everything else about this event, the date, too, was dubious. The reason for the proposed extravaganza was obvious: to reduce the genealogical insecurity of the 'Light of the Aryans', a favourite self-description of the shah. The chosen venue was historic: the ruins of the ancient Persian capital of Persepolis.

Most of the guests showed up. Emperors Haile Selassie and Hirohito from Ethiopia and Japan, less exalted kings from the Benelux countries and Scandinavia, and lesser still, the kings of Morocco, Jordan and Nepal, Charles Windsor, the heir to the British throne, and sundry politicians of every hue. These included the shyster Spiro Agnew (currently the US vice-president), as well as the Soviet president, Podgorny, and a senior representative from the Chinese Politburo. Alone among Europe's politicians, the French leader, Pompidou, decided to stay away. Having just experienced the barricades of May '68 in his own capital, perhaps he saw the future more clearly than his global counterparts. Also present were numerous academic and screen celebrities from the United States and Europe, among them the distinguished British political philosopher Sir Isaiah Berlin, whose bracing pamphlet, *Two Concepts of Liberty*, had been recently published in Tehran to great acclaim from the courtiers. The great man had given a lecture in Tehran to mark the occasion. The fee was not disclosed.

According to media accounts, a good time was had by all those present. The food and 25,000 bottles of wine had been flown from Paris. The only local item on the menu was Iranian caviar, from its share of the Caspian. The bill totalled a paltry $300 million – which must have included the 'expenses' of the non-state celebrities present – enough money to feed the entire population of a third-world country for several months.

The climax of the show was pure kitsch. The guests gasped as the floodlights were switched on to reveal the overdressed occupant of the Peacock Throne as he stood before the tomb of Cyrus. The shah overcame stage-fright as he spoke the sentence that had been endlessly rehearsed:

'Sleep easily, Cyrus, for we are awake.'[29]

---

29 In *The Mantle of the Prophet*, London 1986, a powerful and evocative historical account of the origins of an Islamic intelligentsia in Iran, Roy Mottahedeh contrasts the Orientalist reaction to the Iranian response: 'A joke of the period claimed that an Iranian office worker was so enraptured by reading these words of the shah in his newspaper that he went home unexpectedly early to tell his wife; there he found his wife and his neighbour, Cyrus, asleep together in his bed. Overcome by the drama of the moment he raised his hand and said: "Sleep easily, Cyrus, for we are awake."'

On their return to the prosaic world of the American campus, gushing Orientalists reported that a sudden desert breeze arose after the magic words uttered by the shah. They did not notice that other breezes were stirring. While the shah was being fêted by leaders from West and East, a prescient warning was issued by an Iranian cleric little known outside Iran. From his Iraqi exile, Khomeini sounded the tocsin:

> Ought the people of Iran to celebrate the rule of a traitor to Islam and the interests of Muslims who gives oil to Israel? The crimes of the kings of Iran have blackened the pages of history . . . Even those who were reputed to be 'good' were vile and cruel. Islam is fundamentally opposed to the whole notion of monarchy . . .
>
> People address themselves to us constantly from all over Iran, asking permission to use the charitable taxes demanded by Islam for the building of bathhouses, for they are without baths. What happened to all those gilded promises, those pretentious claims that Iran is progressing on the same level as the more developed countries of the world, that the people are prosperous and content? If these latest excesses continue, worse misfortunes will descend upon us . . .

Inside Iran, where he was both known and feared, it was noticed that the tone was different. In 1963, from his stronghold in Qom, the Ayatollah, angered by references to the mullahs and their poor students in the *madrasas* (religious boarding schools), as 'parasites', had warned his profligate ruler to beware the presence of false friends and change his policies:

> Let me give you some advice Mr Shah! Dear Mr Shah, I advise you to desist . . . I don't want the people to offer up thanks if your foreign master should decide one day that you must leave. I don't want you to become like your father . . . During World War Two the Soviet Union, Britain and America invaded Iran and occupied our territory. The property of the people was exposed and their honour was imperilled. But Allah knows, everyone was happy because the Pahlavi [Shah's father] had gone! . . . Don't you know that if one day some uproar occurs and the tables are turned, none of these people around you will be your friends?

This counsel was disregarded, and the priest who offered it in the spirit of reform was expelled from the country. From his exile in Iraq and, later, France, Khomeini's corrosive tape-recorded messages began to circulate throughout the country. On occasion they were played in the mosques after Friday prayers.

From the end of 1977 Iran had been gripped by a pre-revolutionary ferment that grew with every passing week. In February 1979 a revolution triumphed, and paradoxically lost. A mass struggle against a brutal and corrupt Western favourite culminated in the overthrow of the monarchy. At the crucial moment, the Iranian army had refused to open fire on the people. Crack regiments created to safeguard against such an upheaval were split. The shah of Iran fled into exile, marking the end of the most short-lived dynasty in Iranian history. The prisons were stormed. The political inmates, tortured and numb, could hardly believe that they had finally won.

They had been waiting for almost two years. It had been obvious inside and outside the prisons that the shah had lost, his departure was only a matter of time, but in revolutions time is of the essence. It can determine everything. The prisoners were ready to be liberated.

Triumphant crowds revelled on the streets. Euphoria was everywhere. The scenes were familiar in history. The Parisian crowd outside the Bastille in 1789. The Petrograd workers waiting for their most radical leader to disembark from his train at the Finland Station in 1917. Tsarist regiments refusing to open fire and steady desertions to the Bolshevik cause. October 1949 and Beijing, excited and eager, waiting for Mao Zedong and his armies to enter the city and proclaim the triumph of the Chinese Revolution. Havana in 1959: the dictator and his mafia colleagues fleeing the country and the triumphant entry of the guerrilla army. Saigon in April 1975: the Vietnamese communists arriving, the Stars and Stripes being taken down and United States helicopters evacuating personnel from their embassy.

Tehran in 1979 seemed no different. The familiar images deceived many, especially leftists and liberals in Iran and elsewhere: throughout Western Europe (and especially strong in West Germany) there had been, from the early Sixties, a campaign of solidarity with Iranian political prisoners who demonstrated against the shah whenever he travelled abroad. Naturally, there was great excitement at the news from Tehran.

True, the icon of this revolution was a bearded priest on his way home from a Parisian suburb, but surely he could not last too long. He was a Girondin, a Father Gapon, a Kerensky, who would soon be swept aside into the dustbin of History. The clerics would be replaced by workers and citizens councils, or the left in alliance with the secular liberals of the National

Front, or radicalised officers in the army or whatever. Anyone would succeed but Khomeini.

It was impossible for the Iranian left to imagine that the people who participated in the gigantic mass mobilisations that secured the revolutionary
victory could be serious when they chanted *Allahu Akbar* (God is Great) or
Long Live Khomeini, or when they cheered the turbaned clerics who spoke
of creating the Islamic Republic. Useful idiots from the Western European
left who had arrived to participate in the fateful events were carried away by
the fervour and excitement and began to chant the same slogans to demonstrate their solidarity. Because they didn't believe in them they assumed
that the Iranian masses, too, were being opportunistic. All this religion was
empty froth; it would be blown away by newer and stronger breezes. It was
a form of false consciousness, soon to be corrected by a large dose of class
struggle. Khomeini's political programme was irrelevant; it was his actions
that mattered. It was not thus, of course, but many wanted it to be so.

Within three months the contours of the new regime had become visible: it was the stern and intransigent face of Islamic Jacobinism. Nothing
like this had been seen since the victory of Protestant fundamentalism in
seventeenth-century England. The difference in time-span was important.
This was a revolt against History, against the Enlightenment, 'Euromania',
'Westoxification' – against Progress. It was a postmodern Revolution before
postmodernism had grown fashionable. Foucault, amongst the first to recognise this affinity, became the most visible European defender of the Islamic
Republic. How had it come to this?

The deposed shah's father had attempted to destroy the clerics through
repression: any dissent on their part had been dealt with by public floggings.
The son had been more careful and had attempted, with some success, to
buy them off with grants and endowments. The real problem was not the
clergy but the conditions in which the bulk of the population lived in town
and country. In the drawing-rooms of Iranian society, religion may have
been an underprivileged extra, but in the servants' quarters it dominated the
stage. Shi'ite orthodoxy encouraged escapism.

The arrival of the Imam of the Age – a Shi'ite messiah – was eagerly
awaited in a countryside where the peasants had been ground down by
oppression and injustice. But the revolution was almost entirely an urban
phenomenon. Indeed, until late in the day the shah had been able to

mobilise a degree of peasant support against the streets. One reason for this was the 1960s land reform, which had given land to some peasants and driven the rest to a semi-proletarian existence in the towns. They had been uprooted to provide labour for the 1970s industrialisation, but most of them could not be absorbed by the factories and became a marginal layer, leading a precarious existence. It was these dispossessed former peasants who became the vanguard of the Islamic revolution in the towns.

The local mosque and its endowments provided the only contact with a world outside their immediate preoccupations. They looked to the sky-god and his earthly followers to provide them with a better life after death. Not that they necessarily followed all the prescriptions. Exhausted after a week's work, they often relaxed with a bottle of arak, making sure to rinse their mouths carefully afterwards in case they encountered a mullah on their way home. Shi'ism was just as fierce in punishing adultery but, unlike its Sunni counterpart, it softened the blow by institutionalising one-night stands: *en route* to a brothel or a hotel room, men could obtain a special religious certificate to sanctify their 'temporary marriage'.

The crisis of the Iranian economy in 1975–6 indicated the failure of the shah's much-lauded 'reforms'. A parasitic state structure was consuming much of the oil wealth. Expenditure on armaments was particularly high at a time when a million people were unemployed and inflation had risen to 30 per cent. The bazaar traders felt victimised by the restriction of bank credits and the relaxation of import-controls. They decided to back the clergy with funds to overthrow the regime.

The clergy's promises of social justice, an end to corruption and a cultural cleansing of the country appealed to the urban poor. They were the only alternative, they insisted; both nationalism and communism had failed. Egypt and Cambodia were used as the prime examples. Only Islam remained. It could rise again if people supported its project. Since communism had not officially collapsed at the time, the Islamists shamelessly stole part of its wardrobe. The phrase 'classless society' was often used by the more radical wings of the religious movement. The most vociferous defenders of the classless society were the mujahidin – a unique development in the Islamic world. Inside the prisons they refused to fraternise with the mullahs and other religious prisoners who refused to sit and eat with the 'unclean' left. At one stage the mujahidin had moved so close to Marxism that both inside and outside the prisons they renounced Islam and declared themselves revolutionary Marxists. This group, Peikar, was the third largest group on the Iranian left.

The combination of bazaar support, the entry of unemployed and employed workers into the struggle and the redemptive ideology of Shi'ism became a potent and irresistible force in Iranian society. In February 1979 the clerics seized the time. This time they knew the shah could never return. They spent the next year and a half building up their repressive apparatuses, which included the Revolutionary Guards, and began to purge the factories, offices, schools and army units of all left-wing influence. While this was happening the Tudeh still could not see the future. They applauded the repression of the 'ultra-left'.

It had been different in 1951. Then the left and secular-liberal-nationalists had won, Mossadegh became prime minister, and the shah fled into exile. But the government failed to mobilise public support to defend the Mossadegh regime against the counter-coup launched by the CIA and British Intelligence. The West had brought the upstart ruler back and destroyed the one chance Iran might have had of moving forward on its own legs. In 1953 the old aristocrat, a direct descendant of the last Qajar king, had finally decided against a test of strength. Mossadegh's guard resisted till the end. The old man, too, had wanted to resist, but he was hoping that the Tudeh cells inside the army – a formidable clandestine presence – would come out and defend him. Their intervention was too half-hearted to succeed. Some party leaders believed that once Mossadegh was out of the way they might take over, but this had been both sectarian and stupid. Once the shah returned the Tudeh organisation in the army was brutally destroyed. The party never fully recovered from this blow.

The CIA had spent five million dollars to help some of the pro-West clerics rent a mob. In the end Mossadegh fell. His crime was the same as Nasser's: he had nationalised Iranian oil. The British government was very angry. Mossadegh had thought that the United States might warn London not to interfere, and for a while Truman and Acheson maintained the pretence of neutrality by advising both sides to remain tranquil. Macmillan noted in his diary: 'Acheson appeals to Britain and Persia to stay calm! As if we were two Balkan countries being lectured in 1911 by Sir Edward Grey!'

That was not the case just yet, but it would be soon. This time London won by playing on Washington's Cold War fears. They stressed the fact that Iranian communists were solidly behind the Mossadegh regime and a future communist victory could not be excluded. The old man was removed from office and placed under house-arrest. With the secular-nationalist alternative removed, the shah obtained a freedom to run the country as he wished provided he remained subservient to Washington's interests in the region. This he did. His main target was the Iranian communists and their supporters. Mass arrests and torture became a feature of the regime. During the 1950s thousands of Iranian students and intellectuals fled into exile. Then in the Sixties came the shah's 'white revolution', which introduced land reforms and gave women the vote. Khomeini opposed both these measures. He was behind the riots of 1963 that got him expelled from the country. Literally. He was taken to the border with Iraq and dumped on the other side. This was one exile who used his enforced departure well.

The hopes aroused by the 1979 revolution amongst many intellectuals, liberal and left-wing students and a section of the religious movement itself were soon destroyed. The new regime had come to power because people were fed up with the social, political and economic situation. But hopes that the radicalism would bypass the clergy were misplaced. While one section of the left paid a heavy price for failing to issue a single warning as to what a clerical dictatorship would entail, other groups who had declared that 'the revolution is dead, long live the revolution' did mobilise people against the clerics. It was one of these groups that picked up 150,000 votes in Tehran in the only relatively free election to the Assembly of Experts which was to prepare the new constitution. The problem with these groups was not so much their lack of understanding of the nature of the clerical regime as their failure to grasp the importance of democracy on the level of the state, society and the party.

The communists of the Tudeh Party and the secular-liberals of the National Front were virtually absent from the mass movement. But this was a problem, not the advantage that some far-left groups hoped. It meant that the mullahs were the only organised force in the movement. Their ideology became dominant. Their victory sealed the fate of all those who had imagined they were fighting for democratic rights, against the oppression of national and religious minorities and for the rights of women. The collapse of the centralised Pahlevi state excited autonomist aspirations, and movements for self-government arose in Khuzestan, Kurdistan, Baluchistan and

Azerbaijan. The clerics fought them with a vigour that exceeded the unitary enthusiasms of the ancien régime.

In the immediate aftermath of the Revolution there had been a flowering of democracy, a proliferation of pamphlets, books, newspapers, public meetings, discussions and committees. Their presence, if not their words, challenged the clerical vision of the Islamic Republic and the 'divine right' of the clerics to rule. They determined to remove the threat permanently, and in this were helped by the uncritical proclamations of the secularists.

The Tudeh Party's opportunist interventions after February 1979 were, to put it mildly, ineffective. In their attempt to create a popular front with the clerics, they disgraced themselves. In March, Khomeini issued an edict demanding that women veil themselves. Within twenty-four hours, 20,000 women came out and demonstrated against the edict. The Tudeh Party denounced 'bourgeois women' for marching in the streets against Khomeini; they lambasted their former liberal allies in the National Front for defending the freedom of the press; they sharply criticised the Kurds and Turcomans for resisting the clerics. The far left groups, too, failed to defend the 'perfumed' women.

Soon they would all be destroyed. In 1981 the radical left and the mujahidin were arrested. The prisons began to overflow, even more than under the shah. In 1983 leaders and members of the Tudeh were arrested, just like the women, the revolutionary left, the Kurds and the Turcomans whose struggles they had mocked. Systematic torture and corporal punishment, prohibited in Iran from the early Twenties to the late Sixties, had returned under the shah. His secret police, Savak, became notorious throughout the world, mentioned each year as gross violators of human rights and dignity by Amnesty International. Religious prisoners and communists both suffered at the hands of the regime, often sharing the same cell. Now the clerics were using exactly the same methods against their 'enemies'.

The shah had sometimes bought off his opponents with cash or exile. The clerics wanted public humiliation. They organised show-trials, tortured prisoners till they agreed to repent on television. One of the saddest episodes in modern Iranian history is the sight of the old Tudeh leadership, veterans of many struggles, appearing on television, denouncing their Satanic past and proclaiming their adherence to Islam and its Shi'ite guardians. They apologised for having referred to clerical leaders of the past as 'reactionaries', 'crazed petty-bourgeois' and 'representatives of the landed gentry'. They denounced their own written work.[30] It is impossible to condemn the victims of torture for their actions, though I have often wondered whether the exaggerated condemnations of themselves were subversive of Shi'ism whose culture is bathed in the blood of martyrs. The refusal of the Tudeh cadres to become martyrs was a clear indication that, for most of them, the 'conversions' were totally fake.

There were others, thousands of left-wing activists who had participated with great courage in the mobilisations that overthrew the shah. They, too, were tortured. They refused to repent and were punished with mass executions.

This was the internal face of the clerical dictatorship, but in the early years it had the support of the majority. In the referendum of March 1979, it had obtained a majority in favour of the Islamic Republic. Some had voted to register their opposition to the shah. The radical left had called for a boycott. The regime was constructing its legitimacy till the time when it could wipe out all opposition to its rule. True, this was a month after the Revolution, but it was indicative. The disarray of the secular forces was complete. It was the fact of this support that led many clerics to justify the terror as a revolutionary expression of the popular will: undoubted shades of Saint-Just and Trotsky.

The fall of the shah's regime was undoubtedly a blow against US interests in the Near and Middle East, but there was a qualitative difference between these events and, for example, the Sandinista victory in Nicaragua.

---

30 In 1984, Ehsan Tabari, the principal theoretician of Iranian communism, a man who had become a Marxist half-a-century before, appeared on television. They had tortured the past out of him: 'Historical materialism – unlike Shi'ism – cannot explain phenomena such as Spartacus and Pugachev.' Unlike his colleagues, who had praised the clerics for their 'anti-imperialism', Tabari's recantation was punctuated by numerous laudatory references to Islam and its Shi'ite thinkers. Nonetheless they kept him in solitary confinement. He produced books to justify his conversion. His anti-Marxist memoirs, whose crudeness surprised the more independent-minded clerics, described his old comrades as Soviet agents, murderers, traitors to Iran, spies for Saddam Hussein, etc. All this was serialised in the mainstream press. The physical and mental pain of torture had produced this result. Tabari died a broken man, without ever being given the opportunity to say his equivalent of 'but it moves . . .'

For Washington was still engaged in the final stages of the Cold War. The threats posed by Havana, Hanoi and Managua were systemic in a way that the Islamic Republic could never be. The danger posed by Tehran affected the United States indirectly. If Tehran fomented Shi'ite uprisings in Iraq, Saudi Arabia and the Gulf states, it could pose problems.

The foreign policy of the Islamic Republic excited Islamists everywhere. It pledged a struggle to the death against the Great Satan (the United States) and the Soviet Union. The former was the protector of Israel and other enemies of true Islam like Saudi Arabia. The latter was the fountainhead of atheism and materialism. Neither assessment was inaccurate, but the main thrust of the clerics was to mobilise thousands outside the US embassy and demand a return of the shah to face trial. This was followed by a theatrical occupation of the embassy and the taking of hostages. It was epic theatre, a demand for vengeance against a hated ruler, but anti-imperialism?

In reality, the mobilisations outside the US embassy became a cover to push through deeply reactionary social measures that would soon lead to the execution of adulterers and homosexuals and a total clampdown on the left, the national minorities (the war in Kurdistan was resumed) and the mujahidin.

How could imperialism ever be threatened by such a social structure? Its real enemies had wanted to transcend the rule of the market and, at the height of their strength, had dramatically reduced its global space: the Soviet Union and the People's Republic of China were no-go areas for world capitalism. Cuba had struck a heavy blow only a few miles from the US mainland, removing itself from the sphere of mafia-capitalism. All these states were striving for a superior social and economic system. Their existence was a challenge to imperialism. In Iran all that was on offer was the anti-imperialism of fools, whose long-term threats were negligible.

A system that claims to rest on divine sanction and in which the clerics are the only interpreters can do what it pleases. Any dissent from within or outside the ranks of the clergy is resisting the injunctions of Allah, who is accountable to no other authority. Khomeini's de facto assumption of total power led to the flight of more liberal Islamists like the first elected president, Bani Sadr, and the placing of dissident ayatollahs under virtual house-arrest. How long could a regime based on a fanatical irrationalism last? What social forces could be mobilised to overthrow it? Just as these questions were beginning to be asked in whispers in prison and in private homes, a real threat emerged.

The West had not favoured a direct military intervention, but it was irritated by the destabilising effects of the Tehran regime. It turned to an unfriendly neighbour. Saddam Hussein was regarded as a semi-reliable relay in a volatile region. Internally he had helped to wipe out the Iraqi Communist Party and marginalised the more radical elements in the Ba'ath. He was happy to talk business with the United States and Britain. Since the fall of the shah, he had begun to receive most-favoured-nation treatment from Washington and London.

Washington feared for the safety of the emirs and sheikhs who ruled the statelets of the Gulf, but it was especially concerned for the 'stability' of the Saudi monarchy. The only legitimacy these rulers enjoyed was the consent of Washington to their rule. At one point, a character in *Cities of Salt* poses a question whose answer is known to all: 'And the emir, was he their emir, there to defend and protect them, or was he the Americans' emir?'

It was because they were, each and every one of them, America's emirs that they became fearful lest the Iranian disease infect their own populations. They knew that if a spirit of defiance seized the hearts of their people, their regimes could fall, despite the Americans and despite the sectarian divide between Sunni and Shia Islam that they had crudely exploited to divide and rule. If Washington was unable to save the mighty shah, how could it save them?

It was these frightened men who now dangled their pregnant purses before the greedy eyes of the hegemon in Baghdad. They flattered Saddam. They bathed him in gold coins. A chorus of sycophants led by a scion of the Kuwaiti ruling family, the poetess Souad el-Sabah, sang his praises in verse, honouring him as the 'sword of Iraq'. They pleaded with him to crush the clerics in Iran, reminded him, as if he needed reminding, that the Shia constituted a majority in Iraq, the site of Karbala, their holiest of holy sites, sprinkled centuries ago with the blood of the martyred Hussein. If the Iranians took Bahrain and Kuwait, they would incite an uprising in Iraq and threaten Riyadh.

The leader of the Iraqi Ba'ath was sympathetic, but non-committal. Only one question interested him. What did the emir in the White House want? Only after he was directly assured that Washington had green-lighted the war and its largest aircraft carrier the *United Kingdom* had been alerted to Iraq's likely military requirements did Saddam Hussein go to war against Khomeini's Iran. Like the rulers of the Gulf, Saddam genuinely believed that the Americans thought of everything.[31]

The Iran–Iraq war was a grim conflict. It lasted eight years, from 1980 to 1988. In its battles, reminiscent of the First World War, more than a million Muslim lives were lost. In 1982 the Tehran regime's successful counter-offensive regained all the territories occupied by Iraq in 1980. In Baghdad the Ba'ath leadership met and isolated Saddam Hussein. They proposed a comprehensive ceasefire which accepted Iranian demands in full. If this had happened Saddam would have fallen. Khomeini, excited by his military triumphs, refused the offer. He believed that if the Islamic Revolution did not expand it might implode, and many of the intellectuals who backed the regime said so publicly. The decision sealed the fate of the Ba'ath oppositionists in Baghdad.

Saddam survived, eliminated internal opposition and continued the war. US naval vessels entered the region and began to engage and destroy the Iranian navy. In an act of totally unjustified terrorism, the United States shot down an Iranian Airlines plane packed with passengers. The Iranians, now fully aware that behind Saddam lay the battleships of Washington and the sparkling munitions of Britain, finally sued for peace. But the regime survived. The stranglehold of the clerics was temporarily strengthened, though dissent surfaced within their own ranks. Most importantly, the fact that the regime had survived meant that its leaders were denied the mantle of martyrdom. They could not blame others for what they had themselves done to their country and its people. The new generation that had never known the shah would draw its own conclusions. The seeds of the Reformation-to-come had been sown by the clerics.

The first sign of the new shoots began to appear on cinema screens at film festivals and arthouse cinemas. This was followed by a student rebellion

---

31 Israel alone remained neutral. 'When *goyim* kill *goyim*', Begin had remarked, 'we can only watch.' He meant, of course, watch and applaud. However, even then, Israel perceived Iraq with its large army as a much greater potential threat than Iran. And so, at a crucial stage of the war, it supplied spare parts to Iran, whose tanks and fighter jets had been supplied by the US arms industry.

demanding reforms. Then women began to defy the restrictions imposed by the religious police. A reformist cleric was elected President. He was able to suggest that banks could pay interest but unable to stop the killings of students and intellectuals by the hard-core thugs of the regime. In 2001 there were 52 street demonstrations against the clerics, one for each week of the year, 370 strikes, one for each day of the year, and open skirmishes between the youth and the hated religious police, a bunch of corrupt sadists. For the last two years the Nauroz festival, the pagan new year, which pre-dates Islam, was openly celebrated by young men and unveiled young women who taunted the religious police to do its worst. This is only the beginning, but what it shows is that people learn through their own experiences. These are much better teachers than American bombs. It is precisely because there is no excuse the regime can offer that a new generation refuses to believe the lies. The hatred that many now feel for the clergy and its religion is truly remarkable.

14

An ocean of terror

In December 1987 a new Palestinian *intifada* began on the West Bank and Gaza. It unsettled Israel, challenging the certainties of Zionism. It also took the Arab regimes by surprise. They thought the days of struggle were long gone. The *intifada* challenged the *infitah*.

As usual it was Qabbani who captured the popular mood. *The Trilogy of the Children of Stones* advised the Palestinians to rely on their own strength:

The children of the stones
have scattered our papers
spilled ink on our clothes
mocked the banality of old texts . . .
What matters about
the children of the stones
Is that they have brought us rain after centuries of thirst,
Brought us the sun after centuries of darkness,
Brought us hope after centuries of defeat . . .
The most important
thing about them is that they have rebelled
against the authority of the fathers,
that they have fled the House of Obedience . . .
O Children of Gaza
Don't mind our broadcasts
Don't listen to us
We are the people of cold calculations
Of addition, of subtraction
Wage your wars and leave us alone

We are dead and tombless
Orphans with no eyes.
Children of Gaza
Don't refer to our writings
Don't read us
We are your parents
Don't be like us.
We are your idols
Don't worship us.
O mad people of Gaza,
A thousand greetings to the mad
The age of political reason
Has long departed
So teach us madness.[32]

The Iraqi regime spoke loudly in favour of the Palestinians and dispatched a great deal of financial aid. The Israeli lobby in the State
Department began a mighty agitation against 'the madness'. They were
aware that if the Palestinians refused to be crushed, an ambitious Arab
leader, dreaming of eternal glory, might just take the risk and ride on their
backs. Arafat was stateless. He could be controlled by concessions, but their
man in Baghdad, was he really their man or did he have ambitions of his
own? Israeli efforts bore fruit. Washington became convinced that the
rearming of Iraq was out of control. It could damage the delicate status quo
in the region. Saddam's wings had to be clipped, but how?

The invasion of Kuwait offered a heaven-sent opportunity, but how did
it actually come about? Every Iraqi government since the mandate of 1922
laid territorial claim to Kuwait, which indeed had been ruled from Baghdad
for the preceding two thousand years. It was widely accepted that the
Kuwaitis were being provocative in their oil dispute with Baghdad. The
Ba'ath leadership came up with a plan that would restore Iraqi sovereignty
and settle the dispute in eternity, but Saddam Hussein's caution, especially in
relation to Washington, is well established. He rarely made a big move
without securing approval in advance. This time, too, he posed his favourite
question. What did Washington think?

---

32 First published by Nizar Qabbani Publications, Beirut, 1988.

To this day senior Iraqi officials insist that Saddam's fatal meeting with US Ambassador April Glaspie was an event of decisive importance. Glaspie was sympathetic to their case, was informed of Iraq's plans and gave her de facto approval. When Saddam's armies invaded on 2 August 1990, Kuwait fell without a struggle. The ruling al-Sabah family fled the country. If Baghdad had supervised immediate elections and devolved power to an assembly it would have won massive support, but democratic accountability was not on the agenda. It had been denied to the people of Iraq for far too long. Permitting it to the Kuwaitis was too dangerous an option.

Nonetheless, the Soviet foreign minister, Yevgeni Primakov, negotiated a deal with Baghdad that would have led to a unilateral Iraqi withdrawal from Kuwait, but the agreement was blocked by the United States. A crumbling and enfeebled Russia discovered it could not insist on anything. The Gulf War erupted. Saddam Hussein, a former ally of Washington, was now branded as 'an Arab Hitler'. The news media of the West took up the refrain and the venal rulers of plucky little Kuwait became part of a propaganda offensive. Saddam's crime was the breach of sovereignty. He had violated international law and the United Nations Charter, which was indeed the case, and had to be punished in public. He did not realise that sovereignty may only be breached by the imperial power. Mimicry in this field is not encouraged.

Liberal apologists for the Gulf War insisted that it was necessary to safeguard the real interests of the people of Iraq. Its outcome would be a democratic regime in Baghdad, albeit after a limited period of direct rule by Washington. Imperialism, we were told, would defeat 'fascism' and restore democracy and was, for that reason, preferable. The emancipatory project was safe in Washington's hands and there was no alternative. This pathetic world-view crumbled within weeks of the war's ending. It became clear that neither Washington nor its clients in Riyadh and the Gulf tributaries, leaving aside Damascus and Cairo, were interested in democracy. This was never a serious consideration in Washington which was always more interested in 'ending the Vietnam syndrome' and establishing a new balance of power in the Middle East by breaking Iraq's backbone and thus convincing Israel to agree a permanent peace with the Palestinians and its neighbours.

Saddam had been taught a lesson. He might be removed, but 'an iron-fisted Iraqi Junta', in Thomas Friedman's phrase, had to be kept in power.

Without such a regime, or so they reasoned, Iraq might become a Lebanon, torn apart by ethnic and sectarian rivalries. As for democracy, banish the thought. Iran could not be provided with a sister Shi'ite republic. The Saudis and the Gulf states could not tolerate that, and nor could the oil companies. In the wake of the Gulf War the United States and its allies averted their eyes as Saddam crushed popular uprisings. Instead they embarked on a cruel campaign to punish the people of Iraq, hoping that the punishment would encourage them to overthrow the regime. Western policies have had the opposite effect.

On 23 May 2000, the British defence minister Geoff Hoon, questioned in the House of Commons about the pattern of Anglo-American attacks on Iraq, replied:

> Between 1 August 1992 and 16 December 1998, UK aircraft released 2.5 tons of ordnance over the southern no-fly zone at an average of 0.025 tons per month. We do not have sufficiently detailed records of coalition activity in this period to estimate what percentage of the coalition total this represents. Between 20 December 1998 and 17 May 2000, UK aircraft released 78 tons of ordnance over the southern no-fly zones, at an average of 5 tons per month. This figure represents approximately 20 per cent of the coalition total for this period.[33]

In other words, over a period of eighteen months the United States and United Kingdom had rained down some 400 tons of bombs and missiles on Iraq. Tony Blair has been dropping deadly explosives on the country at a rate twenty times greater than his Conservative predecessor, John Major. What explains this escalation? Its immediate origins are no mystery. On 16 December 1998 Clinton, on the eve of a vote indicting him for perjury and obstruction of justice in the House of Representatives, unleashed a round-the-clock aerial assault on Iraq, ostensibly to punish the regime in Baghdad for failure to cooperate with UN inspections, in fact to help deflect impeachment. Operation Desert Fox, fittingly named after a Nazi general, ran for seventy hours, blasting a hundred targets.

Thereafter, far from dying down, the firestorm continued. In August 1999 the *New York Times* reported:

---

33 *Hansard*, 24 May 2000.

American warplanes have methodically and with virtually no public discussion been attacking Iraq. In the last eight months, American and British pilots have fired more than 1,100 missiles against 359 targets in Iraq. This is triple the number of targets attacked in four furious days of strikes in December . . . By another measure, pilots have flown about two-thirds as many missions as NATO pilots flew over Yugoslavia in seventy-eight days of around-the-clock war there.[34]

In October 1999 American officials were telling the *Wall Street Journal* they would soon be running out of targets – 'We're down to the last outhouse.' By the end of the year, the Anglo-American air forces had flown more than 6,000 sorties, and dropped over 1,800 bombs on Iraq. By early 2001 the bombardment of Iraq had lasted longer than the US invasion of Vietnam.

A decade of assault from the air has yet been the lesser part of the purgatory inflicted on Iraq. Blockade by land and sea has caused still greater suffering. Economic sanctions have driven a population whose levels of nutrition, schooling and public services were once well above regional standards into fathomless misery. Before 1990 the country had a per capita GNP of over $3,000. Today it is under $500, making Iraq one of the poorest societies on Earth.[35] A land that once had high levels of literacy and an advanced system of health-care has been devastated by the West. Its social structure is in ruins, its people are denied the basic necessities of existence, its soil is polluted by uranium-tipped warheads. According to UN figures of 2001, some 60 per cent of the population have no regular access to clean water, and over 80 per cent of schools need substantial repairs. In 1997 the FAO reckoned that 27 per cent of Iraqis were suffering from chronic malnutrition, and 70 per cent of all women were anaemic. UNICEF reports that in the southern and central regions which contain 85 per cent of the country's population, infant mortality has doubled compared to the pre-Gulf War period.[36]

The death-toll caused by deliberate strangulation of economic life cannot yet be estimated with full accuracy – that will be a task for historians.

---

34 Steven Lee Myers, 'In Intense But Little-Noticed Fight, Allies Have Bombed Iraq All Year', *New York Times*, 13 August 1999. For this and much else besides, see Anthony Arnove's introduction to Arnove (ed.), *Iraq Under Siege: The Deadly Impact of Sanctions and War*, London and Cambridge, MA, 2002, pp. 11–13.

35 Peter Pellett, 'Sanctions, Food, Nutrition, and Health in Iraq', in *Iraq Under Siege*, p. 189.

36 UN Report on the Current Humanitarian Situation in Iraq, March 1999.

According to the most careful authority, Richard Garfield, 'a conservative estimate of "excess deaths" among under five-year-olds since 1991 would be 300,000',[37] while UNICEF – reporting in 1997 that '4,500 children under the age of five are dying each month from hunger and disease' – reckons the number of small children killed by the blockade at 500,000.[38] Other deaths are harder to quantify, but as Garfield points out, 'UNICEF's mortality rates represent only the tip of the iceberg as to the enormous damage done to the four out of five Iraqis who do survive beyond their fifth birthday.'[39] In late 1998 the UN Humanitarian Coordinator for Iraq, former Assistant Secretary General Denis Halliday, an Irishman, resigned from his post in protest against the blockade, declaring that the total deaths it had caused could be upwards of a million.[40] When his successor Hans von Sponeck had the temerity to include civilian casualties from Anglo-American bombing raids in his brief, the Clinton and Blair regimes demanded his dismissal. He too resigned, in late 1999, explaining that his duty had been to the people of Iraq, and that 'every month Iraq's social fabric shows bigger holes'. These holes have continued to tear under the Oil-For-Food sanctions in place since 1996, which allow Iraq $4 billion of petroleum exports a year, when a minimum of $7 billion is needed even for greatly reduced services.[41] After a decade, the throttling of Iraq by the US and UK has achieved a result without parallel in modern history. This is now a country that, in Garfield's words, 'is the only instance of a sustained, large increase in mortality in a stable population of more than two million in the last two hundred years'.[42]

What justification is offered for this murderous revenge on a whole people? Three arguments recur in the official apologetics, and are relayed

---

37 Richard Garfield, 'The Public Health Impact of Sanctions', *Middle East Report*, No. 215, Summer 2000, p. 17. Garfield is Professor of Clinical International Nursing at Columbia University.

38 UNICEF, 'Iraq Survey Shows "Humanitarian Emergency"', 12 August 1999.

39 Garfield, 'The Public Health Impact of Sanctions', p. 17.

40 See Arnove (ed.), *Iraq Under Siege*, pp. 45, 67.

41 See Haris Gazdar and Athar Hussain, 'Crisis and Response: A Study of the Impact of Economic Sanctions in Iraq', Asia Research Centre, London School of Economics, December 1997.

42 Richard Garfield, 'Changes in Health and Well-being in Iraq during the 1990s', in *Sanctions on Iraq – Background, Consequences, Strategies*, Cambridge 2000, p. 36.

through the domesticated media. First, Saddam Hussein is an insatiable aggressor, whose seizure of Kuwait was a violation of international law and a threat to the stability of the entire region; no neighbour will be safe till he is overthrown. Second, his regime was stockpiling weapons of mass destruction, and was about to acquire a nuclear arsenal, posing an unheard-of danger to the international community. Third, Saddam's dictatorship at home is of a malignant ferocity beyond compare, an embodiment of political evil whose continued existence no decent government can countenance. For all these reasons, the civilised world can never rest until Saddam is eliminated. Bombardment and blockade are the only means of doing so, without improper risk to our own citizens.

Each of these arguments is utterly hollow. The Iraqi occupation of Kuwait, a territory often administered from Basra or Baghdad in precolonial times, was no exceptional outrage in either the region or the world at large. The Indonesian seizure of East Timor had been accepted with equanimity by the West for the better part of two decades when the ruling family fled Kuwait. Still more pointedly, in the Middle East itself, Israel – a state founded on an original process of ethnic cleansing – had long defied UN resolutions mandating a relatively equal division of Palestine, repeatedly seized large areas of neighbouring territory, and was in occupation not only of the Gaza Strip, the West Bank and the Golan Heights, but a belt of Southern Lebanon at the time. Far from resisting this expansionism, the United States continues to support, equip and fund it, without a murmur from its European allies, least of all Britain. The end of this process is now in sight, as Washington supervises the reduction of the Palestinians to a few shrivelled bantustans at Israel's pleasure. The lesson is not that aggressive territorial expansion is a crime that cannot be allowed to pay, it is that to conduct it with success a state must act in the interests of the West too: then it can be astonishingly successful. Iraq's seizure of Kuwait was not in the West's interest, since it posed the threat that two-fifths of the world's oil reserves would be controlled by a modern Arab state with an independent foreign policy, unlike the feudal dependencies of the West in Kuwait, the Gulf or Saudi Arabia. Hence Desert Storm.

So much for expansionism. As for the deadly threat from Iraqi weapons programmes, there was little out of the way about these either. So long as the regime in Baghdad was regarded as a friend in Washington and London – for some twenty years, as it crushed communists at home and fought Iranian mullahs abroad – few apprehensions about its armaments drive were expressed: chemical weapons could be used without complaint, export licences were granted, extraordinary shipments winked at. Nuclear capability was another question, not from any special fear of Iraq, but because since the Sixties the United States has sought, in the interests of big-power monopoly, to prevent their spread to lesser states. Israel, naturally, has been exempted from the requirements of 'non-proliferation' – not only stockpiling a large arsenal without the slightest remonstration from the West, but enjoying active support in concealing its programme.

Once the Iraqi regime had turned against Western interests in the Gulf, of course, the possibility of it acquiring nuclear weapons suddenly moved up the ordinary US agenda to the status of an apocalyptic danger. Today there is no shred left on this scarecrow. On the one hand, the nuclear monopoly of the big powers, always a grotesque pretension, has – as it was bound to do – collapsed with the acquisition of weapons by India and Pakistan, with Iran no doubt soon to follow. On the other hand, Iraq's own nuclear programme has been so thoroughly eradicated that even the super-hawk Scott Ritter – the UNSCOM inspector who boasted of his collaboration with Israeli intelligence, and set up the raids that triggered Desert Fox – now says there is no chance of its reconstitution, and the blockade should be dropped.

Last, there is the claim that the domestic enormities of Saddam's regime are so extreme that any measure is warranted to get rid of him. Since the Gulf War ended without a march on Baghdad, Washington and London have not been able to proclaim this officially, but they let it be understood with every informal briefing and insider commentary. No theme is more cherished by camp-followers of officialdom on the left, given to explaining that Saddam is an Arab Hitler, and since 'fascism is worse than imperialism' all people of good sense should unite behind Strategic Air Command. This line of argument is, in fact, the *ultima ratio* of the blockade; in Clinton's words, 'sanctions will be there until the end of time, or as long as Saddam lasts'.[43] That the Ba'ath regime is a brutal tyranny no one could doubt –

---

43 See Barbara Crossette, 'For Iraq, a Dog House with Many Rooms', *New York Times*, 23 November 1997.

however long Western chancelleries looked away while Saddam was an ally. That it is unique in its cruelties is an abject fiction. The lot of the Kurds in Turkey, where not even the Kurdish language is permitted in schools and the army has displaced 2 million people from their homelands in its war against the Kurdish population, has always been worse than in Iraq, where – whatever Saddam's other crimes – there has never been any attempt at this kind of cultural annihilation. Yet as a valued member of NATO and candidate for the EU, Ankara suffers not the slightest measure against it, indeed can rely on Western help for its repression. The kidnapping of Ocalan supplies a fitting pendant to that of Vanunu, accompanied by soothing reportage in the Anglo-American media on Turkey's progress towards responsible modernity. Who has ever suggested an Operation Urgent Rescue around Lake Van, or a no-fly zone over Adana, any more than a pre-emptive strike on Dimona?

If the fate of its Kurds has attracted most attention abroad, Ba'ath oppression has certainly not spared the Arab populations of Iraq either. But what of the firm Western ally on its southern borders? The Saudi kingdom makes not even a pretence of human rights as understood in Harvard, or elections as in Westminster, not to speak of the condition it accords women, which would not pass muster in medieval Russia. Yet no state in the Arab world is more toasted in Washington. In killing and torture, Saddam was never a match for Suharto, whose massacres in Indonesia far exceeded any in Iraq. But no Third World regime was more prized by the West, from its bloody inception right through the years when Saddam's rule was declared such an iniquity that its removal was a moral imperative of the whole 'international community'. In 1995, while American and British air power were pounding the outlaw in Baghdad, Clinton and Gore were receiving an old friend from Djakarta with open arms.[44] In London, Blair was dispatching arms to

---

44 Suharto – 'the aging, military-backed leader of Indonesia, and a man who also knows a good deal about how to keep dissenters under control' – was a star attraction, reported the *New York Times*. 'When he arrived at the White House on Friday for a "private" visit with the President, the Cabinet room was jammed with top officials ready to welcome him. Vice President Gore was there, along with Secretary of State Warren Christopher; the Chairman of the Joint Chiefs of Staff, Gen. John Shalikashvili; Commerce Secretary Ronald H. Brown; the United States trade representative, Mickey Kantor; the national security adviser, Anthony Lake, and many others. "There wasn't an empty chair in the room," one participant said. "No one used to treat the Indonesians like this, and it said a lot about how our priorities in the world have changed."' The *New York Times*

the Indonesian dictatorship down to 1997, and on the very eve of Suharto's fall he welcomed his regime at the Euro-Asian Summit in London – while barring the Burmese junta – whose victims may be modest by comparison, but whose attitude to foreign investors is less enlightened – as beyond the pale.

But if not a single leg of the argument for the bombardment and block-ade of Iraq stands up, there is still the most widespread fall-back of all. So what? Other states may be equally expansionist, seek nuclear weapons more effectively, maltreat or kill larger numbers of their citizens, but what follows? Not all injustices can be cured at one stroke. An evil elsewhere is not mended by a failure to do good here. Even if we only do the right thing once, isn't it better than not doing it at all? Rather double standards than no standards. Such is now the orthodox casuistry among loyal factotums, columnists and courtiers of the Clinton and Blair regimes, to be heard on those occasions when denial of inconvenient – that is: Saudi, Israeli, Indonesian, Turkish or any other – realities becomes impossible. 'We need to get used to the idea of double standards,' writes Blair's Personal Assistant for Foreign Affairs, ex-diplomat Robert Cooper, quite openly.[45] The under-lying maxim of this cynicism is: we will punish the crimes of our enemies and reward the crimes of our friends. Isn't that at least preferable to univer-sal impunity? To this the answer is simple: 'punishment' along these lines does not reduce but breeds criminality, by those who wield it. The Gulf and Balkan wars are copybook examples of the moral blank cheque of a selective vigilantism.

left no doubt about what these were. Suharto, it went on, was 'sitting on the ultimate emerging market: some 13,000 islands, a population of 193 million and an economy growing at more than 7 percent a year. The country remains wildly corrupt and Mr Suharto's family controls leading businesses that competitors in Jakarta would be unwise to challenge. But Mr Suharto, unlike the Chinese, has been savvy in keeping Washington happy. He has deregulated the economy, opened Indonesia to foreign investors and kept the Japanese, Indonesia's largest supplier of foreign aid, from grabbing more than a quarter of the market for goods imported into the country. So Mr Clinton made the requisite complaints about Indonesia's repressive tactics in East Timor, where anti-Government protests continue, and moved right on to business, getting Mr Suharto's support for market-opening progress during the annual Asian Pacific Economic Cooperation meeting in Osaka in mid-November. "He's our kind of guy," a senior Administration official, who deals often on Asian policy, said'. See David Sanger, 'Real Politics: Why Suharto is In and Castro is Out', *New York Times*, 31 October 1995.

45 Robert Cooper, *The Post-Modern State and World Order*, London 1996, p. 42.

The two cases are not identical, since there were no strategic minerals in Yugoslavia. But if their origins differ, a single ideology embraces both. Cooper sets it out with admirable clarity. On the one hand, he explains without inhibition that 'the reasons for fighting the Gulf War were not that Iraq had violated the norms of international behaviour' – annexations by other states, he notes, might be tolerable enough – but lay in the West's need to keep a tight grip on 'vital oil supplies'. On the other hand, he continues, the West should not confine itself to such clear-cut cases of material interest, but should range more widely. 'Advice to post-modern states: accept that intervention in the pre-modern is going to be a fact of life,' he writes. 'Such interventions may not solve problems, but they may salve the conscience. And they are not necessarily the worse for that.'[46] Here is the script for Kosovo, written in advance of the NATO blitz. The cost of 'conscience' was, quite predictably, far more death and destruction – not to speak of permanent ethnic cleansing – than the ostensible occasion for 'salving' it. Actually the phrase itself, however damning, needs some adjustment to capture the realities of Western intervention in the Balkans, as 'credibility' became the key, officially expounded, reason why NATO had to persist for months with an air assault it had initially promised, in the words of its secretary-general, was going to be a matter of hours: 'saving face' would be as good a way of putting it. The mind-set behind this posture is graphically expressed by the British prime minister, in confidential memoranda to his aides. '*Touchstone issues.* There are a clutch of issues – seemingly disparate – that are in fact linked. They are roughly combining "on your side" with toughness and standing up for Britain.' Blair goes on: 'We really cannot think we have any chance of winning the "Standing Up for Britain" argument if we appear to be anti-defence.' Likewise with 'asylum and crime: these may appear to be unlinked to patriotism, but they are; partly because they are toughness issues; partly because they reach deep into British instincts.' The remedies? 'Kosovo should have laid to rest any doubts about our strength on defence [*sic*]', and 'we are taking tough measures on asylum and crime'. Refugees from the Balkan War, beneficiaries of one kind of toughness, can now enjoy the fruits of another: 'On asylum we need to be

---

46 Ibid., pp. 44–5.

highlighting removals – also if the benefits bills really start to fall, that should be highlighted.' The thoughts of Britain's pipsqueak bombardier conclude with the peerless instruction: 'I should be personally associated with as much of this as possible.'[47] We might be in the Piazza di Venezia in the Twenties:

For all the devastation it has caused, without hope of durable solution, the upshot of intervention in the Balkans pales besides the balance-sheet in Iraq. There, the result has been a veritable Massacre of the Innocents. Let us take the vanity of our leaders at its word. Clinton and Blair are personally responsible for the deaths of hundreds of thousands of small children, callously slaughtered to save their joint 'credibility'. If we take a low-range figure of 300,000 children under five, and enter a provisional estimate of the premature death toll among adults at another 200,000, we arrive at one of the largest mass killings of the past quarter-century. Moderate figures like Dennis Halliday put the total much higher, at a million or more. By comparison, the Gulf War itself was a small affair: not more than 50,000 dead. Saddam's bloodiest crime – the one that enjoyed Western complicity – was his attack on Iran, which cost his people 200,000 casualties. The genocide in Rwanda wiped out some 500,000. It is sufficient to say that the number of infants and adults destroyed by the siege of Iraq appears to be in that league. If we want a more exact political accountability, Clinton – in power since 1992 – can be apportioned nine-tenths of the dead, Blair – in office since 1997 – two-fifths. Since without America and Britain the blockade would have been lifted long ago, the role of other Western leaders, craven though it is, need not be reckoned.

In 1964, within a few months of the Wilson government coming to power, the socialist political theorist Ralph Miliband warned the Sixties generation, many elated by the end of thirteen years of Conservative rule

---

47 Memoranda from 'TB' of December 1999 and 29 April 2000, published by *The Times*, July 16 and 27 July 2000. 'On crime we need to highlight the tough measures,' the prime minister reiterates obsessively. 'Something tough with immediate bite, which sends a message through the system – maybe the driving licence penalty for young offenders. But this should be done soon and I, personally, should be associated with it.' The documents are an inventory of the mental furniture of Britain's ruler; the phrase describing him above is the pithy coinage of Alexander Cockburn: *Counterpunch*, 16–30 May 1999.

and willing to take any signs of reform at home as the tokens of a progressive administration, that it was a fatal mistake to lose sight of Labour's foreign policy, already quietly locked on to Washington. That, he predicted, would be likely to define the whole experience of the regime. Within a year he was proved right. Wilson's support for the American war in Vietnam, once Johnson had dispatched the US expeditionary force in 1965, exposed to view the full extent of the political rot within Labourism. The miserable end of Old Labour, after a decade of barren office, was written in advance in this futile, servile collusion with a vicious imperial war. In the United States, the struggle against the Vietnam War finished off Johnson and in the end, indirectly, Nixon too; in Britain, it ensured Wilson, Callaghan and their colleagues the complete disdain of anyone of spirit under twenty-five, not to speak of disillusioned elders.

The siege of Iraq is not another war in Vietnam. Its target, scale and means are all lesser. But there is another difference too. This time, Britain is not just lending diplomatic and ideological support to American barbarities, it is actively participating in them as a military confederate. The record of Old Labour, shameful as it was, is little beside the odium of its successor.

In the aftermath of the 11 September events, military planners in the Pentagon once again raised the question of removing Saddam Hussein from power. If a new war is waged against Iraq, the so-called 'war against Terrorism' will turn into its opposite. The combination of anger and despair will lead to more and more young people in the Arab world and elsewhere feeling that the only response to state terror is individual terror.

PART III

The Nuclear Wastelands
of South Asia

This is how my sorrow became visible:
its dust, piling up for years in my heart,
finally reached my eyes,
the bitterness now so clear that
I had to listen when my friends
told me to wash my eyes with blood
Everything at once was tangled in blood –
each face, each idol, red everywhere.
Blood swept over the sun, washing away its gold.
The moon erupted with blood, its silver extinguished.
The sky promised a morning of blood,
and the night wept only blood . . .
Let it flow. Should it be dammed up,
there will only be hatred cloaked in colours of death.
Don't let this happen, my friends,
bring all my tears back instead,
a flood to purify my dust-filled eyes,
to wash this blood forever from my eyes.

Faiz Ahmed Faiz (1911–84), *Lines on the Massacres
in East Pakistan (Bangladesh), March 1971*

Pakistan is like Israel, an ideological state. Take out Judaism from Israel and it will collapse like a house of cards. Take Islam out of Pakistan and make it a secular state; it would collapse. For the past four years we have been trying to bring Islamic values to this country.

General Zia-ul-Haq (1916–89), Chief Martial Law Administrator, Pakistan, 1981

Goodness is nothing else than love born of sympathy.

Spinoza

The case of Anwar Shaikh

In 1989 Khomeini's fatwa against Salman Rushdie had put literature and critical thought on the defensive. The world of Islam was gripped by an oppressive silence. Free speech, already restricted, was further smothered in Cairo and Algiers. But the fear also gripped New York and London. There is a limited analogy here with the atmosphere in the United States after 11 September. Then, as now, there have been several instances of self-censorship by publishers. Shocked authors tell of abandoned literary projects, of fearful groups of intellectuals forced to speak in whispers, of faded smiles on obedient lips, of hurried changes of name: a jazz record label, Jihad, has rebranded; the Islamo-American rock group 'Dr Jihad and the Intellectual Muslim Guerrillas' decided to drop the name after the Pentagon was hit. Anwar Shaikh is a man who refuses to be defeated by fear.

In his youth, he was devout, an ardent believer. Now his quarrel with the religious establishment has become the central feature of his biography. For almost two decades in the Welsh capital, Cardiff, this former bus conductor has been conducting an unremitting one-man campaign against 'the mullahs and politicians who use Islam as a cloak to justify their grisly deeds'. And having a considerable impact.

I first heard of Shaikh several years ago. An old friend from Lahore, a professor in Islamic Law at a Swedish university, was visiting Britain and we met to discuss the state of our world. He asked if I had heard of Anwar Shaikh. I pleaded ignorance. The professor was genuinely surprised. In these bad times, how could I be so ignorant? The man in Cardiff was defending the values of the Enlightenment with such courage and vigour that he deserved our respect. 'Don't you ever read the *Daily Jang?*' my friend asked with some irritation. He was referring to a conservative Urdu daily published in London and distributed all over Europe. He read it in Stockholm to keep abreast of South Asian politics. I explained that my contact with Pakistan was more direct. A daily phone conversation with my mother in Lahore was bad for my overdraft, but kept me well ahead of the *Daily Jang*. It was true, however, that she had never mentioned Anwar Shaikh. Nor was she aware that Shaikh's pamphlets were causing such disquiet within Islamic fundamentalist circles in Western Europe and South Asia.

In the weeks following this encounter, I obtained a set of clippings from the Urdu press in Britain. It became obvious that it wasn't just the hardliners who were agitated. Muslims in Stockholm, Copenhagen, Berlin, Paris and Amsterdam, as well as in London, Birmingham, Bradford and Glasgow, were circulating Shaikh's writings and discussing their blasphemous nature. News had spread largely by word of mouth. The angry letters to the Urdu press confirmed the ferment.

Shaikh had published *Eternity*, his first book, in March 1994. Published, publicised and distributed it himself. It was not in the shops. It could only be ordered through a PO box number in Cardiff. I ordered a copy. The central thesis of the book was straightforward: Shaikh, like the Mu'tazilites of the ninth century, questioned the validity of the revelation. He challenged the divinity of the Koran. The response of the *Daily Awaz* of London was an equally straightforward headline:

ANWAR SHAIKH OF CARDIFF IS A RENEGADE
AND DESERVES TO BE KILLED.

Given the political temperature within the community, what genuinely surprised me was that the tone of the letters denouncing Shaikh in the Muslim press was fairly moderate. Encouraged by the response, Shaikh produced a new pamphlet. The response to this revealed the anxieties of the Muslim community. The *Daily Jang* of 19 August 1997 published a letter from a Mr Abdul Latif in Oldham, Lancashire. The sub-editor's helpful caption, 'A Sordid Anti-Islamic Campaign', was at odds with the actual tone of the letter – a plea for help, which provided a rare insight into the thinking of diaspora Muslims, who are believers without being fanatics:

Several letters have been published in *Jang* about Anwar Shaikh's book: 'Islam, The Arab National Movement'. Ordinary Muslims have been begging their scholars to give crushing answers to the contents of this book, but surprisingly they have remained silent. Is there not a single Muslim scholar in Britain who can rebut Anwar Shaikh's criticism of Islam?

Our scholars must note that the time to frighten the Islam-bashers with fatwas is over. In modern times, public opinion will only be satisfied with arguments. Another reason for writing this letter is that my post-graduate son, who was recently a pious Muslim, no longer cares about Islam. I have learnt that a Christian missionary gave him Anwar Shaikh's book. It is the study of this book which has turned him against Islam . . .

The truth is that we, the Muslims, protested against the accursed Rushdie's book foolishly because Rushdie is nothing compared to Anwar Shaikh. Rushdie forged untruths to make his novel attractive and we were able to satisfy our children on this ground. Anwar Shaikh, by contrast, has founded his work on quotations from the Holy Koran and the *hadiths* which are the cornerstone of our faith.

A week later, the same newspaper published a letter along similar lines from M. Anwar, a Muslim in Amsterdam. This too was a plea to the divines and scholars of Islam to provide a detailed critique of Anwar Shaikh's heresies, lest the infection spread to the younger generation and detach them from their faith. The note of desperation in this letter was a common trope of letter-writers to the Urdu press. While correspondents from most of Western Europe denounced Shaikh, the vast majority did not call for him to be killed, or even for his 'blasphemous' books to be burnt. They demanded an authoritative rebuttal.

While branding Shaikh an apostate, a crime which the *shari'a* punishes with death, Muslim leaders were reluctant to publicise the affair. Believers were advised to remain calm. Qari Sayyad Hussain Ahmed in Leeds argued:

We have been deceived once. The satan Rushdie was an obscure person. We issued a fatwa and fixed a reward for his head. Had we not done so, Rushdie would have reached the end of his tether. As a result, his type of madman could not even have thought of insulting the Prophet. Rushdie and Shaikh belong to the same tribe. People should not organise protests lest Anwar Shaikh receives international fame.

The analogy between Shaikh and Rushdie is misplaced. Shaikh regards himself as a serious historian, not a weaver of fictions. Rushdie was denounced as a corrupted modernist, a product of Rugby School and Cambridge, a man remote from the lives of ordinary Muslims. Shaikh is a Punjabi of peasant stock. His youth was spent in the heart of subcontinental Islam. He knows his subject well. Too well.

His prose is repetitive and, on occasion, an incoherence seeps into his argument, but this can be effective if written for an audience used to religious texts and sermons that are always repetitive and incoherent. His books and pamphlets circulate throughout the Muslim communities in Western Europe and Pakistan like samizdats in the former Soviet Union or Aaron MacGruder's cartoons in the post-September United States. They are read, copied, passed on, endlessly discussed. It is this that makes Shaikh a dangerous opponent of orthodoxy. He *is* the enemy within. When I finally met up with him, I was taken aback by his self-confidence: 'They will never succeed in gagging my mouth, because I speak for millions of silent Muslims.'

In his pamphlet *Islam: The Arab National Movement*, Shaikh's intent is to torpedo the fundamentals of Islam. He does this by separating Muhammad from Allah. His claim that in so doing he is simply obeying a Koranic injunction – 'Bring your argument, if you are one of the truthful' – is disingenuous. His project is to deconstruct the theological architecture of Islam so that the twin towers – the Koran and the Prophet – collapse simultaneously. His model is the seventeenth-century Jewish philosopher Spinoza, who unravelled the Old Testament in similar fashion and, as a consequence, was excommunicated by the elders of the Amsterdam Synagogue. When I inform Shaikh (a) that despite repeated attempts by Jewish scholars, the excommunication has still not been revoked and (b) that there is no excommunication in Islam, only the executioner's sword, his response is a deep, throaty chuckle.

In his texts he argues that the ancient Semitic tradition of Revelation creates more problems than it solves. He sees 'revelation as the device which makes a man (the revelationist) divine, but reduces the stature of God, who becomes dependent on the revelationist, i.e. the prophet, to execute His will'. He cites chapter and verse from the Koran and the *hadiths* of the Prophet, to demonstrate that Allah accepts the political and material needs of Muhammad far too easily for a Supreme Being. In Shaikh's view it is the Prophet and not Allah who stands at the centre of Islam. Unaware of the pedigree of such ideas – the debates sparked off by Ibn Rawandi and the Mu'tazilites a thousand years ago – Shaikh sees himself as a pioneer. 'My arguments are like a dagger pointing at the heart of fundamentalism.'

Mufti Mohammed Saeed Ahmad Saeed, president of World Muslim Unity, after declaring Shaikh a renegade, an apostate and an infidel, went on to declare:

> Anwar Shaikh has claimed he believes in God, but not the Prophet. This is like someone who says I acknowledge my mother, but not my father. Such a person is commonly known as a bastard.

Allah as Mother and the Prophet the Father? Statements of this sort only strengthen Shaikh in his belief that Islam is a topsy-turvy religion.

So who is Anwar Shaikh? When I went to meet him in Cardiff, I did not know what to expect. Might he be a bearded mirror-image of the mullahs he so mercilessly torments? Instead I discovered a relaxed old Punjabi extremely attached to his Doberman pinscher and proud of his large, beautiful garden. The home-made wine was disappointing. Cardiff grapes lack the potency of the written word. After lunch we discussed his evolution.

'How did all this begin?'

I should have known. His writings betray the ardour of a new convert to rationalism. Shaikh was brought up as an orthodox Sunni Muslim. He was born in 1928 in a small village four miles from Gujrat in the Indian province of the Punjab. His birthday coincided with the day of Hajj (the Muslim pilgrimage). He announces that 'I was born circumcised, which was regarded as auspicious by my family.' He was named Haji Mohammed, later changed to Mohammed Anwar Shaikh. At a very young age he learnt to recite the Koran, but he had already learnt Arabic so that, unlike the majority of Indian Muslims, he understood the recitation.

In 1947, the year of independence and Partition, nineteen-year-old Anwar Shaikh was working as an accounts clerk at Lahore railway station. He was a staunch Muslim, angered by the confessional cleansing that was taking place in the Punjab, one of the two Indian provinces (the other was Bengal) which had been divided along religious lines. The non-Muslim minorities in Western Punjab and Muslims in Eastern Punjab were compelled to abandon villages and towns where they had lived for centuries.

Each community had its own version of bloodcurdling tales, of killings, executions, rapes, looting of homes and, of course, heroic martyrdoms. The
precarious situation in which everyone lived heightened Anwar Shaikh's
awareness of the religious divide. Fifty years later he retained a clear memory
of what he witnessed in the summer of 1947. His eyes became moist as he
spoke: 'Trains were arriving at Lahore station from India every day. I used to
hear people waiting for the trains on the platform screaming. They were
heart-rending screams. I would rush out and there was the train, full of
corpses. All the Muslim refugees had been slaughtered. It was a two-way
traffic, of course. Sikhs and Hindus fleeing from our side were also brutally
massacred.'

At the time, however, the nineteen-year-old boy could only see the
events from his side. Possessed by rage and a desire to avenge the deaths of
his fellow Muslims, he went out into the streets of Lahore and killed three
innocent Sikhs. The first two he battered to death with a club, near
Anarkali bazaar, the medieval shopping centre in Lahore. His third victim
was bludgeoned to death with a spade on the Ravi Road near the river. For
days afterwards he wandered around in a daze. Was he scared of being
caught and punished?

'No. You know a madness gripped us in 1947. A madness. I was part of
it. When I was killing them all I could think of was revenge. I was not
frightened of being caught and killed in return. I knew I was destined for
the Islamic paradise, where scores of houris were waiting for me. Seventy
virgins with upright breasts and Allah would give me enough virility for
eighty-four years. What more could a young man want? So you see, not
only was I unafraid, but even looking forward to continuous sex in heaven.
You don't believe me? Please believe me. I believed it at that time. I was
young and impressionable.'

Could he really have believed that at the time? It sounded like a later
rationalisation. Revenge, madness, religion I could understand, but not the
seventy virgins. He was only nineteen. A young man has more romantic
dreams at that stage, usually centred on one or two people. The seventy virgins and twenty-eight-year-long erections are for old men. Perhaps the idea
had come into Shaikh's mind as we were talking that day. Perhaps.

After the turmoil was over and the new state of Pakistan had come into
existence, life became settled again. It was then that Anwar Shaikh realised

the enormity of his crime. He knew he would never be punished and so he began to punish himself. Torment and regret began to eat his soul. He was still a believer, but becoming infected with scepticism. He could not carry on living in Pakistan. It was easy to travel in search of work in those days. There were no immigration controls within the Commonwealth and no visa requirements. He arrived in Cardiff in 1956 with £25 in his pocket, found himself a job as a labourer, and later worked for three years as a bus conductor. Always in search of self-improvement, he graduated at the Institute of Transport in London.

He had married a Welsh woman and begun to build a new life. He invested his savings in property and within a few years – it was now the mid-Sixties – had become an extremely successful property developer. It was a success story.

He had everything now. An easy life, a family, lots of friends. He could have relaxed and seen the world, but he was haunted by the past. The trauma had gone deep. He still couldn't forget the awful summer of 1947, when corpses littered the countryside and blood flowed down the streets of the old city in Lahore. He tried, but could not seal the cellars of his memory.

'I kept thinking, as I still do, that I had destroyed three innocent lives. They might still have been alive had it not been for me. I don't even know who they were. And I began to think. All this had happened because of religion. I had never given up reading the Koran. Now I read it with wide open eyes. One day I read something I had read hundreds of times before: "O Believers, do not walk in front of the Prophet. Do not raise your voice above his." And I asked myself why? Why should Allah raise one human above others? Well, once you ask why, you can never stop. The spell was broken.'

Anwar Shaikh became a familiar face in the libraries of Cardiff. He read Spinoza, Freud and Marx. He did not agree with everything they wrote, but the act of reading them and others expanded his intellectual horizon.

Then he reread the Koran, but not just the Koran. While he was recounting this part of his life, he grabbed me by the arm and took me into the garden once again. Hidden away was a tiny room packed with books in Arabic, Urdu and English. These were the *hadiths*, or traditions as they are known: accounts of the words and actions of the Prophet, which Muslims have used to supplement the Koran and find guidance for their own conduct.

'I have read all these books. I know more about our religion and its traditions than most of these crazed fundamentalists. That's why they can't
answer me. I challenge them now. Wherever and whenever they want I will
debate them. Let us do it in front of a hundred per cent Muslim audience.
Fine by me. Let us do it on radio or television. But they won't. Why?'

Perhaps, I suggest, they don't want to give him any publicity.

'But the mullahs have already pronounced fatwas against me at the Friday
prayers in all the British mosques. So the believers already know of my existence. No, the reason they do not wish to debate me is because the house
they have built for themselves is on weak foundations.'

Shaikh's hostility is directed at the mullahs and politicians who exploit
Islam for their own ends. He is aware of some of the secular traditions of
Islamic culture. He is also only too aware that a rampant Christian and
Hindu fundamentalism, not to mention the Serb and Croat fanatics, could
use his books to service their own nefarious needs. He knows all this, but he
refuses to remain silent any longer.

'For too long we Muslims have taken cover underneath a veil of ignorance. It has held us back for some centuries. Kemal Ataturk understood this
when he sought to modernise Turkey, but he did so without the ideological basis for secularising our culture. That is all I wish to do. I write not just
for today, but for tomorrow. I don't want our children to ever do what I did
in 1947.'

He regularly receives threatening calls, mainly in Punjabi, warning him
that traditional Islamic punishments are on the way. Is he not scared?

'I am sixty-eight years old. I've had heart surgery and seven bypasses. My
life's work is now finished. Whatever happens I will die honourably. My
latest book has been deposited in two bank vaults. Once that is published,
I will be happy.'

A new book?

Shaikh smiled. 'I have called it *Islam and Sexuality*. I think Islam is the
most sex-obsessed religion in the world.'

Chapter 4 of the manuscript is headed 'The Sexual Orientation of the
Prophet'. The argument here is that the Prophet Muhammad's political
and military genius dominated his life to such an extent that he only found
true happiness through an above-average sexual drive. Shaikh writes:

Since my purpose is constructive and reformative, I will not resort to gossip or insolence; the narrative shall be based on the authority of the *hadith*, the Koran and Muslim scholars.

There follow a set of fairly explicit and candid quotations from the *hadith* which discuss the Prophet's virility and his sexual habits. None of the material is exactly new, but this is the first time it has been collated in this fashion by someone who has emerged from within Islam. It is this that makes Shaikh a dangerous interlocutor. Even after 11 September, I doubt whether a Western publisher would touch *Islam and Sexuality*, but Shaikh is unconcerned. He has his own publishing outfit. He will publish and let them damn him. When he started off he was like the swimmer who plunges into a swollen river, not sure whether he'll reach the other shore. Now he is sure and at peace with himself.

'Whatever happens now I will die confident in my humanist and rationalist beliefs, and if my writings have weaned even a few dozen people away from religous hatred and fanaticism I feel I will have partially redeemed myself, even though nothing, nothing can bring my three victims back to life. I don't worry for myself. I worry for others. Look what we did to each other with our bare hands. With nuclear weapons they could destroy everything in the name of religion. They might, you know. They might . . .'

16

Plain tales from Pakistan

Conceived in a hurry and delivered prematurely – a last-minute Caesarean by doctors tending the British empire – Pakistan emerged in August 1947, its birth accompanied by a massive loss of blood. In its first year, the new state was deprived of a limb (Kashmir) and then lost its father (Mohammed Ali Jinnah). Then, like its tougher and more ruthless confessional twin, Israel, it decided to accept the offer of a permanent nurse. It was assumed that the only route to survival was to become a Cold War patient under the permanent supervision of Western imperialism. As the British empire faded, the United States assumed responsibility for Pakistan.

Soon after this transition, Saadat Hasan Manto, the country's most gifted Urdu short-story writer, died in January 1955 from cirrhosis of the liver. He was forty-three years old. During the last year of his life he registered the change from 'John Bull to Uncle Sam' by writing a set of nine, satirical open 'Letters to Uncle Sam'. The English translation, by the journalist Khalid Hasan, was published for the first time a few weeks prior to 11 September 2001 in Islamabad. As one reads the 'Fourth Letter' written on 21 February 1954, the coincidence is striking:

Dear Uncle:
I wrote to you only a few days ago and here I am writing again. My admiration and respect for you are going up at the same rate as your progress towards a decision to grant military aid to Pakistan. I tell you I feel like writing a letter a day to you.

Regardless of India and the fuss it is making, you must sign a military pact with Pakistan because you are seriously concerned about the stability of the world's largest Islamic state since our mullah is the best antidote to Russian communism. Once military aid starts flowing you should arm these mullahs. They would also need American-made rosaries and prayer-mats, not to forget small stones that they use to soak up the after-drops following nature's call . . . I think the only purpose of military aid is to arm these mullahs. I am your Pakistani nephew and I know your moves. Everyone can now become a smartass thanks to your style of playing politics.

If this gang of mullahs is armed in the American style, the Soviet Union that hawks communism and socialism in our country will have to shut shop. I can visualise the mullahs, their hair trimmed with American scissors and their pyjamas stitched by American machines in strict conformity with the *Sharia*. The stones they use for their after-drops [of urine] will also be American, untouched by human hand, and their prayer-mats, too, will be American. Everyone will then become your camp-follower, owing allegiance to you and none else . . .

From 1951 till the end of the Cold War in 1989–90, few important decisions were left to the Pakistan elite alone. The major exception was the decision taken by the country's first elected prime minister, Zulfiqar Ali Bhutto, during his period in office (1971–7) to acquire nuclear capability. During a vist to Lahore in August 1976, the US secretary of state, Henry Kissinger, offered Bhutto material and political support if he abandoned all nuclear plans. Bhutto, referring to himself in the third person, would later describe this approach as follows: 'This was the carrot – the stick was held out brazenly when, in reply to the Prime Minister's refusal to accept dictation on policies considered vital for Pakistan, Kissinger said "we can destabilise your government and make a horrible example out of you."' Kissinger kept his word. Within six months of the threat, Bhutto was destabilised, then his government was removed via a military coup, he was charged with murder, subjected to a rigged trial and found guilty in a 4–3 verdict by debased Supreme Court judges who followed military dictates rather than the law of precedent. Two years later the Pakistani prime minister was executed. This was the second death of Pakistani democracy. The first had taken place in 1971. The third in 1999. However, before revisiting those events, a brief explanation is necessary.

As the twentieth century dawned the British noted a change of mood in the urban population. Liberal notions of freedom and democracy spread wide after the First World War. The Indian National Congress was already

in existence. It was constitutionalist, it was secular, it appealed to most educated Indians. The Congress demand for India to become a self-governing
dominion on the Australian and Canadian model was firmly rejected,
though some reforms were conceded, but it worried the men who ruled
India. The consuls of the empire began to wonder whether the alliances
they had so carefully constructed might one day crumble. Was that day far
off?

It is often forgotten that the actual British presence in India never
exceeded 0.5 per cent of the population: in 1805 it numbered 31,000, in
1911 there were 164,000, and in 1931 the contingent had risen slightly to
168,000. The bulk of them were soldiers, but the figure is tiny compared
with the millions of Indians. This thin red-and-blue presence necessitated a
policy of local alliances. Without these British rule could not have lasted for
a hundred and fifty years, or defeated the coalition of native rulers who
raised the banner of revolt in 1857.

The native chiefs and rulers, leftovers of the old Mughal aristocracy,
were the natural allies of the raj, and in many princely states they were left
to misrule their subjects as long as British interests were not adversely
affected. British India transformed tribal chiefs into a landed gentry that
could and did serve as a pillar of the colonial state. Its domination of the
peasantry was vital both to ensure the continuous production of wheat,
sugar cane, cotton and rice staple foods and to facilitate the recruitment of
Indian peasants to the British army.

The formation of the Congress was, so far, only an irritation, but the
more farsighted servants of the empire sensed the dangers that lurked below.
They did not like unnecessary risks. Some preventive measure was required:
a new political instrument that could prevent the Congress from dominating the political scene. The British authorities approached Muslim notables
to discuss the formation of a loyal, separatist Muslim organisation, and the
Aga Khan was delighted to become the viceroy's principal conduit. An
obese loafer, he was the head of the wealthy Ismaili community of Muslims,
which was relatively modern except in its worship of the Aga Khan. There
was a reason for the latter's obesity. Sheer greed. Each year, on his birthday,
a special ceremony took place. The Aga Khan was seated on a comfortable
chair, placed on a scale and weighed against diamonds and bars of gold and
silver, donated by fawning devotees to prove their loyalty to the Ismaili

cause. After the weighing, these were gifted to him. Rarely has the process of accumulation been so transparent.

On the viceroy's behalf, the Aga Khan assembled a bunch of faded, servile and inert mediocrities – each one outstanding for his spinelessness – to create the Muslim League in 1906. The deputation described its own class origins with perfect accuracy: 'We the nobles, Jagirdars, Taluqdars, Zamindars, Lawyers and Merchants, subjects of His Majesty the King-Emperor in different parts of India'. The new organisation made no effort to conceal its principal aim: 'to foster a sense of loyalty to the British empire among the Muslims in India'. This it sought to do and achieved in a permanent alliance with English commissioners, deputy commissioners, magistrates, etc.

In the decades that followed, a majority of nationalist-minded Muslims would snub the League and align themselves with the Congress. These included the Kashmiri Sheikh Abdullah and a brilliant Muslim lawyer, Mohammed Ali Jinnah, who couldn't have imagined that one day he would become the founding father of Pakistan. In the Twenties he was hailed as 'the ambassador of Hindu–Muslim unity'. In the Thirties he walked away from the Congress and joined the Muslim League. In the Forties he came up with the 'two nations' theory and demanded a separate state for Muslims, managed to put one together and died a year after his triumph.

Why did he do all this? He was a liberal constitutionalist, fastidious in his tastes, dress and politics. He was an arrogant agnostic, contemptuous of all religious fundamentalisms. All these sensibilities were offended by the Congress's turn to mass civil disobedience and street politics. Jinnah preferred to deploy arguments in elite assemblies. The Congress leadership had decided that words, however reasonable, and arguments, however unanswerable, were not weapons respected by the British empire. A display of mass anger was needed, which had to be channelled into a movement for national independence. This meant mobilising the peasantry. Gandhi's blatant use of Hindu religious imagery to awaken the countryside worried Jinnah. He felt that people like him would ultimately be sidelined and overwhelmed by the 'Hindu element'. So he joined the Muslim League and appealed to other Muslim professionals to do the same as part of a bid to transform the organisation, removing it from the grip of the collaborationist landlords and notables of the United Provinces. Despite a number of early setbacks, Jinnah's enterprise succeeded. The Muslim League won new recruits, but without a total rejection of its past. It preferred gentlemanly negotiations with the British rather than abject surrender.

Pakistan was born out of a struggle waged largely by middle-class Muslim professionals and traders who feared they would be orphaned after the British left India. The Hindus would dominate politics and economics. Without access to power and money, the Indian Muslims would die on the vine. The demand for Pakistan was initially devised by the Muslim League as a bargaining chip to gain maximum concessions from the imperial power. Pakistan was achieved largely due to a combination of the Second World War, Congress Party intransigence, and Britain's hasty departure. The Muslim League had supported the British war effort, while Gandhi and Nehru had launched a civil disobedience movement demanding that the British 'Quit India'. Pakistan was the consolation prize received by the League for standing shoulder to shoulder with the raj during the war. Till 1946, however, Jinnah was prepared for a constitutional settlement that preserved the unity of India, while accepting the principle of provincial autonomy. Gandhi, too, favoured the deal, and was even prepared to offer Jinnah the prime ministership of a united India, but the Congress high command overruled him.

Jinnah's conception of the new state was that of a 'little India', except that in Pakistan the Muslims would be a majority. In retrospect it appears totally naïve, but it is nonetheless a fact that Jinnah had no idea that the carving of the subcontinent along confessional lines would lead to religious cleansing on both sides. Though his vision was flawed it was never theocratic, and it was for that reason that the forces of Islamic fundamentalism in India were hostile to the notion of Pakistan. For some, a separate Muslim state marked a breach with the universalism inherent in their faith. In orthodox eyes, 'Muslim' nationalism was a forbidden hybrid. For others, an Islamic state carved out of India was acceptable, but the Muslim League was regarded as a secular nationalist party and its version of Pakistan was deemed intolerable.[48]

The founder of the Jamaat-e-Islami (the Islamic Party), Maulana Abul Ala Maududi (1903–79), loathed Jinnah and despised the Muslim League. He

---

48 One is again reminded of the analogy with Israel. Like the Muslim League leadership, the founding fathers of Israel were secular Jewish nationalists. Ben-Gurion was denounced by many orthodox Jews who never accepted the idea of a 'Jewish state'.

came from a family that felt spiritually and materially disenfranchised after the defeat of the 1857 mutiny/uprising which had led to the formal closure of the Mughal court and the exile of the last emperor, Bahadur Shah Zafar, to Burma. Maududi's father, a lawyer and a modernist, had turned his back on the world and become a Sufi ascetic. He did not want his children to be influenced by Western culture and values and so restricted his son's education to Urdu and Arabic. Maududi imbibed the Deobandi interpretation of Islam, which was completely orthodox, rejected modernity and stressed the Koranic message, but soon afterwards he decided to learn English and study the thought of Western philosophers. Initially, like Jinnah, he supported the Congress, but after the disbandment of the Ottoman caliphate the twenty-one-year-old Maududi became obsessed with this defeat and its effects in India.

Even those Indian Muslims who had accepted the defeat of the Mughal empire would often look in the direction of Istanbul. When that came to an end they felt disorientated. This feeling even affected men like the poet-philosopher Muhammad Iqbal (1877–1938). As a graduate attending the elite Government College in Lahore, he studied philosophy under the gifted and generous-spirited orientalist scholar, Thomas Arnold. It was he who encouraged the young poet to visit Europe and improve his mind further. Iqbal accepted the advice and spent three years (1905–8) at Heidelberg, where his interest in philosophy was further heightened and began to infect his poetry.

His choice of poetic forms was usually conditioned by the intellectual environment. In his secular nationalist phase he wrote a powerful and evocative *Hymn for India*, which became a Nehru favourite and is still recited by secular Muslim leaders in India to prove their loyalty. The hymn was endlessly repeated on All-India Radio during the Sino-Indian conflict in 1960. Iqbal may have publicly revoked the anthem in favour of one written for the Muslims alone, but its intensity and genuineness ensured its survival. Another poem, *New Temple*, was written during the same period:

I shall tell the truth, O Brahman, but take it
Not as an offence:
The idols in thy temple have decayed.
Thou hast learnt from these images to bear
Ill-will to thine own people,
And God has taught the mullah
the ways of strife

My heart was sick: I turned away
both from the temple and the Ka'aba,
From the mullah's sermons and from
thy fairy tales, O Brahman.
To thee images of stone embody the divine –
For me, every particle of my country's
dust is a deity . . .
Come, let us build a new temple in this land.

This mood changed too, soon after his return from Europe. He saw the end of the Ottoman empire and wrote his famous Complaint, addressed to Allah. Like those to whom it was addressed, the poem was boastful, self-pitying and filled with despair. It celebrated the triumphs of ancient Islam and was a complaint against its decay. Muslims alone had defended monotheism, and with only their swords to provide them with shade, they had taken Allah's message to all the known continents. Why then had He so cruelly deserted them? 'Thou art used to songs of praise; now hear a note of protest too.'

Though the Seljuks had their empire, the
Turanians their sway,
Though the Chinese ruled in China, the
Sassanian in Iran.
Though the Greeks inhabited broad, fruitful
Acres in their day
And the Jews possessed their cubit, and the
Christians owned their span,
Who upraised the sword of battle in Thy
Name's most sacred cause,
Or who strove to right the ruined world by
Thy most hallowed laws?
It was we and we alone who marched the
soldiers to the fight,
Now upon the land engaging, now
embattled on the sea,
The triumphant call to Prayer in Europe's
Churches to recite,
Through the wastes of Africa to summon
Men to worship thee,
All the glittering splendour of great

emperors we reckoned none;
In the shadow of our glinting swords we
Shouted 'God to One.'
Tell us this, and tell us truly – who
uprooted Khyber's gate?
Or who overthrew the city where great
Caesar reigned in pride?
Who destroyed the gods that hands of
Others laboured to create,
Who the marshalled armies of the
unbelievers drove aside?
Who extinguished from the altars of Iran
that sacred flame,
Who revived the dimmed remembrance of
Yazdan's immortal name?

The poem appealed to the mood of Indian Muslims, but the clerics saw in it the traces of apostasy. Up went the shout: Iqbal has become an Unbeliever. The poet, who had intended to give voice to a community depressed by its decaying religion, now had to write a new poem, *Reply to the Complaint,* in which Allah responded to destroy every doubt. If Muslims were feeling forlorn it was their own fault. They had become too addicted to earthly pleasures and abandoned the teachings of their Prophet. But this phase, too, did not last long. Iqbal's intellect was restless.

In his social-revolutionary period his imagination organised a meeting between Lenin and Allah. Each was surprised by the other. Allah listened closely to Lenin's account of the class wars that dominated the Earth and was touched. In these lines from *God's Commandment* – quoted by South Asian socialists and communists to this day – Allah orders the angel Gabriel:

Arise, awaken the wretched of this earth
Shake the foundations, tremble the walls
of the mansions in which the wealthy sleep;
And in every field where a peasant starves,
There go and burn every bushel of wheat.[49]

---

49 The translations of Iqbal are those of M. Mujeeb, A.J. Arberry and the author respectively.

Iqbal's response to the crisis of Islam was contained in his poetry and his philosophy. He was remarkably undogmatic. His ideas were constantly in flux. In *The Reconstruction of Religious Thought in Islam* he argued for modernising the old religion. Prophecy had reached its zenith with the birth of Islam and abolished itself. Islamic culture could only move forward if it became dialectical and synthetic, concentrating on the finite and the concrete as it had done in its youth. This was a view that found favour with Jinnah. Official culture in Pakistan has destroyed the critical essence in Iqbal by making him a semi-divine icon of the state: a tragedy for the poet and the state.

The modernism of Iqbal and Jinnah was not unchallenged. Maududi, too, accepted that Islam was in decline. For him the remedy was simple. The only answer possible lay in the revival of Indian Islam. When Jinnah's Muslim League passed the Pakistan Resolution in Lahore in 1940, Maududi decided that the only possible riposte to this provocation was to lay the foundations of the Jamaat-e-Islami (JI) as a 'counter-League'. If Pakistan was to become a true Muslim state then it needed a Maududi, not a Jinnah, to be its head. He denounced Jinnah and the Muslim League as blasphemers who were misusing Islam to promote a secular nationalism.

Maududi's own views were remarkably similar to those of the eighteenth-century Arab preacher, Ibn Wahhab. The fall of Islam was the result of abandoning the purity of the Koran. Its undefiled message and pristine prescriptions were the *only* basis for exercising political power. Over the centuries, Islam had become a palimpsest, accreting foreign traditions and cultures and abandoning its initial aim. In this lay its tragedy. Hence the need for a total reversal. Only the corrective measures of an 'Islamic state' could reverse the decline.

Such a state could not be achieved simply through propaganda and social welfare projects. It required a political party. During his time in the princely state of Hyderabad, the preacher had observed the functioning of the clandestine Communist Party with great interest. He greatly admired the dedication of its cadres and their ability to work with and influence peasants and workers who were far removed from any understanding of Marxism. He was also impressed by Lenin's writings on the party and party-building. The party of Islam would have its own ideology, but its internal life and structure was modelled on the Bolsheviks, even though it pledged to work inside the existing constitution. Maududi's party, unlike Lenin's, was never designed to overthrow and transform the state machine, but to 'Islamise' the men who led society and infiltrate its institutions, initially the all-powerful civil service, and later the army.

On 26 August 1941, seventy-five carefully chosen Muslim men met at a private house in Lahore to pledge their allegiance to the faith and their loyalty to the new party and community that was about to be created. They agreed to the election of an emir, but limited his powers by subjecting him to a ruling council. After some debate it was agreed that Maududi be elected as the first emir, but tensions developed within the first year. The new group had decided that it could not breathe in the cosmopolitan atmosphere of Lahore. Secularism was too well established and temptations were rife.

As Muhammad had once abandoned Mecca and migrated to Medina, so now Maududi and his colleagues decamped from Lahore and established a refuge in Pathankot in eastern Punjab. The first differences to emerge prefigured postmodernity. They concerned a key aspect of life-politics: money, appearance and style. Since funds were in short supply the new Muslim commune lived frugally. They shared quarters, cooked their own food and ate communally. The emir lived separately in a small house he shared with his wife. The couple employed a male servant. Maududi was earning adequate royalties from his books as well as from sales of his magazine. His main rival, Maulana Numani, a devout scholar-journalist from Lucknow, insisted that all earnings should be the common property of the community: the contrasting lifestyles within a single commune were unacceptable. Maududi vigorously defended the principle of private ownership, citing Koranic verses to defend himself. This was a doctrinal issue and he refused to budge. The intellectual property in question belonged to him, not to the party, or by extension to any state the party might create. Numani disagreed, but had to retreat. Here, in a nutshell, is a contradiction that plagues Islamic fundamentalists to this day.[50]

Having failed to defeat Maududi on the key issue of property rights,

---

50 In his videos, which circulate clandestinely throughout the Arab peninsula, Osama bin Laden denounces the squandered oil revenues of Saudi Arabia. He refers to oil as the common property of the Muslim community, but his demand is that it be privatised and handed over to smaller groups throughout the region. In a way this is understandable, since in Saudi Arabia nationalisation has only meant control by the royal kleptocracy, but there is no demand that, after the royal family is overthrown, the oil revenues be owned collectively and administered by an Islamic Republic. The doctrine of Osama bin Laden, and Maududi before him, may be tinged with self-interest, but their interpretation of the scripture was pretty accurate.

Numani extended the attack to the emir's lack of piety. He laid three new charges: (a) Maududi's beard was the wrong size (i.e. not 7 cm) and shape; (b) Maududi was usually late for the dawn prayers; and (c) his wife was immodestly attired in the presence of a male servant, i.e., she did not veil or cover herself.

On these questions the emir was far more conciliatory and muttered a few self-critical phrases, but refused to either repent or resign. Numani summoned a special meeting of the council/central committee, and in the faction fight that ensued he appeared to have won over the majority. Maududi offered now to resign as emir, or he suggested they could dissolve the party and go their separate ways. Numani, who would have won had he restricted himself to demanding a resignation, fell into the trap and insisted on the dissolution of the Jamaat. This was rejected. Numani and his group split and denounced Maududi publicly. The effect of this was to make the emir reconsider the structures of the party and some years later the council was neutered and the emir became the dominant figure: a combination of Stalin and Khomeini.

Even before he founded the Jamaat, its future emir was aware of his place in Islamic history. In 1940 he had obtained the services of an Arabist and begun to have his writings translated into Arabic so that the Muslim world at large could benefit from his ideas. Soon echoes of Maududi were heard in Cairo and Jiddah. The Muslim Brotherhood made good use of his texts: Sayyid Kutb openly acknowledged his debt to the Indian scholar. The links between Maududi and Saudi clerics were institutionalised soon after the formation of Pakistan in 1947. By the Fifties, an Islamist triangulation was in place: Wahhabism, Maududi's JI and the Muslim Brothers dominated Islamist discourse. These were the groups seen by Washington as an essential ideological bulwark against communism and radical nationalism in the Muslim world.[51]

---

51 When the Jamaat-e-Islami and other religious groups spearheaded agitation in Pakistan in favour of an Islamic Constitution, denouncing what was on offer as secular and hence unacceptable, the US ambassador in a dispatch to Washington referred to the fundamentalist 'Constitution Day' protest as 'the only effort in Karachi on behalf of the Constitution'. My father was at the time editor of *The Pakistan Times*, the country's largest daily, owned by a left-wing group, Progressive Papers Limited. The bulk of its employees were socialists or communists. Iskander Mirza,one of the senior bureaucrats resisting the mullahs, who later became president, met my father at a social occasion and admonished him: ' You should be much sharper in reporting the debate on the constitution. If we ever agreed to what these bastards want then the mullahs who are at the moment happily engaged in buggering little boys behind their mosques would want to run the country.'

All the armed Sunni-Islamist groups who, at the time of writing, are engaged in the jihad against other Muslims and the Great Satan are the children of this constellation.

Maududi's group did not flourish in the new Pakistan. Government employees were barred from joining political parties. The JI was soon making pragmatic adjustments to its programme. Prevented from infiltrating state institutions, they appointed themselves as the caretakers of Islam in the new state. Since the Sikhs and the overwhelming majority of Hindus had left the areas that were now Pakistan, depriving Islamists of an infidel enemy, religious sectarianism turned inwards on itself. One such campaign was to demand the outlawing of the Ahmadiya sect within Islam, a subject which Maududi had, till now, ignored. The Ahmadiya were followers of Mirza Ghulam Ahmad (c. 1835–1908), a Muslim preacher who claimed that he too had experienced a divine revelation. Since the Koran explicitly stated that Muhammad was the last Prophet, this was viewed by the orthodox scholars at the Deoband seminary as an outrageous blasphemy. As Mirza's followers began to increase, the Deobandis campaigned against the new heresy, even though on all other issues apart from the disputed revelation the Ahmadiya believed in exactly the same things as any other Muslim, with regional variations.

In a Muslim state, the orthodox argument was that the Ahmadiya be declared a religious minority outside Islam, accorded the same rights as Christians or Hindus, but banned from appearing or recruiting as Muslims. A campaign against the Ahmadiya was started by the religious groups in league with unscrupulous and ambitious politicians, in particular the Oxford-educated chief minister of the Punjab, Mumtaz Daultana. It soon began to turn nasty. Pakistan's foreign minister, Zafarullah Khan, was a member of the sect and, to his credit, refused to retreat under fundamentalist pressure. He publicly acknowledged his affiliation by addressing an Ahmadi conference in Karachi.

Maududi, who had initially viewed the question with distaste, realised that he could be outflanked by his rivals and entered the fray in characteristic style. He sat down and composed a virulent text entitled, *The Ahmadi Problem*. In the eighteen days before it was banned, the book sold 57,000 copies. Its inflammatory message excited orthodox passions, making Maududi a central figure in what followed.

In early 1953, a series of carefully orchestrated riots shook the Punjab. It is my first memory of religious rioting. The shoe-shop below our family apartments in Lahore was rented and managed by an Ahmadi family. One day as I returned from school I saw it being attacked by an ultra-violent mob, while the police watched. I was dragged away from the scene by my father. The next day I noticed the shop-front had been totally destroyed. The manager had escaped with a few wounds.

That same week the central government imposed martial law and a curfew in Lahore. Soldiers opened fire on bearded mobs. Within two days the disturbances had been quelled. Maududi and his colleague Kausar Niazi were arrested and charged with treason. Both were found guilty, but Maududi was sentenced to death, later commuted to some years in prison. Maududi's offence was his book. Kausar Niazi had indulged in violent and obscene rhetoric at a public rally, and stoked the crowd to such a fury that a mob surrounded and lynched an on-duty policeman.[52] For his role in encouraging the riots to further his factional interests in the Muslim League, Chief Minister Mumtaz Daultana was forced to resign, his political career effectively at an end.

A public court of inquiry was appointed, with Justice Muhammad Munir as president and Justice M.R. Kayani a member,[53] to investigate the 'causes of the anti-Ahmadi disturbances'. Its 387-page Report, published in April 1954, is the only modernist text in the country's history. Instead of lying buried in the archives, it should be part of the university curriculum, or at least made available to the library of the Military Staff College in Quetta. Munir and Kayani were fearless in their recommendations. They mocked the confusion of the mullahs, and warned the country that an Islamic state would be a disaster. Nothing like this was ever produced again in Pakistan.

---

52 Kausar Niazi subsequently broke with the Jamaat and in 1972 joined Bhutto's party. He became minister of religious affairs and Bhutto's adviser on how to deal with Islamists. It was Niazi's advice that led to the Bhutto regime declaring that the Ahmadiya were non-Muslims. Bhutto thought he would outflank the mullahs, but by this appalling decision he had paved the way for them.

53 During the first military dictatorship in Pakistan, M.R. Kayani, then retired chief justice of the Lahore Court, began to give a series of speeches that completely undermined the Ayub regime. Any event where he was due to speak was packed with students. I heard him on three occasions. His Pashtun voice was very soft, there was never a trace of demagogy in what he said, and each sentence was carefully constructed. When he died in 1963, we all wept.

The disturbances referred to were instigated by a number of religious leaders (*ulama*) in pursuance of their demand that the government officially classify Ahmadis as a non-Muslim minority community, and take certain other actions against members of this movement. Referring to the *ulama*'s call for Pakistan to be run as an official 'Islamic' state, and to their demands against Ahmadis, the Report stated:

> The question, therefore, whether a person is or is not a Muslim will be of fundamental importance, and it was for this reason that we asked most of the leading *ulama* to give their definition of a Muslim, the point being that if the *ulama* of the various sects believed the Ahmadis to be *kafirs* [unbelievers], they must have been quite clear in their minds not only about the grounds of such belief but also about the definition of a Muslim because the claim that a certain person or community is not within the pale of Islam implies on the part of the claimant an exact conception of what a Muslim is. The result of this part of the inquiry, however, has been anything but satisfactory, and if considerable confusion exists in the minds of our *ulama* on such a simple matter, one can easily imagine what the differences on more complicated matters will be. Below we reproduce the definition of a Muslim given by each *alim* in his own words. (p. 215)

The Report reproduces verbatim the answers given by various *ulama* to the question: How do you define a Muslim? The judges were obviously enjoying themselves by this stage. Their conclusion was suitably deadpan:

> Keeping in view the several definitions given by the *ulama*, need we make any comment except that no two learned divines are agreed on this fundamental. If we attempt our own definition as each learned divine has done and that definition differs from that given by all others, we unanimously go out of the fold of Islam. And if we adopt the definition given by any one of the *ulama*, we remain Muslims according to the view of that *alim* but *kafirs* according to the definition of everyone else. (p. 218)

Later, under the heading Apostasy, the Report refers to a view held by the *ulama* that, in an Islamic state, a Muslim who becomes a *kafir* is subject to the death penalty. The Report refers to the country's foreign minister, Zafarullah Khan and states :

> According to this doctrine, Chaudhri Zafarullah Khan, if he has not inherited his present religious beliefs but has voluntarily elected to be an Ahmadi, must be put

to death. And the same fate should befall Deobandis and Wahabis, including Maulana Muhammad Shafi Deobandi, Member, Board of Talimat-i-Islami attached to the Constituent Assembly of Pakistan, and Maulana Daud Ghaznavi, if Maulana Abul Hasanat Sayyad Muhammad Ahmad Qadri or Mirza Raza Ahmad Khan Barelvi, or any one of the numerous *ulama* who are shown perched on every leaf of a beautiful tree in the fatwa, Ex. D.E. 14, were the head of such Islamic State. And if Maulana Muhammad Shafi Deobandi were the head of the State, he would exclude those who have pronounced Deobandis as *kafirs* from the pale of Islam and inflict on them the death penalty if they come within the definition of *murtadd*, namely, if they have changed and not inherited their religious views.

The genuineness of the fatwa, Ex. D.E. 13, by the Deobandis which says that Asna Ashari Shias are *kafirs* and *murtadds*, was questioned in the course of inquiry, but Maulana Muhammad Shafi made an inquiry on the subject from Deoband, and received from the records of that institution the copy of a fatwa signed by all the teachers of the Darul Uloom, including Maulana Muhammad Shafi himself which is to the effect that those who do not believe in the *sahabiyyat* of Hazrat Siddiq Akbar and who are *qazif* of Hazrat Aisha Siddiqa and have been guilty of *tehrif* of Quran are *kafirs*. This opinion is also supported by Mr Ibrahim Ali Chishti who has studied and knows his subject. He thinks the Shias are *kafirs* because they believe that Hazrat Ali shared the prophethood with our Holy Prophet. He refused to answer the question whether a person who being a Sunni changes his view and agrees with the Shia view would be guilty of *irtidad* so as to deserve the death penalty. According to the Shias all Sunnis are *kafirs*, and Ahl-i-Quran, namely, persons who consider *hadith* to be unreliable and therefore not binding, are unanimously *kafirs*, and so are all independent thinkers. The net result of all this is that neither Shias nor Sunnis nor Deobandis nor Ahl-i-Hadith nor Barelvis are Muslims and any change from one view to the other must be accompanied in an Islamic State with the penalty of death if the Government of the State is in the hands of the party which considers the other party to be *kafirs*. And it does not require much imagination to judge of the consequences of this doctrine when it is remembered that no two *ulama* have agreed before us as to the definition of a Muslim.

If the constituents of each of the definitions given by the *ulama* are given effect to, and subjected to the rule of 'combination and permutation' and the form of charge in the Inquisition's sentence on Galileo is adopted *mutatis mutandis* as a model, the grounds on which a person may be indicted for apostasy will be too numerous to count. (p. 219)

Those were early days in the life of the country. Judges could not yet be manipulated by politicians, mullahs, army officers or bribes. The Munir

Report was a bold defence of modernity and secularism. It denounced religious sectarianism as 'perfidious' and virtually argued that Islam was the stranger in the house: its intervention was unwarranted, its recourse to violence had created a political crisis and it could only impede the development of the new state. Therefore it should be excluded from Pakistan's politics and institutions. A separation between religion and the state was crucial if the country was to move forward. Maududi's leading lieutenant, Mian Tufail, retorted: 'Our religion is our politics, our politics is our religion.'

Who would decide? The citizens of Pakistan would, if given a chance. All the political parties in the country, with the exception of the Muslim League, favoured an immediate general election, but the military–bureaucratic–US embassy elite was nervous and with good reason. The 'counter-League' was not going to be the religious element under Maududi's leadership. The Muslim League might retain the Punjab, but it was widely expected that a coalition of nationalist and left parties would win everywhere else.

The first test came with the provincial elections of 1954. The big worry for the elite was the Bengali province of East Pakistan, separated from the West by 1,000 miles of Indian territory but inhabited by 60 per cent of the country's population. A large majority of these were Muslims, but there was also a sizeable Hindu minority. Not all of them had fled to India after Bengal was partitioned. In fact, East Pakistan came much closer to Jinnah's original vision for the new state than its Western flank where the bulk of the ruling elite was based.

In March 1954 the fears of Pakistan's rulers were realised. East Pakistan voted for the United Front parties, inflicting a severe defeat on the bureaucracy and its weak political instrument, the Muslim League. Out of 309 seats, the League won only 10. All the provincial ministers, including the chief minister, failed to get elected. The Communist Party had won 4 seats of the 10 contested. Interestingly enough all the communists of Muslim origin had been defeated. The communists of Hindu origin had won all four seats, including one in Sylhet where the local branch of the Jamaat-e-Islami was very strong. The communists had also been working inside other parties and had won 22 seats, bringing their total to 26, more than double that of the Muslim League, the party that had founded Pakistan. The Jamaat-e-Islami failed completely.

One of the first controversies in the provincial parliament concerned the bilateral military pact Pakistan was preparing to sign with the United States. 162 members signed a motion denouncing the proposed agreement. Two months later, the central government dissolved the legislative assembly of East Pakistan and proclaimed governor's rule in the province. The US–Pakistan Military Pact was signed a week later.

The new governor was the veteran bureaucrat, Iskander Mirza. He had played a central role in repressing the Islamists. They had represented a tiny minority. He was now determined to do the same to a large majority of the country. Several hundred members of the United Front were arrested. The elected chief minister and several provincial ministers were kept under close house arrest. The Communist Party was banned and employers instructed to sack all known communists in the factories. They complied willingly, and used the occasion to sack non-communist trade-union militants at the same time.

In 1955, after a series of shoddy compromises, the provincial assembly was restored, but the events had shaken the confidence of most Bengalis in the new state. In the same year the Constituent Assembly of Pakistan, which was discussing a new constitution for the country, heard and ignored the warning of an ultra-conservative Bengali leader:

> Sir, I actually started yesterday and said that the attitude of the Muslim League coteries here was of contempt towards East Bengal, towards its culture, its language, its literature and everything concerning East Bengal . . . In fact, Sir, I tell you that far from considering East Bengal as an equal partner, the leaders of the Muslim League thought we were a subject race and they belonged to a race of conquerors.

This was true, but the Muslim League was alienating West Pakistan as well. In successive by-elections, League candidates were being defeated. The bureaucracy began to panic. Their biggest fear was that if the smaller provinces of Sind, Baluchistan and the North-West Frontier produced anti-Muslim League coalitions they could, together with the Bengalis, rule the country. Locally this threatened the political and economic control of the Punjabi landlords, bureaucrats and a developing class of new capitalist entrepreneurs. On a global level an elected Pakistani government might well withdraw from the Cold-War alliances that had been negotiated by the army and bureaucracy. There was only one solution. To forget about democracy altogether.

It had been agreed by the Constituent Assembly that the country's first-ever general election would be held in March 1959. To pre-empt the establishment of a democratically elected government, the army, under the instructions of the bureaucracy and the United States, seized power in October 1958. General Ayub Khan became the de facto ruler of the country. That he was intellectually challenged was hardly a secret in Pakistan. Despite this knowledge his opening remarks as Head of State startled the citizenry. It was a unique contribution to political geography: 'We must understand that democracy cannot work in a hot climate. To have democracy we must have a cold climate like Britain.' The Punjabi poet Ustad Daman mocked the new rulers: 'Now each day is fair and balmy/Wherever you look: the army.' He was imprisoned for reciting this couplet, but his poet's instinct told him that the uniforms were there to stay. The country was going to suffer.

No such doubts surfaced in the mainstream US media. The *New York Times*, generous as always to pro-US military dictators, failed to see the implicit threat in the stupidity. Ayub was publicly saying farewell to democracy. On 12 October 1958 the newspaper commented editorially on the new regime:

> In Pakistan both President Mirza and the army's head General Ayub Khan have stated clearly that what they propose and wish to do is establish in due course a fine, honest, and democratic government. There is no reason to doubt their sincerity.

Ayub's 'due course' lasted ten years. A decade under a military dictatorship, backed by China and the West. A decade of repression and war and a one-sided economic development. In those days it would not have occurred to even the weakest of Western liberals to demand outside intervention. They and everyone else knew that the reason for the pro-West dictatorships in Asia, Africa and Latin America was very simple: the liberal democracies of the West feared democracy everywhere else. The beast was removed, not by outside interference but through an epic struggle waged by its own people.

A student revolt that began on 7 November 1968 spread rapidly and, despite the massive repression, grew in strength, drawing in other social layers. The workers joined the movement in January 1969, by which time it had embraced every major city in West and East Pakistan. Soon lawyers, doctors, teachers, judges and prostitutes had come out to fight for democracy. Prevented from exercising their right to choose their own government, the people had united from below. It was the only time in the short history of the old Pakistan that its people were united. In March 1969 the self-appointed field marshal accepted defeat and resigned. Victory. People came out and danced on the streets of every city. When I arrived at Karachi airport the atmosphere was exhilarating. It seemed even to have affected the officer corps.

As I was waiting to get a flight to Lahore, I ran into an old acquaintance, a distant cousin of my mother's and a colonel in the army. He was uniformed, on his way back to GHQ after a spell at the Military Staff College in Quetta. I had not seen him for several years. As he greeted me warmly, I gave him a mock salute. He laughed. Six months before he would have looked straight through me. Over breakfast he told me that he had just finished reading Isaac Deutscher's trilogy: the three-volume biography of Trotsky. I expressed amazement. He informed me that they had to study the Red Army and he had found the books in the Staff College library. 'One thing puzzles me greatly,' he confessed. 'Trotsky was a brilliant leader during the Civil War. Tukhachevsky was a brilliant military commander. You agree?' I did. 'Then explain why they didn't use the Red Army to defeat Stalin.' I explained. 'I disagree with you,' he said. 'Bonapartism under Trotsky and Tukhachevsky would have been much better than bloody Stalin. How can you be so naïve?'

I began to laugh, slightly hysterically, which both annoyed and slightly unnerved him. 'Can't you see the joke?' I said. 'Your commander-in-chief banned me from returning here. I'm back because he's gone. We've just witnessed a successful uprising that has removed your boss from power and you're asking me why Trotsky didn't opt for a military dictatorship in 1923?'

He became slightly defensive, but refused to budge. Some years later he had to retire in a hurry for an act of sexual Bonapartism. He kept on dispatching a junior officer on spurious missions in order to pursue an affair with his wife. The guilty couple were discovered and the junior dislodged my cousin's nose. His military career ended in disgrace. A pity. In seven years' time one could have encouraged him to play Tukhachevsky against Zia's Kornilov.

For six weeks I travelled extensively throughout East and West Pakistan, met the men and women who had brought down the regime, spoke to the politicians. On platforms in West Pakistan, I was usually accompanied by the popular poet Habib Jalib, whose verses had actually sparked off the movement in various towns. Some years before the movement began, Jalib had denounced military rule at several *mushairas*[54]: 'This system, this night without a dawn/ I will never accept it, I will never obey.' Or 'Only one slogan, one request/President, don't love the USA best.' No other poet was dragged in and out of prison as much as Jalib. He refused to capitulate. During the movement Maududi's supporters had been completely sidelined. Their slogan, which rhymed in Urdu, never caught the public imagination: 'What is the meaning of Pakistan? There is only one Allah.' Jalib devised a reply which also rhymed, but was chanted by millions: 'What is the meaning of Pakistan? Food, clothing and medicines.' Later he mocked the mullahs quite openly.

On some platforms, when we were addressing audiences of twenty thousand people or more, he would whisper in my ear: 'They're mainly workers and peasants today. Tell them about Vietnam. Show them we can win.' I would do as he asked and he would afterwards recite *Vietnam's Burning*: 'O lovers of Human Rights, where are you?/Humanity is on the edge/ Vietnam is alight, Vietnam is alight/ Don't be silent, speak up now/The clouds of war are heading this way.'

In West Pakistan the Muslim League and all traditional parties had been bypassed by the upsurge. The only popular politician was Zulfiqar Ali Bhutto. He had been sacked from Ayub Khan's cabinet and now emerged at the head of the mass movement. His rhetoric was ultra-radical. He threatened to destroy capitalism, pledged land reforms and 'Food, Clothing and Shelter for All' became the leitmotif of his campaign. Democracy and social justice was a potent mixture. It was obvious travelling through the country that Bhutto's party would easily win the majority in this part of Pakistan.

---

54 Public poetry readings. In Pakistan where adult literacy levels were very low, tens of thousands sometimes showed up to hear the poets.

Ayub's successor, General Yahya Khan, had immediately announced the date for a general election. March 1970. The country rejoiced.

When I arrived in Dhaka, the capital of East Pakistan, the mood was equally euphoric, but with this difference. The students, intellectuals and working-class leaders with whom I spoke were divided. The nationalists were fed up with the Pakistani elite. The Bengali left had been divided during the movement, with the Maoists abdicating from the struggle on the ground that Field Marshal Ayub was an 'anti-imperialist' because of his friendship with China. The weaknesses of the once-strong left had enabled the nationalists of the Awami League to dominate the struggle. They had demanded total autonomy from the West and insisted that unless the Six-Point charter incorporating these demands was met, they would carry on the struggle. Wherever I went the story was the same. Bengal had been mis-treated so often that it was ready to break. When I spoke to the students at Dhaka University, they insisted I do so in English and not the hated Urdu that the Centre had tried to impose on them. A few shouted: 'Learn Bengali, please.' Standing under the *amtala* tree where the movement had begun on this campus, I told them that there was not the slightest chance of the military accepting their Six Points. They should have no illusions on this score. If that was what they wanted they had better be prepared to go the whole way. I could see I had stunned them.

Afterwards some leftists came and remonstrated that my speech had encouraged the Awami League students. Heated discussions continued over the next few days. When I met the Awami League leader, Sheikh Mujibur Rahman, a few days later, he knew exactly what I had said at the university. 'You're sure?' he asked. 'What if we win the next election?' I reminded him that they had won in 1954 as well. True, conditions were different now, but I doubted very much if the army would ever accept the Six Points. I pre-dicted a bloodbath. He wasn't convinced. Nor was the peasant leader Maulana Bhashani, with whom I had toured the countryside for over a fort-night. I feared the worst. It happened.

The elections took place in December 1970. In West Pakistan, Bhutto won a big majority. In East Pakistan the Awami League got over 90 per cent of the popular vote. They were the largest party in the country. Sheikh Mujib should have been asked to form the next government, but Yahya Khan and his fellow generals refused to accept the verdict. To his lasting discredit, Bhutto did a deal with them. If he had backed Mujib, the story might have been slightly differ-ent. Instead the army prepared to invade and occupy its own Eastern Province. This was the end. Within the army, the soldiers were injected with the poison of ethnic hatred. They were told that Bengalis were only recent con-verts to Islam, that Hinduism was in their blood, that this was the reason they wanted to break away from Pakistan. Nobody said: but we seem to be breaking away from them.

Soldiers were incited to mass-rape the women in order to mutate the Hindu Bengali gene. This is what was said by Punjabi officers to Punjabi sol-diers. This is what they did. In March 1971, West Pakistan invaded East Pakistan. Rapes and massacres took place. In one night alone, occupying sol-diers, accompanied by Jamaat-e-Islami collaborators, invaded the student hostels at the university. Hundreds of students disappeared. Left-wing intel-lectuals were traced and shot. Sheikh Mujib was arrested and brought to a West Pakistani prison. His party went underground and prepared to resist. Pakistan's greatest poet, Faiz Ahmed Faiz, wrote of 'eyes washed with blood'.

And, ten years later, in *Midnight's Children*, Salman Rushdie immortalised the first day of West Pakistan's military offensive against East Pakistan:

Midnight, March 25, 1971: past the University, which was being shelled, the buddha led troops to Sheikh Mujib's lair. Students and lecturers came running out of hostels; they were greeted by bullets, and Merchurichrome stained the lawns . . . And while we drove through the city streets, Shaheed looked out of windows and saw things that weren't-couldn't-have-been-true: soldiers entering women's hostels without knocking; women dragged into the street, were also entered, and again nobody troubled to knock . . .

When thought becomes excessively painful, action is the finest remedy . . . dog-soldiers strain at the leash, and then, released, leap joyously to their work. O wolfhound chases of undesirables! O prolific seizings of professors and poets! O unfortunate shot-while-resisting arrests of Awami Leaguers and fashion corre-spondents! Dogs of war cry havoc in the city . . . Farooq Shaheed Ayooba take turns at vomiting as their nostrils are assailed by the stench of burning slums . . . no undesirable is safe tonight; no hiding place impregnable. Bloodhounds track the fleeing enemies of national unity; wolfhounds, not to be outdone, sink fierce teeth into their prey . . .

A number of my Bengali friends had disappeared. Everywhere there was chaos. Abroad a few of us from West Pakistan organised protests against the brutalities in Britain and the United States: together with Aijaz Ahmed, Feroz Ahmed, Eqbal Ahmed, I wrote and spoke and appealed for support, but the West remained silent. Nixon had ordered Kissinger (or perhaps it was the other way round) to 'tilt towards Pakistan'. Beijing tilted in the same direction. As the war raged, millions of refugees were provided with temporary accommodation in the Indian province of West Bengal. Finally, the Indian army crossed the border and defeated its Pakistani counterparts. General Niazi chose to surrender. He did not want to fight. It was a sensible decision. Too much blood had already been spilt. The Indian troops were greeted by the Bengalis as liberators. Pakistan was dead. Bangladesh was born.

This single event had alienated me totally from the 'new' Pakistan. In the past one had fought against the elite, but this time a large section of the population was infected with an ugly chauvinism. It was not the Baluch or the Pashtuns as much as the Punjab and, to a certain extent, Sind. The failure of the Punjabis to protest against the crimes being committed in their name made them complicit. Some were no doubt frightened, but how could they be when they had only recently moved mountains, defied fear, toppled a dictatorship? It was something else. It was Bhutto. Having followed him during the movement, voted for him, they could not betray him. They assumed he must be right and so remained silent. It was then that I made my own personal decision to stay away from them. The blood of Bengal separated us.

Pakistan has yet to acknowledge these crimes and apologise to the people of Bangladesh. For its own sake, not only for theirs. Official histories in Pakistan continue to lie. They write of how India had decided to break up Pakistan. Not true. It was the Pakistan army backed by the bureaucracy and the majority People's Party led by Zulfikar Ali Bhutto who took the risk and lost. They did not succeed in implanting 'pure Muslim genes' via the 'pure Muslim sperm' of the Punjabi soldiery.

Bhutto got what he wanted. He became the leader of a truncated country, promised a great deal, delivered very little in real terms to his supporters.[55] Once the United States had decided to dump him, it was obvious that the instrument they used would be the army. Bhutto, always

---

[55] I have discussed old and new Pakistan at length in two books: *Pakistan: Military Rule or People's Power?*, 1971, and *Can Pakistan Survive?*, 1983.

a weak judge of character and susceptible to flattery, had promoted General Zia-ul-Haq above four other generals. He assumed that Zia, a Uriah Heep figure, was 'in his pocket'. But Zia was a Fort Bragg-trained officer. His loyalties stretched beyond national boundaries. He had already shown his mettle in September 1970 by leading an armed attack and inflicting a heavy defeat on the Palestinian resistance in Jordan. The operation to save Hussein of Jordan had been masterminded by the United States and Israel. On that occasion, Brigadier Zia-ul-Haq had not been too worried about the cause of Islam. Seven years later, General Zia seized power in Pakistan and removed Bhutto, who was arrested, and later charged with murder. Overnight he became popular again. When a High Court bench granted Bhutto bail, the deposed politician flew to Lahore to consult friends. When his plane landed hundreds of thousands of people lined the streets to welcome his release. This support proved to be his death-warrant.[56] Zia knew that Bhutto alive would return to power one day. It was a case of two men, one coffin.

Zia's military dictatorship, once again fully backed by the United States, was the worst period in the country's history. Zia's men were dense, deaf and heartless. The new regime had decided to use Islam as its battering ram, and its bearded supporters, often incredibly stupid, were opportunist to the marrow of their bones. They combined religion with profanities of the vilest kind. Under Zia, despotism and lies mutilated a whole generation. Islamic punishments were introduced, public floggings and hangings instituted. The political culture of Pakistan was brutalised. It has still to recover. Washington and London watched from the sidelines as the country's elected leader was executed. Work on the nuclear programme continued, but Washington now chose to ignore the process because by now the pro-Moscow Afghan left had seized power in Kabul.

The Cold War had reached the Pamirs. The temptation to provoke, isolate and defeat Moscow proved too strong. A squalid military dictator became the instrument through which this campaign would be conducted. Everything else was subordinated to this single aim. In order to defeat the

---

56 Bhutto was shaken and touched by the response. At dinner that night he told my father how humbling the experience had been: 'They still come out for me after what I've done to them.'

Soviet Union, two countries – Pakistan and Afghanistan – were totally wrecked. Fundamentalist Islam and heroin production grew apace.

In 1988, General Zia marked the tenth anniversary of his rule by informing the country that he had no intention of retiring. The following year he was assassinated. A plane specially built to security specifications exploded in the sky. Apart from Zia, another general and the US ambassador Arnold Raphael, who were travelling with him, were also killed. Who killed Zia? His wife was in the habit of informing visitors that 'he was killed by our own people', implying that the military was involved. Inquiries proved fruitless. Neither US nor Pakistan intelligence have unravelled this particular murder mystery.

The reaction in Pakistan, barring Zia's supporters and the Islamist groups he had nurtured, was unrestrained joy. Sweets were distributed in many cities to celebrate the death. His successor was compelled to announce a general election. Benazir Bhutto and the People's Party had already launched a movement against the dictatorship and she had been arrested yet again. Now her campaign began to attract massive crowds. Her opponent, Nawaz Sharif, was a creature of the former military dictatorship. Benazir won the election and became prime minister, to the great annoyance of the military High Command, but she was hemmed in by the military on one side and a hostile bureaucracy on the other. The president was a man who had helped to have her father executed. The important province of the Punjab had been won by Nawaz Sharif. The mullahs were up in arms. On her own side, she was surrounded by mediocrities and bandwagon careerists of every description. After a few years her paralysed government was dismissed. The bureaucracy helped Nawaz Sharif back to power. The rivalry between Bhutto's daughter, Benazir, and Muhammad's son, Nawaz, has rich antecedents.

Since 1947, Lahore had been the home town of the Sharif family. They were blacksmiths in East Punjab (now in India) and sought refuge in the new Muslim homeland. They worked hard. Their foundries prospered. They were businessmen, uninterested in politics. One day in 1972 Benazir's father, Zulfiqar Ali Bhutto, was advised to nationalise the Sharif family factory. It was an economically inept decision, but it pleased party loyalists and it distracted attention from the fact that Bhutto had failed to push through badly-needed land reforms in the countryside. The landlords were only too pleased to support the half-baked nationalisations of industries large and

small. One of the results was to make Muhammad Sharif, the family patriarch, a lifelong enemy of Bhutto. When General Zia took over in July
1977, the Sharif clan cheered loudly. When Zia ordered the execution of
Bhutto after a rigged trial, the Sharif family gave thanks to Allah for answer-
ing their prayers.

Nawaz Sharif became a protégé of the late General Zia, and was brought
into politics as the clumsy, dirty boot of Inter Services Intelligence (ISI), the
most powerful institution in the country. After Benazir's first removal, he
became the prime minister of Pakistan. His brother, Shahbaz, the clever one
in the family, was kept on the sideline. But this government didn't last long
either. Benazir was voted back into power and with a large majority. This
time there were no excuses. She could have pushed through badly-needed
reforms. Instead the government became mired in corruption.

When I was in Pakistan, in 1997, the surface calm was deceptive. As I was
lunching my mother in her favourite Islamabad restaurant a jovial mousta-
chioed figure, Senator Asif Zardari, the state minister for investment, came
over to greet us from an adjacent table. His wife, Benazir Bhutto, was
abroad on a state visit. He was responsible for entertaining the children and
had brought them out for a special treat. An exchange of pleasantries
ensued. I asked how things were proceeding in the country. 'Fine,' he
replied with a charming grin. 'All is well.' He should have known better.
Behind closed doors in the capital, Islamabad, a palace coup was in motion.
Benazir Bhutto was about to be luxuriously betrayed. Her handpicked president, Farooq Leghari, after secret consultations with the army and the
leaders of the opposition, was preparing to dismiss her government.

During dinner that same week, an old acquaintance, now a senior civil
servant and very fond of Benazir, was in a state of despair. He described how
the president had sought to defuse the crisis by asking for a special meeting
with the prime minister. Benazir, characteristically, turned up with her
husband, Senator Zardari. This annoyed Leghari, since one of the subjects he
had wished to discuss with her was her husband's legendary rapaciousness and
greed. Despite the irritation, he remained serene while attempting to convince
the First Couple that it was not simply their traditional political enemies or
smaller-sized brains who were demanding action. The scale of the corruption
and the corresponding decay of the administration had become a *national*
scandal. As president of the country, he was under pressure from the army and

concerned groups of citizens to act against her government. In order to resist them, he needed her help. He pleaded with her to discipline her husband and other out-of-control ministers. At this point Zardari, stubbornly consistent in defending his own material interests, grinned and taunted the president with the remark that nobody in Pakistan, including Leghari, had a clean slate. The threat was obvious. You touch us and we'll expose you.

Leghari felt that the dignity of his office had been insulted. He began to tremble with anger. He suggested that the minister for investment leave the room. Benazir nodded and Zardari walked out. Alone now with his prime minister, except for the discreet presence of a civil servant, he once again entreated her to restrain her turbulent husband. She smiled patronisingly and gave her president a little lecture on how much she valued loyalty. The people who were complaining, she told him, were jealous of her husband's business acumen. They were professional whiners, has-beens, rogues resentful at being bypassed when top jobs were being allocated. She made no concessions.

By Pakistani standards Leghari was an honest, straightforward man. He had been Benazir's choice as president only because she thought he lacked ambition and would do her will. He would be a good dog. Disappointed aspirants were told: 'He may not be very bright, he's a bit limited, but his heart is in the right place.'

During a brief conversation in January 1999, Leghari told me that this meeting, the last of many, had been decisive. His patience had evaporated. He could no longer tolerate her excesses. He believed that if she continued in office the army would intervene and murder democracy for the fourth time in the country's chequered history. Reluctantly, he decided to utilise the hated Eighth Amendment (a gift to the nation from the late dictator, General Zia-ul-Haq, which gave the president powers to dismiss an elected government) and dismissed the government. New elections were to be held within ninety days.

The chief charge levelled against Benazir and her husband was that of corruption. It was alleged that the couple had used Prime Minister's House to build a large private fortune and transfer their assets abroad. The value of this gift from destiny is usually put at one billion dollars.

Immediately after her fall, Senator Zardari was arrested. To this day he languishes in a Karachi prison, charged with a series of offences for which government lawyers have yet to find proof acceptable in a Pakistani court, where standards of evidence are exceptionally low. The state still lacks a reliable witness. Zardari's business associates and friends have remained loyal. In what now seems like a dress rehearsal of the Enron scandal, one of them, the chairman of Pakistan Steel, chose to commit suicide rather than bear witness against his former patron.

Some of Benazir's closest supporters – and they exist – are insistent that her political prestige was squandered by a husband who is a fraud, a poseur, a wastrel, a philanderer and much worse. Back in the opposition, while addressing a friendly gathering at a seminar in Islamabad, Benazir attempted to defend the quondam minister for investment. He was much misunderstood, she said, but before she could continue the members of the audience began to shake their heads in disapproval and shout 'No! No! No!' She paused and then said with a sigh: 'I wonder why I always get the same reaction whenever I mention him?' Either the question was tongue-in-cheek or lust is truly blind.

I don't think Zardari was the only reason for her unpopularity. Unfortunately, her People's Party government did little for the poor of town and country that constitute its natural constituency. Most of her ministers on national and provincial level were so busy lining their own pockets that they failed to notice how the lining of the stomachs of starving children was being affected by the shortage of food and the lack of a proper diet. Infant mortality figures remained unchanged throughout her period in office.

Benazir, permanently encircled by cronies and sycophants, had become isolated from her electorate and oblivious to reality. In the general election following her removal from power, her People's Party suffered a humiliating defeat. The Pakistani electorate may be largely illiterate, but its political sophistication has never been in doubt. The mood was one of disillusion. Disappointment had created apathy and weariness. Benazir's supporters refused to vote for her, but they could not bring themselves to vote for the enemy. Instead, they stayed at home. The Muslim League won its giant majority (they hold over two-thirds of the seats in the National Assembly) on the basis of a minority vote. Under 30 per cent of those eligible bothered to visit the polling-booths.

The Sharifs were back in power. This time while Nawaz became prime minister, younger brother Shahbaz became the chief minister of the Punjab. Their *Abaji* ('dear father'), Muhammad Sharif, amused himself in his dotage by sponsoring the appointment of old cronies as ambassadors and even selected the president of the country: a bearded simpleton called Rafiq Tarrar, one of *Abaji*'s factotums. What made Tarrar dangerous was his open sympathy for a fundamentalist Muslim sect, the Ahle-Hadis, which had its own armed organisation.

Of the two brothers, Shahbaz was perceived as a more sophisticated politician. The US embassy helpfully organised a trip to Washington for a meeting with Sandy Berger at the White House. It became an open secret that Washington would like to swap the brothers by sending Shahbaz to the Prime Minister's House and giving Nawaz his old job in Lahore. But *Abaji* could not be won over to the plan.

Little changed after the Sharif brothers won the last election, but then few expected anything to happen. Corruption, its tentacles spreading from the top downwards, is so widespread that visiting economists from the World Bank and IMF are, like Kurtz in Conrad's *Heart of Darkness*, traumatised by the scale of the horror. Local wits express bewilderment at the news that Nigeria heads the list of the world's most corrupt countries. 'Even here,' they say as they shed mock tears, 'we can't quite make the top. Why didn't we bribe the agency compiling the statistics?'

The elite, led by the politicians, continued to loot the country's wealth. Benazir's gang had its turn and then it was back to the Brothers Sharif. Less than 1 per cent of the population paid any income tax. The politicians, many of whom are landlords, refused to countenance a serious agricultural tax. State-owned banks were shamelessly pillaged. Forced by successive governments to loan money to politicians, landlords and businessmen, the banks were not encouraged to retrieve the money. Bad bank loans stood at 200 billion rupees (£1 = 85 rupees), which is the rough equivalent of 70 per cent of the total revenue base of the country's budget. Pakistan marked the new millennium with a foreign debt of $42 billion and a domestic debt of $70 billion, a combined figure that was $50 billion higher than the Gross Domestic Product of the country.

And underneath all this the country continued to rot. A state that has never provided free education or health can now no longer guarantee sub-sidised wheat, rice or sugar, nor can it protect innocent lives from random killings. The country's largest city, Karachi, has been in a state of virtual civil war for an entire decade. On one side are the Urdu-speaking children of the refugees who trekked to the new homeland from India in 1947. Their organisation, the MQM (Muhajir Quami Mahaz – National Organisation of Refugees), has waged war on indigenous Sindhis as well as the government. Several thousand on both sides have died in armed encounters.

In these conditions people have to fend for themselves. The suicide rate is soaring, usually poor women and men driven insane by poverty which rendered them incapable of feeding their children. In January 1999 a transport worker in Hyderabad, Sind, who had not been paid his salary for two years, went to the Press Club, soaked himself in petrol and set himself alight. He left behind a letter:

> I have lost patience. Me and my fellow-workers have been protesting the non-payment of our salaries for a long time. But nobody takes any notice. My wife and mother are seriously ill and I have no money for their treatment. My family is starving and I am fed up with quarrels. I don't have the right to live. I am sure the flames of my body will reach the houses of the rich one day.

This abdication of its traditional role by a corrupt and decaying state combined with the fundamentalist neo-liberal economic prescriptions handed down by the ayatollahs of the IMF and World Bank helped to unlock the space for political Islam. In successive general elections, the people voted against hardline religious parties. The Pakistan electorate, for instance, casts proportionately fewer votes for religious fundamentalists than voters in Israel. The strength of religious extremism has till now been derived from state patronage rather than popular support. The groups that have paralysed the country for two decades were the creation of the late General Zia-ul-Haq, who received political, military and financial support from the United States and Britain throughout his eleven years as dictator of Pakistan. The West needed Zia to fight its Afghan war against the former Soviet Union. Nothing else mattered. The CIA turned a blind eye to the sale of heroin, supposedly to fund the Afghan war. The number of officially registered heroin addicts in Pakistan rose from 130 in 1977 to 30,000 in 1988.

It was during this period (1977–89) that a network of *madrasas* was established throughout the country, most of them funded at first by foreign aid from a variety of sources. These religious boarding schools became the training ground for a new-style religious 'scholar'. Since board and lodging were free, it was not only the children of poor Afghan refugees who flocked to receive their privileged and unique instruction. Poor peasants' families were only too happy to donate a son to the *madrasas*. They thought it would be one mouth less to feed at home, and the boy would be educated and might find a job in the city or, if he was really lucky, in one of the Gulf states.

Together with verses from the Koran (learnt by rote) and the necessity to lead a devout life, these children were taught to banish all doubts. The only truth was divine truth, the only code of conduct was that written in the Koran and the *hadiths*, virtue lay in unthinking obedience. Anyone who rebelled against the *imam* rebelled against Allah. The aim was clear. These *madrasas* had a single function. They were indoctrination nurseries designed to produce fanatics. The primers, for example, stated that the Urdu letter *jeem* stood for *jihad*; *tay* for *tope* (cannon); *kaaf* for *kalashnikov* and *khay* for *khoon* (blood).

As they grew older the pupils were instructed in the use of sophisticated hand weapons and taught how to make and plant bombs. ISI agents provided training and supervision. They could also observe the development of the more promising students or *taliban*, who were later picked out and sent for more specialised training at secret army camps, the better to fight the 'holy war' against the unbelievers in Afghanistan.

The Jamaat-e-Islami had grown in influence during the Zia years. Its leaders assumed that they would run the schools. The party has always prided itself on its cadre organisation, built on the underground 'Leninist model' of small cells. It shunned mass membership, but this may have been because it, in turn, was shunned by the masses. Its leaders now thought their time had come. They saw the students as potential recruits. They were to be disappointed. New problems arose. Since dollars were freely available, different Islamic factions emerged and began to compete with each other for mastery in these schools and a division of the spoils. The ISI became the arbiter of intra-religious disputes and favoured some groups against others.

For a time the Afghan war consumed their energies. After the first war was over, the Pakistani state refused to accept a coalition government in Afghanistan. It was Benazir Bhutto's government that unleashed the Taliban, backed by Pakistan army commando units, in an attempt to take Kabul. The United States, fearful of Iranian influence in the region, had backed this decision.

The dragon seeds sown in 2,500 *madrasas* produced a crop of 225,000 fanatics ready to kill and to die for their faith when ordered to do so by their religious leaders. General Nasirullah Khan Babar, minister for the interior during Benazir Bhutto's second period in office, confided to friends that since the Taliban were becoming a menace inside Pakistan, he had decided that the only solution to the problem lay in giving the extremists their own country. This argument was disingenuous at the time, but in the light of what has happened over the last years, Babar deserves to be tried as a war-criminal.

With the collapse of the Soviet Union, the Cold War came to an end, bequeathing orphan-states on every continent. The effect in Pakistan was catastrophic. The fundamentalist groups had served their purpose and, unsurprisingly, the United States no longer felt the need to supply them with funds and weaponry. Overnight the latter turned violently anti-American and began to dream of revenge. Pakistan's political and military leaders, who had served the United States loyally and continuously from 1951 onwards, felt humiliated by Washington's indifference. A retired general summed it up succinctly for my benefit: 'Pakistan was the condom the Americans needed to enter Afghanistan. We've served our purpose and they think we can just be flushed down the toilet.'

The Pakistan army – one of the Pentagon's spoilt brats in Asia – refused to be relegated to the status of Kuwait. In order to gain attention it threw a nuclear tantrum. The explosion had the desired effect. Pakistan is back on the 'B list' of countries in the US State Department.

On 29 November 1998 Foreign Minister Sartaj Aziz attempted to soothe Western opinion: 'I see no possibility of an accidental nuclear war between Pakistan and India . . . Pakistan has an effective command and control system.' This is pure nonsense on a scientific level, but even if one were to accept the statement, a political question is immediately posed. What if reality began to imitate our nightmares and hardline Islamists took over the Pakistan army? Every political leader in Pakistan is aware of the danger. Nawaz Sharif's crude attempt to pre-empt political Islam by stealing some of its clothes ended in predictable failure.

The irony of the present situation is that religion in the Punjab always was a relaxed affair. The old tradition of Sufi mysticism, with its emphasis on individual communion with the Creator and its hostility to preachers, had found deep roots in the countryside. The tombs of the old Sufi saints, for centuries the site of annual festivals during which the participants sang, danced, drank, inhaled *bhang* and fornicated to their heart's content, were placed under martial law by General Zia. The people were to be denied simple pleasures.

This peculiarly non-Punjabi form of religious overkill did not arrive in Pakistan from nowhere. It was approved by Washington, funded by Saudi petrodollars and carefully nourished by General Zia. The result was the birth of madness. The twisted and self-destructive character of the groups that have mushroomed over the last five years is hardly in doubt. Ninety per cent of Pakistan's Muslims are Sunnis. The rest are mainly Shias. The Sunnis themselves are divided into two major schools of thought. The Deobandis represent orthodoxy. The Barelvis believe in a more synthetic Islam, defined and changed by local conditions. For many years these were literary disputes, often debated in public by mullahs and religious scholars. No longer. Every faction now lays claim to Islam, a moral and political claim. Disputes are no longer settled through discussion, but resolved by machine-guns and massacres. Some Deobandi factions want the Shias to be declared as heretics, and preferably physically exterminated. A sectarian civil war has been raging for many years. The Sunni Sipah-e-Sahaba (Soldiers of the First Four Caliphs) has attacked Shia mosques in the heart of Lahore and massacred the Shia faithful at prayer. The Shias have responded in kind. They formed the Sipah-e-Muhammad (Soldiers of Muhammad), drummed up Iranian backing and began to exact a gruesome revenge. Several hundred people have died in these intra-Muslim massacres, mainly Shias.

In January 1999 an armed Taliban faction seized a whole group of villages in the Hangu district of Pakistan's North-West Frontier province. They declared the area under 'Islamic laws' and promptly proceed to organise the public destruction of TV sets and dish antennae in the village of Zargari. This was followed by the burning of 3,000 'obscene' video and audio cassettes in the small square in Lukki.

There is something slightly comical in this hostility to television, and it reminds one of a Situationist spectacle in the Sixties, but humour, alas, is not congenial to the Taliban. The leader of the movement, Hussain Jalali, wants to extend the Afghan experience to Pakistan. After the television burning, he declared: 'The hands and feet of thieves will be chopped off and all criminals brought to justice in accordance with Islamic laws . . .'

'What can we do?', a supporter of the Sharif brothers asked me, wringing his hands in despair. 'These bastards are all armed!'

I pointed out that some of the bastards were being armed by the government to create mayhem in neighbouring Kashmir, but our bloated army was also armed. Why weren't they asked to disarm these groups? Here the conversation ended. For it is no secret that the fundamentalists have comprehensively penetrated the army. What distinguishes them from the old-style religious groups is that they want to seize state power, and for that they need the army.

In fact one of the most virulent of the groups is a creation of the ISI. Its political wing, Ahle-Hadis, wants the Saudi model implanted in Pakistan, but without the monarchy. They have supporters and mosques throughout the world, including Britain and the United States, whose aim is to supply cadres and money for the worldwide 'jihad'. This is the most orthodox of the Sunni sects, and is in a minority except that the president of the country is a supporter and government ministers grace its meetings. Their sub-office was at the time at 5 Chamberlaine Road in Lahore. I was tempted to go and interview them, but the sight of thirty heavily-armed guards decided me against the venture.

Its armed wing, the Lashkar-i-Tayyaba (Soldiers of Medina), could not exist without the patronage of the army. It has a membership of 50,000 militants and is the leading group in the 'jihad' to 'liberate' Indian Kashmir. The foot soldiers are trained by the army at eight special camps in Azad (Pakistani-controlled) Kashmir and are funded by Saudi Arabia and the government of Pakistan. They recruit teenagers from poor families, and have lost several hundred members in Kashmir. The government pays them 50,000 rupees (£500 approx.) for each corpse returned. Fifteen thousand rupees go to the family of the 'martyr' and the rest helps to fund the organisation.

The Harkatul Ansar (Volunteers Movement), once funded by the United States and backed by the ISI, was declared a terrorist organisation by the State Department in 2001. It promptly changed its name to Harkatul Mujahideen. Its fighters were amongst the most dedicated Taliban, and it has shifted its training camps from the Punjab to Afghanistan. Its leader, Osama bin Laden, continued to maintain close contacts with the ISI until 11 September 2001. Prior to that day his supporters have warned the government that any attempt to abduct him or ban his organisation would lead to an immediate civil war in Pakistan. They boast that the army will never agree to be used against them, but the hits against America changed all that and isolated, albeit temporarily, the Islamists inside the army.

These groups wanted to take over Pakistan. They dreamt of an Islamic Federation that would impose a Pax Talibana stretching from Lahore to Samarkand, but avoiding the 'Heretics' Republic of Iran'. For all their incoherence and senseless rage, their message is attractive to those layers of the population who yearn for some order in their lives. If the fanatics promise to feed them and educate their children they are prepared to forgo the delights of CNN and BBC World.

It is their truly frightening craving for a head-on clash, an explosive encounter, even if they turn out to be the victims of such an encounter, that marks the new wave of Islamic militants in Pakistan. Mercifully, they still constitute a minority in the country, but all that could change if nothing else changes. Something did change.

It was something old, something new. Yes, it was another coup, but with a difference. This was the first time the army had seized power without the approval of Washington. In October 1999, Nawaz Sharif, with US support, attempted to remove General Musharraf as chief of staff of the Pakistan army. They chose to do so while he was in Sri Lanka on an official trip. The plan backfired. The generals refused to support the sacking of their chief. Musharraf swooped home in dramatic fashion and took over the country. The Sharif brothers were locked up. The new military chief executive soon discovered that it was not easy to wipe out corruption, modernise the country or, most important of all, to curb the armed fundamentalist groups. And then, on 11 September 2001, a small group of Islamists decided to blow up the Pentagon and the Twin Towers of New York. The United States wanted revenge. Vultures descended on the region. For a short time, Pakistan once again became a key player, and once again the reason for its elevation was Afghanistan.

The destabilising effects of the war in Afghanistan were always likely to be felt here first. The Pashtun population in Pakistan's North-West Frontier Province shares linguistic and ethnic ties with the region that formed the principal base of the Taliban in Afghanistan. The same brand of Deobandi Islam is strong on both sides of the border. It is worth stressing that there was less actual fighting on the ground in the last three months of 2001 than there has been over the last quarter century. The bearded ones chose not to fight. A sizeable section of the Taliban forces simply came home to Pakistan. Some of them are undoubtedly demoralised and happy to be alive, but there is probably a large minority that is angered by Islamabad's betrayal and eager to link up with the armed fundamentalist groups already active in the country.

The leaders of the most virulent *jihadi* sects were arrested, but who will disarm their militants? Until December 2000, some of the Islamist leaders were boasting that they had chosen twenty Pakistani cities on which Islamic laws would be imposed. The unstated threat was clear. If any authority attempted to interfere, they would unleash a civil war. When the Afghan war began in October 2001, Washington made no secret of its fear that a massive Western intervention in Afghanistan that overtly used Pakistan as a launching-pad might trigger major unrest, or even a coup against a collaborationist regime. The US did everything to maintain decorous appearances for General Musharraf, Pakistan's ruler, while making sure of the practical compliance of Islamabad. In return for this, sanctions were lifted and money and the latest weaponry began to flow into Pakistan once again.

But once the Taliban have been defeated, can anyone be sure that the various fig-leaves will really shield Pakistan from the wrath of the faithful? Everything depends on the unity of the officer corps. To some degree, though difficult to gauge, Sunni fundamentalism has also penetrated the ranks of the armed forces. Across the country, radical Islamism of one kind or another is a vocal, if minority, force. General Musharraf's military regime itself is, moreover, a very recent and none-too-strong creation, with little positive civilian support and now dependent, once again, on Washington.

The abandonment of its own creation in Afghanistan is a bitter pill for many in the army, especially at junior levels of command, where religious influence is strongest. Even more secular-minded officers were not pleased at the outcome. The Taliban takeover in Kabul had been the Pakistan army's only victory. Privately the ruling elite – officers, bureaucrats and politicians – congratulated each other for having gained a new province. It almost made up for the 1971 defection of Bangladesh. As if to rub salt into the wounds, Afghanistan's Northern Alliance and its Washington-selected prime minister, Hamid Karzai, declared their intention of forging close relations with India, as was the case from 1947 to 1989. This has further weakened the political position of the generals ruling Pakistan.

At more senior levels, the American crusade against the Taliban has been seen as a godsend, for at a stroke it has allowed the Pakistani generals to recover their traditional regional priority for Washington, assured them of credits they desperately need, and dissolved opposition to their nuclear arsenal. Unlike its Arab counterparts, the Pakistani army has never seen a coup mounted by captains, majors or colonels – when it has seized power, as so often, it has always done so without splits, at the initiative and under the control of its generals (a tradition of discipline inherited from the raj).

At all events, short of a break in this long-established pattern, it seems unlikely that the top brass of the Pakistani regime will suffer much bruising from the pieces of silver with which they have been showered. However, the scale of the Pakistani defeat is such that, once the flow of money and weapons ceases, General Musharraf could well be toppled from within. Power-hungry generals have never been a rare commodity in Pakistan.

This is what makes the tension with India potentially dangerous. The irony is that Pakistan is led by a secular general and India by a fundamentalist Hindu politician: an ideal combination to make peace. Yet on one level it would suit both sides to have a small war. General Musharraf could prove that he was not a total pawn and Atal Bihari Vajpayee, India's prime minister, could win an election. The Kashmiris would continue to suffer. But who could guarantee a small war?

Pakistan's infiltration of *jihadi* groups, such as the Lashkar-i-Tayyaba and the Jaish-e-Muhammad, into Indian-occupied Kashmir has created an alternative military apparatus that Islamabad funds and supplies but can't fully control – just like the Taliban. It's obvious that the attack on the Indian Parliament was carried out by one of these groups to provoke a more serious conflict. Some of the *jihadis* don't much care for Pakistan as an entity. Their aim is to restore Muslim rule in India. Crazy? Yes, but armed and capable of wreaking havoc in both countries.

If Washington can wage its 'war on terrorism', why can't Delhi? Just because it can't get retrospective sanction from the UN? But as any Second World politician will tell you, for UN read US. The threat of an Indo-Pak war has concentrated minds in Washington: how to give the Indians their pound of flesh without destabilising Pakistan? General Musharraf can obviously be sacrificed in the name of a return to democracy in Pakistan. The problem is that no civilian politician there is strong or incorruptible enough to challenge the army, which has ruled the country longer than any political party.

17

Afghanistan: between hammer and anvil

Coveted in the late nineteenth century by Russian tsar and British viceroy alike, Afghanistan's impassable fastnesses enabled it to avoid occupation by either colonial power. Two British invasions were repelled – a warning to both London and St Petersburg. Eventually an expanding Tsarist empire and the British empire in India accepted Afghanistan, still a pre-feudal confederacy of tribes with its own king, as a buffer state. The British, as the more powerful force, would keep a watchful eye on Kabul. This arrangement suited all three parties at the time. The result was that Afghan society never underwent even a partial imperial modernisation, remaining more or less stationary for over a century. A mosaic of competing tribes and nationalities – ranging from the dominant Pashtuns (themselves bitterly divided), the Tadjiks and the Uzbeks, to Hazaras (of Mongol descent), Nuristanis and Baluch – ensured that no central authority maintained its power for too long. The gulf between Kabul and the countryside was rarely, if ever, breached.

When change finally came, the catalysts were external. The Russian Revolution of 1917 and the overthrow of the Ottoman caliphate by Kemal's new model army in 1919 stirred modernising ambitions in the young Afghan King Amanullah. Chafing under British tutelage, and surrounded by radical intellectuals who looked to Enlightenment ideals from Europe and the bold example from Petrograd, Amanullah briefly united a small educated elite with the bulk of the tribes, and won a famous military victory against British arms in 1919. This also won him ten years on the throne.

Success in the field gave Amanullah the confidence to launch a Reform Programme, partially inspired by Kemal's revolution in Turkey. A new Afghan constitution was proclaimed, promising universal adult franchise. If implemented, it would have made Afghanistan one of the first countries in the world to give all women the right to vote. Following the Turkish example, Amanullah had pushed through measures which dispensed with the veil, encouraged men to wear Western clothes, sent Afghans to study abroad and authorised mixed education in Kabul schools. Simultaneously, emissaries were dispatched to Moscow to seek assistance. Though the Bolshevik leaders were themselves beleaguered by multiple armed interventions from the Entente powers, they treated the Afghan overtures quite seriously. Sultan-Galiev received the messengers from Kabul warmly on behalf of the Comintern, while Trotsky sent a secret letter to the Central Committee of the Russian Communist Party from his armoured train at the front line of the civil war. In this remarkable dispatch, he wrote:

> There is no doubt at all that our Red Army constitutes an incomparably more powerful force in the Asian terrain of world politics than in the European terrain. Here there opens up before us an undoubted possibility not merely of a lengthy wait to see how events develop in Europe, but of conducting activity in the Asian field. The road to India may prove at the given moment to be more readily passable and shorter for us than the road to Soviet Hungary. The sort of army which at the moment can be of no great significance in the European scales can upset the unstable balance of Asian relationships of colonial dependence, give a direct push to an uprising on the part of the oppressed masses and assure the triumph of such a rising in Asia ... The road to Paris and London lies via the towns of Afghanistan, the Punjab and Bengal.

A hallucinatory document by one of Trotsky's military specialists proposed the creation of an anti-imperialist cavalry corps of 30–40,000 riders to liberate British India.

Nothing came of such schemes. No doubt the failure of Tukhachevsky's march into Poland two years later had a sobering effect in Moscow. Amanullah got no more than friendship and advice from the Bolsheviks. The British, understandably nervous, were now determined to overthrow him. New Delhi imported T.E. Lawrence as an adviser, purchased the services of a couple of leading tribes, fomented religious opposition to the king, and finally toppled him with a military coup in 1929.[57] The Comintern journal *Inprekorr* commented that Amanullah had only survived for a decade because of 'Soviet friendship'; more pertinently, the senior Bolshevik Raskolnikov remarked that Amanullah had introduced 'bourgeois reforms without a bourgeoisie', whose cost had fallen on peasants whom he had failed to win over with an agrarian reform, allowing Britain to exploit social and tribal divisions in the country.

As the imperial power in the region, Britain was not popular even among those tribal chiefs it supported. During the Second World War, Afghanistan remained neutral. A document from the German Foreign Office, dated 3 October 1940 (cracked by the Enigma decoder during the Second World War), makes fascinating reading. It is from State Secretary Weizsäcker to the German legation in Kabul.

> The Afghan Minister called on me on September 30 and conveyed greetings from his Minister president and the War Minister, as well as their good wishes for a favourable outcome of the war. He inquired whether German aims in Asia coincided with Afghan hopes; he alluded to the oppression of Arab countries and referred to the 15 million Afghans [Pashtuns, mainly in the North-West Frontier Province – TA] who were forced to suffer on Indian territory. My statement that Germany's goal was the liberation of the peoples of the region referred to, who were under the British yoke, as well as the restoration of their rights, was received with satisfaction by the Afghan Minister. He stated that justice for Afghanistan would be created only when the country's frontier had been extended to the Indus; this would also apply if India should secede from Britain . . . The Afghan remarked that Afghanistan had given proof of her loyal attitude by vigorously resisting English pressure to break off relations with Germany. Today he wanted to present Afghanistan's wishes as a matter of precaution, but he requested strict secrecy; he called a fulfilment of these wishes a matter for the future.

The king who had dispatched the minister to Berlin was the twenty-six-year-old Zahir Shah. The minister-president was his uncle Sardar Muhammad Hashim Khan. What is interesting in the German dispatch is

---

57 Among other things, Lawrence had fabricated photographs of Queen Sorayya (a staunch feminist) in 'compromising poses' and distributed these amongst the tribesmen.

not so much the hatred for Britain, which was normal at that time. It is the desire for a Greater Afghanistan by the incorporation of what is now Pakistan's North-West Frontier Province and its capital Peshawar.[58]

Fifty years after Amanullah came to the throne, history repeated itself, with a grimmer outcome. In the early Seventies the reigning King Zahir Shah was ousted by his cousin Daud, who declared a republic with the support of the local communists and financial aid from the USSR. When, in April 1979, the shah of Iran convinced Daud to turn against the communist factions in his army and administration, they staged a self-defensive coup. Bitterly divided amongst themselves – inner-party disputes were sometimes settled with revolvers – the Afghan communists had no social base outside Kabul and a few other cities. Their power rested on control of the army and air force alone. Nonetheless they did begin to implement a reform programme. Education, in particular, received an important boost from the new regime. Girls began to be educated in the villages and some co-educational institutions were also established. In 1978, male illiteracy was 90 per cent, while female illiteracy stood at 98 per cent. Ten years later it had been substantially reduced. A new generation of young Afghan men and women emerged as doctors, teachers, scientists and technicians. Despite its many negative features – especially a crazed Pol Pot style purge of those who opposed the reforms – the PDPA regime had restarted the process of modernisation, which had been disrupted with the overthrow of King Amanullah.

The United States, taking over the historic role of Britain, soon started to undermine the regime by arming the religious opposition to it, using the Pakistani army as a conduit. This increased the violence in the villages as tribesmen were given money and arms to start a civil war. Under mounting pressure, the Afghan communists broke into violent internecine strife. At this juncture, Brezhnev took the plunge that had been beyond the Bolsheviks – dispatching a massive military column to Kabul to salvage the regime.

---

58 Behind the scenes, Zahir Shah's return has been strongly resisted by Pakistan. They know that the king never accepted the Mortimer–Durand Line, not even as a temporary border. They remain concerned that he might revive Pashtun nationalism.

This was exactly what Carter's National Security chief Zbigniew Brzezinski had been hoping for. The interview published by the French weekly *Le Nouvel Observateur* of 15–21 January 1998 leaves little room for doubt:

Q: The former director of the CIA, Robert Gates, stated in his memoirs [*From the Shadows*] that American intelligence services began to aid the Mujahidin in Afghanistan 6 months before the Soviet intervention. In this period you were the national security adviser to President Carter. You therefore played a role in this affair. Is that correct?

Brzezinski: Yes. According to the official version of history, CIA aid to the Mujahidin began during 1980, that is to say, after the Soviet army invaded Afghanistan, 24 Dec. 1979. But the reality, secretly guarded until now, is completely otherwise: Indeed, it was 3 July 1979 that President Carter signed the first directive for secret aid to the opponents of the pro-Soviet regime in Kabul. And that very day, I wrote a note to the president in which I explained to him that in my opinion this aid was going to induce a Soviet military intervention.

Q: Despite this risk, you were an advocate of this covert action. But perhaps you yourself desired this Soviet entry into war and looked to provoke it?

B: It isn't quite that. We didn't push the Russians to intervene, but we knowingly increased the probability that they would.

Q: When the Soviets justified their intervention by asserting that they intended to fight against a secret involvement of the United States in Afghanistan, people didn't believe them. However, there was a basis of truth. You don't regret anything today?

B: Regret what? That secret operation was an excellent idea. It had the effect of drawing the Russians into the Afghan trap and you want me to regret it? The day that the Soviets officially crossed the border, I wrote to President Carter: We now have the opportunity of giving to the USSR its Vietnam War. Indeed, for almost 10 years, Moscow had to carry on a war unsupportable by the government, a conflict that brought about the demoralisation and finally the breakup of the Soviet empire.

Q: And neither do you regret having supported Islamic fundamentalism, having given arms and advice to future terrorists?

B: What is most important to the history of the world? The Taliban or the collapse of the Soviet empire? A few crazed Muslims or the liberation of Central Europe and the end of the Cold War?[59]

The Russian leaders fell headlong into the trap. Politburo documents from that period make interesting reading. Till two days before the decision was taken, the entire Politburo was opposed to military intervention. Something happened to change their minds. What this was has yet to be revealed, but the answer probably lies in the CIA archives. What is most likely is that US disinformation implying that the Afghan leader, Hafizullah Amin, was on the verge of changing allegiances played a big part in shifting the Politburo. Moscow did state that Amin was a CIA agent, but at the time this was dismissed as the usual blackening of names that precedes all Big Power interventions. The entry of Soviet troops into Afghanistan transformed an unpleasant civil war funded by Washington into a jihad enabling the mujahidin ('holy warriors') to appear as the only defenders of Afghan sovereignty against the foreign army of occupation. Brzezinski was soon posing for photographs in a Pashtun turban on the Khyber Pass and shouting 'Allah is on your side', while Afghan fundamentalists were being fêted as 'freedom-fighters' in the White House and Downing Street.

Washington's role in the Afghan war has never been a secret, but few citizens in the West were aware that the United States utilised the intelligence services of Egypt, Saudi Arabia and Pakistan to create, train, finance and arm an international network of Islamic militants to fight the Russians in Afghanistan. A former Middle East correspondent for the *Christian Science Monitor* and ABC Television, John Cooley, who gained easy access to retired and serving officials in the states mobilised, has written a fascinating account of this final episode of the Cold War.[60] Although he does not always cite his sources, and some of what he says should be viewed with scepticism, his information corroborates much that was widely bruited in Pakistan during

---

59 Contempt for the rights and lives of ordinary people elsewhere in the world – a trademark of the Washington outlook before, during and after the Cold War – could not be more pithily expressed, though I wonder how the citizens of New York would have responded to the question after 11 September 2001.

60 John Cooley, *Unholy Wars: Afghanistan, America and International Terrorism*, London 1999.

the Eighties. According to his account, the US drew in other powers to the anti-Soviet jihad. Cooley contends that Chinese help was not restricted to the provision of weapons, but extended to the provision of listening-posts in Xinjiang, and even dispatch of Uighur volunteers whose costs were covered by the CIA. Some form of Chinese assistance was privately always acknowledged by the generals in Islamabad, though Beijing has never admitted it. Cooley even suggests that the People's Republic has not been immune to the post-Soviet withdrawal syndrome: Islamic militants turning on the powers that armed them. However, the country not mentioned by Cooley is Israel, whose role in Afghanistan remains one of the best-kept secrets of the war. In 1985, Ahmed Mansur, a young Pakistani journalist working for *The Muslim*, accidentally stumbled across a group of Israeli 'advisers' at the bar of the Intercontinental Hotel in Peshawar. Aware that the news would be explosive for the Zia dictatorship, he informed his editor, some friends and a visiting WTN correspondent. A few days later the mujahidin, alerted by Pakistan's Inter Services Intelligence, captured and killed him.

Cooley also describes a meeting in 1978 in Beirut with Raymond Close, former station chief of the CIA in Saudi Arabia, who clearly charmed him. If he had questioned him more closely, he would have discovered that Close had previously been posted to Pakistan, where his father had been a missionary teacher at the Forman Christian College in Lahore. His son was fluent in Persian, Urdu and Arabic. In nominal retirement, he would have been ideally placed to help orchestrate operations in Afghanistan, and their backup in Pakistan, where the Bank of Credit and Commerce International (BCCI) functioned as a channel for CIA funding of clandestine activities, and laundered profits from the heroin trade.

Afghanistan itself, a decade after Soviet withdrawal, was still awash with factional violence. Veterans of the war helped to destabilise Egypt, Algeria, the Philippines, Sudan, Pakistan, Chechnya, Daghestan and Saudi Arabia. Well before 11 September they had bombed targets in the United States and declared their own war against the Great Satan. Osama bin Laden became the bugbear of US official and popular fantasies only after starting his career as a Saudi building tycoon with links to the CIA. When the Pakistani generals pleaded with the Saudi dynasty to send a princeling from the royal family to lead the holy war, no volunteers were forthcoming. Osama was sent as a friend of the palace instead. Doing better than expected, he was to surprise his patrons in Riyadh and Foggy Bottom. Cooley concludes with the following advice to the US government:

> When you decide to go to war against your main enemy, take a good, long look at the people behind you whom you chose as your friends, allies or mercenary fighters. Look well to see whether these allies already have unsheathed their knives – and are pointing them at your own back.

His pleas are unlikely to move Zbigniew Brzezinski, who repudiates regrets.

After the Soviet withdrawal in 1989, the de facto alliance of states that had backed different factions of the mujahidin soon fell apart. Islamabad did not want any broad government of reconstruction, preferring – with US and Saudi support – to impose its own pawn, Gulbuddin Hekmatyar, on the country. The result was a series of vicious civil wars, punctuated by unstable ceasefires, as Hazaras (backed by Iran), Ahmad Shah Masud (backed by France), and the Uzbek General Dostum (backed by Russia) resisted. When it became obvious that Hekmatyar's forces were incapable of defeating these foes, the Pakistan army shifted its backing to the Taliban it had been training in religious schools in the North-West Frontier since 1980. In 1992 the chief minister of the North-West Frontier Province told me that the juvenile fanatics in the *madrasas* might or might not 'liberate' Afghanistan, but they would certainly destabilise what was left of Pakistan.

The Taliban were orphans of the war against the Russian infidel. Trained and dispatched across the border by the ISI, they were to be hurled into battle against Muslims they were told were not true Muslims. In his now cult text, Ahmed Rashid captured their outlook vividly:

> These boys were a world apart from the Mujaheddin whom I had got to know during the 1980s – men who could recount their tribal and clan lineages, remembered their abandoned farms and valleys with nostalgia and recounted legends and stories from Afghan history. These boys were from a generation who had never seen their country at peace. They had no memories of their tribes, their elders, their neighbours nor the complex ethnic mix of peoples that was their homeland. They admired war because it was the only occupation they could possibly adapt

---

61 Ahmed Rashid, *Taliban, Islam, Oil and the New Great Game in Asia*, London 1999.

to. Their simple belief in a messianic, puritan Islam was the only prop they could hold on to and which gave their lives some meaning.[61]

This deracinated fanaticism – a kind of bleak Islamic cosmopolitanism – made the Taliban a more effective fighting force than any of their localised adversaries. Although Pashtun in origin, the Taliban leaders could be sure their young soldiers would not succumb to the divisive lure of ethnic or tribal loyalties, which even the Afghan left had found it hard to shed. When they began their sweep from the frontier, a war-weary population often greeted them with an element of relief: citizens in the larger towns had lost faith in all the other forces that had been battling at the expense of civilian life since the Soviet departure.

If the Taliban had simply offered peace and bread, they might have won lasting popular support. Soon, however, the character of the regime they were bent on imposing became clear to the bewildered population. Women were banned from working, collecting their children from school and, in some cities, even from shopping: effectively, they were confined to their homes. Girls' schools were closed down. The Taliban had been taught in their *madrasas* to steer clear of the temptation of women – male brotherhood was a condition of tight military discipline. Puritanism extended to snuffing out sexual expression of any kind; although this was a region where homosexual practices had been common for centuries, recruits guilty of the 'crime' were executed by the Taliban commanders. Outside their ranks, dissent of any sort was brutally crushed with a reign of terror unmatched by any preceding regime. The Taliban creed is a variant of the Deobandi Islam professed by a sectarian strain in Pakistan – more extreme in some respects even than the Wahhabi strain, since not even the Saudi rulers have deprived half their population of all civic rights in the name of the Koran. This has been one of Osama's complaints against them. They had become soft. For him the 'Emirate of Afghanistan' was closer to the original Wahhabi philosophy than the desert kingdom. The severity of the Afghan mullahs has been denounced by Sunni clerics at al-Azhar in Cairo and Shi'ite theologians in Qom as a disgrace to the Prophet. Faiz Ahmed Faiz, whose father had spent his early life in the Afghan court and who always spoke knowledgeably about Kabul and Kandahar, could have written his lines from prison about Afghanistan under the Taliban:

Bury me underneath your pavements, oh my country
Where no person now dare walk with head held high,
Where true lovers bringing you their homage
Walk furtively in fear of life and limb;
A new-style law-and-order is in use
Stones and bricks are locked up and dogs turned loose –
Villains are judges and usurpers both,
Who speaks for us?
Where shall we seek justice?

Certainly not from the commander-in-chief in the White House or his aide-de-camp in Downing Street. Before 11 September, little was heard from these pulpits for human rights as the women of Afghanistan were subjected to a vile persecution. A few mild words of criticism from Hillary Clinton, during her husband's reign, were more designed to soothe American feminists during the Lewinsky scandal – not a very demanding task – than to alter the situation in Kabul or Kandahar or Herat, ancient towns where women had never before been reduced to such depths of misery. American business was less hypocritical. Responding to complaints about the pipeline it is constructing from Central Asia through Afghanistan to Pakistan, a spokesman for the US oil giant Unocal explained why capitalism is gender-blind: 'We disagree with some US feminist groups on how Unocal should respond to this issue . . . We are guests in countries who have sovereign rights and their own political, social, religious beliefs. Walking away from Afghanistan would not solve the problem.' Nor, of course, improve the rate of return on its projected investments.

The Taliban could not have swept across Afghanistan without the military and financial backing of Islamabad, sustained in turn by Washington. The top Taliban commander Mullah Omar, the one-eyed ruler of Kabul till the latest Afghan war, was long on the direct payroll of the Pakistani regime. The conquest of power, however, had an intoxicating impact on the Afghan zealots. The Taliban have their own goal for the region – a Federation of Islamic Republics that would enforce a Pax Talibana from Samarkand to Karachi. They controlled sufficient revenues from the heroin trade to fund their land campaigns, but they wanted access to the sea and made no secret of their belief that Pakistan with its nuclear arms would fall to them one day.

Relations between Pakistan and the Taliban had been tense since

October 2000, when in an effort to cement friendship, Pakistan dispatched a football team to play a friendly against Afghanistan. As the two teams faced each other in the stadium at Kabul, the security forces entered and announced that the Pakistani footballers were indecently attired. They were wearing football shorts, and some had long hair in the fashion of European football stars, whereas the Afghan team were wearing long shorts that came down well below the knees. Perhaps the security police felt that the heaving thighs of the Pakistanis might cause upheavals in the all-male audience. Who knows? No football was played that day. The Pakistani team was arrested, their heads were shaved and they were all flogged in public, while the stadium audience was forced to chant verses from the Koran. This was Mullah Omar's way of firing a shot across the Pakistan army's bow.

And then came 11 September 2001 and a new war. Initially the United States demanded the head of Osama bin Laden. Mullah Omar, cheekily but correctly, demanded to see the evidence involving bin Laden. None was supplied because none existed at the time. Washington then threatened the Taliban regime directly, though a week before the bombing began Donald Rumsfeld, the US defence secretary, was talking in terms of 'a moderate wing of the Taliban'. Once the war began the only serious question was how long it would take for Kabul to fall.

After 11 September, Pakistan's military rulers attempted to convince the Taliban to hand over Osama bin Laden and avoid the castastrophe in store. They failed. The more interesting question was whether Pakistan, after withdrawing its own soldiers, officers and pilots from Afghanistan, had managed to split the Taliban and withdraw those sections totally dependent on its patronage. This was a key aim of the military regime if it was to maintain its influence in a future coalition government in Kabul. It succeeded in pulling out a large chunk of the Taliban fighters. Some returned to Pakistan. Others were instructed to shave their beards and join some of the factions jockeying for power in Kabul.

I've never believed in the myth of Afghan invincibility. True, they defeated the British twice during the nineteenth century, but helicopters, bomber jets and cruise missiles had not then been invented. The Soviet army was defeated because of the massive military and economic aid provided by the United States and the direct military intervention of Pakistan's

ISI. The notion that the Taliban could resist this assault was laughable. In fact, soon after the bombing began, I suggested in the *Guardian* that:

> The bombing of Kabul and Kandahar by the United States will not have affected the fighting strength of the Taliban or bin Laden's special brigade consisting of Arabs. Nonetheless the Taliban are effectively encircled and isolated. Their defeat is inevitable. Both Pakistan and Iran are ranged against them on two important borders. It is unlikely if they will last out more than a few weeks.
>
> As for the supposed aim of this operation – the capture of Osama bin Laden – this might be less easy than it appears. He is well-protected in the remote Pamir mountains and since he has had three weeks to plot his course, he might well disappear. But victory will still be proclaimed. The West will rely on the short memory of its citizens. But let us even suppose that bin Laden is captured and killed. How will this help the 'war against terrorism'? Other individuals will decide to mimic the events of 11 September in different ways.

Sustaining a new client state in Afghanistan will not be an easy affair given local and regional rivalries. The first attempt was made after the year-long mujahidin civil war that had followed the collapse of the PDPA regime. In March 1993 the Saudi king, Pakistan and Iran brought the warring Islamic factions together. A detailed semi-constitutional plan based on power-sharing and the creation of a national army which would take over all heavy weaponry was solemnly agreed in Islamabad. It was also agreed that an Election Commission would be set up to prepare the election of a Grand Constituent Assembly, which would vote on a new constitution. Even though rival warlords could barely conceal their distaste at being present in the same room, the Pakistani prime minister, Nawaz Sharif, was so excited by his own success that he suggested they all fly off together to Mecca and seal the agreement in the Holy City itself. The warlords – leaders of the nine mujahidin factions – smiled benignly and boarded the plane. The Mecca Accord was duly signed in the presence of King Fahd, who was *compos mentis* at the time. Nawaz Sharif told the Afghans that history and Allah would never forgive anyone who violated an agreement signed in Mecca. But it didn't work. Hardly had they returned to Afghanistan than fighting broke out between the main factions. General Syed Rafaqat of the Pakistan army provided an interesting, if inadequate, explanation for the civil war:

Five evils gradually slipped out of the holy womb of jihad: weakening of Afghan identity, sharpened focus on ethnicity, emergence of sectarian aspect, the cult of warlordism, and the habit of foreign powers to interfere in the internal affairs of Afghanistan. The first undermined the pride, which all people of Afghanistan had in being known and called Afghans.

Much more had emerged from the 'holy womb': an addiction to ready supplies of cash, weaponry and heroin. The first two had dried up once the Soviet Union was defeated. The third remained, and all the mujahidin factions were involved in it in one capacity or another: cultivation, processing, distribution. The factions' supply routes varied. The Pashtuns used the Pakistani port of Karachi. The Hazaras and Tadjiks found it easier to work with the powerful Russian mafia which controlled distribution in all the former Soviet republics and had a massive base to supply Europe in Albania and, later, Kosovo. Rivalry between the groups was not based so much on ethnic hostility as simple greed. When the Taliban did a deal with the United States in 2000 and agreed to burn the poppy fields under their control in return for $43 million, their rivals in the Northern Alliance were delighted. They now had the monopoly. The Russian mafia had defeated the heroin merchants of Pakistan.

The old warlords who had assembled in Mecca in 1993 were not in evidence at Bonn in 2001. Some were dead. Others preferred to stay at home. This time their representatives, carefully vetted by Western intelligence agencies, handpicked by a veteran UN fixer, Lakhdar Brahimi, and carefully dressed in smart Western suits, were quite happy to mouth a rhetoric that pleased their new hosts. In Mecca, they had thanked Almighty Allah for their triumph against the infidel. This time they were thanking the 'infidel' for their victory against the 'bad seed of Noah' and 'false Muslims'. This time they spoke in honeyed tones of 'one country, one nation, at peace with itself, marching confidently on the road to modernity, and no threat to its neighbours'.

Napoleon's mother, on being congratulated by courtiers for having so many children seated on the thrones of Europe, responded tartly: 'But will it last?'

The facts are these: the situation in Afghanistan is inherently unstable. Only fantasists could suggest otherwise. The notion that the Alliance in its present form could last out a few years is risible. Turf wars have already begun in 'liberated' Kabul, though open clashes have been avoided. There is too much at stake. The West is watching. Money has been promised. Putin and Khatami are urging caution. But the dam will burst sooner rather than later. The former CIA collaborator Hamid Karzai can always get a job modelling chic Pashtunwear in North America and Europe, the US pro-consul Zalmay Khalizad can return to the White House or Unocal, but what of the dying and suffering people of Afghanistan? Once the Marines depart, with or without the head of bin Laden, the Alliance will discover that there is no money for anything these days except waging war. The boy-scout propaganda that 'we're remaking the world' is designed for domestic consumption. Schools and hospitals and homes are not going to be sprouting next spring or the one after in Afghanistan or Kosovo. I fear that this story, too, is not done.

18

The story of Kashmir

Only the graveyard breezes blow in the valley of Kashmir. Murder tours the region in different guises, garbed sometimes in the uniform of the Indian army or in the form of bearded men, armed and infiltrated by Pakistan, speaking the language of jihad – Allah and Fate rolled into one. The background presence of nuclear missiles offers a ghoulish comfort to both sides. Kashmir, trapped in this Neither–Nor predicament, suffocates. Depressed and exhausted by the decades of violence, many Kashmiris have become passive. The beauties of spring and summer pass unnoticed by listless eyes. Fearful even of medium-term possibilities, they prefer to live in the present. Oppressed by Neither–Nor they are silent in public, speaking the truth in whispers. They fear that old Kabul might move to Srinagar and, in the name of a petrified religion, ban all poetry and music, outlaw the public appearance of unveiled women, close down the university and impose a clerical dictatorship. It is difficult to imagine a Talibanised Kashmir, but it was once equally difficult to imagine a Talibanised Afghanistan. A complicated and unpredictable combination of circumstances does sometimes enable the enemies of light to triumph. Unless . . .

I was thinking about this on a balmy October evening in New York during the dying days of the Clinton presidency, wondering if there was an alternative to Neither–Nor and what, if anything, the Empire had in store for its South Asian satrapies. Provincial at the best of times, the country was immersed in its own election campaign.

Strolling down Eighth Avenue in search of sustenance I was halted between 40th and 41st by a tacky, twinkling neon-lit sign: K-A-S-H-M-I-R. An adjacent, non-twinkling arrow signalled a fast-food dive in the basement below. I decided to risk the food. Attached to the austere eating zone was an extension in the shape of a raised wooden platform. A slab on the wall proclaimed this to be the Jinnah Hall, inaugurated in 1996 by Nawaz Sharif, the prime minister of Pakistan. I asked the young Kashmiri woman sitting behind the cash-desk underneath the slab, whether this could possibly be the same Nawaz Sharif who was sitting at the time in a Pakistani prison on charges of corruption and attempted murder. She smiled, but did not reply. Instead she turned her eyes to the 'Hall', where a meeting was in progress. The place was nearly full. About twenty or so South Asian men and a single white woman. The top table was occupied by an assortment of beards dressed in traditional baggy trousers and long shirts. I felt for one of them. Afflicted with the dreaded dhobi's itch, he was engaged in his own private jihad, scratching away at his testicles throughout the evening.

At the lectern, next to the top table, a clean-shaven white American was already in full flow. His gestures and rancid rhetoric suggested a politician, who could have belonged to either party. He turned out to be a Democratic Congressman, 'a friend of the people of Kashmir'. Recently returned from a visit to the country, he had been 'deeply moved' by the suffering he had witnessed and was now convinced that 'the moral leadership of the world must take up this issue'. The beards nodded vigorously, recalling no doubt the help the 'moral leadership' had given in Kabul and Kosovo. The Congressman paused; he didn't want to mislead these people: what was on offer was not a 'humanitarian war' but an informal Camp David. 'It needn't even be the United States,' he continued. 'It could be a great man. It could be Nelson Mandela . . . or Bill Clinton.'

The beards were unimpressed. One of the few beardless men in the audience rose to his feet and addressed the Congressman: 'Please answer honestly to our worries,' he said. 'In Afghanistan we helped you defeat the Red Army. You needed us then and we were very much loyal to you. Now you have abandoned us for India. Mr Clinton supports India, not human rights in Kashmir. Is this a good way to treat very old friends?'

The Congressman made sympathetic noises, even promising to tick Clinton off for not being 'more vigorous on human rights in Kashmir'. He needn't have bothered. A beard rose to ask why the US government had betrayed them. The repetition irritated the Congressman. He took the offensive, complaining about this being an all-male meeting. Why were these men's wives and daughters not present? The bearded faces remained impassive Feeling the need for some fresh air, I decided to leave. As I went up the stairs the Congressman had changed tack once again, speaking now of the wondrous beauty of the valley he had recently visited.

Damn the beauty, I thought, stop the killings. Was the Congressman or attendant beards aware of Kashmir's turbulent past, Islamic and pre-Islamic? Did they know that the Mughal kings had never regarded religion as a cornerstone of empire-building? Were they aware of the strong women who had resisted rulers in the past, or why Kashmir had been sold for a pittance by the East India Company to a corrupt local ruler? And why had it all ended so badly? Could the beards seriously imagine that the Empire would intervene and transform Srinagar into Sarajevo, occupied by Western troops while India and China watched calmly from the sidelines? Or did they believe that one day a totally bearded Pakistan would use nuclear missiles to liberate them?

'The buildings of Kashmir are all of wood,' the Mughal Emperor Jehangir wrote in his memoirs in March 1622. 'They make them two, three and four-storeyed, and covering the roofs with earth, they plant bulbs of the black tulip, which blooms year after year with the arrival of spring and is exceedingly beautiful. This custom is peculiar to the people of Kashmir. This year, in the little garden of the palace and on the roof of the largest mosque, the tulips blossomed luxuriantly . . . The flowers that are seen in the territories of Kashmir are beyond all calculation.' Surveying the lakes and waterfalls, roses, irises and jasmine, he described the valley as 'a page that the painter of destiny had drawn with the pencil of creation'.

The first Muslim invasion of Kashmir took place in the eighth century and was defeated by the Himalayas. The soldiers of the Prophet found it impossible to move beyond the mountains' southern slopes. Victory came unexpectedly five centuries later, as a result of a palace coup. Rinchana, the Buddhist chief from neighbouring Ladakh who carried out the coup, had sought refuge in Kashmir and embraced Islam under the guidance of a Sufi with the pleasing name of Bulbul ('Nightingale') Shah. Rinchana's conversion would have been neither here nor there had it not been for the Turkish mercenaries who made up the ruler's elite guard and were only too pleased to switch their allegiance to a co-religionist. But they swore to obey only the new ruler, not his descendants, so when Rinchana died, the leader of the mercenaries, Shah Mir, took control and founded the first Muslim dynasty to rule Kashmir. It lasted for seven hundred years.

The population, however, was not easily swayed, and despite a policy of forced conversions it wasn't until the end of the reign of Zain-al-Abidin in the late fifteenth century that a majority of Kashmiris embraced Islam. In fact, Zain-al-Abidin, an inspired ruler, ended the forced conversion of Hindus and decreed that those who had been converted in this fashion be allowed to return to their own faith. He even provided Hindus with subsidies enabling them to rebuild the temples his father had destroyed. The different ethnic and religious groups still weren't allowed to intermarry, but they learned to live side by side amicably enough. Zain-al-Abidin organised visits to Iran and Central Asia so that his subjects could learn bookbinding and woodcarving and how to make carpets and shawls, thereby laying the foundations for the shawlmaking for which Kashmir is famous. By the end of his reign a large majority of the population had converted voluntarily to Islam and the ratio of Muslims to non-Muslims – 85 to 15 – has remained fairly constant ever since.

The dynasty went into a decline after Zain-al-Abidin's death. Disputes over the succession, unfit rulers and endless intrigues among the nobility paved the way for new invasions. In the end the Mughal conquest in the late sixteenth century probably came as a relief to most people. The landlords were replaced by Mughal civil servants who administered the country rather more efficiently, reorganising its trade, its shawlmaking and its agriculture. On the other hand, deprived of local patronage, Kashmir's poets, painters and scribes left the valley in search of employment at the Mughal courts in Delhi and Lahore, taking the country's cultural life with them.

What made the disappearance of Kashmiri culture particularly harsh was the fact that the conquest itself coincided with a sudden flowering of the Kashmiri court. Zoonie, the wife of Sultan Yusuf Shah, was a peasant from the village of Tsandahar who had been taken up by a Sufi mystic enchanted with her voice. Under his guidance she learned Persian and began to write her own songs. One day, passing with his entourage and hearing her voice in the fields, Yusuf Shah, too, was captivated. He took her to court and prevailed on her to marry him. And that is how Zoonie entered the palace as queen and took the name of Habba Khatun ('loved woman'). She wrote:

I thought I was indulging in play, and lost myself.
O for the day that is dying!
At home I was secluded, unknown,
When I left home, my fame spread far and wide,
The pious laid all their merit at my feet.
O for the day that is dying!
My beauty was like a warehouse filled with rare merchandise,
Which drew men from all the four quarters;
Now my richness is gone, I have no worth:
O for the day that is dying!
My father's people were of high standing,
I became known as Habba Khatun:
O for the day that is dying.

Habba Khatun gave the Kashmiri language a literary form and encouraged a synthesis of Persian and Indian musical styles. She gave women the freedom to decorate themselves as they wished and revived the old Circassian tradition of tattooing the face and hands with special dyes and powders. The clerics were furious. They saw in her the work of Iblis, or Satan, in league with the blaspheming, licentious Sufis. While Yusuf Shah remained on the throne, however, Habba Khatun was untouchable. She mocked the pretensions of the clergy, defended the mystic strain within Islam and compared herself to a flower that flourishes in fertile soil and cannot be uprooted.

Habba Khatun was queen when, in 1583, the Mughal emperor, Akbar, dispatched his favourite general to annex the kingdom of Kashmir. There was no fighting: Yusuf Shah rode out to the Mughal camp and capitulated without a struggle, demanding only the right to retain the throne and strike coins in his image. Instead, he was arrested and sent into exile. The Kashmiri nobles, angered by Yusuf Shah's betrayal, placed his son, Yakub Shah, on the throne, but he was a weak and intemperate young man who set the Sunni and the Shia clerics at one another's throats, and before long Akbar sent a large expeditionary force, which took Kashmir in the summer of 1588. In the autumn the emperor came to see the valley's famous colours for himself.

Habba Khatun's situation changed dramatically after Akbar had her husband exiled. Unlike Sughanda and Dida, two powerful tenth-century queens who had ascended the throne as regents, Habba Khatun was driven out of the palace. At first she found refuge with the Sufis, but after a time she began to move from village to village, giving voice in her songs to the melancholy of a suppressed people. There is no record of when or where she died – a grave, thought to be hers, was discovered in the middle of the last century – but women mourning the disappearance of young men killed by the Indian army or 'volunteered' to fight in the jihad still sing her verses:

> Who told him where I lived?
> Why has he left me in such anguish?
> I, hapless one, am filled with longing for him.
> He glanced at me through my window,
> He who is as lovely as my ear-rings;
> He has made my heart restless:
> I, hapless one, am filled with longing for him.
> He glanced at me through the crevice in my roof,
> Sang like a bird that I might look at him,
> Then, soft-footed, vanished from my sight:
> I, hapless one, am filled with longing for him.
> He glanced at me while I was drawing water,
> I withered like a red rose,
> My soul and body were ablaze with love:
> I, hapless one, am filled with longing for him.
> He glanced at me in the waning moonlight of early dawn,
> Stalked me like one obsessed.
> Why did he stoop so low?
> I, hapless one, am filled with longing for him!

Habba Khatun exemplified a gentle version of Islam, diluted with pre-Islamic practices and heavily influenced by Sufi mysticism. This tradition is still strong in the countryside and helps to explain Kashmiri indifference to the more militant forms of religion.

The Mughal emperors were drawn to their new domain. Akbar's son, Jehangir, lost his fear of death there, since Paradise could only transcend the beauties of Kashmir. While his wife and brother-in-law kept their eye on the administration of the empire, he reflected on his luck at having escaped the plains of the Punjab and spent his time smoking opium, sampling the juice of the Kashmir grape and planning gardens around natural springs so that the reflection of the rising and setting sun could be seen in the water as it cascaded down specially constructed channels. 'If on earth there be a paradise of bliss, it is this, it is this, it is this,' he wrote, citing a well-known Persian couplet.

By the eighteenth century, the Mughal empire had begun its own slow decline and the Kashmiri nobles invited Ahmed Shah Durrani, the brutal ruler of Afghanistan, to liberate their country. Durrani obliged in 1752, doubling taxes and persecuting the embattled Shia minority with a fanatical vigour that shocked the nobles. Fifty years of Afghan rule were punctuated by regular clashes between Sunni and Shia Muslims.

Worse lay ahead, however. In 1819 the soldiers of Ranjit Singh, the charismatic leader of the Sikhs, already triumphant in northern India, took Srinagar. There was no resistance worth the name. Kashmiri historians regard the twenty-seven years of Sikh rule that followed as the worst calamity ever to befall their country. The principal mosque in Srinagar was closed, others were made the property of the state, cow-slaughter was prohibited and, once again, the tax burden became insufferable – unlike the Mughals, Ranjit Singh taxed the poor. Mass impoverishment led to mass emigration. Kashmiris fled to the cities of the Punjab: Amritsar, Lahore and Rawalpindi became the new centres of Kashmiri life and culture. (One of the many positive effects of this influx was that Kashmiri cooks much improved the local food.)

Sikh rule didn't last long: new conquerors were on the way. Possibly the most remarkable enterprise in the history of mercantile capitalism had launched itself on the Indian subcontinent. Granted semi-sovereign powers – i.e. the right to maintain armies – by the British and Dutch states, the East India Company expanded rapidly from its Calcutta base and, after the battle of Plassey in 1757, took the whole of Bengal. Within a few years the Mughal emperor at the Fort in Delhi had become a pensioner of the Company, whose forces continued to move west, determined now to take the Punjab from the Sikhs. The first Anglo-Sikh war in 1846 resulted in a victory for the Company, which acquired Kashmir as part of the treaty of Amritsar, but, aware of the chaos there, hurriedly sold it for 75 lakh rupees (10 lakhs = 1 million) to the Dogra ruler of neighbouring Jammu, who pushed through yet more taxes. When, after the 1857 uprising, the East India Company was replaced by direct rule from London, real power in Kashmir, and other princely states, devolved to a British Resident, usually a fresh face from Haileybury College, serving an apprenticeship in the backwaters of the empire.

Kashmir suffered badly under its Dogra rulers. The corvée was reintro-
duced after the collapse of the Mughal state and the peasants were reduced to
the condition of serfs. A story, unconfirmable, told by Kashmiri intellectuals
in the 1920s to highlight the plight of the peasants revolved round the
maharaja's purchase of a Cadillac. When His Highness drove the car to
Pehalgam, admiring peasants surrounded it and strewed fresh grass in front of
it. The maharaja acknowledged their presence by letting them touch the car.
A few peasants began to cry. 'Why are you crying?' asked their ruler. 'We are
upset,' one of them replied, 'because your new animal refuses to eat grass.'

When it finally reached the valley, the twentieth century brought new
values: freedom from foreign rule, passive resistance, the right to form trade
unions, even socialism. Young Kashmiris educated in Lahore and Delhi
were returning home determined to wrench their country from the stranglehold of the Dogra maharaja and his colonial patrons. When the Muslim
poet and philosopher Iqbal, himself of Kashmiri origin, visited Srinagar in
1921, he left behind a subversive couplet which spread around the country:

> In the bitter chill of winter shivers his naked body
> Whose skill wraps the rich in royal shawls.

Kashmiri workers went on strike for the first time in the spring of 1924.
Five thousand workers in the state-owned silk factory demanded a pay rise
and the dismissal of a clerk who'd been running a protection racket. The
management agreed to a small increase, but arrested the leaders of the protest.
The workers then came out on strike. With the backing of the British
Resident, the opium-sodden Maharaja Pratap Singh sent in troops. Workers
on the picket-line were badly beaten, suspected ringleaders were sacked on
the spot and the principal organiser of the action was imprisoned, then tortured to death.

Some months later a group of ultra-conservative Muslim notables in
Srinagar sent a memorandum to the British viceroy, Lord Reading, protesting the brutality and repression:

> Military was sent for and most inhuman treatment was meted out to the poor,
> helpless, unarmed, peace-loving labourers who were assaulted with spears, lances
> and other implements of warfare . . . The Mussulmans of Kashmir are in a mis-
> erable plight today. Their education is woefully neglected. Though forming 96

per cent of the population, the percentage of literacy amongst them is only 0.8 per cent . . . So far we have patiently borne the state's indifference towards our grievances and our claims and its high-handedness towards our rights, but patience has its limit and resignation its end.

The viceroy forwarded the petition to the maharaja, who was enraged. He wanted the 'sedition-mongers' shot, but the Resident wouldn't have it. As a sop he ordered the immediate deportation of the organiser of the petition, Saaduddin Shawl. Nothing changed even when, a few years later, the maharaja died and was replaced by his nephew, Hari Singh. Albion Bannerji, the new British-approved chief minister of Kashmir, found the situation intolerable. Frustrated by his inability to achieve even trivial reforms, he resigned. 'The large Muslim population,' he said, 'is absolutely illiterate, labouring under poverty and very low economic conditions of living in the villages and practically governed like dumb driven cattle.'

In April 1931 the police entered the mosque in Jammu and stopped the Friday *khutba* which follows the prayers. The police chief claimed that references in the Koran to Moses and Pharaoh quoted by the preacher were tantamount to sedition. It was an exceptionally stupid thing to do and, inevitably, it triggered a new wave of protests. In June the largest political rally ever seen in Srinagar elected eleven representatives by popular acclamation to lead the struggle against native and colonial repression. Among them was Sheikh Abdullah, the son of a shawl-trader, who would dominate the life of Kashmir for the next half-century.

One of the less well-known speakers at the rally, Abdul Qadir, a butler who worked for a European household, was arrested for having described the Dogra rulers as 'a dynasty of blood-suckers' who had 'drained the energies and resources of all our people'. On the first day of Qadir's trial, thousands of demonstrators gathered outside the prison and demanded the right to attend the proceedings. The police opened fire, killing twenty-one of them. Sheikh Abdullah and other political leaders were arrested the following day. This was the founding moment of Kashmiri nationalism.

At the same time a parturition was taking place on the French Riviera. Tara Devi, the fourth wife of the dissolute and infertile Maharaja Hari Singh – he had shunted aside the first three for failing to produce any children – gave birth to a boy, Karan Singh. In the Srinagar bazaar every second

person claimed to have fathered the heir-apparent. Five days of lavish entertainment and feasting marked the infant heir's arrival in Srinagar. A few
weeks later, public agitation broke out, punctuated by lampoons concerning
the maharaja's lack of sexual prowess, among other things. The authorities
sanctioned the use of public flogging, but it was too late. Kashmir could no
longer be quarantined from a subcontinent eager for independence.

The viceroy instructed the maharaja to release the imprisoned nationalist leaders, who were carried through the streets of Srinagar on the shoulders
of triumphant crowds. The infant Karan Singh had been produced in vain;
he would never inherit his father's dominion. Many years later he wrote of
his father:

> He was a bad loser. Any small setback in shooting or fishing, polo or racing,
> would throw him in a dark mood which lasted for days. And this would inevitably
> lead to what became known as a *muqaddama*, a long inquiry into the alleged inef-
> ficiency or misbehaviour of some hapless young member of staff or a servant . . .
> Here was authority without generosity; power without compassion.

On their release from jail, Sheikh Abdullah and his colleagues set about
establishing a political organisation capable of uniting Muslims and non-
Muslims. The All-Jammu and Kashmir Muslim Conference was founded in
Srinagar in October 1932 and Abdullah was elected its president. Non-
Muslims in Kashmir were mainly Hindus, dominated by the Pandits,
upper-caste Brahmins who looked down on Muslims, Sikhs and low-caste
Hindus alike, but looked up to their colonial masters, as they had to the
Mughals. The British, characteristically, used the Pandits to run the administration, making it easy for Muslims to see the two enemies as one.
Abdullah, though a Koranic scholar, was resolutely secular in his politics.
The Hindus might be a tiny minority of the population, but he knew it
would be fatal for Kashmiri interests if the Brahmins were ignored or per-
secuted. The confessional Muslims led by Mirwaiz Yusuf Shah broke away –
the split was inevitable – accusing Abdullah of being soft on Hindus as well
as those Muslims regarded by the orthodox as heretics. From the All-India
Kashmir Committee in Lahore came an angry poster addressed by the poet
Iqbal to the 'dumb Muslims of Kashmir'.

No longer constrained by the orthodox faction in his own ranks, Sheikh
Abdullah drew closer to the social-revolutionary nationalism advocated by

Nehru. He wasn't the only Muslim leader to do so: Khan Abdul Ghaffar Khan in the North-West Frontier Province, Mian Iftikharuddin in the Punjab and Maulana Azad in the United Provinces all decided to work with the Indian National Congress rather than the Muslim League, but it was not enough to tempt the majority of educated urban Muslims away from the Muslim League.

The Muslims had arrived in India as conquerors. They saw their religion as infinitely superior to that of the idol-worshipping Hindus and Buddhists. The bulk of Indian Muslims were nonetheless converts: some forced and others voluntary, seeking escape, in Kashmir and Bengal especially, from the rigours of the caste system. Thus, despite itself, Islam in India, as in coastal Africa, China and the Indonesian archipelago, was affected by local religious practices. Muslim saints were worshipped like Hindu gods. Holy men and ascetics were incorporated into Indian Islam. The Prophet Muhammad came to be regarded as a divinity. Buddhism had been especially strong in Kashmir, and the Buddhist worship of relics, too, was transferred to Islam, so that Kashmir is the home today for one of the holiest Muslim relics: a strand of hair supposedly belonging to Muhammad. The Koran expressly disavows necromancy, magic and omens, and yet these superstitions remain a strong part of subcontinental Islam. Many Muslim political leaders still have favourite astrologers and soothsayers.

Muslim nationalism in India was the product of defeat. Until the collapse of the Mughal empire at the hands of the British, Muslims had dominated the ruling class for over five hundred years. With the disappearance of the Mughal court in Delhi and the culture it supported, they were now merely a large religious minority considered by Hindus as lower than the lowest caste. There was an abrupt retreat from the Persian–Hindu cultural synthesis they had created, orphaning the scribes, poets, traders and artisans who had flourished around the old Muslim courts. The poet Akbar Allahabadi (1846–1921) became the voice of India's dispossessed Muslims, speaking for a community in decline:

> The Englishman is happy, he owns the aeroplane,
> The Hindu's gratified, he controls all the trade,
> 'Tis we who are empty drums, subsisting on God's grace,
> A pile of biscuit crumbs and frothy lemonade.

The angry and embittered leaders of the Muslim community asked believers to wage a jihad against the infidel and to boycott everything he represented. The chief result was a near-terminal decline in Muslim education and intellectual life. In the 1870s, Syed Ahmad Khan, pleading for compromise, warned Muslims that their self-imposed isolation would have terrible economic consequences. In the hope of encouraging them to abandon the religious schools where they were taught to learn the Koran by rote in a language they couldn't understand, in 1875 he established the Muslim Anglo-Oriental College in Aligarh, which became the pre-eminent Muslim university in the country. Men and women from all over northern India were sent to be educated in English as well as Urdu.

It was here, at the end of the 1920s, that Sheikh Abdullah had enrolled as a student. The college authorities encouraged Muslims to stay away from politics, but by the time Sheikh Abdullah arrived in Aligarh, students were divided into liberal and conservative camps and it was difficult to avoid debates on religion, nationalism and communism. Even the most dull-witted among them – usually those from feudal families – got involved. Most of the nationalist Muslims at Aligarh University aligned themselves with the Indian National Congress rather than the Muslim League, set up by the Aga Khan on the viceroy's behalf.

To demonstrate his commitment to secular politics, Sheikh Abdullah invited Nehru to Kashmir. Nehru, whose forebears were Kashmiri Pandits, brought with him Abdul Ghaffar Khan, the 'Frontier Gandhi'. The three leaders spoke at consciousness-raising meetings and addressed groups of workers, intellectuals, peasants and women. What the visitors enjoyed most, however, was loitering in the old Mughal gardens. Like everyone else, Nehru had a go at describing the valley:

> Like some supremely beautiful woman, whose beauty is almost impersonal and above human desire, such was Kashmir in all its feminine beauty of river and valley and lake and graceful trees. And then another aspect of this magic beauty would come into view, a masculine one, of hard mountains and precipices, and snow-capped peaks and glaciers, and cruel and fierce torrents rushing to the valleys below. It had a hundred faces and innumerable aspects, ever-changing, sometimes smiling, sometimes sad and full of sorrow . . . I watched this spectacle and sometimes the sheer loveliness of it was overpowering and I felt faint . . . It seemed to me dreamlike and unreal, like the hopes and desires that fill us and so

seldom find fulfilment. It was like the face of the beloved that one sees in a dream and that fades away on wakening.

Sheikh Abdullah promised liberation from Dogra rule and pledged land reform; Nehru preached the virtues of unremitting struggle against the empire and insisted that social reform could come only after the departure of the British; Ghaffar Khan spoke of the need for mass struggle and urged Kashmiris to throw fear to the wind: 'You who live in the valleys must learn to scale the highest peaks.'

Nehru knew that the main reason they had been showered with affection was that Abdullah had been with them. There was now a strong political bond between the two men, unlike as they were. Abdullah was a Muslim from a humble background whose outlook remained provincial and whose political views arose from a hatred of suffering and of the social injustice he perceived to be its cause. Nehru, a product of Harrow and Cambridge, was a lofty figure, conscious of his own intellectual superiority, rarely afflicted by fear or envy, and always intolerant of fools. He was a left-wing internationalist and a staunch anti-fascist. Yet the ties established between the pair proved vital for Kashmir when separatism took over the subcontinent in 1947.

In a hangover from Mughal days, and to make up for their lack of real power, the Muslims of India had developed an irritating habit of inflating their leaders with fancy titles. In this scheme Sheikh Abdullah became Sher-i-Kashmir, the Lion of Kashmir, and his wife Akbar Jehan Madri-i-Meharban, the Kind Mother. The Lion depended on the Kind Mother to impress famous visitors, to receive them during his frequent absences in prison, and to give him sound political advice. Akbar Jehan was the daughter of Harry Nedous, an Austro-Swiss hotelier, and Mir Jan, a Kashmiri milkmaid. The Nedous family had arrived in India at the turn of the last century and invested its savings in the majestic Nedous Hotel in Lahore – later there were hotels in Srinagar and Poona. Harry Nedous was the businessman; his brothers, Willy and Wally, willied and wallied around; his sister, Enid, took charge of the catering and her pâtisserie at their Lahore hotel was considered 'as good as anything in Europe'.

Harry Nedous first caught sight of Mir Jan when she came to deliver the milk at his holiday lodge in Gulmarg. He was immediately smitten, but she was suspicious. 'I might be poor,' she told him later that week, 'but I am not for sale.' Harry pleaded that he was serious, that he loved her, that he wanted to marry her. 'In that case,' she retorted wrathfully, 'you must convert to Islam. I cannot marry an unbeliever.' To her amazement he did so, and in time they had twelve children (only five of whom survived). Brought up as a devout Muslim, their daughter Akbar Jehan was a boarder at the Convent of Jesus and Mary in the hill resort of Murree. Non-Christian parents often packed their daughters off to these convents because the education was quite good and the regime strict, though there is evidence to suggest they spent much of their time fantasising about Rudolph Valentino.

In 1928, when a seventeen-year-old Akbar Jehan had left school and was back in Lahore, a senior figure in British Military Intelligence checked in to the Nedous Hotel on the Upper Mall. Colonel T.E. Lawrence, complete with Valentino-style headgear, had just spent a gruelling few weeks in Afghanistan destabilising the radical, modernising and anti-British regime of King Amanullah. Disguised as 'Karam Shah', a visiting Arab cleric, he had organised a black propaganda campaign designed to stoke the religious fervour of the more reactionary tribes and thus provoke a civil war. His mission accomplished, he left for Lahore. Akbar Jehan must have met him at her father's hotel. A flirtation began and got out of control. Her father insisted that they get married immediately; which they did. Three months later, in January 1929, Amanullah was toppled and replaced by a pro-British ruler. On 12 January, Kipling's old newspaper in Lahore, the imperialist *Civil and Military Gazette*, published comparative profiles of Lawrence and 'Karam Shah' to reinforce the impression that they were two different people. Several weeks later, the Calcutta newspaper *Liberty* reported that 'Karam Shah' was indeed the 'British spy Lawrence' and gave a detailed account of his activities in Waziristan on the Afghan frontier. Lawrence was becoming a liability and the authorities told him to return to Britain. 'Karam Shah' was never seen again. Nedous insisted on a divorce for his daughter and again Lawrence obliged. Four years later, Sheikh Abdullah and Akbar Jehan were married in Srinagar. The fact of her previous marriage and divorce was never a secret: only the real name of her first husband was hidden. She now threw herself into the struggle for a new Kashmir. She raised money to build schools for poor children and encouraged adult education in a state where the bulk of the population was illiterate. She also, crucially, gave support and advice to her husband, alerting him, for example, to the dangers of succumbing to Nehru's charm and thus compromising his own standing in Kashmir.

Few politicians in the 1930s believed that the subcontinent would ever be divided along religious lines. Even the most ardent Muslim separatists were prepared to accept a federation based on the principle of regional autonomy. In the 1937 elections the Congress Party swept most of the country, including the Muslim-majority North-West Frontier Province, where Ghaffar Khan's popularity was at its peak. The Muslim-majority provinces of the Punjab and Bengal remained loyal to the raj and voted for secular parties controlled by the landed gentry. Contrary to Pakistani mythology, separatism wasn't at this stage an aim so much as a bargaining tool to ensure that Muslims received a fair share of the post-colonial spoils.

The Second World War changed everything. India was included in Britain's declaration of war against Germany and the Congress Party was livid at His Majesty's government's failure to consult them. Nehru would probably have argued in favour of participating in the anti-fascist struggle provided the British agreed to leave India once it was all over, and London would probably have regarded such a request as impertinent. As it was, the Congress governments of each province resigned. Gandhi, who despite his pacifism had acted as an efficient recruiting-sergeant for the British during the First World War, was less sure what to do this time. A hardline ultra-nationalist current within the Congress led by the charismatic Bengali Subhas Chandra Bose argued for an alliance with Britain's enemies, particularly Japan. This was unacceptable to Nehru and Gandhi. But when Singapore fell in 1942, Gandhi, like most observers, was sure that the Japanese were about to take India by way of Bengal and argued that the Congress had to oppose the British empire, whatever the cost, in order to gain a position to strike a deal with the Japanese. The wartime coalition in London sent Stafford Cripps to woo the Congress back into line. He offered its leaders a 'blank cheque' after the war. 'What is the point of a blank cheque from a bank that is already failing?' Gandhi replied. In August 1942 the Congress leaders authorised the launch of the Quit India movement. A tidal wave of civil disobedience swept the country. The entire Congress leadership, including Gandhi and Nehru, was arrested, as were thousands of organisers and workers. The Muslim League backed the war effort and prospered. Partition was the ultimate prize.

When Nehru and Ghaffar Khan revisited Srinagar as Abdullah's guests in the summer of 1945 it was evident that divisions between the different nationalists were acute. The Lion of Kashmir had laid on a Mughal-style welcome. The guests were taken downriver on lavishly decorated *shikaras* (gondolas). Barred from gathering on the four bridges along the route, Abdullah's local Muslim opponents stood on the embankment, dressed in *phirens*, long tunics which almost touched the ground. In the summer months it was customary not to wear underclothes. As the boats approached, the male protesters, who had not been allowed to carry banners, faced the guests and lifted their *phirens* to reveal their pencils of creation, while the women turned their backs and bared their buttocks. Muslims had never protested in this way before, and have not done so since. Ghaffar Khan roared with laughter, but Nehru was not amused. Later that day Ghaffar Khan referred to the episode at a rally and told the audience how impressed he had been by the wares on display. Nehru, asked at a dinner the next day how he compared the regions he had visited most recently, replied: 'Punjabis are crude, Bengalis are hysterical and the Kashmiris are simply vulgar.'

The confessional movement was gaining strength, however. Mohammed Ali Jinnah, the founding father of Pakistan, had left the Congress in the 1930s partly because he was uneasy about Gandhi's use of Hindu religious imagery. He had then joined the Muslim League in a partially successful attempt to wrest it from the collaborationist landlords of the United Provinces. Jinnah had half-hoped, half-believed that Pakistan would be a smaller version of India, but one in which Muslims would dominate, with Hindus and Sikhs still living there and forming a loyal minority. Had a confederal solution been adopted this might have been possible, but once the decision to split had been accepted as irrevocable by the departing British, it was out of the question. Bengal and the Punjab were mixed provinces and so they, too, would have to be divided. As they were.

Crimes were committed by all sides. Those who were reluctant to abandon their villages were driven out or massacred. Trains carrying refugee families were attacked by armed gangs and became moving coffins. There are no agreed figures, but according to the lowest estimates, the slicing of the subcontinent cost nearly a million lives. No official monument marks the casualties of Partition, there is no official record of those who perished. Amrita Pritam, an eighteen-year-old Sikh, born and brought up in Lahore but now forced to become a refugee, left behind a lament in which she evoked the medieval Sufi poet and free-thinker, Waris Shah, whose love-epic *Heer-Ranjha* was (and is) sung in almost every Punjabi village on both sides of the divide:

> I call Waris Shah today:
> 'Speak up from your grave,
> From your Book of Love unfurl
> A new and different page.
> *One* daughter of the Punjab did scream
> You covered our walls with your laments.'
> Millions of daughters weep today
> And call out to Waris Shah:
> 'Arise you chronicler of our inner pain
> And look now at your Punjab;
> The forests are littered with corpses
> And blood flows down the Chenab.'

Kashmir is the unfinished business of Partition. The agreement to divide the subcontinent had entailed referendums and elections in the Muslim majority segments of British India. In the North-West Frontier Province, which was 90 per cent Muslim, the Muslim League had defeated the anti-Partition forces led by Ghaffar Khan. It did so by intimidation, chicanery and selective violence. The Muslim League never won a free election there again, and Ghaffar Khan spent much of the rest of his life – he died in the 1980s – in a Pakistani prison, accused of treason. His defeat seemed to prove that secular Muslim leaders, despite their popularity, were powerless against the confessional tide. Would Sheikh Abdullah be able to preserve a united Kashmir?

In constitutional terms, Kashmir was a 'princely state', which meant that its maharaja had the legal right to choose whether to accede to India or to Pakistan. In cases where the ruler did not share the faith of a large majority of his population it was assumed he would nevertheless go along with the wishes of the people. In Hyderabad and Junagadh – Hindu majority, Muslim royals – the rulers wobbled, but finally chose India. Jinnah began to woo the maharaja of Kashmir in the hope that he would decide in favour of Pakistan. This enraged Sheikh Abdullah. Hari Singh vacillated.

Kashmir's accession was still unresolved when midnight struck on 14 August 1947 and the Union Jack was lowered for the last time. Independence. There were now two armies in the subcontinent, each commanded by a British officer and with a very large proportion of British officers in the senior ranks. Lord Mountbatten, the governor-general of India, and Field Marshal Auchinleck, the joint commander-in-chief of both armies, made it clear to Jinnah that the use of force in Kashmir would not be tolerated. If it was attempted, Britain would withdraw every British officer from the Pakistan army. Pakistan backed down. The League's traditional toadying to the British played a part in this decision, but there were other factors: Britain exercised a great deal of economic leverage; Mountbatten's authority was resented but could not be ignored; Pakistan's civil servants hadn't yet much self-confidence. And, unknown to his people, Jinnah was dying of tuberculosis. Besides, Pakistan's first prime minister, Liaquat Ali Khan, an upper-class refugee from India, was not in any sense a rebel. He had worked too closely with the departing colonial power to want to thwart it. He had no feel for the politics of the regions that now comprised Pakistan and he didn't get on with the Muslim landlords who dominated the League in the Punjab. They wanted to run the country and would soon have him killed, but not just yet.

Meanwhile, something had to be done about Kashmir. There was unrest in the army and even secular politicians felt that Kashmir, as a Muslim state, should form part of Pakistan. The maharaja had begun to negotiate secretly with India and a desperate Jinnah decided to authorise a military operation in defiance of the British high command. Pakistan would advance into Kashmir and seize Srinagar. Jinnah nominated a younger colleague from the Punjab, Sardar Shaukat Hyat Khan, to take charge of the operation.

Shaukat had served as a captain during the war and spent several months in an Italian POW camp. On his return he had resigned his commission and joined the Muslim League. He was one of its more popular leaders in the Punjab, devoted to Jinnah, extremely hostile to Liaquat, whom he regarded as an arriviste, and keen to earn the title of 'Lion of the Punjab' that was occasionally chanted in his honour at public meetings. An effete and vainglorious figure, easily swayed by flattery, Shaukat was a chocolate-cream soldier. It was the unexpected death of his father, the elected prime minister of the old Punjab, that had brought him to prominence. He was not one of those people who rise above their own shortcomings in a crisis. I knew him well: he was my uncle. To his credit, however, he argued against the use of irregulars and wanted the operation to be restricted to retired or serving military personnel. He was overruled by the prime minister, who insisted that his loud-mouthed protégé, Khurshid Anwar, take part in the operation. Anwar, against all military advice, enlisted Pashtun tribesmen in the cause of jihad. Two extremely able brigadiers, Akbar Khan and Sher Khan from the 6/13th Frontier Force Regiment ('Piffers' to old India hands), were selected to lead the assault.

The invasion was fixed for 9 September 1947, but it had to be delayed for two weeks: Khurshid Anwar had chosen the same day to get married and wanted to go on a brief honeymoon. In the meantime, thanks to Anwar's lack of discretion, a senior Pakistani officer, Brigadier Iftikhar, heard what was going on and passed the news to General Messervy, the C-in-C of the Pakistan army. He immediately informed Auchinleck, who passed the information to Mountbatten, who passed it to the new Indian government. Using the planned invasion as a pretext, the Congress sent Nehru's deputy, Sardar Patel, to pressure the maharaja into acceding to India, while Mountbatten ordered Indian army units to prepare for an emergency airlift to Srinagar.

Back in Rawalpindi, Anwar had returned from his honeymoon and the invasion began. The key objective was to take Srinagar, occupy the airport and secure it against the Indians. Within a week the maharaja's army had collapsed. Hari Singh fled to his palace in Jammu. The 11th Sikh Regiment of the Indian army had by now reached Srinagar, but was desperately waiting for reinforcements and didn't enter the town. The Pashtun tribesman under Khurshid Anwar's command halted after reaching Baramulla, only an hour's bus ride from Srinagar, and refused to go any further. Here they embarked on a three-day binge, looting houses, assaulting Muslims and Hindus alike, raping men and women and stealing money from the Kashmir treasury. The local cinema was transformed into a rape centre; a group of Pashtuns invaded St Joseph's Convent, where they raped and killed four nuns, including the mother superior, and shot dead a European couple sheltering there. News of the atrocities spread, turning large numbers of Kashmiris against their would-be liberators. When they finally reached Srinagar, the Pashtuns were so intent on pillaging the shops and bazaars that they overlooked the airport, already occupied by the Sikhs.

The maharaja meanwhile signed the accession papers in favour of India and demanded help to repel the invasion. India airlifted troops and began to drive the Pakistanis back. Sporadic fighting continued until India appealed to the UN Security Council, which organised a ceasefire and a Line of Control (LOC) demarcating Indian and Pakistan-held territory. Kashmir, too, was now partitioned. The leaders of the Kashmir Muslim Conference shifted to Muzaffarabad in Pakistan-occupied Kashmir, leaving Sheikh Abdullah in control of the valley itself.

If Abdullah, too, had favoured Pakistan, there wouldn't have been much that the Indian troops could have done about it. But he regarded the Muslim League as a reactionary organisation and rightly feared that if Kashmir became part of Pakistan, the Punjabi landlords who dominated the Muslim League would stand in the way of any social or political reforms. He decided to back the Indian military presence, provided the Kashmiris were allowed to determine their own future. At a mass rally in Srinagar, Nehru, with Abdullah at his side, publicly promised as much. In November 1947, Abdullah was appointed prime minister of an emergency administration. When the maharaja expressed nervousness about this, Nehru wrote to him, insisting that there was no alternative: 'The only person who can deliver the goods in Kashmir is Abdullah. I have a high opinion of his integrity and his general balance of mind. He may make any number of mistakes in minor matters, but I think he is likely to be right in regard to major decisions. No satisfactory way out can be found in Kashmir except through him.'

In 1944 the National Conference had approved a constitution for an independent Kashmir, which began:

We the people of Jammu and Kashmir, Ladakh and the Frontier regions, includ-ing Poonch and Chenani districts, commonly known as Jammu and Kashmir State, in order to perfect our union in the fullest equality and self-determination, to raise ourselves and our children for ever from the abyss of oppression and poverty, degradation and superstition, from medieval darkness and ignorance, into the sunlit valleys of plenty, ruled by freedom, science and honest toil, in worthy participation of the historic resurgence of the peoples of the East, and the working masses of the world, and in determination to make this our country a dazzling gem on the snowy bosom of Asia, do propose and propound the fol-lowing constitution of our state . . .

But the 1947–8 war had made independence impossible, and Article 370 of the Indian Constitution recognised only Kashmir's 'special status'. True, the maharaja was replaced by his son, Karan Singh, who became the non-hereditary head of state, but it was a disappointed Abdullah who now sat down to play chess with the politicians from Delhi. He knew that most of them, apart from Gandhi and Nehru, would like to eat him alive. For the moment, though, they needed him. Since the split with the confessional element in the Jammu and Kashmir Conference, Abdullah had moved to the left. As the elected chief minister of Kashmir he pushed through a set of major reforms, the most important of which was the 'land to the tiller' legislation, which destroyed the power of the landlords, most of whom were Muslims. They were allowed to keep a maximum of 20 acres, provided they worked on the land themselves: 188,775 acres were transferred to 153,399 peasants, while the government organised collective farming on 90,000 acres. A law was passed prohibiting the sale of land to non-Kashmiris, thus preserving the basic topography of the region. Dozens of new schools and four hospitals were built, and a university was founded in Srinagar with perhaps the most beautiful location of any campus in the world.

These reforms were regarded as communist-inspired in the United States, where they were used to build support for America's new ally, Pakistan. A classic example of US propaganda is *Danger in Kashmir*, written by Josef Korbel. Korbel had been a Czech UN representative in Kashmir before he defected to Washington. His book was published by Princeton in 1954, and in the second edition, in 1966, he acknowledged the 'substantial help' of several scholars, including Mrs Madeleine Albright of the Russian Institute at Columbia University – his daughter.

In 1948 the National Conference had backed 'provisional accession' to India, on condition that Kashmir was accepted as an autonomous republic with only defence, foreign affairs and communications conceded to the centre. A small but influential minority, made up of the Dogra nobility and the Kashmiri Pandits, fearful of losing their privileges, began to campaign against Kashmir's special status. In India proper, they were backed by the ultra-right Jan Sangh (which in its current reincarnation as the Bharatiya Janata Party heads the coalition government in New Delhi). The Jan Sangh provided funds and volunteers for agitation against the Kashmir government. Abdullah, who had gone out of his way to integrate non-Muslims at every level of the administration, was enraged. His position hardened. At a public meeting in the enemy stronghold of Jammu on 10 April 1952, he made it clear that he was not willing to surrender Kashmir's partial sovereignty:

> Many Kashmiris are apprehensive as to what will happen to them and their position if, for instance, something happens to Pandit Nehru. We do not know. As realists, we Kashmiris have to provide for all eventualities . . . If there is a resurgence of communalism in India how are we to convince the Muslims of Kashmir that India does not intend to swallow up Kashmir?

Abdullah was mistaken only in his belief that Nehru would protect them. When the Indian prime minister visited Srinagar in May 1953 he spent a week trying to cajole his friend into accepting a permanent settlement on Delhi's terms: if a secular democracy was to be preserved in India, Kashmir had to be part of it. Nehru pleaded. Abdullah wasn't convinced: Muslims were a large minority in India even if Kashmiris weren't included. He felt that Nehru shouldn't be putting pressure on him but on politicians inside the Congress who were susceptible to the chauvinistic demands of the Jan Sangh.

Three months later, Nehru gave in to the chauvinists and authorised what was effectively a coup in Kashmir. Sheikh Abdullah was dismissed by Karan Singh and one of his lieutenants, Bakhshi Ghulam Mohammed, was sworn in as chief minister. Abdullah was accused of being in contact with Pakistani intelligence and arrested. Kashmir erupted. A general strike began which was to last for twenty days. There were several thousand arrests and Indian troops repeatedly opened fire on demonstrators. The National Conference claimed that more than a thousand people were killed: official statistics record sixty deaths. An underground War Council, organised by Akbar Jehan, orchestrated demonstrations by women in Srinagar, Baramulla and Sopore.

The unrest subsided after a month, but now Kashmiris were even more suspicious of India. The situation was no happier in Pakistani-controlled Kashmir, which had the additional disadvantage of being made up of the least attractive part of the old state, a barren moonscape. Appalling living conditions gave rise to large-scale economic migration. Today, more Kashmiris live in the English cities of Birmingham and Bradford than in Mirpur or Muzaffarabad. An Islamist Kashmiri sits in the House of Lords as a New Labour peer; another Kashmiri stood as a Tory candidate in the 2001 British general elections.

Sheikh Abdullah, detained for four years without trial, was released without warning one cold morning in January 1958. Declining the offer of government transport, he hired a taxi and was driven to Srinagar. Within days he was drawing huge crowds at meetings all over the country, which he used to remind Nehru of the promise he had made in 1947. 'Why did you go back on your word, Panditji?' Abdullah would ask, and the crowds would echo the question. By spring, he had been arrested again. This time the Indian government, using British colonial legislation, began to prepare a conspiracy case against him, his wife and several other nationalist leaders. Nehru vetoed Akbar Jehan's inclusion: her popularity made it inadvisable. The conspiracy trial began in 1959 and lasted more than a year. In 1962 the special magistrate transferred the case to a higher court with the recommendation that the accused be tried under sections of the Indian penal code for which the punishment was either death or life imprisonment.

In December 1963, with the higher court still considering the conspiracy charges, the single hair of the Prophet's head was stolen from the Hazrat Bal shrine in Srinagar. Its theft created uproar: an Action Committee was set up and the country was paralysed by a general strike and mass demonstrations. A distraught Nehru ordered that the strand of hair be found – and it was, within a week. But was it the real thing? The Action Committee called on religious leaders to inspect it. Faqir Mirak Shah, regarded as 'the holiest of the holy men', announced that it was genuine. The crisis abated. Nehru concluded that a lasting solution had to be found to the problem of Kashmir. He had the conspiracy case against Abdullah dropped, and the Lion of Kashmir was released after six years in prison. A million people lined the streets to mark his return: Nehru spoke of the necessity of ending hostilities between India and Pakistan.

Kashmir troubled Nehru's conscience. He met Abdullah in Delhi and told him that he wanted the problem of Kashmir resolved in his lifetime. He suggested that Abdullah visit Pakistan and sound out its leader, General Ayub Khan. If Pakistan was ready to accept a solution proposed by Abdullah, then Nehru would, too. For a start, India was prepared to allow free movement of goods and people across the ceasefire line. Abdullah flew to Pakistan in an optimistic mood. After a series of conversations with Ayub Khan he felt progress was being made. On 27 May 1964 he reached Muzaffarabad, the capital of Pakistani-controlled Kashmir, and was cheered by a large crowd. He was addressing a press conference when a colleague rushed in to inform him that All India Radio had just announced Nehru's death. Sheikh Abdullah broke down and wept. He cancelled all his engagements and, accompanied by Pakistan's foreign minister, Zulfiqar Ali Bhutto, flew back to Delhi to attend his old friend's funeral.

Fearing that there would be no peaceful solution without Nehru, Abdullah travelled around the world, trying to get international support, and was received in several capitals with the honours accorded a visiting head of state. His meeting with the Chinese prime minister Zhou Enlai ('Chew and Lie' in the ultra-patriotic sections of the Indian press) created a furore in India. And so, on his return, Abdullah was imprisoned again. This time he and his wife were sent to prisons far away from Kashmir. The response was the usual: strikes, demonstrations, arrests and a few deaths.

Encouraged by this, the military regime in Pakistan dispatched several platoons of irregulars in September 1965, hoping to spark off an uprising. As usual, they had misjudged the situation. The unrest was not an expression of pro-Pakistan sentiments. The Pakistan army crossed the Line of Control, aiming to cut Kashmir off from the rest of India. The military high command was confident. On the eve of the invasion, the self-appointed Field Marshal Ayub Khan had boasted that they might even be able to take Amritsar – the Indian town closest to Lahore – as a bargaining chip. A senior officer present (another of my uncles) muttered loudly: 'Give him a few more whiskies and we'll take Delhi as well.' The Indian army, caught by surprise, suffered serious reverses. They responded dramatically by crossing the Pakistan border near Lahore. Had the war continued, the city would have fallen, but Ayub Khan appealed to Washington for support. Washington asked Moscow to bring pressure on India and a peace agreement was signed in Tashkent under the watchful eye of Alexei Kosygin.

The war had been Bhutto's idea. Ayub Khan, publicly humiliated at home and abroad, sacked his foreign minister. Bhutto had always been the most awkward member of the government and, embarrassed at having to serve under a general, he had ratcheted up his nationalist rhetoric. Government ministers, fearing trouble, tended to avoid the universities, but a few years before this, in 1962, Bhutto had decided to address a student meeting on Kashmir at the Punjab University in Lahore, at which I was present. He spoke eloquently enough, but we were more concerned with domestic politics. We began to talk to each other. He was offended. He stopped in mid-flow and glared at us aggressively. 'What the hell do you want? I'll answer your questions.' I raised my hand. 'We're all in favour of a democratic referendum in Kashmir,' I began, 'but we would like one in Pakistan as well. Why should anybody take you seriously on democracy in Kashmir when it doesn't exist here?'

He glared at me angrily, but wouldn't be drawn, pointing out that he had only agreed to speak on Kashmir. At this point the meeting erupted, with everyone demanding a reply and chanting slogans. At one point Bhutto took off his jacket and challenged a heckler to a boxing match outside. This was greeted with jeers and the meeting came to an abrupt halt. That night Bhutto cursed us roundly as one drained whisky glass after another was hurled against the wall, an affectation he had picked up during an official trip to Moscow. Many months later he told me that the encounter had made him realise how powerful the students were.

A week after Bhutto's dismissal in spring 1966 – by which time I was a student in the UK – I received a phone call from J.A. Rahim, Pakistan's ambassador to France. He needed to see me in Paris the next day. He would pay my return ticket and offered the bribe of a 'sensational lunch'.

An embassy chauffeur picked me up at Orly and drove me to the restaurant. His Excellency, a cultured Bengali in his late fifties, greeted me with a conspiratorial warmth, which was surprising since we had never met. Halfway through the hors-d'oeuvres he lowered his voice and asked: 'Don't you think the time has come to get rid of the Field Marshal?' Concealing my surprise, not to mention fear, I asked him to elaborate. He raised his hand above the table, pointed two fingers at me and pulled an imaginary trigger. He wanted me to help organise Ayub Khan's assassination. My instinctive reaction was to forget the main course and leave. How could this be anything other than a set-up? Rahim ordered another bottle of Château Latour, courtesy of the Pakistan government. I pointed out the danger of removing an individual military leader while leaving the institution intact. In any case, I added, it would be difficult for me to organise the assassination from Oxford. He glared at me. 'Drastic action is needed,' he said, 'and you're just trying to avoid the issue. The army is enfeebled after this wretched war. Everyone is fed up. Remove him and anything is possible. I'm surprised at you. I don't expect you to do it yourself. One of your uncles is always boasting about the hereditary assassins in your villages who've acted for your family in the past.'

I tried to talk about Kashmir but Rahim wasn't interested. 'Kashmir,' he said, 'is irrelevant. It's the dictatorship we're after.' A week later, Rahim resigned his ambassadorship. A few months after that he turned up in London with Bhutto and summoned me to the Dorchester. I had heard that Bhutto was depressed, but there was no trace of it that day. Conscious of the shortness of life, he was the sort of man who was determined that it should flash by with brilliance, romance and verve. He could also be silly, arrogant, childish and vindictive – defects that cost him his life.

At one point, when Rahim was out of the room, I began to describe our lunch in Paris, but Bhutto already knew about it. He laughed and insisted that Rahim had just been testing me. Then he whispered: 'When you met Rahim in Paris did he introduce you to his new mistress?' I shook my head regretfully. 'I'm told she's very pretty and very young. He's hiding her from me. I was hoping you might have . . .' Rahim came back with a bulky typescript. It was the manifesto of the Pakistan People's Party, which he had drafted on Bhutto's instructions.

'Go into the next room, read it carefully and tell me what you think,' Bhutto ordered. 'I want you to become a founding member.' I was halfway through it when the author walked in with an apologetic smile. 'Bhutto wants to be alone. He's booked a call to Geneva. Did you know he's got a Japanese mistress there? Have you met her?' I shook my head. 'He's hiding her from me,' Rahim said. 'I wonder why.'

I finished reading the manifesto. It was strong on anti-imperialist rhetoric, self-determination for Kashmir, land reform, nationalisation of industry, but far too soft on religion. I couldn't associate myself with a party that wasn't 100 per cent secular and Rahim smiled in agreement, but Bhutto was angry and denounced us both. Later that evening, during dinner, I asked why he had embroiled the country in an unwinnable war. The reply was breathtaking. 'It was the only way to weaken the bloody dictatorship. The regime will crack wide open soon.'

Subsequent events appeared to vindicate Bhutto's judgement. In 1968 a prolonged uprising of students and workers finally toppled it. The traditional parties on the left had not grasped the importance of what was happening, but Bhutto put himself at the head of the revolt, promised that after the people's victory, they would 'dress the generals in skirts and parade them through the streets like performing monkeys', and prospered politically.

When I met him in Karachi in August 1969, he was in ebullient mood. The stopgap dictator had promised a general election and he was sure his party would win. Once again he mocked me for refusing to join. 'There are only two ways: mine or Che Guevara's. Are you planning to start a guerrilla war in the mountains of Baluchistan?'

Bhutto scored an amazing triumph in the 1970 election, but only in West Pakistan. In what was then East Pakistan and is now Bangladesh the nationalist leader Sheikh Mujibur Rahman and his Awami League won virtually every seat. Since 60 per cent of the population lived in East Pakistan, Mujib gained an overall majority in the National Assembly and expected to become prime minister. The Punjabi elite refused to hand over power and instead arrested him. General Yahya ('fuck-fuck' in Lahori Punjabi) Khan attempted to crush the Bengalis, and Bhutto, desperate for power, supported him. It was, as I have suggested in a previous chapter, his most shameful hour. A Bangladeshi government-in-exile was set up in neighbouring Calcutta. Millions of refugees poured into the Indian province of West Bengal and, finally, at the request of the Bengali leaders in exile, the Indian army moved into East Pakistan to be greeted by the population as liberators. Pakistan surrendered and Bangladesh was born.

Bhutto came to power in a truncated Pakistan, but the old game was over: in 1972, at the Indian hill resort of Simla, he agreed to the status quo in Kashmir and in return got back the 90,000 soldiers who had been captured after the fall of Dhaka in what had been East Pakistan. In Kashmir every political group, with the exception of the confessional Jamaat-e-Islami, was shocked by the brutalities inflicted on fellow Muslims in Bengal. Had a referendum been held at this point, a majority would have opted to remain within the Indian Federation, but Delhi refused to take the risk. Pakistan's reputation continued to sink when its third military dictator, the Washington implant Zia-ul-Haq, executed Bhutto in 1979 after a rigged trial. A large rally in Srinagar turned into a prayer meeting for the dead leader.

Sheikh Abdullah (released from prison on grounds of ill-health in the mid-1970s) had made his peace with Delhi and was again appointed chief minister in 1977, courtesy of Mrs Gandhi, who forced Congress yes-men in the Kashmir Assembly, themselves elected by dubious means, to switch sides and vote for him. The changeover was calm: Kashmiris were pleased at Abdullah's return, but mindful of the fact that Mrs Gandhi was calling the tune.

Abdullah seemed stale and tired; his time in prison had affected both his health and his politics. He now mimicked other subcontinental potentates by attempting to create a political dynasty. It's said that Akbar Jehan insisted he do so and that he was too old and weak to resist. At a big rally in Srinagar he named his oldest son, Farooq Abdullah – an amiable doctor, fond of wine and fornication, but not very bright – as his successor.

As he lay dying in 1982, Sheikh Abdullah told an old friend of a dream that had haunted him for the past thirty years. 'I am still a young man. I'm dressed as a bridegroom. I'm on horseback. My bridal party leaves our home with all the fanfare. We head in the direction of the bride's house. But when I arrive she's not there. She's never there. Then I wake up.' The missing bride, so it has alway seemed to me, was Nehru. Abdullah had never fully recovered from his betrayal.

In 1984 I asked Indira Gandhi about India's loss of nerve over Kashmir. She didn't offer any explanation for the failure to hold a referendum and agreed that 1979 might have been the time to take the risk, but, she reminded me with a smile, 'I was not in power that year. If I had been prime minister,' she added, 'I would not have let them hang Bhutto next door.'

When I met Sheikh Abdullah's son Farooq at a conclave of opposition parties in Calcutta, he was scathing about Delhi's failures, but still convinced that a referendum would not go Pakistan's way. 'She's getting too old,' he said about Mrs Gandhi. 'Look at me. Who am I? In Indian terms a nobody. A provincial politician. If she had left me alone there would have been no problems. Her Congressmen in Kashmir were bitter at having been defeated so they began to agitate, but for what? For power which the electorate had denied them. I met Mrs Gandhi a number of times to assure her that we were loyal, intended to remain so and wanted friendly relations with the centre. Her paranoia was such that she wanted one to be totally servile. That was impossible. So she gave the Kashmir Congress the green light to disrupt our government's functioning. It was she who made me a *national* leader. I would have been far happier left alone in our lovely Kashmir.'

When I passed this on to her, Mrs Gandhi snorted derisively. 'Yes, yes, I know that's what he *says*. He said similar things to me, but he acts differently. Tells too many lies. The boy is totally untrustworthy.' Meanwhile her 'sources' had informed her that Pakistan was preparing a military invasion of Kashmir. Could this be so? I doubted it. General Zia-ul-Haq was brutal and vicious, but he wasn't an idiot. He knew that to provoke India would be fatal. In addition, the Pakistan army was busy fighting the Soviet Union in Afghanistan. To open a second front in Kashmir would be the height of irrationality.

'I'm surprised at you,' she said. 'You of all people believe that generals are rational human beings?'

'There is a difference between irrationality and suicide,' I said (a judgement I have since had cause to revise).

She smiled, but didn't reply. Then, to demonstrate the inadequacies of the military mind, she described how after Pakistan's surrender in Bangladesh her generals had wanted to continue the war against West Pakistan, to 'finish off the enemy'. She overruled them and ordered a ceasefire. Her point was that in India the army was firmly under civilian control, but in Pakistan it was a law unto itself.

Later that evening – I was staying in Delhi – I received a phone call from a civil servant. 'I believe you had a very interesting discussion with the PM. We have an informal discussion club meeting tomorrow and would love you to come and talk to us.' The members of the club were civil servants, intelligence operatives and journalists from both the US and Soviet lobbies. They tried to convince me that I was wrong, that the Pakistani generals were planning an attack. After two hours of argument and counter-argument I began to tire. 'Listen,' I said, 'if you lot are preparing a pre-emptive strike against Zia or the nuclear reactor in Kahuta, that's your decision. You might even win support in Sind and Baluchistan, but don't expect the world to believe you acted in response to Pakistani aggression. It's simply not credible at the moment.' The meeting came to an end. Back in London I described these events to Bhutto's daughter, Benazir. 'Why did you deny that Zia was planning to invade Kashmir?' she interrupted.

Four months later Mrs Gandhi was assassinated by her Sikh bodyguards. A civil servant I met in Delhi the following year told me they had evidence linking the assassins with Sikh training camps in Pakistan set up with US

assistance with a view to destabilising the Indian government. He was sure
the US had decided to eliminate Mrs Gandhi in order to prevent a strike
against Pakistan that would have derailed the West's operation in
Afghanistan. Bhutto certainly believed that Washington had orchestrated the
coup which toppled him. He smuggled out a testament from his death-cell
which included Kissinger's threat to 'make a horrible example' of him
unless he desisted on the nuclear question. Many people in Bangladesh still
insist that the CIA, using the Saudis as a conduit, was responsible for Mujib's
downfall. Mujib's daughter Haseena, currently prime minister of
Bangladesh, was out of the country and thus the only member of the family
to survive. The US may or may not have been involved, but it was a remarkable hat-trick: in the space of a decade three populist politicians, each
hostile to US interests in the region, had been eliminated.

After the breakup of 1971, Pakistan appeared to lose interest in Kashmir
and South Asia as a whole. A young and ambitious State Department official visited the country in 1980, a year after Bhutto's execution, and advised
Zia to look towards the petrodollar surplus being accumulated by Saudi
Arabia and the Gulf states. Pakistan's large army was well positioned to
guarantee the status quo in the Gulf. The Arabs would pay the bill. Francis
Fukuyama's position paper, 'The Security of Pakistan: A Trip Report', was
taken very seriously by the military dictatorship. Officers and soldiers were
dispatched to Riyadh and Abu Dhabi to strengthen internal security.
Salaries were much higher there, and a posting to the Gulf was much
sought after. Pakistan also exported carefully selected prostitutes, recruited
from elite women's colleges. Islamic solidarity recognised no bounds.

With Islamabad's attention elsewhere, the Indian government could have
reached an amicable settlement in Kashmir. But during the 1980s India
interfered in the region with increasing ferocity, dismissing elected governments, imposing states of emergency, alternating soft and hard governors.
Delhi's favourite despot, Jagmohan, was responsible for the suppression of
the ultra-secular Jammu and Kashmir Liberation Front and the imprisonment and torture of its leader, Maqbool Bhat. Young Kashmiri men were
arrested, tortured and killed by Indian soldiers; women of all ages were
abused and raped. The aim was to break the will of the people, but instead
many young men now took up arms without bothering where they came
from.

I had met Bhat in Pakistani-controlled Kashmir in the early 1970s. He seemed equally hostile to Islamabad and New Delhi and determined to remake a Kashmir that was not a helpless dependant of either. He was a great admirer of Che Guevara, and when I talked to him, in the euphoric aftermath of the 1969 uprising in Pakistan that had led to the fall of Ayub Khan, he was dreaming of a quick victory in Kashmir. I suggested that the rickety enthusiasm of a tiny minority was not enough. He reminded me that every revolutionary group (Cuba, Vietnam, Algeria) had started off as a minority.

The Indian authorities arrested Bhat in 1976, and charging him with the murder of a policeman, sentenced him to death. He was kept in prison as a bargaining counter until 1984, when he was executed in response to the kidnapping and murder of an Indian diplomat by Kashmiri militants in Birmingham. The vacuum he left would soon be filled by the men with beards, infiltrated, armed and funded by Pakistan.

By the late 1990s, after years of intra-Muslim factional violence, Afghanistan had come under the control of the Taliban – themselves funded, armed and sustained by the Pakistan army. Pakistan itself was in the grip of corrupt politicians, and sectarian infighting was claiming dozens of lives each month. In India, the Congress Party had lost its hold on national politics, paving the way for the Hindu fundamentalist Bharatiya Janata Party (BJP). In Kashmir the number of armed Islamist groups multiplied as more and more veterans of the Afghan war came across the border to continue their fight for supremacy there. The main rivals were the indigenous Hizbul Mujahidin and the Pakistani-sponsored and armed Lashkar-i-Tayyaba and Harkatul Mujahidin. The groups killed each other's militants, kidnapped Western tourists, drove Kashmiri Hindus out of regions where they had lived for centuries, punished Kashmiri Muslims who remained stubbornly secular, and occasionally knocked off a few Indian soldiers and officials. Each group was willing when convenient to make terms with Delhi rather than combine with other groups to inflict punishment on the Indian government. Governor Jagmohan responded by making it as hard as he could for these Muslim groups to find new recruits. Night-long house-to-house searches became a part of everyday life. Young men were abducted by Indian soldiers, never to be seen again. In his self-serving memoirs, *Frozen Turbulence*, Jagmohan explained: 'Obviously, I could not walk barefoot in a valley full of scorpions. I could leave nothing to chance.' The result of his policy was to win support for the gunmen.

Kashmir was ruled, more or less unhappily, by Delhi until 1996, when Farooq Abdullah came back to power – most of the other parties boycotted the elections. Since then his collaboration with the BJP has destroyed his remaining reputation, and if a free election were permitted, his career as a politician would soon be over.

The Indian and Pakistani armies are among the largest in the world. In September 1998, the Pakistani high command decided to test Indian border defences in the virtually undefended Kargil-Drass region, a Himalayan wasteland 14,000 feet above sea-level where Kashmir meets Pakistan and China. The region is one of mountain ridges and deep valleys, with temperatures averaging −20°C; it is also an area colonised by wild yellow roses, which bloom for a month each summer; the petals are eaten by villagers, who believe the rose nourishes the body and heals the soul. Most of the villagers are Shi'ite Muslims or Buddhists who live quiet, harmonious lives, sharing, among other things, an aversion to the Sunni fundamentalist imports from next door. The Pakistani army, wholeheartedly backed by Nawaz Sharif's government, crossed the Line of Control accompanied, just as it had been in 1947 and 1965, by soldiers disguised as irregulars and Lashkar-i-Tayyaba contingents, and occupied several ridges and villages. The Indian army moved troops to the area from Srinagar and artillery duels became a daily nightmare for the locals.

Why had Pakistan embarked on an adventure of such obvious strategic futility? There was no possibility of triumphant entrances by victorious generals or politicians. Most Pakistani citizens, other than the Islamists, knew very little about what was happening in the mountains. Nor were they particularly interested in the fate of Kashmir. The real reasons for the war were ideological. Hafiz Mohammed Saeed, the head mullah of the Lashkar, told Pamela Constable of the *Washington Post*: 'Revenge is our religious duty. We beat the Russian superpower in Afghanistan; we can beat the Indian forces too. We fight with the help of Allah, and once we start jihad, no force can withstand us.' His argument was echoed by Pakistani officials. The Indians weren't as powerful as the Russians, and since they no longer possessed a nuclear monopoly in the region there was no danger that a limited war would escalate. Second, and more important, Pakistan's actions would internationalise the conflict and bring the United States 'on side', as in Afghanistan and the Balkans.

In the war-zone itself, India suffered initial reverses, then brought in more troops, helicopter gunships and fighter jets and began to bomb Pakistani installations across the border. If NATO could overfly borders without any legal sanction, so could they. By May 1999, as the yellow roses were about to bloom, the Indian army had retaken most of the ridges it had lost. A month later its forces were poised to cross the Line of Control. Pakistan's political leaders panicked and, falling back on an old habit, made a desperate appeal to the White House.

A US general was sent to Pakistan to have a quiet word with the military, and Nawaz Sharif was summoned to the White House. Clinton told him to withdraw all his troops, as well as the fundamentalists, from the territory they had occupied. Nothing was promised in return. No pressure on India. No money for Pakistan. Sharif capitulated. His information minister, Mushahid Hussain, had told the press just before the Washington visit that 'we did not start insurgency in Kashmir which is populous [sic], spontaneous and indigenous and we cannot stop it.' But they did. The dispute had indeed been internationalised, though not exactly as Pakistan had wanted. With China as the main enemy, Washington had dumped on Pakistan and was leaning heavily in India's direction.

In private, Sharif told the Americans that he supported a rapprochement with India and had resisted the Kargil war, but had been outmanoeuvred by the army. The lie went down well in Washington and Delhi, but angered the Pakistani high command. When he got home, Sharif hatched a plan to replace the commander-in-chief of the army, General Pervaiz Musharraf, with one of his placemen, General Khwaja Ziaudin, head of the Inter Services Intelligence (ISI). Sharif's brother Shahbaz made an unpublicised visit to Washington with Ziaudin in tow in order to get approval for Ziaudin's appointment. The two men were received at the White House, and the Pentagon and the CIA and made many rash promises.

On 11 October 2000, while Musharraf was on his way back from a three-day official visit to Sri Lanka, Nawaz Sharif announced his dismissal and Ziaudin's promotion. The authorities at Karachi airport were instructed to divert the general's plane to a tiny airstrip in the interior of Sind, where he would be taken into custody. But the army refused to accept Ziaudin's authority and the Karachi commander occupied the airport and ordered the plane to land. Musharraf was received with full military protocol. The army commander in the capital arrested the Sharif brothers and General Ziaudin. This was the first coup d'état carried out in the face of explicit American instructions to the contrary: in a statement issued three days before these events, Clinton had warned against a military takeover. In Pakistan the fall of the Sharif brothers was celebrated on the streets of every city.

Musharraf pledged to wipe out corruption and restore standards in public life; in an unguarded interview he stressed his affinity with Kemal Ataturk, the founder of secular Turkey. No restrictions were placed on the press or political parties. Nearly two years later, Musharraf's early anti-corruption zeal has dissipated. The fiercely incorruptible General Amjad was transferred from the Accountability Bureau to a military command in Karachi: he had amassed evidence revealing extensive corruption in every institution in the country. Supreme Court judges were for sale to the highest bidder (defence lawyers asked clients for six-figure sums as the 'judge's fee', payable before a trial began); many senior civil servants were on the payroll of big business and the narco-barons; businessmen pocketed bank loans worth billions of rupees; senior military officers had succumbed to bribery. Amjad insisted to no avail that the new regime clean up the armed forces. Unless retired and serving officers were tried, sentenced and punished, he believed, Pakistan would remain a failed state, dependent on foreign handouts and a black economy fuelled by narco-profits. His transfer shows that he lost this battle.

Many people in Pakistan had assumed that Musharraf would disarm the Islamists and restore a semblance of law and order in the big cities. Here, too, the regime has made little progress, because it underestimated Islamist penetration of the army. When I was in Lahore in December 1999, I was told about a disturbing incident. The Indians had informed their Pakistani counterparts that one of the peaks in Kargil-Drass was still occupied by Pakistani soldiers, contrary to the ceasefire agreement. A senior officer went to investigate and ordered the captain in charge of the peak to return to the Pakistani side of the Line of Control. The captain accused his senior officer and the military High Command of betraying the Islamist cause, and shot the officer dead. The Islamist officer was finally disarmed, tried by a secret court-martial and executed.

If, as is widely agreed, between 25 and 30 per cent of the army are Islamists, its reluctance to act against the *jihadis* is understandable: it is nervous of provoking a civil war. Musharraf has a serious problem – and it's not just his problem. The fundamentalists' boast that in ten years' time they will control the army and hence Pakistan conjures a deadly image: an Islamist finger on the nuclear trigger. This is what has concentrated minds in Washington, Delhi and Beijing, but so far with little to show for it.

Neither Pakistan nor India favours the cause of Kashmiri independence. Nor does Beijing, worried about the ramifications in Tibet. And yet independence is what the Kashmiri people appear to want. In the valley itself, Farooq Abdullah and his BJP chums, backed by Karan Singh, are plotting a Balkanisation of the province, dividing it into eight units along religio-ethnic lines. The J&K Liberation Front meanwhile has published a map showing its favoured boundaries for an independent Kashmir, made up of territory currently occupied by India, Pakistan and China. Hashim Qureshi, one of the leaders of the organisation, told me that they did not want all the paraphernalia of a modern state. They weren't interested in having an army. They would be happy for their frontiers to be guaranteed by China, India and Pakistan, so that Kashmir, the cause of three wars, could become a secular, multicultural paradise, open to citizens of both India and Pakistan.

At the moment it is a noble but utopian hope. The political landscape is exceptionally bleak. (A pamphlet issued by a *jihadi* group in Pakistan a few weeks ago calls for donations to fund the struggle: the total launch-fee for a jihad is Rs 140,000; the price of a Kalashnikov is given as Rs 20,000; a single bullet is Rs 35; a Kenwood wireless is Rs 28,000.)

11 September has not changed anything for the people who live here. The Jaish-e-Muhammad group carried out a brutal terrorist act in Srinagar a few days later. Over forty people were killed. It is the same group that, a few weeks later, killed a group of Christians in the Pakistani city of Bahawalpur. The reason this group cannot be disarmed is that it is a creation of Pakistani military intelligence. The links between official and unofficial are inextricable. In retaliation, India bombed a few targets inside Pakistani territory. The message was obvious. If the West can inflict punishment bombing on Afghanistan, then India can do the same to Pakistan. The terrorist attack on the Indian Parliament by one of these groups in December 2001 almost led to a war between the two countries. Pakistan

acted against the leaders of the fundamentalist armies, but the membership has ominously disappeared.

The chapter of South Asian history that opened with the Partition of 1947 needs to be closed. Most people want a durable peace. There are now three large states in the region: India, Pakistan and Bangladesh, with a combined population of well over a billion human beings. On the periphery there is Nepal, Bhutan and Sri Lanka. Linguistically diverse, the region shares a culture and a history in common. Economic and political logic dictates the formation of a South Asian Union, a voluntary confederation of republics. Within such a framework, where no state fears a challenge to its sovereignty, Kashmir could be guaranteed complete autonomy, as could the Tamil region in Sri Lanka. Shared sovereignty is better than none at all. A massive reduction in military expenditure and trade deals with China and the Far Eastern bloc could even benefit the continent as a whole. The empire prefers to play the role of supreme arbiter these days, but its solutions put its own interests first. It would make much more sense for the South Asian states and China to forgo the mediation of the empire and speak with each other directly. If they fail to do so they might discover, sometime later this century, that over the benign gaze of the empire, the forces of rampant capitalism are breaking up both China and India. Now there's a thought.

19

The colour khaki

Pakistan's fifty-four-year-old history has been a series of lengthy duels between general and politician, with civil servants acting as seconds for both sides. Statistics reveal the winner. Unaccountable bureaucrats and their tame politicians ran Pakistan for eleven years; the Army has ruled the country for twenty-nine years; while elected representatives have been in power for fifteen years. It is a dismal record. In the last analysis Pakistan's generals have remained loyal to the institution that produced them and its international backers rather than to any abstract ideas like democracy, Islam or even Pakistan. The present state is a truncated version of what existed between 1947 and 1970. The breakup of the old state and the defection of a majority of its population (to Bangladesh) was the direct outcome of a military refusal to recognise the will of the electorate. In the circumstances, the army's self-image as the only institution that holds the country together is somewhat grotesque.

When the Pakistan Army seized power in October 1999, there was some rejoicing at home and abroad. It was the fourth coup in as many decades, but the first that had occurred in the face of serious US displeasure. This, coupled with the pseudo-modernist rhetoric of the new military ruler and the removal of Nawaz Sharif – the country's most venal politician – encouraged a wave of amnesia. It was as if the army had either ceased to exist or been miraculously transformed. Liberal pundits in New York and Lahore lost their bearings while in the *London Review of Books* Anatol Lieven described Musharraf's administration as being 'the most progressive Pakistan has had in a generation'. The hermaphrodite community of Pakistan distanced itself from this absurd euphoria.

Hermaphrodites have long occupied an unusual place in South Asian culture. For centuries they were invited to weddings to sing bawdy songs and dance suggestively in the presence of both men and women. In a male-dominated society, their jokes and satires were made more acceptable by their special biological status: neither male nor female, they could address both genders with impunity. This permitted them a verbal sexual freedom denied to men and women at public performances in town and country.

In Pakistan, the hermaphrodite minstrels adapted to the *khaki* order by developing a sharp line in political satire. During the first three military dictatorships, many a wedding guest was stunned by their savage attacks on the generals. Less exalted army officers present laughed together with everyone else. After all, it was only the hermaphrodites and everyone knew that their critical view of politics was determined by their material needs. Whatever the reason, the courageous minstrels did not treat Musharraf's coup kindly. After 9/11, they would offer the following riddle to their audiences, to the accompaniment of some extremely vulgar miming: 'What's brown and jumps to attention immediately on being caressed by the white hand of a white man from a White House? General Busharraf.' The bulk of Pakistan's citizens were indifferent to the fate of their politicians and for good reason, but few harboured any illusions as to the role of the army. The instincts of the masses may have been more advanced than the wishful thinking of many liberal and left intellectuals, but the country's wandering hermaphrodite minstrels were ahead of both.

The Chief of Army Staff (COAS), General Pervaiz Musharraf, had taken over the country not merely to save his own position (he had been fired and replaced by the prime minister while on an official visit to Sri Lanka), but to re-assert military supremacy in the political life of the country. Pakistan's military leaders have never tolerated interference from civilian politicians for too long. The last elected leader (Zulfiqar Ali Bhutto) to believe that the army was firmly under his control had to be brutally disabused of the notion: on the orders of General Zia-ul-Haq, an erstwhile favourite whom Bhutto had pole-vaulted above the heads of five more deserving and more senior officers, he was removed from power in 1977 and hanged two years later. Nawaz Sharif was luckier. Washington organised his release from prison and ensured a comfortable exile in Saudi Arabia.

From the day he took over as 'chief executive' of Pakistan, Musharraf's first wish was to come to an agreement with Washington. But the Clinton administration, which had argued against a military take-over, was irritated by the unilateralist display on the part of a long-standing satrap and was in a deep sulk. Then came a regime-change in Washington, followed by the terror attacks of 9/11. The needs of the Empire now required the services of a frontline state and its tried and tested armed forces. And once again it was Afghanistan that required an urgent cleansing. (In 1978–9, the US had organised the destabilisation of a leftist regime in Kabul. Propaganda at the time stressed how communist co-education was wrecking the traditional subordination of Afghan women. On that occasion, the White House had decided to go for a jihad via Osama bin Laden and his cohorts and that war, too, had been mediated through a Pakistani dictator – the ill-fated General Zia-ul-Haq.[62] Western arms had ensured success.)

Now it was time to unravel the gains of the victory. Zia's successors had made sure that Afghanistan became a de facto Pakistani protectorate: the only foreign victory of an army accustomed to defeating its own citizens. But the Taliban protectorate had to be dismantled and Osama bin Laden captured 'dead or alive'. This time Western propaganda underlined the oppression of women as one of the principal crimes of the Taliban and, in a culture that has virtually outlawed history, few citizens could recall how, twenty years ago, both French *philosophes* and White House apparatchiks aggressively defended religious zealotry as a liberating force.

Mercifully for the Pentagon and the Defense Intelligence Agency, the army was already in power in Pakistan. Washington was spared the time and energy needed to organise a new coup. General Musharraf's hour had arrived. Overnight, he became *halal* and was soon being fêted by Bush and

---

62 Zia-ul-Haq, who masqueraded as an Islamist, had in reality been trained in Fort Bragg and was a favourite of the Defense Intelligence Agency (DIA). He had seen active imperial service in Jordan during the Black September of 1973 where he had led a bevy of mercenaries to crush a Palestinian uprising on behalf of Tel Aviv and the Jordanian king. Subsequently he donned a religious cloak to fight against the pro-Soviet regime in Afghanistan and to brutalise Pakistan's political culture. He was assassinated, together with the US Ambassador Arnold Raphael, when a military plane in which the pair were returning to Islamabad after watching military manoeuvres exploded in the sky in August 1988. The 'terrorists' were never discovered.

Blair in the White House and at 10 Downing Street. Reagan and Thatcher had welcomed Osama's friends in the same locations on previous occasions. Alliances and enemies had shifted, but the methods remained the same and it must have been reassuring to have the Pakistan army providing an institutional continuity. For its part, the army high command was united in the view that the born-again alliance with Washington was a severe blow against the Indian enemy.

The Pakistani civilian elite, too, was in jubilant mood. They might be a failed state but at least they were no longer pariahs. A new imperial war, with their very own army as the principal proxy and the whole country as a base of operations, meant they were needed again. That meant money and possibly a rescheduling of the country's debt. The more liberal wing of the elite dreamt of a permanent Pentagon–Musharraf axis that would destroy the hold of the dreaded Islamists in Pakistan, and this time for ever. Its representatives, overlooking how many times their illusions had been betrayed in the past, now travelled to Washington in order to plead that their region never be left unprotected again. Emissaries from the disgraced politicians Nawaz Sharif and Benazir Bhutto became familiar, if pathetic, figures at Foggy Bottom, urging junior functionaries of the State Department not to trust the Army.

Musharraf's own popularity became asymmetrical: the more he was appreciated by the State Department the less inclined he felt to undertake any serious measures at home. Like his uniformed predecessors he had promised to end corruption, reform the countryside, tax the middle classes, end poverty, educate the poor and restore real democracy. The Pakistani road to absolutism is always paved with the same intentions. Why were so many liberal commentators deceived? Partially it was desperation. They wanted to be deceived. Partially it was his rhetoric, replete with admiring references to Kemal Ataturk, that misled them. And partially it was Musharraf's socio-cultural background. Unlike most of the military high command, Musharraf was not of Punjabi stock. He had no links with the traditional landed elite that has dominated the country. Nor was he on the payroll of a heroin-millionaire or close to an untainted industrialist. He spurned the offer of political godfathers. He belonged to an educated and secular refugee family that had left India during the Partition of 1947 to find shelter in the Land of the Pure. After her son's rise to fame his mother casually revealed, in the course of a newspaper interview, how in the Fifties, during her own youth, she had been greatly influenced by progressive intellectuals such as Sajjad Zaheer and Sibte Hassan.[63] She never said that her views had been genetically transmitted to her boy, but despairing liberals are always in search of a straw.

Within a few months of the new regime there was a strong indication that nothing substantial would change. Musharraf had appointed a friend and colleague, General Amjad, to head the National Accountability Bureau (NAB) – an organisation designed to curb and punish corrupt officials, politicians and businessmen. Amjad is probably one of the few senior officers in the army with clean hands. His insistence on 'playing by the rules' had made him a maverick figure even as a junior officer. On one celebrated occasion he had, despite insistent requests, refused to allow a general to borrow the mess silver for a private dinner party. His colleagues, shocked by his probity, laughed at him in public while respecting him in private. Musharraf's decision to put him in charge of the NAB was far from light-hearted. Within a fortnight, Amjad had hired the services of a radical, non-establishment American lawyer, William F. Pepper, to track and unearth the money spirited abroad by Benazir Bhutto and her errant husband Asif Zardari, while in

---

63 The information had little impact in a country where its own history is barely taught in school or university. Sajjad Zaheer and Sibte Hassan were two of the finest literary critics of the subcontinent. Both had joined the Communist Party of India during the Thirties and were members of its Central Committee in 1947. After Partition, as senior communists of Muslim origin, they were despatched to Pakistan to help organise the Communist Party which had been denuded of its cadres, the bulk of whom consisted of Hindus and Sikhs. The intellectual skills of Sajjad Zaheer and Sibte Hassan did not transfer automatically to the organisational plane. Under pressure to achieve results (after the surreal putschist turn by the Cominform in 1948), both comrades went underground. Zaheer became a professor of Urdu literature and hid in our house. My mother's uncle, then Inspector-General of the country's police force, met him there accidentally and was charmed by him. Later both comrades participated in a half-baked attempt to take power in league with nationalist elements in the army. An unreliable brigadier lost his nerve and informed his superiors. A general and several junior officers were court-martialled, the Communist Party was banned and Sibte Hassan, Sajjad Zaheer and the poet Faiz Ahmed Faiz ended up in prison. The Inspector-General was not amused to see that his name was fifth on a list of notables to be executed without trial. He was even less pleased to discover that the friendly professor he had met during a family dinner had compiled the list. The Indian prime minister, Jawaharlal Nehru – a family friend of Zaheer – intervened and the latter was released and returned to India. It was quite bold of Musharraf's mother to claim friendship with two convicted 'traitors'.

occupation of the prime minister's house in Islamabad. Simultaneously, Amjad ordered the arrest of industrialists who had borrowed money from the banks and failed even to pay the interest; a list of politicians who had done the same was published in every newspaper. The naming and shaming was punishing psychologically, but not sufficient to deal with the cancer. Amjad told his boss that the only serious way to deal with the problem was to create at least one clean institution in the country. Only then would civil servants and politicians take them seriously. This meant arresting serving and former generals, admirals and air marshals who had been engaged in large-scale corruption. Amjad was ready to push through Operation Clean-Up, but Musharraf baulked at the scale of the enterprise. It would divide and demoralise the top brass of the armed services and could lead to a break-down in discipline and once discipline went they would be no different from a Middle Eastern or Latin American army where any Johnny, regardless of rank, thought he could seize power. Amjad disagreed. He was removed from the NAB and returned to the army as a corps commander. The imprisoned capitalists were released; the shamed politicians heaved a collective sigh of relief and it was, in every sense of the phrase, back to business as usual.

Musharraf was making his own history, but in heavily circumscribed conditions. Internationally, there was the overwhelming might of the American Empire and its financial institutions. At home he had to contend with the baggage handed down by previous military dictators. The decision to sideline General Amjad had appeased local capitalism; the appointment of a New York banker, Shaukat Aziz, as the country's finance minister pleased the World Bank and the IMF. But, there was still the problem of how the country should be governed. Like Generals Ayub and Zia before him, Musharraf now attempted to make himself impregnable. He temporarily discarded his uniform, dressed himself in native gear, replete with a stupid and unconvincing turban, and launched his political career at a 'public' rally which consisted of peasant-serfs bussed in to a large field by a friendly landlord in Sind. The referendum is a time-honoured weapon of dictators in search of legitimacy. The decision to rig a plebiscite in his own favour disillusioned most of his liberal supporters. The majority of the electorate stayed at home, while civil servants, soldiers and serfs trooped to the polls and transformed the chief executive into an elected president. Nothing changes.

The next stage was also preordained. What does a dictator need in order to provide a civilian façade to his regime? Top of the list is a political party, which the surrounding sycophants assure him is not a serious problem. A crude instrument can be easily fashioned from the debris of the past. Like an out-of-work courtesan, the Muslim League – the country's foundational party – is given a shower, provided with a wig, dusted with powder, heavily made up and shown to the ever-growing queue of potential suitors. General Ayub named his party the Convention Muslim League; General Zia preferred the Pakistan Muslim League and he allowed the Sharif family to manage it on his behalf; General Musharraf ditched the Sharifs and had to get a new name. A time-server suggested the Quaid-i-Azam[64] Muslim League and so it came about that this old–new entity entered the lists as the General's Party in the General's Election of October 2002. Its personnel were hardly unfamiliar. They consisted of bandwagon careerists of every stripe. In the countryside it was still the old landed gentry, eager to please the new ruler. In the town it was local notables who had accrued a great deal of money (usually through illegal means) and had become procurers of power and influence. Whereas in the past a father or uncle had supported Ayub or Zia, now the son or son-in-law was eager to act as a prop for Musharraf. In the face of mass apathy the bureaucracy, past masters in the art of electoral manipulation, set out to ensure the required outcome.

The results of the *khaki* election were much closer than anticipated. Despite the low turn-out (under 20 per cent according to independent observers) and skilful ballot-rigging, the official Muslim League (Quaid-i-Azam) failed to secure an overall majority in the National Assembly: they won 115 seats out of 324. The Pakistan People's Party (the PPP, under Benazir Bhutto) secured 80 seats, and the remnants of the Muslim League that had remained loyal to Nawaz Sharif retained 19 seats. It was the Islamists who scored a really big hit. Their united front, the Muttahida

---

64 Quaid-i-Azam (the Supreme Leader or Die Grossen Führer) was the appellation inflicted on Mohammed Ali Jinnah, the founding father of Pakistan, by his devoted fans. The title stuck and is today almost better known than the name: Jinnah is usually referred to in Pakistani publications as the Quaid.

Majlis Amal (MMA – Unified Action Conference), gained the highest ever complement of Islamist parliamentarians in the history of the Islamic Republic. Bedecked in colourful turbans and wearing long beards, they had changed the complexion of parliamentary politics. True, they were helped by the first-past-the-post system, but this had been inherited from the mother of democracies where Margaret Thatcher and Tony Blair have both benefited from it without too many complaints. More importantly, the MMA emerged as the largest political force in the North-West Frontier Province (NWFP) and a dominant influence in Baluchistan, the two regions bordering Afghanistan: the provincial governments in Peshawar and Quetta are presided over by Islamist chief ministers.

Power brokers acting on behalf of Musharraf finally managed to organise a rickety coalition government at the centre. A block of PPP Members of the National Assembly was offered inducements in the shape of senior ministries in the new cabinet and detached from the parent organisation. Mir Zafarullah Khan Jamali, a Baluch landlord and a hockey enthusiast, who supervised the brutal repression of peasants in 1977 (ten were killed in clashes with the police), was anointed as the new prime minister. A couple of decades earlier, Jamali had worked really hard to achieve the same position under General Zia, but Zia was not keen on hockey and preferred to employ the cricket-loving Nawaz Sharif as his factotum.

Given that 70 per cent of Musharraf's new cabinet (including Jamali) had, not so long ago, featured prominently on General Amjad's list of corrupt politicians, the widespread public cynicism was hardly a surprise. Far from regenerating democracy, the *khaki* election has bared the sordid reality of Pakistani politics and a large majority feels both disenfranchised and alienated from those who govern on its behalf.

The election campaign itself was largely lacklustre, if not totally apolitical. The mainstream parties did not differ from each other on ideology or practical policies on either the domestic or the international level. The People's Party had long abandoned its populism. Benazir Bhutto, wanted in Pakistan on charges of corruption, attempted to rule the roost from her base in Dubai. Her chosen proxy, Makhdoom Amin Fahim, is a *Pir*-cum-landlord from Sind – politician and religious divine in one, but hardly a social liberal.

Uniquely, even for Pakistan, all his four brothers-in-law are the Koran.[65] Like the different Muslim Leagues on offer, the PPP was concerned with power as a means to offer patronage and enlarge its clientele. The Islamist alliance had no disagreements on the IMF prescriptions for the economy (there is, after all, a neo-liberal reading of the Koran), but they campaigned vigorously in defence of Islamic laws and against the US presence in the region. There was hardly a day without a newspaper headline highlighting MMA leader Maulana Fazlur Rehman's hostility to US troops: 'Fazl demands expulsion of US commandos from tribal areas', 'West bent on initiating civilisations clash: Fazl', 'Fazl says sovereignty mortgaged to US', 'Fazl demands halt to US army operations', 'Fazl urges US troops withdrawal', 'MMA vows to block hunt for al-Qaeda', etc. Much of this was pure bluster, but it proved to be helpful electorally. The Maulana has admitted that it was not religion that won him new support, but his foreign policy stance. During his discussions with Musharraf, he declared his willingness to establish a coalition with himself as prime minister. When the general pointed out that his anti-Americanism posed a serious problem, the cleric is reported to have said: 'Don't worry about that now. We've worked with the Americans in the past. Make me prime minister and I'll sort everything out.' The offer was declined.

The MMA is a six-party alliance, with the Jamaat-Ulema-Islam (JUI – Party of Islamic Scholars) and the Jamaat-e-Islami (JI – Islamist Party) as its two main pillars. Both parties have been actively engaged in politics for several

---

65 Fahim's family claims descent from the first Muslims to enter the subcontinent, the cohort of the Muhammad bin Kasim who took Sind in 711. Since women in early Islam – prior to the codification of the *Shari'a* – both owned and shared inherited property equally, this tradition also took root in parts of Sind. In order to preserve family property, the Sindhi landowners who observed this unusual custom needed to prevent the women from marrying outside the family. This was not always simple and could lead to a parcellisation that destroyed a landholding. An ingenious solution was devised. Young women were to be married off to the Koran (similar to nuns who became brides of Christ; they could, at least, fantasize with the aid of the crucifix, but in the Muslim case the marriage was to The Book, which despite bordering on the surreal restricted the possibility of fantasies). This preserved their virginity, which in turn was purifying and provided them with magical powers to heal and cure, but above all ensured that the property remained under the control of men. The problems posed by the four sisters of the PPP leader were disposed of in this fashion. It is difficult sometimes not to sympathise with the Wahhabi contempt for all this nonsense.

decades. Traditionally, the JUI considered itself anti-imperialist and was, in the Seventies, under the leadership of Maulana Mufti Mahmood (Fazlur Rehman's father), involved in coalition governments with radical secular parties. Its strength was concentrated in the frontier provinces of NWFP and Baluchistan. It was always hostile to the JI, regarding it as an instrument of the US and Saudi embassies in Islamabad. And it had opposed the military dictatorships of both Ayub and Zia. Mufti Mahmood had, on occasion, visited Moscow and Beijing to attend peace conferences. His own death preceded the collapse of the communist world by a few years. His son inherited the organisation. As a student Fazl had dabbled in poetry, writing verses in both Pashto and Urdu and declaring publicly that the left-wing Faiz Ahmed Faiz was his favourite poet. After his father's death he continued the old man's policies. In the mid-Nineties he worked closely with Benazir Bhutto's government, but whereas the farthest old Mufti had gone was making sure that he collected his dollar *per diems* at international conferences, the son (like Benazir Bhutto and her consort) was, as befitted the new times, more market-oriented. In return for actively supporting Ms Bhutto, he demanded and obtained his pound of flesh in the shape of a lucrative diesel franchise covering large parts of the country and, after the Pakistan–Taliban victory, Afghanistan as well. This earned him the sobriquet of Maulana Diesel. Soon the rotund, bearded and cheerful Diesel had become a great favourite of Benazir's interior minister, General Naseerullah Babar, the architect of the Taliban triumph in Kabul. Fazlur Rehman's political, ideological and commercial links with the Taliban leadership always remained close. This also enabled him to outflank his local rivals, the Jamaat-i-Islami, whose pawn, Gulbuddin Hekmatyar (a great 1980s' favourite of Ronald Reagan and Margaret Thatcher), had been effectively sidelined by the bearded *wunderkind* in Kabul.

Then came 11 September. In its wake, the bulk of the Taliban accepted Musharraf's advice and left Afghanistan. Fazlur Rehman was livid, but powerless. He had run out of diesel. Many of the Taliban returnees swelled the ranks of the JUI and other Islamist organisations. In Pakistan, the JUI took the lead in organising mass rallies against the 'foreign occupiers'. It was Fazlur Rehman who realised that if the Islamists remained divided, they could be wiped out electorally. The alliance was his initiative and he was duly elected as its Secretary-General, even though at forty-nine he is fifteen years younger than his main coalition rival, Qazi Hussain Ahmed.

Qazi Hussain's election as amir of the Jamaat-e-Islami marked a generational shift in an organisation that had remained under the control of its founder Maulana Maudoodi and his deputy Mian Tufail since its foundation in 1941. Where the JUI was populist, had support in the villages and collaborated with the left, the JI was built on the Leninist model. It was an organisation of cadres whose recruits were both literate and carefully vetted. Most of them were students from urban petty-bourgeois backgrounds; many had been tried and tested in campus struggles with opponents of every variety. During the 1960s and 1970s, various factions of the left dominated the schools and universities, and it was the left too which was at the forefront of the Action Committees, which had led the struggle in the semi-insurrection of 1968–9 that had toppled the dictatorship. To support the JI in those days required a real commitment to its cause and its motto: 'religion is our politics and politics is our religion'.

Qazi Hussain was a leader of the JI student faction in Islamia College, Peshawar and his formative years were dominated by battles against the left, which sometimes became physical. He joined the parent body in 1970, a decisive year in Pakistani history. The JI's branch in East Pakistan collaborated fully with the army during the attempt to destroy the Bengali nation. Their cadres in Dhaka, Chittagong and Sylhet compiled lists of 'undesirables' for military intelligence, which were then used to physically eliminate the opposition. 'Chairman Mao supports us, not you' was a taunt they regularly hurled at their opponents on the Bengali left at the time. China and the United States had supported the Pakistan Army's assault on its own country in order to nullify a dramatic election victory by the Bengali nationalist Awami League. If, in the past, the Jamaat had believed that it and it alone could defend the 'ideology of Pakistan' it was now forced to concede that another institution possessed more battalions. Neither ideology nor physical force could prevent the breakup of Pakistan. The army's attempt to crush East Pakistan backfired badly. The surgical Indian intervention was successful only because the overwhelming majority of Bengalis greeted the Indian troops as liberators. Nor did the Indians overstay their visit. A few years later attempts by the Indian Foreign Office to pressure Dhaka were greeted by giant demonstrations united by a single chant: 'We are neither Sikkim, nor Bhutan, but Bangladesh, Bangladesh!'

The effect of all this on the JI was to draw it closer to the intelligence apparatuses of the state. After General Zia seized power in 1977 and decided to fight the US jihad in Afghanistan wearing Islamist colours, the JI became the main ideological prop of the regime. The JUI, meanwhile, opposed Zia vigorously and many of its leaders and members were imprisoned as a result. Qazi Hussain defended the new turn. His skills were noticed by his superiors and he began to be promoted within the JI apparatus. A lecturer in geography by training, he abandoned the low-paid chores of the academy after three years and threw himself at the mercy of the market. It was an astute move. His Popular Medical Store in Soekarno Square, Peshawar became an informal meeting point for local JI cadres, but, more importantly, it was also a successful commercial operation. As his business prospered he expanded, first establishing a Popular Medical Laboratory and later twinning it to a Popular X-Ray Clinic.[66] Was the recurring word an early indication of a suppressed desire for a Popular Jamaat-e-Islami? His enterprises were certainly popular. Profits rose and some, one assumes, were ploughed back into the JI, but could his entrepreneurial talents be transferred to a political organisation? Could a vanguard party that had always prided itself on its elite character now be re-branded and marketed in a more popular style? This was the task that Qazi Hussain now set himself. He knew that in politics as in business there is always an element of risk when you decide to enlarge your outfit. His decision to join an alliance of Islamist parties must have been as carefully calculated as the size of his own regulation pure-white beard, in marked contrast to the wilder, salt-and-pepper version sported by Maulana Diesel.

---

66 These medical facilities undoubtedly made a handsome profit, but they also served a useful political function. The poor were sometimes provided with free medicines and treatment, which they naturally identified with the JI. In Cairo last year, an Islamist parliamentarian boasted of how his organisation controlled the leadership of the doctors' union. We were conversing in his clinic where a majority of those waiting to see him were the Cairene poor. Like some sections of the Latin American church, these Islamists try and provide a substitute for the dismantled welfare functions of the state. Their efforts can only be limited, but the psychological impact they have in the poor quarters should not be underestimated.

But can a bearded provincial government do anything except rage? Incapable of serious opposition to either Musharraf or his backers in Washington, the MMA concentrates its fire against women. It has declared its intention to ban cable channels and co-education and institute the *shari'a* in the provinces under their control. Given the disaster that befell a more extreme version of the same policies in neighbouring Afghanistan, this could be pure rhetoric designed to keep their followers inebriated while embarrassing the occupant of President's House. The MMA's triumph may or may not have been the result of some independent campaigning by sections of the ISI, but its effect has undoubtedly been to put pressure on the regime to release Islamist militants accused of killing fellow-Muslims, indigenous Christians and foreigners. They had been imprisoned when Musharraf joined the 'war against terror,' but some of the most diehard Sunni terrorists have been freed from prison.

More striking still was the MMA's success in dragooning the entire newly elected National Assembly (with two exceptions) to stand with bowed heads and observe a minute's silence in memory of the 'martyred Aimal Kansi', whose body was returned for burial by the US after receiving a lethal injection in a federal penitentiary.[67] Prior to this, 70,000 people had attended the funeral prayers in Quetta, the capital of Baluchistan. These, too, had been organised by the MMA.

One reason for the MMA's ideological offensive is that on domestic policy issues there is little that divides them from the Muslim League or the

---

67 The case itself is not without interest. Aimal Kansi and his father were recruited in Baluchistan to work for the CIA during the First Afghan War (1979–89). Once US aims in the region had been accomplished it dumped most of its unofficial agents, while continuing to work with and through the Inter Services Intelligence. Kansi's family felt betrayed. Perhaps they were expecting a pension. Kansi decided to avenge the insult. He flew to the United States, targeted two senior CIA officials in Langley, Virginia, shot them dead and flew back to Pakistan. Whatever else, Kansi was a well-trained agent and the CIA deserves the credit. But a big reward was offered for his capture and he was ultimately betrayed by his brother-in-law, captured by the ISI and handed over to the US authorities. He did not deny the crime, was found guilty and sentenced to death. Was it a private intra-CIA grudge? What made him a martyr? And why did the National Assembly mourn him? Pakistan, after all, has not outlawed capital punishment, so it could hardly be seen as a liberal protest. The simple answer is that the MMA's success has worried its opponents and they think they can defeat the Islamists on their own ground. Bhutto *père* made a similar error in the 1970s and paid the price.

People's Party. All three have abased themselves before the market. None offers even a moderate social alternative to the existing system. None is capable of mobilising support to defend even the most elementary needs of the population, let alone social rights that were taken for granted. A striking example of this can be seen in the failure of the political parties to defend a two-year struggle being waged by tenants working on state farms leased to the army. Rarely has an event spotlighted the bankruptcy of traditional politics in Pakistan so vividly.

Almost a hundred years ago, the British colonial administration leased what were then known as 'Crown lands' and set up military farms in the Punjab to produce grain and dairy products at subsidised prices for the British Indian Army. After Partition, the management of the farms in Lahore, Okara, Sahiwal, Khanewal, Sargodha and Multan (largely in Southern Punjab) passed on to the Ministry of Defence and the Government of the Punjab. The army controlled 26,274 acres; the remaining 32,000 acres were leased to the Punjab Seed Corporation. The tenant families who have worked the farms to feed and clothe the army are the direct descendants of the tenants who were first taken there in 1908. The de facto merger of army and state on virtually every level has meant that the generals in *khaki* act as a collective landlord, the largest in the country, determining the living conditions of just under a million tenants. Forty per cent of them are Christians: mosques and churches function side by the side. The religious parties have failed miserably in these regions and the peasants have, since the Seventies, tended to vote for the People's Party.

Not any longer. Globalisation arrived over four years ago. The authorities, *khaki* and civilian, have been attempting to loosen the grip of the tenants over the land and the produce by offering short-term contracts and replacing '*battai*' (whereby the tenants are allowed one-half of what they produce) by cash-rents. Till now, the colonial administration's Punjab Tenancy Act of 1887 has safeguarded their rights: under the terms of this Act male tenants and their direct descendants who had cultivated the land for more than two generations (twenty years) had the right of permanent occupancy. It was illegal to eject them from the land.

The aim of the 'modernisation' in Okara and Sargodha – just as in Rio Grande de Sul – is deregulation, privatisation and the destruction of tenant solidarity. And this after the managers had spent the whole of the 1990s ordering excessive use of fertilizers, pesticides and blaming the tenants when the yields were reduced. The functionaries of the *khaki* state bullied, cheated and mistreated their tenants: the latter were denied permission to construct brick dwellings, their women were molested, they required management approval to electrify their villages or to build schools and roads for which state subsidies were neither offered nor demanded. The corrupt and callous managers had institutionalised a system of bribery. The tenants became embroiled in a growing debt burden. The exploitation was ruthless. Its unconcealed purpose was to drive the tenants off the land, so that it could be divided into private landholdings. Many serving and retired generals and brigadiers had long viewed these lands with greed-filled eyes; some of them had only joined the army in order to use it as a base for the primitive accumulation of property. Others felt they had done their service to the state and wanted to retire as gentleman farmers. They reassured each other that, when the time came, they would, of course, re-employ the evicted tenants as farm-serfs. It would be better for everyone. Hardly surprising that in these circumstances many tenants realised that conditions on the state farms had been qualitatively better during British rule. It was an undeniable fact. There was usually a method to late-colonial plunder. Post-colonial looting, regardless of the continent, has always been anarchic.

Despite the misery inflicted on their families, the tenants defied all attempts to divide them along religious lines and remained united in a single body: the Anjuman-i-Muzaireen Punjab (Punjab Tenants Organisation), which was set up in 1996. When I met two of their leaders, Dr Christopher John (Senior Vice-President) and Younis Iqbal (General Secretary), in Lahore in December 2002, both stressed that religious divisions had played no part whatsoever in their conflict with the state. Church and mosque had alternated as meeting places and on these occasions, as Iqbal told me with a smile, 'You couldn't tell the difference between a Muslim tenant and a Christian tenant.'

The story I heard was remarkable. In an unnoticed corner of Pakistan a chamber epic was in progress: the GHQ of the Pakistan Army versus a tenant organisation. The army decided to change the status of its employees. In June 2000, without any consultations whatsoever, the *khaki* landlords announced the conversion from a system of shared-produce to cash-rents. The tenants were outraged. Every evening, there were informal assemblies to discuss the resistance. These involved the entire village: women and children were to play a leading role in this rural *intifada.*

Angered by the daily harassment, the tenants refused to defend the status quo. They retaliated by demanding complete ownership of the land. Their slogan, 'Malkiyat ya Maut' ('Ownership or Death'), echoed that of similar struggles in other continents over the last few centuries. The first public protest took place on 7 October 2000: a four-hour sit-in on the lawn of the office of the Deputy Commissioner (the second most-powerful post-colonial bureaucrat) of Okara by a thousand tenants protesting the new scheme. Two days later, the Deputy Director of the Military Farms rang the local police chief and informed him that the tenants were threatening violence and had, in some villages, prevented the managers from removing (i.e. pilfering) wood. The Frontier Constabulary and the Elite Force Rangers (whose main function is to prevent smuggling on the border with India) arrived in the village and began to mistreat the tenants. As women and children saw their fathers, brothers and husbands being abused and kicked, they came out of their homes and began to hurl stones at the police. A number of tenant activists were captured and imprisoned. As news of this confrontation spread to neighbouring villages, the protests began to grow. Attempts by the authorities to divide and buy off tenants were a miserable failure.

During the first six months of 2002, the Rangers opened fire on tenants, killing some of them, and arrested some organisers and beat up others in full view of their families. Women – Christian and Muslim – carrying wooden bats (used to beat clothes while they were washed) marched to Okara and surrounded the police station. Nothing like this had been seen before and the army soon realised that, short of a massacre, it could have a protracted struggle on its hands. And a massacre of Christian peasants might be misread in Washington, where a fundamentalist Christian regime was in power and 'civilizational' concerns were high on the ideological agenda. On 9 June 2002 an armed gang of a thousand policemen and Rangers surrounded the village of Pirowal. The siege lasted for seven hours, but the police failed to capture the organisers, despite threats to burn the entire cotton crop of the village. They had underestimated the power of peasant solidarity.

In a sharply worded editorial the Karachi daily, *Dawn,* commented on 24 June 2002:

To win back the confidence of the restive and distraught farmers, the police force sent to harass and terrorise them should be withdrawn immediately and any ill-conceived notion of teaching them a 'lesson' must be abandoned. Cases should be registered against government and farm management officials who ordered the police action that led to deaths. . . . Once these confidence-building measures have been taken, the government should sit down and negotiate with the tenants, perhaps through the Punjab Tenants Organisation, on how to grant the owner-ship rights due to them.

The generals ignored the advice of a newspaper that has usually been sympathetic to their needs. Instead, leaders of the Punjab Tenants Organisation were arrested and the harassment and siege of the villages continued. As did the struggle. While the mainstream political parties have ignored the conflict, it has been supported by many independent groupings, one of which, Asr (Impact), organised a successful solidarity conference and public demonstration in Lahore in mid-December.

Musharraf's new status as the trusted ally of the West was now used against the tenants. Some of their leaders were charged under the new 'anti-terrorist' legislation. While releasing the real terrorists, most of whom have, at one time or another, been on the payroll of the military intelligence services, the men in *khaki* resorted to denouncing non-violent tenants as 'terrorists'. Despite the fact that Pakistan is a regular stomping ground of mainstream media pundits from the West, none of the visiting journalists deemed this struggle worthy of attention. It was too unfashionable and distracted from concentrating on the beards. But the beards are most effectively marginalized when people see them as irrelevant to their real needs – as the Punjabi tenants of the military farms have demonstrated. Christopher John and Younis Iqbal now want to internationalise their struggle. They want the world to take notice and they are desperate for global solidarity, which has so far been absent.

What the lack of synchronisation between the recent elections and a two-year struggle involving a million peasant families suggests is the flimsy nature of the polity. The political screen created by Musharraf is designed not to conceal, but rather to emphasize the institutional power that rules the coun-try. If any of the regimes that Pakistan has suffered since 1977 had actually improved living conditions for the majority of its citizens there would be some room for a utilitarian argument to determine whether military or civilian governments work best. But even the massaged and doctored official figures reveal a country living through a long and deep social crisis, regardless of who is in power.

In the past there were, at least, a few attempts to grapple with reality. An official government *Survey of Shelterless Persons in Karachi* published in 1959 (when a form of social-democratic ideology was the common sense of global capitalism) makes poignant reading, compared to the callous indifference exhibited by today's rulers:

> A farmer provides his one yoke of oxen with properly sheltered space covering more than 445 yards . . . those who live in *jhuggies* or similarly improvised tenements in Karachi do not enjoy even that much space or comfort. For though the *jhuggie* is also 4 x 5 yards its average density is 4.2 persons. . . . Even the earliest human dwellings discovered by archaeologists were bigger and more comfortable than the ones we had the painful duty to survey.

Given the rapid rise of population density since then, it is hardly surprising that providing shelter has ceased to be a priority since General Zia's coup of March 1977. The Malthusian policies of successive governments – the virtual absence of health care for over half the population, the appalling living conditions in town and country, the inability to educate the country (70 per cent of women and 41 per cent of men are officially classified as illiterate and the real figures are probably much higher) – have wrecked the country, but failed to reduce the size of the average family. According to the last census, the country has a population of 148.7 million. The United Nations Family Planning Association estimates that by 2050 this will have grown to 344.2 million, making Pakistan the world's fourth most populated state after China, India and the USA.

The hierarchical divisions in Pakistani society have accelerated sharply over recent decades. The only serious breach in the wall dividing an English-educated civilian and military elite, with access to Western universities, medical schools and military academies, and the rest of the population, semi-literate (largely, but not exclusively, the product of *madrassahs* or religious schools) or illiterate, has been courtesy of the 'black economy'. Throughout the 1980s and 1990s, the cultivation of poppy fields in Afghanistan and the NWFP produced a fine crop of heroin-millionaires, who laddered their way to the top. Many of them were of peasant or urban petty-bourgeois stock, but their money funded every political party and penetrated the armed forces.[68] Money, Kalashnikovs and Pajeros (a Japanese version of the Range-Rover) were scattered liberally amongst them all. In return the humble heroin merchants were loaded with honours and public displays of affection. It may have been too late for them, but they made sure their children were properly educated and became part of the elite. The upward mobility of this layer slightly altered the composition of the property-owning elite, without changing much else. Money remained the great leveller in the upper reaches of society, while the price of urban land reached astronomical heights. To buy an apartment in the Defence Colony of Karachi or the fashionable Parade Ground in Lahore is not too different from buying one in New York or Berlin.

During the 1990s the heroin had been despatched to Europe and North America via two routes. The first lay through the Grand Trunk Road from Peshawar to Karachi and thence via container ships to Mediterranean ports. The second, policed by the Russian mafia, went from Afghanistan via Central Asia and Russia to the Balkans and then to the capitals of the Western world. The defeat of the Taliban following 11 September has meant that Pakistani heroin networks have virtually collapsed. The Northern Alliance now monopolises the trade and it is their old Russian friends who prosper, while Kosovo becomes the main distribution point for most of the world.[69] The Pakistani economy has withstood the blow only because of the new money that has arrived with American troops. US foreign policy in Pakistan rests on a skilful combination of military force and funds, but what will happen if soldiers and money are needed on other fronts and this equilibrium can no longer be preserved?

---

68 The mass production of heroin was a by-product of the First Afghan War. The money it generated was utilised to fund the mujahideen against the godless soldiers of the former Soviet Union. The foundation and rapid growth of the Bank of Credit and Commerce International (BCCI) was necessitated by the needs of the Cold War and the drug barons. Money was laundered on a massive scale: heroin money from Pakistan and cocaine cash from Colombia was used to bribe and reward bankers and politicians in every Western country as well as funding the Contra operation in Nicaragua and the beards in Afghanistan.

69 It would not come as a total surprise to discover one fine evening that Western soldiers and civil servants, policing the Balkan protectorates on behalf of the *basileus* in Washington, were also benefiting from the poppy trade.

Apologists of the American Empire often talk of hard choices in the world of market-states. For the Islamic world this means either a democracy decked in the chains of free trade and intellectual property rights and privatising anything that matters, or a reversion to bearded barbarism. But the 'bearded barbarians' rarely raise objections to the economic model of the West. What threatens them is the social side of the equation. They know that to concede on issues related to gender and sexuality would destroy their influence in the Islamic world. For this reason, they violently reject the freedoms permitted women and, more recently, homosexuals.[70] The main difference between the beards and the Pakistani liberals who support the United States is that the latter accept both sides of the coin. The real problem lies in the coinage. Pakistan is a failed state because its ruling elites have failed its people. Public offices can be bought in the marketplace and the money paid recouped through oppressive and exacting bribes; justice is sold or badly administered; the capitalist system serves the needs of the wealthy; tax returns from businessmen small or big are scanty; nutritious food, education, health and shelter are the preserve of those who can pay; defence expenditure is totally out of control and each budget is dominated by the requirements of 'national security'. There appears to be no escape from this vicious circle. The result is deep misery and insecurity, accompanied by murder and brigandage.

One of the army's worst failures has been its inability to restore even a semblance of law and order in town or village. Self-appointed social supe-

---

70 Sheikh Fahd bin Abd Al-Rahman Al-Abyan, a Wahhabi preacher much loved by Pakistani Islamists, recently addressed his flock in the Al-Riyadh mosque in the Saudi kingdom with a statement that Maulana Diesel would happily endorse:

Some people have been influenced by the putrid ideas spread by the infidel West about man's custodianship over the woman [a reference to a famous passage in the Koran – TA]. On the face of it these ideas appear to protect women's rights. In truth, their aim is to push the people into a sinful liberty that has caused the downfall of entire civilisations [probably a reference to Sodom and Gomorrah – TA]. This false liberation has been engendered by a society in which crime is a hobby, adultery is an entertainment and murder a means of sublimating rage; a society in which the woman does as she pleases even if she is married and in which under-age girls know and do what married women know and do and even more. . . . These putrid ideas – no more than conceptual trash disseminated by the West – have begun to appear in the whorish journals of our world and on the Arab satellite channels.

riors rape young men and women at will as a punishment for supposed mis-deeds or infringing the Islamic code of conduct. One so-called violation is punished with a violation that is only too real. In almost every case, both mullah and local police chief protect the perpetrators. These crimes are casually referred to in the press as 'punitive rapes'. Add to this the failure to curb or contain the Islamo-terrorist sects who have attacked and killed Pakistani Christians, visiting foreigners and technicians and carried out two serious attempts on Musharraf's own life. The failure to curb these obscurantist excesses lies in the composition of the army and the octopus it created (the Inter Services Intelligence – ISI) during the First Afghan War. The ISI became an army within an army, accountable only to its own high command and controlling its own budget, much of which used to be supplied directly by Washington. It was the ISI that supervised the Taliban take-over in Kabul; it was the ISI that controlled the infiltration of skilled terror merchants into Indian-held Kashmir; it was the ISI that maintained a direct connection with Osama bin Laden and his group.

The reason the army cannot curb the violence inside Pakistan is because if some of the leads were followed they would flow directly to the headquarters of its own organisation. The MMA victories in the NWFP and Baluchistan were also a victory for sections of the ISI. They could now continue to sow discord within the army itself.

The generals blame the crisis on the politicians and vice versa. Both are right. The politicians were milking the country's resources for private gain and were uninterested in the social welfare of those who had elected them. On assuming power, General Musharraf promised transparent government, financial growth and an end to corruption. He has failed on every count. Government statistics, always understated, admit that the rate of unemployment has increased by 2 per cent since the military assumed direct control. The investment–GDP ratio is the lowest since 1966 and the much-promised investment has yet to arrive, though 9/11 undoubtedly helped to shore up the country's foreign exchange reserves, which currently stand at $6 billion.

The problem is structural. Low productivity in agriculture can be reversed only with the implementation of serious land reforms, but the alliance of the *khaki* state with local landlords makes such a move virtually impossible. This view is not confined to the left. The Economist Intelligence Unit report on

Pakistan (2002) commented on the lamentable state of the country's agriculture:

> Change is hindered, however, not least because the status quo suits the wealthy landowners who dominate the sector, as well as federal and provincial parliaments. Large landowners own 40% of the arable land and control most of the irrigation system. Yet assessments by independent agencies, including the World Bank, show them to be less productive than smallholders. They are also poor taxpayers, heavy borrowers and bad debtors.[71]

The last sentence is an accurate description of the cabinet ministers in the new government.

Since the foundation of the country in 1947, the Pakistani army has been the spinal cord of the state apparatus. The weakness of political institutions, the absence of a bourgeoisie and the domination of the country's politics by a rural elite – a parasitical excrescence of the worst sort – led to an over-reliance on the civilian bureaucracy and the army. Since there was no real consent for landlord rule, force had to be used both directly and indirectly. Both institutions had been created by the colonial power and formed in its mould.[72] Whereas the civil service was soon mired in corruption, the army held out for a bit longer. The impression was created that while individual officers might be susceptible to bribes (and after all they were human) the institution itself was clean. Two long periods of military rule destroyed that image. General Ayub Khan's family became extremely wealthy during his rule (1958–69), as did some of his collaborators, and from 1977–89 at least two of General Zia's corps commanders were centrally involved in the heroin trade and gun-running. Corruption on a lesser scale spread through

---

71 Country Profile 2002, The Economist Intelligence Unit, London.

72 The needs of the post-1858 civil servants of the Raj were supplied by the colonial state precisely in order to prevent the corruption that had characterised the rule of the East India Company and led to the vilification and prosecution of its most successful agents, Robert Clive and Warren Hastings. The hierarchical discipline of the British Indian Army was combined with its subordination to the senior civilian ruler – the Governor-General or Viceroy. The only breach in this custom was the celebrated clash between Kitchener and Curzon, which the former won: the youngest Viceroy was recalled to London.

the junior ranks of the army like a vicious cancer. The failure to crack down on these practices was hardly accidental. The generals adopted a materialist approach to the problem. They were aware that it was an easy way to preserve the unity of the army. The loot could not be equally shared since that might promote egalitarian tendencies amongst the colonels and majors, but at the same time the subalterns could not be denied some protection money. For was it not the army as a whole that protected Pakistan?

As it gained more experience in running the country, the *khaki* elite began to see itself as a party/army. On the rare occasions that it had to agree to an election, a political front organisation was rapidly assembled, but its rule was heavily circumscribed by the needs of the military. A civilian government ruled only in name. The defence allocation in successive budgets survived every regime change. The official figures over the last ten years may well be doctored but are revealing nonetheless. In 1988–9, defence spending was six times that of the expenditure on education and health. In 1998–9 the figure had altered by a single percentage point in favour of defence. It was now seven times as high, though in real terms it was probably three times higher. For security reasons the money is never itemised. Thus the citizenry remains unaware of how much is spent on anything, let alone nuclear weapons and delivery systems. The infrastructure required to sustain a five-million-strong army, with two armoured divisions, dozens of brigades, nearly three thousand tanks and armoured personnel carriers, among much else, has to be huge. The air force has four hundred combat planes divided into ten fighter squadrons as well as missile systems bought from France and the United States. There is also the navy, which is relatively small: nine submarines and a few destroyers and frigates.

Does Pakistan really need such a large defence establishment? The *khaki* ideologues insist that ever since Partition there has been a permanent military threat from India. As I have often argued elsewhere, this notion is pure rubbish.[73] On all three occasions (Kashmir twice and Bangladesh) when the two countries have fought a war, the initiative was taken by Pakistan. In 1971 the Indian army could have taken West Pakistan, but was not allowed

---

73 See *Pakistan: Military Rule or People's Power?*, London and New York 1971; *Can Pakistan Survive?*, London 1983.

to cross the international border by its own political leaders. With both coun-tries in possession of nuclear delivery systems it is obvious that neither the Kashmir issue nor any other dispute can be resolved through a war. Even an India dominated by Hindu chauvinism and led by slightly crazed men in saffron is hardly likely to attempt a conquest of Pakistan. Why should they? Whose interests would it serve? It might have been different if Pakistan had suddenly discovered unlimited quantities of oil lying just beneath the surface, but what else does it offer? In reality there is no rationale behind this fear of India. It serves only one purpose: the maintenance of the huge military–industrial complex that sprawls the country and sustains *khaki* political hegemony. In reality the threat to the army's domination has always come from its own people. The only time the old Pakistan was seriously united was during an uprising from below which saw students and workers in Dhaka and Karachi, Chittagong and Lahore, topple the dictatorship of Field Marshal Ayub Khan. The army never forgave its Bengali citizens this act of treachery and when they elected their own lead-ers, unhindered by the state, the army embarked on a bloodbath. It is worth stressing that an army, which demands limitless amounts of protection money to preserve the state, actually provoked its breakup in 1971. This is usually glossed over in recent accounts of both the army and the country.

When the party/army realised that the defence budget alone was insufficient to meet its insatiable requirements, it decided to embark on a corporate career, followed soon after by its junior partners, the navy and the air force.[74] The army has always had its social-welfare foundations, another colonial inheritance, but their aims were limited to helping retired soldiers and officers with pensions and grants as well as re-integrating them into civil society. Ten per cent of all public sector jobs were reserved for the army. There is nothing unusual in this and the British and US armies have their own versions of the same.

The oldest of these foundations is the Fauji (Army) Foundation, which

---

74 A gifted Pakistani scholar, Dr Ayesha Siddiqa-Agha, has now skilfully documented the entire process – see *Pakistan's Arms Procurement and Military Build-up, 1979–99: In Search of a Policy*, London 2001. See also her paper 'Power, Perks, Prestige and Privileges: Military's Economic Activities in Pakistan', presented at an international conference, 'Soldiers in Business: Military as an Economic Actor', held, appropriately enough, in Jakarta, in October 2000. Also her essay 'Political Economy of National Security', in the *Economic and Political Weekly*, 2–9 November 2002. All the figures quoted above are the result of her meticulous research.

was established as a charity in 1889 and has become a giant entrepreneur in its own right with controlling shares in sugar mills, energy, fertilizer, cereals, cement and other industries. The sum of its combined assets is 9.8 billion rupees. Despite its heavy presence in the private sector, the Foundation's board is headed *ex-officio* by the Federal defence secretary. Interestingly enough, its current managing director is General Amjad, who has retired from active service. Whether his reputation for probity survives his tenure at the Foundation remains to be seen. Another trust became operational in 1977 during General Zia's dictatorship. The Army Welfare Trust controls real estate, rice mills, stud farms, pharmaceutical industries, travel agencies, fish farms, six different housing schemes, insurance companies and an aviation outfit. Its assets have been valued at 17 billion rupees.

Irritated by *khaki* domination of the trusts, which had originally been designed for the entire armed services, the air force and navy chiefs met, demanded and obtained from General Zia the right to establish their own troughs, once again under the old Charitable Endowments Act of 1889. This meant that none of these organisations was taxed until the rules were changed in 1991. Whereas the smaller naval and air force outfits were asked to pay 33 per cent, the army foundations were taxed at 20 per cent. Whether any taxes were paid at all is a moot point. No figures are available. When the enterprises run by the foundations made a loss the generals dipped into the public purse and removed money from the annual allocation for defence in the national budget.

Most of these foundations have been involved in rackets of one sort or another. Scandals have only erupted, however, when private businessmen have become too greedy in exploiting the foundation or where the fall of a government has exposed shady deals, as in the case of Benazir Bhutto's spouse Asif Zardari involving the air force's Shaheen Foundation in a media venture via an intermediary subsequently accused of short-changing the Foundation. Another case concerned the Navy Foundation, and its purchase of urban land and housing developments. It emerged that, in the process of defrauding the Foundation, a private businessman had bribed senior naval personnel. A lawyer petitioned the Supreme Court to outlaw all use of military, naval and air force insignia and involvement in private enterprise. He accused the foundations and their partners of collusion and corruption. He demonstrated how the foundations contravened the Companies Ordinance (1984) and pleaded with the court to outlaw all commercial activities by the armed services. Unable to contest his argument, the judges dismissed the case on a technicality, thereby revealing their own subordination to the colour *khaki*.

The army's domination of the country is now complete. It is the only ruling institution. But how long can it rule? Till now it has managed to preserve the command structure inherited from the British. Pakistani generals often boast of its inviolability when compared to the Middle East or Latin America. But a great deal has changed since the Sixties. The officer corps is not the exclusive domain of the landed gentry. A majority of officers come from urban backgrounds and are subject to the same influences and pressures. It is the privileges that have kept them loyal, but the processes that destroy politicians are already at work. Whereas in the recent past it was Nawaz Sharif and his brother or Benazir Bhutto and her husband who demanded kickbacks before agreeing to various deals, it is now General Musharraf's office that sanctions key projects. When a cosmetic change becomes necessary to preserve the status quo, he too will go the way of his civilian and military forebears. But is the history of Pakistan nothing more than a series of endless repetitions, each more debased than its predecessor? The answer does not lie in Pakistan alone. It will be partially determined by how and where India moves over the next decade. And partially by the American overlord itself. The Musharraf regime cannot aspire to play the same role as regional satrap that Zia once enjoyed. Pakistan has been ousted as imperial instrument in Afghanistan, and checked from compensating with renewed incursions in Kashmir. But if Islamabad has been forced into a more passive posture along its northern borders, its strategic importance for the US has, if anything, increased. For Washington has now made a huge political investment in the creation of a puppet regime in Kabul, to be guarded by US troops 'for years to come', in the words of General Tommy Franks – not to speak of its continuing hunt for Osama bin Laden and his lieutenants. Pakistan is a vital flank in the pursuit of both objectives, and its top brass can look forward to the kind of lavish emoluments, public and private, that the Thai military received for their decades of collusion with the American war in Indochina. Still, Washington is pragmatic and knows that Benazir Bhutto and Nawaz Sharif were just as serviceable agents of its designs in Kabul as Zia himself. Should he falter domestically, Musharraf will be ditched without sentiment by the suzerain. The Phoenixes of sleaze will be revived again. The *Pax Americana* can wage war with any number of proxies. It will take an uprising on the scale of 1969 to shake Pakistan free of them.

PART IV

A Clash of Fundamentalisms

It is terrible to see our middle-class journals and speakers calling for the destruction of Delhi, and the indiscriminate massacre of prisoners . . . To read the letters of our officers at the commencement of the outbreak [the 1857 rebellion against British rule in India – TA], it seemed as if every subaltern had the power to hang or shoot as many natives as he pleased, and they spoke of the work of blood with as much levity as if they were hunting wild animals . . . It will be a happy day when England has not an acre of territory in Continental Asia . . . where do we find even an individual who is not imbued with the notion that England would sink to ruin if she were deprived of her Indian Empire? Leave me, then, to my pigs and sheep, which are not labouring under any such delusions . . .

Letter from Richard Cobden to John Bright,
22 September 1857

Their [English bourgeois] character has been molded in the course of centuries. Class self-esteem has entered into their blood and marrow, their nerves and bones. It will be much harder to knock the self-confidence of world rulers out of them. But the American will knock it out just the same, when he gets seriously down to business.

In vain does the British bourgeois console himself that he will serve as a guide for the inexperienced American. Yes, there will be a transitional period. But the crux of the matter does not lie in the habits of diplomatic leadership but in actual power, existing capital and industry. And the United States, if we take its economy, from oats to big battleships of the latest type, occupies the first place. They produce all the living necessities to the extent of one-half to two-thirds of what is produced by all mankind . . .

Leon Trotsky, Izvestia, 5 August 1924

Lesley Stahl: 'We have heard that half a million children have died in Iraq. I mean, that's more children than died in Hiroshima. And you know, is the price worth it?'
Madeleine Albright: 'I think this is a very hard choice, but the price? We think the price is worth it.'

CBS News, 1996

The ruling to kill the Americans and their allies – civilians and military – is an individual duty for every Muslim who can do it in any country in which it is possible to do it.

Osama bin Laden, 1998

20

A short-course history of US imperialism

In a world dominated by conflicting ideologies and social systems, debate on the relative demerits of each or both was normal. Capitalism, socialism, communism, anti-imperialism and anti-communism were for or against some recognised aspect of reality. This confrontation dominated world politics as well as intellectual discourse, making it impossible to institutionalise the routine disinformation or no-information that prevails today: the less you know, the easier to manipulate. With the triumph of one ideology and the total collapse of the other, the space for debate and dissent has narrowed dramatically.

The ideological dominance of the United States, backed by its military ascendancy, has now grown so pronounced that many of those who were once critical of the way this power was used are reduced to fond purring and trite eulogies. Sweeping generalisations are drawn from incidental or trivial occurrences, and many leading American and supporting European journalists have abandoned unbiased observation and independent thinking in favour of an imperial superpatriotism. US pundits are forever on the lookout for evidence that things are worse abroad than at home, and reporting from the various outposts of the Empire – London, Sarajevo, Riyadh, Cairo, Lahore, Seoul, Tokyo – they yearn in chorus for the familiar American reality they have left behind. Those Americans – Gore Vidal, Susan Sontag, Noam Chomsky amongst many others – who assert their independence from chauvinism or refuse to conform by drawing attention to some of the flawed and grim realities of the Empire are viciously denounced by the superpatriots.

In this ideological atmosphere, criticisms of US foreign policy are treated as displays of 'anti-Americanism' or, in more recent coinage, 'Occidentalism'. Both terms are used to denote a blind hatred for Americans and all secular aspects of US life, politics and culture. This is undoubtedly the view of many religious fundamentalists, regardless of the religion. What else explains the first reactions of the fundamentalist TV evangelists in the United States who explained the hits of 11 September as 'God's punishment' for the sin of tolerating homosexuality and abortion, etc.? How else is one to explain the confusion of the relatively moderate preacher, Billy Graham? As he flanked President Bush at the New York memorial to honour the dead, Reverend Graham informed the gathering of stars and megastars that he had been deluged with letters and queries since the events. People wanted him to explain 'why God had let them hit America'. The preacher's response was straightforward. He confessed his bewilderment. He told his flock he had no answer.[75]

Religious fundamentalists do not single out the United States for special treatment for any other reason than its hegemonic power. They apply the same stringent criteria to other societies. For Islamists, none of the rulers of existing Muslim states today are 'true' Muslims. Not a single one. Hence the struggle to change the existing regimes and replace them with holy emirates. Some orthodox Jews regard the very existence of Israel as a disgrace. Others, belonging to the Israeli settlers movement, claim scriptural sanction and are fuelled by the eschatological belief that reclaiming the land will hasten the coming of the Messiah. Hindu revivalists are extremely dissatisfied with their own prime minister for being too soft on India's 130 million Muslims and not permitting the Hindutva to record a total triumph of Hindu culture against 'the foreigners' by tearing down all the old mosques in India and building temples on the ruined foundations. The born-again Christian sects

---

75 Why had God allowed Allah to permit the hits? Why had Allah permitted God to bomb Afghanistan and destroy the 'Emirate of the Faithful'? The US religious fundamentalists did have an answer. *Their* country was not being governed according to the laws of God and his prophets. The Islamic fundamentalists in Afghanistan had no such excuse. They had done their best to follow their own interpretations of Koranic prescriptions. And yet I doubt that the leaderships of the Islamist groups will be racked by crises as a result. They are hard-headed politicos who use religion effectively. Whether a majority of them believe it literally is an open question.

in the United States are far from satisfied merely with having one of their own occupying the White House. They bemoan the corrupt and anti-Christian laws that defile the United States. Some of them sanction the bombing of abortion clinics and the assassination of doctors who work in them.

But the secular priests of the Empire are not referring only to religious bigotry when they excoriate 'anti-Americans' and 'Occidentalists'.[76] They are speaking of those liberal critics and leftists who will not have it that the collapse of the Soviet Union means bending the knee before the Caesar in the White House. For the Americophiles, no criticism of the Empire matters that is not conducted within the framework of loyalty. This is then internalised and affects all their activities in the public domain. Their self-image is that of loyal but disinterested advisers to the politicians in power: if only they followed this disinterested advice all would be well in the world. The historic compromise with integrity that this form of Americophilia entails transmutes the friendly critic into a slave of power, always wanting to please. S/he becomes an apologist, expecting the Empire to actually deliver on its rhetoric. Alas, the Empire, whose fundamental motivation today is economic self-interest, may sometimes disappoint the more recent converts to its cause. They feel betrayed, refusing to accept that what has been betrayed is their illusions. What they dislike most is to be reminded of the sour smell of history. An argument often deployed is that one must back the United States because 'it's the only game in town' and more enlightened than those it seeks to destroy. This display of historical amnesia refuses to recall the time of US imperialism's birth, gestation and early banditry, long before the Russian Revolution transformed international relations after 1917.

The history of migrations and conquests has been closely interwoven for thousands of years. Most of the modern world is a product of immigration and imperialism. For two and a half centuries, what is now the United States

---

76 'Occidentalism' is the coinage of Ian Buruma and Avashai Margalit, two veteran contributors to the *New York Review of Books*. It reminds one of the concoctions that used to appear in *Pravda*, rather than *Novy Mir*, and which would lump all the 'enemies' of the Soviet Union into a single spurious target. Buruma and Margalit are, of course, not as crude, but they serve a smarter market.

remained a self-sufficient world, nurtured by the leftovers of European civilisation and helped by a group of strongly motivated immigrants. Religious
fundamentalists in the first phase, political refugees fleeing persecution in
Europe in the second, and later, those whose only drive was gold. It was a
potent mixture, but its wealth of possibilities could only be made profitable
by a combination of internal imperialism (genocide of the native population) and armed trading on the African coasts (slavery). That genocide was
the preferred method of technologically more advanced new arrivals to
assert their superiority over the native people is well established, though
even as late as the twentieth century, liberal historians and educationalists
often denied this fact, preferring to believe that their ancestors had come to
'virgin lands'. In October 1948, President Conant of Harvard University
informed the New York Herald Tribune Forum that:

> In the first place, this nation, unlike most others, has not evolved from a state
> founded on military conquest. As a consequence we have nowhere in our tradi-
> tion the idea of an aristocracy descended from the conquerors and entitled to rule
> by right of birth. On the contrary we have developed our greatness in a period
> in which a fluid society overran a rich and empty continent . . .

Thinly populated, yes, but empty? In whose eye? Were the Indian wars
not real? Were they phantom struggles? Or was it that Protestant fundamentalism provided a moral justification for large-scale theft of land held in
common by different native tribes, as well as the mass murder of 'hea-
thens'? The land on which Harvard University was built had been taken
from Indians through 'military conquest'. The remapping of North America
was a long process, which has been tracked with great care by the historian
Oliver LaFarge in his classic work, *As Long as the Grass Shall Grow*:

> The roster of massacres of Indian men, women and children extends from the Great
> Swamp Massacre of 1696 in Rhode Island, through the killing of the friendly
> Christian Indians in Wyoming, Pennsylvania, when the republic was young, on
> through the friendly Arivaipas of Arizona, the winter camp of the Colorado
> Cheyennes, to the final dreadful spectacle of Wounded Knee in the year 1870.

Catholic fundamentalism played a similar role in the Spanish conquest of
South America, though their policies were more nuanced. They enslaved,

killed and let die in large numbers, but they also inaugurated a campaign of mass conversions to Catholicism. It was this that enabled the Indian population to survive. In Mexico, Bolivia, Peru and Ecuador, it remained a majority. Elsewhere it was diluted through the emergence of *mestizo* elites, dominated by people of Spanish descent. In Argentina alone were the indigenous people completely exterminated. The Catholic Church was better prepared to deal with its New World conquests than its Protestant counterparts in the North. It had, after all, moved outwards only after orchestrating a bloody dress-rehearsal at home. The wars of Reconquest in the Iberian peninsula, followed by mass expulsions and forced conversions of Hispanic Muslims and Jews, had trained and prepared the fundamentalist warriors who conquered South America.

The earliest manifestations of America's imperial destiny became visible in the nineteenth century, first in relation to Latin America, later in the Pacific with the conquest of the Philippines and an early declaration of interest in Japan. Some of the most effective criticism of the first phase of US empire-building was to come from an insider, someone whose credentials could not be challenged by even the most ardent Americophile. This was Major General Smedley Butler (1888–1940) of the US Marine Corps, described by General Douglas MacArthur as 'one of the really great generals in American history' and twice awarded the Medal of Honor. MacArthur's admiration extended to naming the US base in Okinawa after Butler. Would Butler have been equally impressed by the Viceroy of Japan and the defender of the Korean Peninsula? His writings would suggest the opposite. After he retired from the US army, General Butler spent some time in reflecting on his career before he concluded: 'Like all members of the military profession, I never had a thought of my own until I left the service. My mental faculties remained in suspended animation while I obeyed the orders of higher-ups. This is typical with everyone in the military service.'

His first book was entitled *War as a Racket*. Its thesis was simple. He was no longer in favour of offensive wars. He would defend his country, but he would never again become 'a racketeer for capitalism'. 'War is just a racket. A racket is best described, I believe, as something that is not what it seems to the majority of the people. Only a small inside group knows what it is about. It is conducted for the very few at the expense of the masses.' In a speech in 1933, General Butler expounded his 'anti-American' or proto-Occidentalist views with remarkable clarity, spelling out the nature of US imperialism in Latin America:

> There isn't a trick in the racketeering bag that the military gang is blind to. It has its 'finger-men' to point out enemies, its 'muscle-men' to destroy enemies, its 'brain men' to plan war preparations and a 'Big Boss' Super-Nationalistic-Capitalism.
>
> It may seem odd for me, a military man, to adopt such a comparison. Truthfulness compels me to. I spent thirty-three years and four months in active military service as a member of this country's most agile military force, the Marine Corps. I served in all commissioned ranks from Second Lieutenant to Major General. And during that period, I spent most of my time being a high class muscle-man for Big Business, for Wall Street and for the Bankers. In short, I was a racketeer, a gangster for capitalism.
>
> I suspected I was just part of a racket at the time. Now I am sure of it.
>
> I helped make Honduras 'right' for American fruit companies in 1903. I helped make Mexico, especially Tampico, safe for American oil interests in 1914. I helped make Haiti and Cuba a decent place for the National City Bank boys to collect revenues in. I helped in the raping of half a dozen Central American republics for the benefits of Wall Street. The record of racketeering is long. I helped purify Nicaragua for the international banking house of Brown Brothers in 1909–1912. I brought light to the Dominican Republic for American sugar interests in 1916. In China I helped to see to it that Standard Oil went its way unmolested.
>
> During those years, I had, as the boys in the back room would say, a swell racket. Looking back on it, I feel that I could have given Al Capone a few hints. The best he could do was to operate his racket in three districts. I operated on three continents.

This was, of course, a long time ago. It's all changed now. Has it? A voice which could not be more different in tone and politics from General Butler's, and which is heard regularly from the pulpit of the *New York Times*, is that of its star columnist, Thomas Friedman. He too is an Americophile, but refreshingly blunt: never is a *burqa* used to soften his vision of reality. General Butler would have greatly appreciated these words of Friedman from *New York Times Magazine* article of 28 March 1999:

> For globalization to work, America can't be afraid to act like the almighty superpower that it is. The hidden hand of the market will never work without a

hidden fist. McDonald's cannot flourish without McDonnell-Douglas, the designer of the F-15, and the hidden fist that keeps the world safe for Silicon Valley's technology is called the United States Army, Air Force, Navy and Marine Corps.

How did it become an 'almighty superpower'? US intervention in the First World War was deeply unpopular at home. Many considered it unnecessary. Others, of German descent, did not see any reason why the United States should intervene to help the king of England rather than the Kaiser. Important sections of the elite would have preferred to wait and watch the two European empires bleed each other to a stalemate that would have economically advantaged the United States, whose capitalists were heavily involved in both countries. Despite the loss of 128 American lives and the exchange of diplomatic notes with Germany, it was not the sinking of the *Lusitania* by a German submarine in 1915 that pushed them in Europe's direction. True, they were nervous of an outright German victory for commercial reasons, since that would have made Germany a formidable opponent. It was the news from Russia that was decisive. A revolution had broken out in February 1917 and overthrown Tsarism. The country was in turmoil. Morale inside the army had collapsed and Russian soldiers were deserting the front in droves. Bolshevik agitators were hard at work encouraging more desertions and telling the soldiers that the enemy was at home.

The timing of the US declaration of war could not have been more symbolic. On 6 April 1917, just as Wilson announced from Washington that his country was at war with Germany, an important event was taking place in Petrograd. The Central Committee of the Bolshevik Party was in session to discuss Lenin's 'April Theses', which argued for the careful preparation of an insurrection in order to make a socialist revolution and take power. A number of Wilson's colleagues were not convinced by his decision to go and make war in Europe. Some of Lenin's closest comrades opposed all talk of insurrection as a wild and irresponsible fantasy. The doubters were to be proved wrong in both cases. Had the Russian Revolution not already been in motion, it is unlikely that President Wilson, who had been trying hard to mediate a peace between England and Germany, would have intervened with the same vigour.

The United States entry in the war of 1914–18 was the first big step towards becoming a world power. It would learn quickly. The rotting corpses on the fields of Europe would help to concentrate its mind. As it grew into its inheritance, its methods of operation would alter and in time the world 'being' would envelop its American 'consciousness'. Henceforth it would not think too hard before flexing its economic muscle to create a military machine that would attempt to throttle all challenges to the world capitalist order.

Interestingly enough, it was the Bolshevik leaders who understood the importance of the change that was taking place, long before the rulers of Britain and France. The old European powers looked at the United States with a mixture of scorn and snobbery, the way an old aristocrat whose estate is mortgaged views a *nouveau riche* entrepreneur. Lenin and Trotsky were contemptuous of the European bourgeoisie, but they admired the energy and capacity of American capitalism. Both men were keen students of economic history. They studied the figures of descent and ascent and were happy to share this knowledge with anyone prepared to listen. This is Trotsky explaining the future of oil in an address to conference delegates in 1924:

> Oil, which now plays such an exceptional military and industrial role, totals in the United States two-thirds of the world output, and in 1923 it had even reached approximately 72 per cent. To be sure, they complain a lot about the threats of the exhaustion of their oil resources. In the initial post-war years, I confess I thought that these plaints were merely a pious cover for coming encroachments on foreign oil. But geologists actually do confirm that American oil at the current rate of consumption will, according to some, last twenty-five years, according to others, forty years. But in twenty-five or forty years, America with her industry and fleet will be able to take away oil from all the others ten times over again.[77]

The Second World War of 1939–45 was the result of a German attempt to reverse the conditions imposed on it by the defeat it had suffered twenty years before. If its war-aims had remained restricted to that achievement and had it possessed a more rational captain at the helm, it might have succeeded, possibly even without a war: an influential section of the British

---

77 *Izvestia*, 5 August 1924.

imperial elite was keen on an Anglo-German alliance. But Germany's capitalist barons, extremely nervous of the communist enemy within, had entrusted their state to the demented leadership of German fascism. It was this that made a London–Berlin axis impossible. There were two reasons why London favoured such a pact. The first was to guard the continent against Bolshevism, the second was to keep the United States at bay. The 'anti-Americanism' of the British ruling class at that time should not be underestimated.

The United States was fully aware of these machinations. Not only did it not enter the war immediately, but it expected a quick German triumph. Until the US entered the war, liberal opinion there was deeply hostile to British imperialism, which angered British liberals. The *New Republic* published a number of anti-imperialist articles which stressed the moral equivalence between Japanese and English marauding in China, and an editorial made clear that its dislike of German fascism was of the same measure as its dislike of British imperialism: both parties were villainous. Enraged by this, the distinguished liberal economist John Maynard Keynes stopped writing for the paper. Six decades later, a few undistinguished American liberals expressed a similar distaste for a series of comments critical of US foreign policy published by the *London Review of Books* after 11 September. Two of them stopped writing for the paper. Liberal universalism, it would appear, does not hold good for the actions of imperialist powers.

During the early stages of the war, President Franklin Roosevelt, in an affectionate gesture, asked Churchill to ensure that, in the event of a likely German victory, the British fleet was hurried to safer shores on the other side of the Atlantic. It was not till later, when he observed that Britain and, more importantly, the Soviet Union had survived the Nazi assault that Roosevelt managed to manipulate a series of disputes with Japan and provoke a conflict which brought the United States into the Second World War.[78]

The United States emerged as the economic victor of the two world wars. Its major competitors had been enfeebled: Germany divided, Japan

---

78 This is, of course, a contentious issue but I am here following Gore Vidal's arguments in the *New York Review of Books* and elsewhere which convinced me.

occupied, the British empire in terminal decline. Its own economy prospered more than ever: immensely rich in raw materials, enjoying a greater equilibrium between industry and agriculture, a geography and demography that enabled it to practise economies of scale on mass-production lines, within an inviolable mainland.

But the political and ideological leaders of the United States did not use their economic or military superiority in 1945 to crush the competition. The heightened prestige of the Soviet Union, its expansion into Eastern Europe and its occupation of East Germany, together with the unfinished revolutions and wars/struggles for national liberation in China, Vietnam, Indonesia, Malaya, the Korean peninsula and India, were indications of a world that was crying to be remade.[79] In this turmoil, politics and ideology were awarded pride of place in the conflict between capitalism and its enemies.

What this meant concretely was the revival of a capitalist Europe devastated by the war. If the rulers of the US had been guided by a necessity to assert the primacy of economics, there would have been no Marshall Plan. This was not an enterprise designed to ensure the pastoralisation of Western Europe. It had two functions: to establish the political hegemony of the United States and to reconstitute capitalist Europe as an autonomous economic entity. In order to defend its global interests, Washington must recreate the market. It was the lesser evil. To permit France, Italy, Western Germany, Greece and Japan to collapse would have meant handing them over on a platter to the Soviet Union. The Marshall Plan and NATO were the Siamese twins designed to fight a protracted war against the old enemy.

The self-sufficiency in essential raw materials that characterised the United States came to an end after the Second World War. The phenomenal surge in industrial production that helped to supply the Allied armies

---

79 Instead it was to be destroyed. During the Korean War (1950–3) and as early as 1951, General Emmett O'Donnell, the chief of Bomber Command declared that 'all or nearly all of the whole Korean peninsula is a terrible mess. Everything is destroyed, there's nothing left standing.' This was not totally accurate. The twenty irrigation dams vital to harvesting rice for the civilian population of the North had not been touched. This was remedied in 1953, when five dams were bombed and destroyed, causing a lightning flood that ravaged the greater part of a valley.

during the Second World War could not be sustained by domestic materials. The United States needed to import oil, iron ore, bauxite, copper, manganese and nickel. The need for oil meant the domination of parts of Latin America, the Middle East and Nigeria; iron ore was obtained from other parts of Latin America and West Africa and other minerals from Canada, Australia and South Africa.

Politics and economics became more intertwined. The need for raw materials meant more and more political interventions. Coups d'état, local wars, establishment of US military bases, clinging tenaciously to the oligarchy in Venezuela, the generals in Brazil and Chile and the al-Saud clan in Saudi Arabia offered the simplest way to fight against the communist enemy and to protect the US economy. The strategy did not always work as intended. The Chinese communists took the country in October 1949; an upsurge in Korea led to US intervention, the division of the peninsula and a bitter UN-backed war leading to a stalemate that has yet to be resolved; the mafia-run dictatorship in Cuba was defeated by the guerrilla armies of Fidel Castro and Che Guevara in 1959; the Vietnamese refused to capitulate and finally defeated the United States after a fifteen-year war in April 1975.

The role of global gendarme assumed by the United States after the Second World War was to have a major impact domestically. It created a permanent arms economy which stimulated heavy industry and encouraged research in electronics, aircraft, chemistry and space. This industry produced goods whose sole purchaser was the American state. Nothing could be supplied to other parts of the world without the sanction of this state. The economic merits are obvious. The arms industry creates a stable sector, unaffected by the fluctuations of the economy. It helps to cushion the impact of the recessions that have been a regular feature of capitalism and, it has also been argued, guarded the economy against a catastrophic crisis of 1929 proportions. All the defence monopolies are thus guaranteed an automatic profit. This has meant that defence contractors will do almost anything to safeguard their investments. A symbiosis developed between the defence industry, the senior officer corps within the armed forces and the politicians, leading to the existence of a powerful military–industrial–political nexus.

The first warning of the dangers this process posed to the functioning of democracy came from another general. But unlike Butler, this one was not radical by any standards. In fact he had been elected president of the United States in the Republican interest. It was in his farewell speech to the nation on 17 January 1961 that Eisenhower alerted the country:

> We now stand ten years past the midpoint of a century that has witnessed four major wars among great nations. Three of these involved our own country. Despite these holocausts America is today the strongest, the most influential and most productive nation in the world. Understandably proud of this pre-eminence, we yet realize that America's leadership and prestige depend, not merely upon our unmatched material progress, riches and military strength, but on how we use our power in the interests of world peace and human betterment . . .
>
> Until the latest of our world conflicts, the United States had no armaments industry. American makers of plowshares could, with time and as required, make swords as well. But now we can no longer risk emergency improvisation of national defense; we have been compelled to create a permanent armaments industry of vast proportions. Added to this, three and a half million men and women are directly engaged in the defense establishment. We annually spend on military security more than the net income of all United States corporations.
>
> This conjunction of an immense military establishment and a large arms industry is new in the American experience. The total influence – economic, political, even spiritual – is felt in every city, every Statehouse, every office of the Federal government. We recognize the imperative need for this development. Yet we must not fail to comprehend its grave implications. Our toil, resources and livelihood are all involved; so is the very structure of our society.
>
> In the councils of government, we must guard against the acquisition of unwarranted influence, whether sought or unsought, by the military–industrial complex. The potential for the disastrous rise of misplaced power exists and will persist.
>
> We must never let the weight of this combination endanger our liberties or democratic processes. We should take nothing for granted. Only an alert and knowledgeable citizenry can compel the proper meshing of the huge industrial and military machinery of defense with our peaceful methods and goals, so that security and liberty may prosper together.

An 'alert and knowledgeable citizenry' did emerge a few years later, during the Vietnam war, and it extended far wider than the organised anti-war movement. When Senator William Fulbright conducted his Senate hearings on the war, they were broadcast regularly on the US networks. This enabled an alert citizenry to also become knowledgeable. It challenged the fantasies of its generals, rebutted the untruths spun by its leaders, and helped to bring the war to an end. This was the high tide of American democracy. Many of the soldiers who returned home from the war had been disabled by the conflict, but had begun to think for themselves, just like General Smedley Butler thirty years previously.[80] But this rejection of imperialist fundamentalism was not an overnight birth. It took five years to mature. It happened because the Vietnamese continued to struggle, refused to be defeated, despite the brutalities inflicted on them. From 1966 onwards, imperialist fundamentalism used chemical warfare against the Vietnamese. The massacre of civilian populations was always an integral part of US war strategy. The use of defoliants, herbicides, toxic gases transformed parts of the countryside into a lunar landscape. Whole areas became uncultivable and remain so to this day.[81] Despite all this, the Vietnamese refused to surrender. It was this knowledge that led those being conscripted, those who had fought and those who had lost friends and relatives in the war to question its motives and efficacy and insist that it be brought to an end. US leaders refused to give up. Nixon and Kissinger extended the war, first to Laos and later Cambodia, hoping to isolate the Vietnamese. They failed. The bombing of Cambodia did, however, create the conditions for the triumph of Pol Pot's fanatical ultra-nationalism. Since he was opposed to the Vietnamese as well, the Western powers provided him with covert support for many years and ignored his crimes.

The Vietnamese triumph of April 1975 created a wave of euphoria in four continents. In Southern Africa, Central America and the Iberian peninsula the mood was revolutionary. The Sandinista victory in Nicaragua in 1979 came as a heavy blow to Washington, which had backed the Somoza dictatorship with weapons and aid. The liberation struggles against colonial rule had produced new possibilities in Angola and Mozambique.

---

80 When American GIs organised themselves in groups like 'GIs against the war' or ' Veterans against the war' and demonstrated outside the Pentagon chanting slogans in favour of the 'enemy' who refused to be defeated, the shock felt inside the building must have been far greater and gone deeper than the hit of 11 September 2001.

81 In spite of repeated demands, no US official, military or civilian, was ever tried for war crimes. Tribunals are usually for the defeated, but not in this case, because the victorious country did not have the support necessary to impose such a Tribunal.

But the fundamentalists in Washington were determined to halt this process. In Africa they collaborated with the South Africans, who sent their army into Angola. The Angolan leadership appealed to Cuba, which sent in troops to defend the regime. These soldiers were transported in Soviet planes and armed with Soviet weaponry. Gradually the South Africans were driven back. Inside South Africa itself the African National Congress had embarked on a campaign of selective terrorism against key military and economic targets. In Nicaragua, the United States armed the Contras in a largely successful attempt to destabilise the country and make it ungovernable.

Fourteen years after the United States had suffered the first real defeat in their entire history, the Berlin Wall collapsed and the Soviet Union disintegrated. The Cold War came to a sudden end, not with a bang, but a whimper. The Warsaw Pact ceased to exist. The fall was both sudden and unexpected. It was not the result of military intervention. The causes were internal: the political and economic bankruptcy of the bureaucratic elite that had led the Soviet Union. The last Soviet leader, Mikhail Gorbachev, had certainly not intended this result. He had wanted reforms on every level. He was prepared to envisage a nuclear-free zone from the Atlantic to the Urals and hoped for a transition from a statist to a mixed economy on the model of European social-democracy of the Fifties, assuming that the West would help in this process. He harboured fatal illusions about Ronald Reagan and Margaret Thatcher. They let him down. The predators took over. What happened? In a recent essay the historian Georgi Derlugian, a former Soviet citizen now resident in Chicago, who had witnessed the process, reflected on this question:

> The Soviet Union was not brought down from without – the West stood watching in amazement. Nor was it undermined either from above or below. Rather it imploded from the middle, fragmenting along the institutional lines of different bureaucratic turfs. The collapse occurred when mid-ranking bosses felt threatened by Gorbachev's flakiness as head of the system, and pressured by newly assertive subordinates beneath them. The eruptions of 1989 in Eastern Europe provided the demonstration prod. In the process of disintegration, it was the particularly cynical apparatchiks of an already decomposed Young Communist League who led the way. In their wake followed the governors of national republics and Russian provinces, senior bureaucrats of economic ministries, and section chiefs all the way down to supermarket managers. As in many declining empires of the

past, the basest servants – emboldened by the incapacitation of emperors and frightened by impending chaos – rushed to grab the assets that lay nearest to hand. Mingling with them were nimble interlopers, ranging from the would-be yuppies to former black marketers and outright gangsters. The luckiest few in this motley *galère* would become the celebrity post-communist tycoons.[82]

Derlugian's pithy comments would probably bring a complacent smile to the face of many a Chinese apparatchik. Their country avoided the same fate. The Politburo in Beijing proved cleverer than the Russians. The two countries had shared similar features: a weak democratic tradition, an apparatus that fused party and state, a long monopoly of power by the Communist Party and the need to crush all manifestations of dissent from below. The leaders of both countries had taken the capitalist road, just as the late Chairman Mao had once predicted, but there the comparison ends.

The Soviet leadership, eager to please its new patrons and desperate to Americanise itself, accepted the 'shock-therapy' being recommended by the witch-doctors from Harvard. A decade later, in 2000, the statistics told the whole story: income inequality had trebled, a third of the population was living below the poverty line, crime and corruption were out of control, and in some parts of the country barter had replaced money as the means of exchange. For the postwar generation this experience had become the most harrowing ordeal of their entire life. And to add to the physical misery their leader, Boris Yeltsin, had turned out to be a fake diamond: an amoral and debauched clown lacking in competence and greedy to boot. The West, fearful of the alternatives, decided to back him. An obedient Western media followed suit.

Crime and corruption were rife in China too, many party bureaucrats were using their power to transform themselves into capitalists by buying up state property, but there was an important difference. Chaos on the Russian model had been avoided. The economy had registered important successes. Chinese capitalism functioned relatively well. Its rate of growth was higher than in a number of Western countries, and in the United States it had found a massive outlet for its goods. China began to look to the future with

---

82 'Recasting Russia' by Georgi Derlugian, *New Left Review* II, 12, November/December 2001. [www.newleftreview.org]

far greater assurance and self-confidence. At the same time the Communist Party had preserved its monopoly of power. In purely capitalist terms, market-Stalinism appeared to work.

Unlike their former Soviet and Eastern European counterparts, the Chinese had been partially insulated by their culture and civilisation. They were not desperate to mimic the West, even though they realised that they could not maintain themselves exclusively through an internal disposition. Their economy required a world equilibrium. This necessitated membership of the World Trade Organisation and close ties with the World Bank and the International Monetary Fund. The downsides were familiar: growing social inequality, corruption, a sea of unemployed labour. Unsurprisingly, out-of-work Chinese – intellectuals and workers – began to migrate to other parts of the world. Despite the barriers, the flow will increase as China integrates itself in the world market. The process was symbolised in an affecting cere-mony held in New York in December 2000 to honour the Chinese dissident Wang Ruowang, who had died in the city. He was eighty-three years old, had spent the bulk of his life trying to improve social and politi-cal conditions in China, but had died in the United States. The funeral oration was delivered by another distinguished exile, the journalist and writer Liu Binyan, whose remarks highlighted the repulsive underbelly of the regime:

> Wang started his life with high ideals and the vigor of youth; he invested these in the Communist Party, whose leaders soon expelled him, then banished him, then imprisoned him, then starved and tortured him, then ruined his family, then 'forgave' him, re-admitted him, re-expelled him, re-imprisoned him, and finally forced him into exile . . .
>
> When we look at China today, do we see the China that Wang and I hoped for sixty years ago? Were we hoping for a China where corruption, deception, cyn-icism are rife? Where exploitation, disease, prostitution and gangsterism have found their ways? Where the rural suicide rate is the highest in the world? Where the 'smart' people have no moral values and no interest in them? Where the nat-ural environment will take decades to recover, if ever?
>
> Ruled by a regime that still will not look squarely at the tens of millions of untimely deaths it caused in the Great Leap famine, but still harshly represses any voice or any organisation that speaks – or even might speak – against it? Is that where Wang Ruowang thought we would end up when he began his life's journey?

A major reason for the success of Chinese capitalism lay in the political and economic deals its leaders had concluded with the United States from the 1970s – when the Great Helmsman was still alive – and which have continued to the present day. The decision of the Chinese leadership to wage war against Vietnam as a punishment for defeating the United States was designed partially to prove their solidarity with their allies in Washington. It had the desired effect. Despite its blatant violations of the most elementary human rights of its citizens, the Chinese regime continued to receive 'most-favoured-nation' treatment from Western capitalism. As we shall see below, such an alliance has its limits, but till now it has served both sides well.

Excepting the war years (1942–5), the Soviet Union had always been a different matter. They had been the historic enemy. Their Revolution had thrown down the gauntlet to the capitalist order and had, seventy years later, dropped off the world map. How would the United States react to the disappearance of the Soviet Union? In its place there was Russia, of course, but also a dozen or so virgin republics, craving to be deflowered by the West. And then there was Eastern Europe. These were rich pickings for the imperial powers, and they had been gained for next to nothing. Mikhail Gorbachev had handed over East Germany without securing anything in return. *Mitteleuropa* awaited its destiny with bated breath.

The triumph of capitalism appeared complete. Even though the Soviet Union had not represented a serious revolutionary threat for many decades, its very existence had given heart to anti-colonial resistance movements in three continents, enabled the Cubans and Vietnamese to resist and survive, armed the ANC in South Africa and provided European social-democracy with a platform to wrest some reforms from the various capitalist elites. The collapse marked the end of an epoch. This was the world, still not fully under its control, on which a triumphant American Empire opened its Pandora's box to release some of its monsters and fears. Who would reorder the globe, and how? Was it possible to maintain the military–industrial complex if there were no more conflicts? Could some enemies be hurriedly manufactured? What was the most effective way to control the continental Europeans? How could Germany and Japan still be kept on a leash?

With the fall of communism, the state-intellectuals of the American Empire began to debate the glorious future. The ideological and economic triumph was complete, but was the world really conflict-free? The first

serious attempt to theorise the victory came in July 1989 with the publication of Francis Fukuyama's essay 'The End of History?' in the *National
Interest*. This was the former State Department employee whose disastrous
advice to the Pakistani military dictator, General Zia-ul-Haq (1977–89), that
he should keep his country as far away from India as possible, had damaged
the liberals and democrats in that country.[83]

His basic thesis, derived from the writings of Hegel and Kojeve, was that
with the defeat of fascism in the Second World War and the disintegration
of the Soviet Union forty-five years later, the victory of liberal-democracy
marked the end of the ideological evolution of humanity.[84] It was the end
because there was nowhere else to go. Nationalism and religious fundamentalism were the flotsam and jetsam of the dead past. Nor was this
triumph confined to the West. In the East, too, the successes of Japan,
South Korea and Taiwan heralded further changes along similar lines. Liberal
democracy was the climax of capitalism's epochal triumph and its structures
would contain the economic competition between states that was likely to
continue till the end of time. Some conflicts would continue, but they
could only be sideshows, pinpricks incapable of challenging liberal hegemony. The success of his essay gave rise to a meteoric bestseller translated
into all the major languages and referred to, if not read, by leader-writers
and columnists everywhere. For a short time it became the catechism of the

---

83 See 'The Story of Kashmir' p. 217.

84 Fukuyama was extremely irritated by crude interpretations of his work which regularly
claimed that he had ruled out all conflicts for all time to come. He denied this vigorously, calmly
informing me during the advertising break in a television programme on which we were debating the US bombing of Belgrade that, sadly, liberals hadn't really understood him. Marxists,
because of their understanding of Hegel, had been much clearer and though he disagreed with
'Professor Anderson's essay, I will admit that he understood my argument better than anyone else'.
For Perry Anderson's critical analysis see 'The Ends of History' in *A Zone of Engagement*, London
and New York 1992. More recently – on 20 September 2001 – Fukuyama signed an 'Open Letter
to the President' together with other defenders of liberal-democratic civilisation such as William
Kristol, Jeane Kirkpatrick, Richard Perle, Martin Peretz, Norman Podhoretz, Charles
Krauthammer and others. The letter gave total backing to Bush, urged him to 'capture or kill
Osama bin Laden' and warned him that failure to invade Iraq and topple Saddam Hussein would
'constitute an early and perhaps decisive surrender in the war on international terrorism'. This
should be done 'even if evidence does not link Iraq directly to the attack . . .' Here was the purest
expression of imperialist fundamentalism, or patriotism as it is known in the United States.

new globalisation. After which the book virtually disappeared as the *cognoscenti* waited for a successor.

It was in the summer of 1993 that Samuel Huntington, one-time counter-insurgency expert for the Johnson administration in Vietnam and later director of the Institute of Strategic Studies at Harvard University, published his article 'The Clash of Civilisations?' in *Foreign Affairs*, which immediately ignited a global controversy. As Huntington subsequently explained, 'the article struck a nerve in people of every civilization'. The essay became a book and later, thanks to Osama bin Laden, a bestseller. The author had become a prophet. Essentially conceived as a polemic – against Francis Fukuyama and 'The End of History?' – Huntington's thesis argued that while the crushing defeat of communism had brought to an end all ideological disputes, it did not signify the end of history. Henceforth culture, not politics or economics, would dominate and divide the world.

He listed eight cultures: Western, Confucian, Japanese, Islamic, Hindu, Slav-Orthodox, Latin American and, perhaps, African. Why perhaps? Because he was not sure whether it was really civilised. Each of these civilisations embodied different value-systems symbolised by religion, which Huntington argued was 'perhaps *the* central force that motivates and mobilises people'. The major divide was between 'the West and the Rest', because only the West valued 'individualism, liberalism, constitutionalism, human rights, equality, liberty, the rule of law, democracy, free markets'. Therefore the West (in reality, the United States) must be prepared to deal militarily with threats from these rival civilisations. The two most menacing were, predictably, Islam and Confucianism (oil and Chinese exports), and if these two were ever to unite, they would pose a threat to the existence of the core civilisation. He concluded on a sinister note: 'The world is not one. Civilisations unite and divide mankind . . . blood and belief are what people identify with and what they will fight and die for.' Other fundamentalists would have no problem agreeing with these sentiments.

This simple but politically convenient analysis provided an extremely useful cover for policy-makers and ideologues in Washington and elsewhere. Islam was seen as the biggest threat because most of the world's oil is produced in Iran, Iraq and Saudi Arabia. At the time Huntington was writing, the Islamic Republic in Iran was fourteen years old and still considered hostile to 'the Great Satan', Iraq's social, economic and military strength was being further eroded in the post-Gulf War syndrome, but Saudi Arabia remained a safe haven, its monarchy protected by American troops. 'Western civilisation' (supported in this case by its Confucian and Slav-Orthodox colleagues) had, as I detailed in an earlier chapter, organised the slow death of 300,000 children in Iraq, while a liberal-democratic-Wahhabi alliance protected the oil wells in the eastern provinces of Saudi Arabia.

There are two basic points to be made in response to Huntington and the civilisation-mongers. First, as I have tried to show in this book, the world of Islam has not been monolithic for over a thousand years. The social and cultural differences between Senegalese, Chinese, Indonesian, Arab and South Asian Muslims are far greater than the similarities they share with non-Muslim members of the same nationality. Over the last hundred years, the world of Islam has felt the heat of wars and revolutions just like every other society. The seventy-year war between United States imperialism and the Soviet Union affected every single 'civilisation'. Communist parties sprouted, grew and gained mass support not only in Lutheran Germany but in Confucian China and Muslim Indonesia. Only the Anglo-Saxon zone, comprising Britain and North America, resisted the infection.

During the Twenties and Thirties, just as they were in Europe, intellectuals in the Arab world were divided between the cosmopolitan appeal of Enlightenment Marxism and the anti-Enlightenment populism of Mussolini and Hitler. Liberalism, perceived as the ideology of the British empire, was less popular. It is the same today. Some Muslim guerrillas in Palestine and Chechnya read the works of Che Guevara and Vo Nguyen Giap. Some Muslim thinkers of the early Sixties – Ali Shariati and Sayyid Kutb – greatly appreciated the writings of the ultra-nationalist Alexis Carrel, a Pétainist whose work is studied avidly today in the training camps of the French National Front.[85]

---

85 Alexis Carrel (1873–1944) was a remarkably gifted but quarrelsome surgeon who left France to make his career in French Canada and later the United States. He was awarded the Nobel Prize for Medicine, which enhanced his credibility and appeal. He began to write on a variety of themes, including eugenics and racial purity. 'Race betterment' and 'whiteness' became regular focuses. He regarded the Scandinavian as one of the most highly civilised races because of the purity of their whiteness (more likely because they had awarded him the Nobel Prize). Later,

After the Second World War the United States backed the most reactionary elements as a bulwark against communism or progressive/secular nationalism. Often these were hardline religious fundamentalists: the Muslim Brotherhood against Nasser in Egypt; the Masjumi against Sukarno in Indonesia, the Jamaat-e-Islami against Bhutto in Pakistan and, later, Osama bin Laden and friends against the secular-communist Najibullah. When the Taliban took Kabul in 1996, one of their first acts was to drag Najibullah out of the UN compound where he had sought refuge and kill him. Once this had been done, his naked body with his penis and testicles stuffed into his mouth was hung up on public display so that the citizens of Kabul would count the high price that an unbeliever had to pay. To the best of my knowledge not a single leader or leader-writer of the West registered a dissenting opinion. Clash of civilisations?

The only exceptions were Iraq and Iran. There was no potential in Sixties Iraq for creating a confessional group. The Communist Party was the most significant social force in the country and it could not be allowed a victory. The United States backed the gangster wing of the Ba'ath Party and encouraged it to decimate first the communists and then the oil-workers' trade unions. Saddam Hussein complied and was rewarded by the West with arms and trade contracts till his fatal misjudgement on Kuwait in 1990. In Iran, as described in an earlier chapter, the West backed a despotic second-generation shah whose modernity came complete with torture instruments specially ordered from British firms. The secular opposition which first got rid of the shah was outfoxed by British Intelligence and the CIA. The vacuum was later occupied by the clerics who rule the country today.

What this reveals is a veteran imperialism that has single-mindedly pursued its own interests – economic, political and military – for a long time.

---

he became a great admirer of Benito Mussolini, despite his distaste for the pigmentation of the Mediterranean races. He regularly denounced liberal democracies for abandoning religion and insisted that this was 'the cause of their weakness and inefficiency'. In 1935 he became a eugenicist and argued that: 'Eugenics is indispensable for the perpetuation of the strong. A great race must propagate its best elements.' During the Second World War he returned to France and worked in support of the Vichy regime, becoming an irregular visitor at the German embassy. He died just before the Liberation, thus avoiding being tried as a collaborator.

Western domination came about because of the advances in science and technology.[86] It did so regionally prior to 1917, on a global scale afterwards, and since the demise of the Soviet Union it has been busy with important readjustments. One of these was NATO enlargement, designed to isolate Russia from the newer republics in the region and to ensure that US interests were properly safeguarded. What other reason is there for NATO to exist except to control the Europeans? And what other reason is there for the massive US arms expenditure than to protect its imperial legacy? It is the most powerful imperialism today. Its defence budget for 2000 was $267.2 billion, an amount greater than the combined military budgets of China, Russia, India, Germany and France. If one adds US military spending to that of NATO, Japan, South Korea and Israel, it is 80 per cent of the world total. The only possible reason for this is to preserve the domination of the United States vis-à-vis its own allies. General Butler's old description is today even more apposite. It is a global protection racket. In return for defending the interests of some of its allies, the US exacts a heavy price. It is Japan's trade-surpluses and dollar reserves, for instance, that have helped to maintain the dollar's status as a global currency.

The distinguished American historian Chalmers Johnson has provided us with a fascinating account of how this system works. Johnson is not the usual 'anti-American' or 'Occidentalist' scholar reviled by both state and power-intellectuals.[87] His credentials are unquestionable. He belongs to a

---

86 The lack of a navy had seriously hindered the development of Indian trade and precipitated the sudden decline of Mughal India in the late seventeenth and eighteenth centuries. Portuguese, Dutch and English traders were armed with the latest technology. The first signs of this were already visible in the mid-seventeenth century when the Portuguese asserted their monopoly of naval power in the Indian Ocean by sinking pilgrim ships bound for Mecca, and later when the British used their guns to silence the Wusung Forts in defence of the narcotics trade in China. Behind the guns stood Christian missionaries, ready to convert the heathen to a superior faith.

87 State-intellectuals are those who have worked for or emerged from the bowels of the US state machine: Kissinger, Brzezinski, Fukuyama and Huntington typify this breed, but many more work in less grand capacities as journalists for the *New York Times* and *Washington Post*. The power-intellectuals fall into a number of categories. A pompous self-description of one is 'historians of the present'. This layer consists of gifted journalists who hover over a world crisis like expectant vultures. Who will get to the corpse first? Their writings are not without merit and often they come up with interesting and useful information, but underlying all their work is a self-denying ordinance: a delicate balance between truth and power must be observed and the imperial

West Coast naval family. His father served in both world wars. Johnson himself was in the Naval Air Reserve and stationed as a member of the fleet in war-defeated Japan. Released to 'inactive duty' he returned home, registered as a graduate student at Berkeley and became a scholar on China and Japan. He was untouched by the campus turbulence of the Sixties and never became a leftist. He supported the United States in Vietnam. It is the post-Cold War mobilisation of the American Empire that has made his one of the most critical voices in the United States, and his latest work, *Blowback*, has been subjected to much mindless criticism from the Americophiles and their patriotic spear-carriers. In *Blowback*, Chalmers Johnson argues that the American Empire is overextended, and the longer it struggles to maintain this status, the more painful the retribution will be. He contrasts the amount spent to defend the Persian Gulf – $50 billion out of the annual US defence budget – with the cost of the imported oil, which is only $11 billion and makes up 10 per cent of US consumption. The same oil accounts for one-quarter of European and one-half of Japanese needs. This is not so much 'post-imperialism' as 'ultra-imperialism'. It may be invisible to the average Western citizen, but the rest of the world knows of its existence. It moves.

There are at the moment 187 member states of the United Nations. The United States has a military presence in 100 countries. One of these is the tiny island of Qatar, which is also the headquarters of al-Jazeera TV. William Arkin described the base to the readers of the *LA Times*:

---

power must never be displeased with what they write. Their writings, presented as objective surveys, appear in publications all over the world, but their regular home is the *New York Review of Books*, whose politics since the Reagan era usually reflect the views of the liberal wing of the State Department. A new type of power-intellectual is the journalist/intellectual from what was once known as the 'third world'. S/he was an anti-imperialist in the past, but has adjusted rapidly to the new order. An expert on the iniquities of Saddam Hussein, this type was much in demand during the Gulf War and Afghanistan and the praise and affection lavished on him by the imperial state and its institutions went to his head. He began to imagine that what he said mattered and he would be able to inflect US policy in a more 'progressive' direction. He entreated the Great Power never to abandon the particular region again. Don't leave us to ourselves is the plea. This is the other side of despair. A whole layer of former radicals no longer believe in the capacity of people to liberate themselves and have become apologists for the new colonialism.

Al Adid is a billion-dollar base. Its 15,000 foot runway is one of the longest in the Gulf Region. Construction began after an April 2000 visit by Defense Secretary William S. Cohen. Qatar already housed equipment for an Army brigade and, in 1996, hosted 30 Air Force fighters on an 'expeditionary' deployment. Though the original justification for Gulf bases such as Al Adid was preparedness for renewed action, a senior defense official said last year that the Qatar facilities were 'not focused on one particular country or the another, but part of a system we would like to have in place' . . . As of September 11, according to Pentagon documents, the United States had formal agreements of this sort with Qatar and 92 other countries.[88]

Chalmers Johnson stretched Eisenhower's prescient warning on the 'military–industrial complex' to suggest that the complex is now a global phenomenon:

One of the things this huge military establishment also does is sell arms to other countries, making the Pentagon a critical *economic* agency of a United States government. Militarily oriented products account for about a quarter of the total U.S. gross domestic product. The government employs some 6,500 people just to co-ordinate and administer its arms sales programme in conjunction with senior officials at American embassies around the world, who spend most of their 'diplomatic' careers working as arms salesmen. The Arms Export Control Act requires that the executive branch notify Congress of foreign military and construction sales directly negotiated by the Pentagon. Commercial sales valued at $14 million or more negotiated by the arms industry must also be reported. Using official Pentagon statistics, between 1990 and 1996 the combination of the three categories amounted to $97,836,821,000. From this nearly $100 billion figure must be subtracted the $3 billion a year the government offers its foreign customers to help subsidize arms purchases from the United States.[89]

Aware of these realities, a senior imperialist ideologue, Zbigniew Brzezinski, warned Russia in 1996: 'Russia is viable as a nation state. I don't think, however, it has much future as an empire. If they're stupid

---

88 'U.S. Air-Bases Forge Double-edged Sword', by William M. Arkin, *Los Angeles Times*, 6 January 2002.

89 Chalmers Johnson, *Blowback: The Costs and Consequences of American Empire*, New York and London 2000, p. 87.

enough to try, they'll get themselves into conflicts that'll make Chechnya and Afghanistan look like a picnic.'[90] But the same rules did not apply to the United States. They did involve themselves in a number of conflicts: Somalia, Bosnia, Kosovo. The first of these was a total disaster. On this occasion the cover of UN sanction for the new doctrine of 'humanitarian intervention' was utilised to intervene in the country.

This war, like those that were to succeed it, was accompanied by a well-orchestrated propaganda campaign. Politics is conducted and presented in the elitist style of intelligence agencies: disinformation, false information, exaggeration of enemy strength and capability, explanation of a TV image with a brazen lie, and censorship. The aim is to delude and disarm the citizenry. Everything is either oversimplified or reduced to a wearisome incomprehensibility. The message is simple. There is no alternative.

In the case of Somalia, the declared intention of Operation Restore Hope was to save Somali lives threatened by famine. The television networks flashed the required images. The world was told that 2 million would die if there was no military intervention to stop the civil conflict and enable food to reach the starving people. Most of the deaths had been caused by malaria. The US troops and the relief agencies arrived without any anti-malaria programme and when the famine itself was already waning. The relief agencies did not want a military presence in the capital, Mogadishu. They asked for a limited, carefully targeted drop in the 'famine triangle', an option that was rejected because, according to James L. Woods, deputy secretary for Defence for African Affairs, 'it failed to meet the US military's new insistence on the application of massive, overwhelming force'.

At the start of the military intervention in 1992, Colin Powell, at the time the chairman of the Pentagon's Joint Chiefs of Staff, called the invasion a 'paid political advertisement' for the Pentagon. It was less than a year since

---

90 *Transition*, 15 November 1996. Ultra-critical of Russia's democracy, Brzezinski had no similar criticisms of Georgia, Ukraine, Azerbaijan, Moldova or Uzbekistan. What explains these double standards? Could it be the fact that Brzezinski is a consultant to Amoco and the Azerbaijan International Operating Company, a cartel whose projected oil pipelines and agreements are central to US interests in the region? And why didn't Brzezinski's star pupil, Madeleine Albright, the scourge of Iraq, ever criticise the regimes in Azerbaijan and Uzbekistan, where there is less democracy than in Russia?

the Cold War had ended and Powell was seeking to maintain the $300-billion-plus budget at the time. The Somalians were the unfortunate guinea-pigs chosen to justify the expenditure. The operation was a disaster. The Somalians have an honourable record of resisting Italian and British colonial oppression. US soldiers began to die, an American pilot was captured and dragged through the streets of Mogadishu, and the TV images rebounded. The US special envoy, Robert Oakley, appeased first one and then another general.[91] The US/UN forces permitted General Mohammed Hersi Morgan, the 'butcher of Hergeisa', to occupy Kismayo, but opened fire on citizens protesting the occupation in Mogadishu. As in the past, the worst atrocities were carried out by Belgian troops. They killed over seven hundred Somalis and numerous incidents of rape were reported. After US helicopters on a rescue mission had opened fire and killed sixty civilians, Major David Stockwell, a UN spokesman, was unapologetic: 'There are no sidelines or spectator seats – the people on the ground are considered combatants.'[92] None of those responsible were charged or tried. If the former Yugoslav president can be tried retrospectively for crimes he is said to have committed, why not the US/UN High Command and the paratroopers responsible? In a devastating critique of the entire operation, Alex de Waal concluded:

> The collapse of the UN–US intervention can only be understood when it is realized just how deeply the UN forces had antagonised a wide swathe of Somali society. When the Marines landed on Mogadishu beach on 9 December 1992, hopes were high . . . but the behaviour of a large number of troops was deplorable. Many countries had sent hardened paratroopers and other combat troops on a mission in which police training and civil engineering skills were needed. In many cases the operation quickly degenerated into routine brutality against Somali civilians . . .
>
> One thing that the US and UN never appreciated was that, as they escalated the level of murder and mayhem, they increased the determination of the Somalis to resist and fight back. By the time of the 3 October battle, literally every inhabitant

---

91 Robert Oakley is still remembered as the US ambassador in Pakistan who behaved more like a pro-consul and was more friendly with generals than with elected politicians.

92 Keith Richburg, 'UN Defends Firing on Somali Crowd', *The Washington Post*, 11 September 1993. Major Stockwell's immortal words were echoed by many Islamists who defended the action of 11 September 2001.

of large areas of Mogadishu considered the UN and US as enemies, and were ready to take up arms against them.[93]

After 11 September there was much talk of re-entering Somalia to avenge the debacle of 1992. On 17 October 2001 a meeting of Hollywood chiefs 'committed themselves to new initiatives in support of the war on terrorism'. The first of these is a disgusting, racist, $90 million film, *Black Hawk Down*, whose design is embarrassingly obvious: to stir primitive patriotic sentiments to justify a war in Somalia if it becomes necessary. Its Washington premiere was graced by Defense Secretary Donald Rumsfeld and veteran war criminal Oliver North.

None of the cultures/civilisations spawned by the three monotheistic religions are monolithic or timeless. Despite the differences between them, they are all affected by the world they cohabit. Times change and they change with them, but in their own way. A striking feature of the present is that no mainstream political party anywhere in the world even pretends that it wishes to change anything significant. If it is true that history and democracy were born as twins in Ancient Greece, will their deaths, too, coincide? The virtual outlawing of history by the dominant culture has reduced the process of democracy to farce. The result is a mishmash of cynicism, despair and escapism. This is precisely an environment designed to nurture irrationalisms of every sort. Over the last fifty years, religious revivalism with a political edge has flourished in many different cultures. Nor is the process finished. A major cause is the fact that all the other exit routes have been sealed off by the mother of all fundamentalisms: American imperialism.

This is something that neither Samuel P. Huntington nor Francis Fukuyama can bring themselves to acknowledge, just as modern Islamist thinkers can be lucid on many subjects, but never accept that their own religion desperately needs a Reformation. In post-11 September essays and interviews, both men have been explaining and modifying their earlier work. Of the two, it is Huntington who is in much greater demand, since many have interpreted the 'war against terrorism' as a civilisational conflict. Huntington himself is not of this view. He has decamped from a position of

---

93 Alex de Waal, 'US War Crimes in Somalia', *New Left Review* I, 230, July/August 1998.

'West versus the Rest', which implied that Western civilisation needed to be cocooned in a giant equivalent of the old 'strategic hamlets' of Vietnam and defended against contamination from everyone else and by any means necessary. He has also, if temporarily, discarded the option that this is a case of 'Islam versus the Rest'. In an essay in the 'Special Davos Edition' of *Newsweek* magazine (Dec. 2001–Feb. 2002) he defines the post-Cold War conjuncture as one of 'Muslim wars', arguing that 'Muslims fight each other and fight non-Muslims far more often than do people of other civilizations'. This simplistic notion leaves his whole conception of 'wars of civilisation' hopelessly mired in a fundamental contradiction. Either we're seeing an 'age of Muslim wars' or a 'clash of civilisations'. It can't be both. In fact it is neither. Huntington's essay highlights two conflicts as marking the beginning of the 'Muslim wars'. The first is the Iraq–Iran war, but as argued earlier in this book, this war could never have taken place if Washington and London had not directly backed and armed Saddam Hussein in the hope that their dictator *du jour* would defeat the clerics and that a pro-Western regime of some sort could be restored.

The second example of a Muslim war is the 1980s anti-Soviet jihad in Afghanistan. Huntington admits that 'this victory was made possible by American technology, Saudi and American money, Pakistani support and training, and the participation of thousands of fighters from other, mostly Arab, Muslim, countries.' Exactly, though he could have added that these included Osama bin Laden and that many of those trained and applauded by the United States at the time later formed the inner core of al-Qaida and decided to break with their former protector. In fact, the entire Afghan war was orchestrated and executed by the United States through the use of totalitarian proxies: Saudi Arabia and General Zia's vicious military dictatorship in Pakistan.[94] Why then characterise this as a 'Muslim war'?

Both the conflicts cited had the total support of the West. Then, as now,

---

94 Contrary to *The Economist* editorial of 19 January 2002, General Zia did not just 'flirt recklessly with fundamentalism', he was a fundamentalist himself, directly responsible for creating and funding the groups that are currently causing mayhem in the region. He instituted public hangings and floggings on the Saudi model and helped to destroy the political culture of Pakistan. He encouraged Islamist penetration of the army and institutionalised the ritual prayer within the army and the civil service. *The Economist* editorials of the period were remarkably indulgent, and for the same reasons that led Washington and London to support him. He was a vital conduit for the anti-Soviet jihad at the time.

individual Muslims as well as Muslim states were happy to follow the war-chariot of the Empire. And when Huntington frankly acknowledges that the 'age of Muslim wars has its roots in more general causes [which] . . . lie in politics, not seventh-century religious doctrines', and correctly explains how these causes include 'American action against Iraq since 1991 and the continuing close relationship between the United States and Israel', his views are closer to those critics of the Empire, who opposed the war of revenge in Afghanistan. The new converts – liberals who have embraced a primitive patriotism – are too busy trying to prove their loyalty to think seriously of world politics.

Huntington must be aware that his latest writings are exploding the foundation of the edifice he had so carefully constructed. This does not apply to rival theorist Francis Fukuyama. He is still convinced of his own conclusions and he carefully positions himself at a respectable distance from Huntington. For Fukuyama, 11 September was an assault against modernity, based on Islamic fundamentalist hatred of all Western values as well as homosexuality, permissiveness and women. He explicitly rejects the view that politics had anything much to do with what happened. Interestingly enough, he is much closer to Huntington's original thesis than Huntington: 'The Islamic world differs from other world cultures today in one important respect. In recent years it alone has repeatedly produced significant radical Islamist movements that reject not just Western policies, but the most basic principle of modernity itself, that of religious tolerance.'[95]

The first point to be made about this is that intolerance or hatred of 'permissiveness' is nothing new and is certainly not confined to Islam. America is supersaturated with religion – 90 per cent of the population regularly declare belief in the deity; 60 per cent believe in angels. There are more believers in the United States than in the whole of Western Europe put together. And religious passions run high, as we saw when American Christian fundamentalists greeted 11 September as God's punishment of a society that tolerated homosexuality and abortion. Whether the United States' traditionally high civil murder rate also punishes the victims' sins, the same Christian sages do not say. Theirs is a pick-and-mix theology. Jewish settlers in the West Bank claim the land in the name of their old scriptures

---

95 *Newsweek*, December–January (2001–2), Special Issue.

and certainly do not believe in religious tolerance. But Fukuyama wants war against the new enemy and, for that reason, he has to stress the 'civilisational' gulf and then go further and characterise Islamism as 'Islamo-fascism'. This is not so much the end of history as a closure of the Western imagination.

Ever since the Second World War the name of Hitler and his philosophy has been recklessly invoked to drum up public support for Western wars. It is an interesting reflection on the recent history of the West that it has to reach over half a century back before it can conjure up a justifiable war and an enemy rooted in popular memory. During the First Oil War (Suez) in 1956, Britain characterised the Egyptian leader, Gamal Abdel Nasser, as the 'Hitler on the Nile'; for the duration of the Third Oil War (aka the Gulf War) the Hitler badge was pinned on the lapel of the Iraqi leader, Saddam Hussein. He only became Hitler when he misread US signals. Throughout the Iran–Iraq war or the internal suppression of the communists and the Kurds, Saddam had been the apple of the State Department's eye. Subsequently, when Madeleine Albright decided that a war was needed in Kosovo and accordingly produced a secret and unacceptable clause to a treaty that had already been accepted by the Yugoslav leadership, the Serbian leader was provided with the familiar sobriquet: Milosevic became Hitler. It was inevitable that, sooner or later, an apologist for the latest war would describe the latest enemy as 'fascist'. The metamorphosis is triggered only when the 'fascists' are opposed to US interests. Had they been 'fascists' in the Eighties then Fukuyama would have had to justify an alliance with 'Islamo-fascists' against the Evil Empire, which might have required some contortion. Or perhaps not. After all important sectors of the liberal-democratic British and French ruling elites were proposing exactly such an alliance with Hitler against the 'Bolshevik menace' in the Thirties. It was the notoriously irrational German leader who let them down on that occasion.[96]

---

96 An Anglo-French-German bloc might well have defeated the Soviet Union, but the new power would have also posed a threat to the imperial ambitions of the United States. The pro-appeasement wing of the English ruling class deeply resented the Americans. In his entertaining *Diaries*, Chips Channon quotes R.A. Butler, a leading appeaser, commenting on Churchill's elevation to 10 Downing Street: 'We have a racial half-breed as Prime Minister.' Churchill's mother was an American heiress. Churchill himself was remarkably soft on Mussolini, and greeted the Duce's victory in 1922 as a triumph against Bolshevism. It was only after the Second World War that fascism became defined as a permanent enemy.

Liberal definitions of fascism adopt the approach of ticking off items from an already printed menu and seeing if they match. But many social-democratic and most Marxist definitions grew out of the actual experience. They explained the rise of Italian, German, Spanish and French fascism as deriving from the overall dynamics of capitalist societies. Fascism was a weapon of last resort, used by a ruling class faced simultaneously with an economic crisis and the threat of a revolutionary labour movement. This was certainly the case in parts of Europe during the interwar period.

The fascist triumph in Germany would not have been possible without the support of big business, which benefited enormously during the first five years of the Third Reich: profits rose from 6.6 billion marks in 1933 to 15 billion in 1938. The destructive delirium of fascist ideology was carefully targeted. It never obstructed the payment of permanent homage to its eco-nomic backers. Even at the height of the war, patriotism was never permitted to deflect the search for profits. In most cases, the Nazi regime obediently capitulated. A classic example is the detailed negotiations between the Flick companies and the government on the price of bazooka shells. The government offered 24 RM per shell. Flick demanded 39.25 RM per shell. Agreement was reached at 37 RM, which meant an extra gain of more than 1 million marks over the period 1940–3.[97]

To dress all new enemies in the black shirts and leather jackets of European fascism is grotesque. It is done because it helps the media to pro-ject the enemy, but the credulity of Western citizens has its limits and the Hitler fix won't work every time. State intellectuals might be better advised to ponder their own back yard. The democracy they boast of is ailing. Politics equals concentrated economics. The author of a recent intellectual biography of Tocqueville concludes thus:

> Far from being valued as symbolising an aspiration towards the democratisation of power and a participatory society of political equals – democracy as subject – democracy would come to be regarded by late-modern power elites as an indis-pensable yet valuable myth for promoting American political and economic interests among premodern and post-totalitarian societies. At home democracy is

---

97 Ernest Mandel, Introduction to *The Struggle Against Fascism in Germany*, by Leon Trotsky, London 1972.

touted not as self-government by an involved citizenry but as economic opportunity. Opportunity serves as the means of implicating the populace in anti-democracy, in a politico-economic system characterised by the dominating power of hierarchical organisations, widening class differentials, and a society where the hereditary element is confined to successive generations of the defenseless poor.[98]

This is what the fanatical preachers of neo-liberalism had always intended. When they began their work in the Sixties and Seventies of the last century they were treated as a joke by Keynesian liberals, scorned by social-democrats and kept at a distance by the conservatives. A majority of Marxist economists did not even deign to take them seriously. But for a quarter of a century, Von Hayek and his loyal followers ignored the ridicule and burrowed away underneath the surface, suddenly to emerge and greet the leaders of the victorious counter-Revolution: Ronald Reagan and Margaret Thatcher. The combination of neo-liberal ideas and the social forces represented by the two politicians transformed the globe.

Hayek was not just the high priest of hard doctrines at home. He favoured military actions to defend US interests abroad. On the domestic front he favoured the invisible magic of a manipulated market. No state intervention against the interests of capital was to be tolerated. But the state was vital to undertake military interventions in the sphere of international relations. The circle of neo-liberals were staunch defenders of the Vietnam war. They supported the US-backed military *coup* in Chile. In 1979, Hayek favoured bombing Tehran. In 1982, during the Malvinas conflict, he wanted raids on the Argentinian capital. This was the creed of neo-liberal hegemony most favoured by its founder.

The cuts in direct taxation, deregulation of financial markets, weak trades-unions and privatised public services were necessary to assert the primacy of consumption – the commodification of all goods and services – which was fuelled by the private sector. The modified capitalist system now accepted speculation as a central feature of economic life in the world's financial markets. The success of the system required that private capital was

---

98 Sheldon Wolin, *Tocqueville Between Two Worlds: The Making of a Political and Theoretical Life*, Princeton 2001.

permitted to penetrate the social fabric with the mass marketing of mutual and pension funds.

Having united the Western world on the necessity to push through neo-liberal 'reforms', the American Empire was to follow through on the need to assert its power globally. In this it was supported to the hilt by its old Trojan Horse in the European Union, otherwise the United Kingdom. For many years now, one of the main priorities of the WTO has been to accelerate the privatisation of education, health, welfare, social housing and transport. With the decline of profit-margins in the once prosperous manufacturing sector, Western capitalism is determined to force entry into a once inviolate public sphere. Giant multinationals have been busy preparing competitive tenders to capture the public services share of the gross domestic product.

In its notorious 1993 development report titled 'Investing in Health', the World Bank described public services as an obstacle to abolishing world poverty. There have been important conflicts between US/Canada and the EU on some of the policies advocated by the WTO which affect the health and safety of citizens, but the multinationals are winning. A few years ago in the hormone-treated beef dispute, the WTO ruled in favour of USA/Canada arguing that EU safety standards were higher than those accepted internationally. In a sharply critical review of WTO policies Professor Allyson Pollock (of the Health Services Research Unit at University College, London) argued in *Lancet,* the leading British medical journal, on 9 December 2000:

> . . . the WTO's national treatment rule was used to define a public-health initiative as protectionist and therefore potentially illegal . . . The new criteria proposed at the WTO threaten some of the key mechanisms that allow governments to guarantee health care for their populations by requiring governments to demonstrate that their pursuit of social policy goals are least restrictive and least costly to trade.

New Labour, like their Thatcherite predecessors, ever desperate to please the United States and its financial institutions, are determined to be the first EU state that fulfils all the WTO conditions. Accordingly, the British public was informed that the Private Finance Initiative (PFI) would be used to create a new structure in the public sector. In other words New Labour declared that it would go further than Thatcher and Major dared and attempt to complete the Thatcher counter-revolution. The air-traffic controllers will be sold off to a few wealthy airlines. The railways, whose privatisation has been a total disaster financially and has led to the breakdown of safety, will not be taken back into any form of public ownership. New laws are being passed to make it possible for any local authority to sell off any school to private industry. At the moment only those schools considered to be 'failing' – i.e. not provided with sufficient resources by the government to teach children from poor families – are handed over to companies. Among the firms directly engaged in teaching children of 'failed' schools are Shell Oil (special lessons in ecology?), British Aerospace (lectures on the arms trade?), McDonalds (healthy eating?).

France and Germany were moving in the same direction. Lionel Jospin and Gerhard Schroeder had come to power repudiating the hard-nosed policies that promoted accumulation and inequality, but their policies have promoted both of them. The privatisation carried out by the French Socialists have exceeded that of the previous six administrations. The German social-democrats have been more hamstrung, but their trajectory is clear.

As they accommodated to neo-liberal fundamentalism at home, they accepted its militarist logic abroad. Britain, France and Germany supported the Third Oil War (1991), the Balkan wars and the 'war on terrorism'. So keen was Germany to become part of the new world order that the Red-Green coalition voted through the re-involvement of the German Republic in military adventures abroad. The dissident Greens in the Bundestag met privately to determine how they could register a few votes against, without threatening the coalition.

It would be illusory to imagine that it is only the Big Three of the EU who line up as obedient retrievers on US hunting missions. The Scandinavian states, once respected throughout the world for their independence, have not wanted to be left behind. Like obedient poodles they follow the leaders of the Empire: Norway was proud of its role in creating Palestinian bantustans, Finland brokered the bombing of Yugoslavia, the Swedish government has been party to the starvation of Iraq, while Denmark supplied a Viceroy in Kosovo.

Meanwhile in the rest of the world, a billion people are undernourished and 7 million children die as a result of the debt owed by the countries in which they live. It is this that accounts for the desperation and hatred that surfaces in large parts of the world against the United States and its allies. Senegal was instructed by the IMF mullahs to withdraw territorial sovereignty from its territorial waters or else its debt would not be rescheduled. It did so. The result? The factory-trawlers of Europe have taken the fish for the supermarkets of the EU. The waters from which the fishermen of Senegal drew sustenance for many thousand years have been taken over by the rich West. The people of this country are suffering because there is now a shortage of fish. Bolivia was ordered to privatise its water. The poor were forbidden to collect the rainwater that had accumulated on their roofs. Water rates became prohibitive. There was a semi-uprising in the town of Cochabamba as a result and some concessions were won. The situation in Ghana is virtually the same. Here the poor have been forced to drink untreated water which has led to disease and death. The Ivory Coast was compelled to withdraw subsidies to its cocoa farmers. This led to massive redundancies. Skilled workers were replaced by indentured children. Two-fifths of the chocolate drunk and eaten by the West is produced by super-exploited child labour.

This is the world in which we live – out of tune with the lucid humanity and the social compassion demanded by anti-globalisation protesters – and beyond which, write the intellectual apologists of this system, no substantial improvement can be imagined. 'Obliterate all political passions', cry the politicians of the globalised world. It reminds me of the title of a poem written seventy years ago by Bertolt Brecht: '700 intellectuals bow before an oil tanker.'

21

September surprise

The events of 11 September have generated a great deal of mediatic hyperbole, but the notion that they represent a new epoch or a historic turning-point is propaganda. Not for the first time, overheated pundits have colluded both to heighten the meaning of an event and thereby to enhance their own self-importance. To accept that the appalling deaths of over 3,000 people in the USA are more morally abhorrent than the 20,000 lives destroyed by Putin when he razed Grozny or the daily casualties in Palestine and Iraq is obscene.

In real terms the terrorist attack has strengthened the domestic and international standing of the Bush administration, which has secured a blank cheque from the UN, support from Russia and China and extended its influence in West and Central Asia. The real test, however, will come in the months and years after the bombing of Afghanistan is over. The delayed blowback in Pakistan, Saudi Arabia and Egypt might destabilise the world order in unexpected ways.

The first time I realised that the US mainland was an untouchable sanctuary, a sacred space that could never be violated was in December–January 1966–7. I was in Northern Vietnam, together with a small group of observers from North America and western Europe. We were investigating US war crimes, which few in the West could believe were taking place, on behalf of a War Crimes Tribunal set up on the initiative of two philosophers, Bertrand Russell and Jean-Paul Sartre.

One day in the southern province of Thanh-Hoa, the bombing was so heavy, the destruction so unbearable and the sight of civilian casualties, mainly women and children, so affecting that I lost my temper at a press conference later that week. I remarked that it was a great pity that US cities had never been bombed in any war. Had this happened I was sure that ordinary American people would realise that tactics of this sort united the population and filled it with hatred against those responsible for such attacks. This might have made them more sympathetic to the Vietnamese. The British Consul-General in Hanoi held a similar view and had calmly told me over tea and sandwiches at the embassy that when he heard the roar of the American bombers his first instinct was to get a rifle and fire at them. However, my remarks shocked a fellow member of the Tribunal, a radical American journalist, Carol Brightman. She reprimanded me in private and warned that remarks like these could be misinterpreted in the United States and would definitely not help the antiwar movement.

The memory of that conversation returned on 11 September. The events certainly united the American people, but far from making them understand that such tactics were ineffective, they were ready to support the revenge bombing of any country and any target anywhere in the world. An old friend in New York described her shock when an Afro-American she met in the street told her: 'We should go and wipe 'em out, just like we did the Injuns.' Many antiwar liberals, too cowardly to defend the new war, became resolute at home as they cheered on the bombers. This was the dominant mood, but many who did not speak were silenced by fear. I noted down the following conversation soon after it had taken place in October, when I was in New York for a conference at the Graduate Center of the City University. I had taken a cab from the airport and was making polite conversation with a white-bearded Latino, whose cab was festooned with Stars and Stripes:

Me: Where were you on September 11th?
He: (looking at me closely in the rear-view mirror) Why do you ask?
Me: I just wondered.
He: Where are you from?
Me: London.
He: No, I mean where are you *really* from?
Me: Pakistan.
He: I'm Taliban. Look at me. No, no. I'm from Central America. Can't you tell?
Me: I just wondered whether you were anywhere near the Twin Towers that day.

He: No, I wasn't but I wouldn't have cared if I was.

Me: What do you mean?

He: It wouldn't have mattered if I had got killed. The important thing is that *they* were hit. I was happy. You know why?

Me: No.

He: You know how many people they've killed in Central America. You know?

Me: Tell me.

He: Hundreds of thousands. Yes, really. They're still killing us. I'm really happy they were hit. We got our revenge. I feel sorry for the ones who died. That's more than they feel for us.

Me: Why do you live here?

He: My son is at school here. I'm working to pay for his education. We had to come here because they left nothing back home. Nothing. No schools. No universities. You think I'd rather be here than in my own country?

These remarks would have shocked many Americans, but not Chalmers Johnson, who had tried to alert his fellow citizens to the dangers that lay ahead. He had done so a whole year before the hijackers hit the Pentagon:

> 'Blowback' is shorthand for saying that a nation reaps what it sows, even if it does not fully know or understand what it has sown. Given its wealth and power, the United States will be a prime recipient in the foreseeable future of all of the more expectable forms of blowback, particularly terrorist attacks against Americans in and out of the armed forces anywhere on earth, including within the United States.

It is the aftermath that concerns us now. A proper balance-sheet will only be possible after a few years, but a few preliminary remarks are necessary. This was the most visible act of violence the world had seen in real time over the last three decades. The world media, which cast their own discreeter veil over the daily violence in other parts of the world, thus rendering it invisible, were drawn straight to the site of the outrage. This was the trial of O.J. Simpson and the death of Princess Diana scaled up by orders of magnitude. Even so, the commentators, hacks and non-hacks alike, supplied an unremitting and familiar chorus. A rain of cliché fell, week after week: 'the world had changed for ever', 'would never be the same again', 'where were you when the first plane hit the first tower?' etc.

Did anything really change after 11 September? Has there been a fundamental shift in world politics? I think not. The modifications in US policy have created further instability in parts of the world without doing anything, so far, to deal with the root causes of the problem. A review of the US response to 11 September does not reveal too much that is original. But that could change if unrest in Saudi Arabia and Pakistan reached a higher level.

The United States has waged war on Afghanistan, removed the Taliban from power and imposed a government of its own. How is this new? General Butler has already enlightened us on how often this was done, and on whose behalf, in Latin America over the last two centuries. New in Asia? Hardly. Mossadegh was toppled in Iran, Bhutto removed in Pakistan, Sheikh Mujib assassinated in Bangladesh, several regimes were imposed and deposed in South-East Asia and Japan was, till recently, established as a de facto one-party state, whose foundations were laid by the former colleagues of General Tojo in collaboration with General Douglas MacArthur. The fact that the United States is behaving like an imperial power is hardly new for most of the world. Some of the criticisms from Europe's 'third-way' supplicants are simply a case of sour grapes. They are nostalgic for the Clinton era because the old stallion was 'more inclusive' and made them feel that, like Monica Lewinsky, they were part of the action, when it was obvious to anyone that they were simply being used. The Bush-men and women are less given to fancy talk.[99]

It is not the person of Osama bin Laden, or even the al-Qaida network, which is minuscule when compared with even the tiniest of Arab armies. The question is why does an educated layer of Saudis, Egyptians and

---

99 In a 45-minute debate with Charles Krauthammer on Canadian Broadcasting Corporation's 'Counter-Spin' programme in November 2001, I found his politics obnoxious but his honesty refreshing. When I suggested that the Afghan war was basically 'a crude war of revenge', he agreed and defended it as such. When I pointed out that the US had created Osama bin Laden and his gang during the first Afghan War, he agreed and argued it was necessary at the time to defeat the Soviet Union. He was not going to apologise to anyone for that, though I did suggest that the people of New York might appreciate the apology. Nonetheless, compared with the gloss and the 'humanitarian' contortions of Messrs Blair, Schröder, Fischer and other assorted European social-democrats, Krauthammer came as a huge relief.. On 12 October 2001, he had written in his *Washington Post* column: 'We are fighting because the bastards killed 5,000 [*sic*] of our people, and if we do not kill them, they are going to kill us again. This is a war of revenge and deter-rence . . . The liberationist talk must therefore be for foreign consumption.' That is for moderate Muslims like the king of Saudi Arabia and moderate Christians like the British prime minister, both of whom share a strong belief in single-faith education.

Algerians gravitate towards individual terrorism and why are they, as individuals, prepared to sacrifice their own lives in the process? The hijackers responsible for the 11 September outrage were not illiterate, bearded fanatics from the mountain villages of Afghanistan. They were all highly skilled, middle-class professionals. Thirteen of the nineteen men involved were citizens of Saudi Arabia. Their names are recognisable. The three Alghamdis are clearly from the Hijaz province of the kingdom, the site of the holy cities of Mecca and Medina. Mohamed Atta, born in Egypt, travelled on a Saudi passport. Regardless of whether he gave the actual order or not, what is indisputable is that the bulk of Osama bin Laden's real cadres (as opposed to foot-soldiers) are located in Egypt or Saudi Arabia, the two principal allies of the United States in the region barring Israel. Support for bin Laden is strong in Saudi Arabia. That is why the Saudi regime, despite its total dependence on the US, is now suggesting politely that American troops be removed from their country. It is here that the effects of the US counter-offensive are being felt most acutely. The royal family is extremely nervous. The Crown Prince, Abdallah bin Abdul Aziz, is openly discussing internal reforms and a war against corruption within the family and the country.

In normal times the Saudi kingdom is barely covered by the Western media or seriously discussed in the academy. Saudi petrodollars have funded many departments of Arabic or Arab studies and Saudi 'generosity' to Western journalists, politicians and diplomats is well-known. It usually requires the imprisonment of an American or British citizen or for a British nurse to be thrown out of a window for attention to focus on the regime in Riyadh, but this is regarded by all sides as a temporary blip and normal business is resumed fairly rapidly. Even less is known about the state religion, which is not an everyday version of Sunni or Shia Islam but, as I have argued, a peculiarly virulent, ultra-puritanical strain. This is the religion of the Saudi royals, the state bureaucracy, the army and air force and, of course, Osama bin Laden, the best-known Saudi citizen in the world, whose current whereabouts are unknown.

A rough equivalent of this in Britain would be if the Church of England was replaced by the United Reformed Church of Dr Ian Paisley, the royal family became ardent Paisleyites and the state bureaucracy and armed services were barred to non-Paisleyites. In the United States it would mean the hiring of Jerry Falwell to become the official chaplain at the White House with the right to overrule any Supreme Court judgement that, in his view, contradicted the basic tenets of his brand of Christian fundamentalism.

That Saudi Arabia needs a thoroughgoing reform is indisputable, but who will carry it out? Is there a Saudi princeling, a desert Gorbachev, skulking somewhere as a deputy governor in a remote Hijazi town, ready to seize the time and push through measures that could turn his world upside down and end the rule of the al-Saud clan? Unlikely. Reforms from above are likely to be timid and cautious, and what is required is a thoroughgoing revolution.

Ten years ago, the exiled Saudi novelist, Abdelrahman Munif was on a rare trip to London, researching the character of H. St John. Philby for one of his novels. We met and talked for a long time over dinner and the next day. He was in a reflective mood. Sad, but lucid and not totally pessimistic about the future of his country. Why was *Cities of Salt* the collective name for all the novels?

> Cities of Salt means cities that offer no sustainable existence. When the waters come in, the first waves will dissolve the salt and reduce these great glass cities to dust. In antiquity, as you know, many cities simply disappeared. It is possible to foresee the downfall of cities that are inhuman. With no means of livelihood they won't survive. Look at us now and see how the West looks at us.
>
> The twentieth century is almost over, but when the West looks at us, all they see is oil and petrodollars. Saudi Arabia is still without a constitution, the people are deprived of all elementary rights, even the right to support the regime without asking for permission. Women, who own a large share of private wealth in the country, are treated like third-class citizens. A woman is not allowed to leave the country without a written permit from a male relative. Such a situation produces a desperate citizenry, without a sense of dignity or belonging. All our rulers do is to increase their own wealth while investing as little as possible in the intellectual development of our people. Why? Because they fear education. They fear change.

In his novels, as discussed earlier, the portraits of the oil-men and their collaborators are savage, surreal and satirical. How far did this hostility stretch, and why?

> As far as the Americans are concerned, my first memories of them go back to the early or mid-1940s. In most cases there was no hostility to them at that stage, but the context in which they appeared changed our way of life and the relationship. In our countries the oil industry is something alien. It has stayed like an island, cut

off from everything around it . . . The presence of oil could have led to real improvements and change, creating the opportunities for a better life and providing everyone with a future. The West is not owed the credit for the riches of the Peninsula and the Gulf. These riches come from within the earth. What happened was that the West discovered these riches and took the lion's share, the larger part, which ought to belong to the people of the region.

Our rulers were brought in by the West, which used them as its instruments. We all know the sort of relationship there is currently between the West and these regimes.

Given his immense knowledge of the Peninsula, had he never thought of writing a straightforward history, or was it too dangerous an enterprise?

My aim is not to create a parallel history of one particular country – not because of fear or lack of interest – because I believe that the novel can give a profound reading of a society that can be more important than political history and certainly than any official history. So my aim is to write novels that would open the eyes of the people of the region and also help others—Americans, Norwegians, Chinese – to understand the nature of our societies, the period in which we live and the character of our people.

As for danger, well all I can say is that a writer has only to write to 'put his life in the palm of his hand' as we say in our part of the world, and it is certainly a gamble. My pen is my only weapon, which shouldn't upset those in power, but it does. Losing my Saudi citizenship caused me real hardship in not being able to move around or live normally. But I have chosen this path and this is part of the price. As to whether I'm kidnapped or killed, that's not my decision. It rests with others. You know what they say about me? I hold political positions of which they disapprove. What is a 'political position'? I have no armed battalions. All I have is the word. An article, a lecture, a book: these are my only weapons. Three important words or slogans I believe in are: Liberty, Equality, Fraternity. How can they be applied? When? By who? At what level? *That's* the question. *That's* the challenge.

There is at this time just one Arab regime. No difference between Right and Left and even these terms are up for review. I'm reminded of a joke. Whenever there is a meeting of Arab ministers of the interior there's always a full house. No minister stays away because the agenda is security. They have to make sure they create a single Arab security!

Denied secular openings in a society where the royal family – a clan with multiple factions and micro-factions – and its tame clerics dominates all aspects of everyday life, there were a number of rebellions in the Sixties and Seventies. One of Munif's novels, *The Trench*, has a striking finale. Two revolutions are being plotted, one of them by angry young men inspired by modern, democratic ideas, the other, invisibly, inside the palace. Everything ends in tears, with curfews and tanks in the street. The young revolutionaries discover that the wrong revolt has succeeded. The reference was to the assassination of King Faisal in 1975 by his own nephew, Prince Faisal Ibn Musaid. Ten years earlier Ibn Musaid's brother Prince Khalid, a fervent Wahhabite, had demonstrated in public against the entry of television into the kingdom. Saudi police entered his house and shot him dead. To this day Prince Khalid is venerated by hardline believers. Twenty years later the Taliban government paid its own unique tribute to the slain prince by ordering all the TV sets in Afghanistan to be publicly hanged and organising street bonfires of audio cassettes and videos. Alas, this was not a protest against 'dumbing down'.

But Wahhabism remains the state religion of Saudi Arabia, imported with petrodollars to fund extremism elsewhere in the world. During the war against the Soviet Union, Pakistani military intelligence requested the presence of a Saudi prince to lead the jihad in Afghanistan. No volunteers were forthcoming and the Saudi leaders recommended the scion of a rich family, close to the monarchy. Osama bin Laden was dispatched to the Pakistan border and arrived in time to hear President Carter's National Security Adviser Zbigniew Brzezinski giving open support to the jihad. One of his first actions as a pro-Western freedom-fighter was a raid on a mixed school, which was burnt to the ground, its headmaster killed and disembowelled.

The religious schools in Pakistan where the Taliban were created were funded by the Saudis, and Wahhabi influence was very strong. In 2000 when the Taliban decided to blow up the old Buddhas there were appeals from the ancient seminaries of Qom and al-Azhar to desist, on the grounds that Islam was tolerant. A Wahhabi delegation from the kingdom advised the Taliban to execute the plan. They did. The Wahhabi insistence on a permanent jihad against *all* enemies, Muslim and non-Muslim, was to leave a deep mark on the young boys who later took Kabul. The attitude of the United States in those days was sympathetic. A Republican Party seething with Christian cults could hardly offer advice on this matter, and both Clinton and Blair were keen on advertising their Christianity. All this is far

removed from the genuinely radical liberation theology currents strong in
Brazil and other parts of Latin America, which have helped to organise the
resistance of the poor without burdening them too much with spiritual
oppression.

After the collapse of the Soviet Union, the internal opposition in Saudi
became totally dominated by religious groups. These core Wahhabis now
saw the kingdom as degenerate because of the American connection.
Others were depressed by the failure of Riyadh to defend the Palestinians.
The stationing of US soldiers in the country after the Gulf War was a signal
for terrorist attacks on soldiers and bases. Those who ordered these were
Saudis, but Pakistani and Filipino immigrants were sometimes charged and
executed in order to appease the United States.

The expeditionary force dispatched to Afghanistan to cut off the tentacles of the Wahhabi octopus may or may not succeed, but the head is safe
and sound in Saudi Arabia, guarding the oil-wells, growing new arms, and
protected by American soldiers and the USAF base in Dhahran.
Washington's failure to disengage its vital interests from the fate of the Saudi
monarchy could well lead to further blowback. In June 1999, one of Fahd's
dissident brothers, Prince Talal bin Abdul Aziz, warned that if a generational
shift was not agreed a ferocious power-struggle could wreck the kingdom.
He suggested a modernisation that would include giving rights to women
and a better education to everyone. He was ignored.

During the early Sixties, Talal had been inspired by Nasser and had called
for radical changes. He had organised a 'Free Princes' movement, but he lost
the fight and went into voluntarily exile in Cairo.[100] At that time the current Crown Prince Abdallah had responded angrily to all talk of reform:

Talal alleges that there is no constitution in Saudi Arabia which safeguards democratic freedoms. But Talal knows full well that Saudi Arabia has a constitution
inspired by Allah and not drawn up by man. I do not believe that there is any

100 Talal had no protectors in the shape of maternal uncles from the local aristocracy. His
mother was an Armenian slave and was isolated within the court. Talal was only one of Ibn Saud's
36 sons. The inner core of the ruling clique is restricted to the children of the al-Sudairi women.
Talal was allowed back from exile on condition that he remained silent. The fact that he has begun
to speak again is one small indication of the crisis faced by the regime. At the time of writing King
Fahd is paralysed beyond repair and being kept alive to delay the succession.

Arab who believes that the Koran contains a single loophole which would permit an injustice to be done. All laws and regulations in Saudi Arabia are inspired by the Koran and Saudi Arabia is proud to have such a constitution . . . As for Talal's statement about socialism, there is no such thing as rightist or leftist socialism; true socialism is the Arab socialism laid down by the Koran. Talal talked at length about democracy. He knows that if there is any truly democratic system in the world, it is the one now existing in Saudi Arabia.

One assumes that Talal is also aware that true globalisation is the Arab globalisation also laid down by the Koran, but times have changed. The Saudi rulers are aware that unless they do something it might be done for them by the contending fundamentalisms. Either a hardline takeover by groups sympathetic to Osama or pre-emptive action by the United States, which could mean the balkanisation of the peninsula. The simplest plan would be to turn the Holy Cities of the Hijaz to the caretakership of the Hashemites in Jordan[101] – the direct descendants of Muhammad – and create a new state in the oil-rich East with a new set of non-Wahhabi locals. It's a dangerous option, one that could easily trigger a 'civil' war, and not just in the region, as other powers and oil companies backed different factions to gain access to the wells.

The second Muslim state seriously affected by the crisis and war inaugurated on 11 September was Pakistan. At the beginning of the new millennium, Pakistan was a failed state. Its education system was dysfunctional, its health services worse than they had ever been, politicians and their clients owed billions of rupees to state-owned banks, law and order had broken down in various parts of the country. Foreign investment was at an all-time low. In the preceding decade, the civil war between armed groups of Sunni and Shia fundamentalists had led to the deaths of over 5,000 people. The condition of women had declined on every level: health, education, legal standing, a massive increase in reported rapes.

The one protected sector was the military. Following the nuclear tests of 1998, the Indian government had allocated $10 billion for defence in its 1999 budget. Pakistan had fought back with $3.3 billion, which was 150 per

---

101 The late King Hussein's brother, Prince Hasan, announced after 11 September that his family were ready to assume their ancestral responsibilities in the region!

cent of the total budgets on education and health spending. Since 1994, Pakistan had paid $1.1 billion to buy three state-of-the-art submarines fully equipped with Exocet missiles. Economists estimated that the two nuclear powers would need to spend $15 billion over ten years to maintain their nuclear armoury. A report suggested that this amount would be 'enough to educate, properly nourish, and provide health care to almost 37.5 million neglected children in South Asia'.[102]

This was the Pakistan whose military elite was pressganged into joining 'Operation Enduring Freedom', a campaign which had already extended its brief and which, as the US ambassador to the UN, John Negroponte, informed the Security Council, was a limitless war: 'We may find that our self-defence requires further action with respect to other organisations and other states.'

Could any other state have had the nerve to inform the UN that it reserved the right to attack whoever and whenever it wanted? The Security Council ventured no opposition. All this was done in the name of combating an enemy which, the American president informed Congress, consisted of tens of thousands of terrorists in sixty different countries. That al-Qaida was not capable of staging another hit on the same scale became clear as the war proceeded. For them to watch Afghan cities crumble under the bombing and not retaliate somewhere in the United States or Western Europe to show their anger and test their strength was inconceivable, unless it was beyond their capacity. The point was sharply stressed in sections of the Indian and Pakistani press, but it did not occur to most of the 'defence specialists' who dominated the television screens during the conflict.[103]

Four months after the war began, the principal war-aim was still remote. Osama bin Laden had eluded capture and death. The leader of the defeated Taliban regime, whose arrest had become a subsidiary objective, had also escaped in a convoy of three motorcycles. By this time attention had already shifted to Pakistan. The destabilising effects of the war in Afghanistan were always likely to be felt here first.

---

102 *Human Development in South Asia*, Oxford 1999.

103 See Aijaz Ahmed, *Frontline*, 9 November 2001. One of the most critical magazines in South Asia, it puts its counterparts in the United States to shame.

The tension between India and Pakistan is potentially dangerous. The irony is that Pakistan is led by a secular general and India by a fundamentalist Hindu politician: in some ways an ideal combination to make peace. Yet at one level it would suit both sides to have a small war. General Musharraf could prove that he was not a total pawn. And Atal Bihari Vajpayee, India's prime minister, could win the next election. But who could guarantee a small war?

The fact is that Pakistan's infiltration of *jihadi* groups such as the Lashkar-i-Tayyaba and the Jaish-e-Mohammed into Indian-occupied Kashmir has created an alternative military apparatus that Islamabad funds and supplies but can't fully control – just like the Taliban. The attack on the Indian parliament in December 2001 was clearly carried out by one of these groups to provoke a more serious conflict. Some of the *jihadis* don't much care for Pakistan as an entity. Their aim is to restore Muslim rule in India. Crazy? Yes, but armed and capable of wreaking havoc in both countries. If General Musharraf won't deal with the menace, Mr Vajpayee has threatened war. This is where the precedent set by Washington after 11 September could lead to disaster. It has already been used retrospectively by the German and British governments to give Colonel Putin a clean bill of health. The death of 30,000 Chechens, the razing of Grozny to the ground, is not a war-crime because the West has so decreed. They were led by terrorists and so 'they had it coming'. Not unnaturally New Delhi, which sees itself as a more important power economically and politically than Russia, wants to join the new Strike-Where-You-Want Club.

The responsibility for a peace initiative rests with India. It is the most powerful state in the region. Its leaders should realise that the natural tendency of globalised capital and its imperialist masters is to break up states, not to unite them. Resistance to this process requires regional alliances and a new form of governance. The war on the edge of the subcontinent has not helped in this regard, but politicians and generals need to think ahead if they are serious about protecting the interests of future generations. India's position in South Asia is unchallenged from without, regardless of which party is in power. The only neighbour of equivalent strength is China, but it has no inclination, and why should it, to quarrel with its neighbour. India's real problems are of its own making: its inability to push through social reforms which end the caste-system, its failure to accept that the Kashmiris are alienated beyond repair, its constant search for scapegoats to justify its own failures. These will not be solved by neo-liberal economics, which heightens competition and increases communal and ethnic tensions. It is politics, not economics, that will deliver in this instance. India's tragedy is that as it seeks to become a global player its politics are controlled by a gang of obscurantists in alliance with opportunists of every hue. Perhaps sometime in the future an Indian government prepared to look beyond its own navel will emerge. If it does I would offer it some advice in the form of a neutral verse, neither Hindu nor Muslim or Christian, but the philosophical poem of the *Tao Tê Ching*, the key text of the Taoist scripture:

> How did the great rivers and seas get their kingship over the hundred
>   lesser streams?
> Through the merit of being lower than they: that was how they got their
>   Kingship.
> Therefore the sage, in order to be above the people,
> Must speak as though he were lower than they.
> In order to guide them
> He must put himself behind them.
> Thus when he is above, the people have no burden,
> When he is ahead, they feel no hurt.

22

Letter to a young Muslim

Dear friend:

Remember when you approached me after the big antiwar meeting in November 2001 (I think it was Glasgow) and asked whether I was a believer? I have not forgotten the shock you registered when I replied 'no', or the comment of your friend ('our parents warned us against you'), or the angry questions which the pair of you then began to hurl at me like darts. All of that made me think, and this little book is my reply for you and all the others like you who asked similar questions elsewhere in Europe and North America. It's heavily interlarded with history, but I hope it will suffice. When we spoke, I told you that my criticism of religion and those who use it for political ends was not a case of being diplomatic in public. Exploiters and manipulators have always used religion self-righteously to further their own selfish ends. It's true that this is not the whole story. There are, of course, deeply sincere people of religion in different parts of the world who genuinely fight on the side of the poor, but they are usually in conflict with organised religion themselves. The Catholic Church victimised worker or peasant priests who organised against oppression. The Iranian Ayatollahs dealt severely with Muslims who preached in favour of a social radicalism.

If I genuinely believed that this radical Islam was the way forward for humanity, I would not hesitate to say so in public, whatever the consequences. I know that many of your friends love chanting the name 'Osama' and I know that they cheered on 11 September 2001. They were not alone. It happened all over the world, but had nothing to do with religion. I know of Argentinian students who walked out when a teacher criticised

Osama. I know a Russian teenager who e-mailed a one-word message – 'congratulations' – to his Russian friends whose parents had settled outside New York and they replied: 'Thanks. It was great.' We talked, I remember, of the Greek crowds at football matches who refused to mourn for the two minutes the government had imposed and instead broke the silence with anti-American chants.

But none of this justifies what took place. What lies behind the vicarious pleasure is not a feeling of strength, but a terrible weakness. The people of Indo-China suffered more than any Muslim country at the hands of the American government. They were bombed for fifteen whole years and lost millions of their people. Did they even think of bombing America? Nor did the Cubans or the Chileans or the Brazilians. The last two fought against the US-imposed military regimes at home and finally triumphed. Today, people feel powerless. And so when America is hit they celebrate. They don't ask what such an act will achieve, what its consequences will be and who will benefit. Their response, like the event itself, is purely symbolic.

I think that Osama and his group have reached a political dead-end. It was a grand spectacle, but nothing more. The United States, in responding with a war, has enhanced the importance of the action, but I doubt if even that will rescue it from obscurity in the future. It will be a footnote in the history of this century. Nothing more. In political, economic or military terms it was barely a pinprick.

What do the Islamists offer? A route to a past which, mercifully for the people of the seventh century, never existed. If the 'Emirate of Afghanistan' is the model for what they want to impose on the world then the bulk of Muslims would rise up in arms against them. Don't imagine that either Osama or Mullah Omar represent the future of Islam. It would be a major disaster for the culture we both share if that turned out to be the case.

Would you want to live under those conditions? Would you tolerate your sister, your mother or the woman you love being hidden from public view and only allowed out shrouded like a corpse? I want to be honest with you. I opposed this latest Afghan war. I do not accept the right of big powers to change governments as and when it affects their interests. But I did not shed any tears for the Taliban as they shaved their beards and ran back home. This does not mean that those who have been captured should be treated like animals or denied their elementary rights according to the Geneva Convention, but as I've argued elsewhere in this book, the fundamentalism of the Empire has no equal today. They can disregard all conventions and laws at will.

The reason they are openly mistreating prisoners they captured after waging an illegal war in Afghanistan is to assert their power before the world – hence they humiliate Cuba by doing their dirty work on its soil – and warn others who attempt to twist the lion's tail that the punishment will be severe. I remember well how, during the Cold War, the CIA and its indigenous recruits tortured political prisoners and raped them in many parts of Latin America. That's what made Philip Agee, a CIA field officer, walk out on them and write *Inside the Company*, which exposed what they were doing in Latin America. During the Vietnam War the US violated most of the Geneva Conventions. They tortured and executed prisoners, raped the women, threw prisoners out of helicopters to die on the ground or drown in the sea, and all this, of course, in the name of freedom. Because many people in the West believe the nonsense about 'humanitarian interventions' they are shocked by these acts, but this is relatively mild compared to the crimes committed in the last century by the Empire.

I've met many of our people in different parts of the world since 11 September. One question is always repeated: 'Do you think we Muslims are clever enough to have done this?' I always answer 'Yes'. Then I ask who they think is responsible, and the answer is invariably 'Israel'. Why? 'To discredit us and make the Americans attack our countries.' I gently expose their wishful illusions, but the conversation saddens me. Why are so many Muslims sunk in this torpor? Why do they wallow in so much self-pity? Why is their sky always overcast? Why is it always someone else who is to blame? Sometimes when we talk I get the impression that there is not a single Muslim country of which they can feel really proud. Those who have migrated from South Asia are much better treated in Britain than in Saudi Arabia or the Gulf States. It is here that something has to happen.

The Arab world is desperate for a change. Over the years, in every discussion with Iraqis, Syrians, Saudis, Egyptians, Jordanians and Palestinians, the same questions are raised, the same problems recur. We are suffocating.

Why can't we breathe? Everything seems static. Our economy, our politics, our intellectuals and, most of all, our religion. Palestine suffers every day. The West does nothing. Our governments are dead. Our politicians are corrupt. Our people are ignored. Is it surprising that some are responsive to the Islamists? Who else offers anything these days? The United States? It doesn't even want democracy, not even in little Qatar, and for a very simple reason. If we elected our own government they might demand that the United States close down its bases. Would it? They already resent al-Jazeera television because it has different priorities from them. It was fine when al-Jazeera attacked corruption within the Arab elite. Tommy Friedman even devoted a whole column in praise of al-Jazeera in the *New York Times*. He saw it as a sign of democracy coming to the Arab world. No longer. Because democracy means the right to think differently, and al-Jazeera showed pictures of the Afghan war that were not shown on the US networks, Bush and Blair put pressure on Qatar to stop unfriendly broadcasts. For the West democracy means believing in exactly the same things that they believe. Is that really democracy?

If we elected our own government in one or two countries people might elect Islamists. Would the West leave us alone? Did the French government leave the Algerian military alone? No. They insisted that the elections of 1990 and 1991 be declared null and void. French intellectuals described the Front Islamique du Salut (FIS) as 'Islamo-fascists', ignoring the fact that they had won an election. Had they been allowed to become the government, divisions already present within them would have come to the surface. The army could have warned that any attempt to tamper with the rights guaranteed to citizens under the constitution would not be tolerated. It was only when the original leaders of the FIS had been eliminated that the more lumpen elements came to the fore and created mayhem. Should we blame them for the civil war, or those in Algiers and Paris who robbed them of their victory? The massacres in Algeria are horrendous. Is it only the Islamists who are responsible? What happened in Bentalha, ten miles south of Algiers, on the night of 22 September 1997? Who slaughtered the five hundred men, women and children of that township? Who? The Frenchman who knows everything, Bernard-Henri Lévy, is sure it was the Islamists who perpetrated this dreadful deed. Then why did the army deny the local population arms to defend itself. Why did it tell the local militia to go away that night? Why did the security forces not intervene when they could see what was going on?[104]

Why does M. Lévy believe that the Maghreb has to be subordinated to the needs of the French republic, and why does nobody attack this sort of fundamentalism? We know what we have to do, say the Arabs, but every time the West intervenes it sets our cause back many years. So if they want to help, they should stay out.

That's what my Arab friends say, and I agree with this approach. Look at Iran. The Western gaze turned benevolent during the assault on Afghanistan. Iran was needed for the war, but let the West watch from afar. The imperial fundamentalists are talking about the 'axis of evil', which includes Iran. An intervention there would be fatal. A new generation has experienced clerical oppression. It has known nothing else. Stories about the shah are part of its prehistory. These young men and women are sure about one thing if nothing else. They don't want the Ayatollahs to rule them anymore. Even though Iran, in recent years, has not been as bad as Saudi Arabia or the late 'Emirate of Afghanistan', it has not been good for the people.

Let me tell you a story. A couple of years ago I met a young Iranian filmmaker in Los Angeles. His name was Moslem Mansouri. He had managed to escape with several hours of filmed interviews for a documentary he was making. He had won the confidence of three Tehran prostitutes and filmed them for over two years. He showed me some of the footage. They talked to him quite openly. They described how the best pickups were at religious festivals. I got a flavour of the film from the transcripts he sent me. One of the women tells him:

> Today everyone is forced to sell their bodies! Women like us have to tolerate a man for 10,000 Toomans. We can't say anything . . . Young people need to be in a bed together, even for ten minutes . . . It is a primary need . . . it calms them down. When the government does not allow it, then prostitution grows. We don't even need to talk about prostitution, the government has taken away the right to speak with the opposite sex freely in public . . . In the parks, in the cinemas, or in the streets, you can't talk to the person sitting next to you. On the streets, if you talk to a man, the 'Islamic guard' interrogates you endlessly. 'Who

---

104 Hugh Roberts, 'Truths about the dirty war', *Times Literary Supplement,* 12 October 2001.

is this guy? How are you related to him? Where are your documents? . . .' Today in our country, nobody is satisfied! Nobody has security. I went to a company to get a job. The manager of the company, a bearded guy, looked at my face and said: 'I will hire you and I'll give you 10,000 Toomans more than the pay-rate.' I said: 'You can at least test my computer skills to see if I'm proficient or not . . .' He said: 'I hire you for your looks!' I knew that if I had to work there, I had to have sex with him at least once a day. I thought to myself it's not worth it! If I work for myself, I can make more money. Wherever you go it's like this! I went to a special family court – for divorce – and begged the judge, a clergyman, to give me my child's custody. I told him 'Please . . . I beg you to give me the custody of my child. I'll be your *Kaniz* . . . (Kaniz means servant. This is a Persian expression which basically means 'I beg you, I am very desperate'.) What do you think the guy said? He said I don't need a servant! I need a woman! What do you expect of others when the clergyman, the head of the court, says this? This guy had 50 kilos of beard and hair on his face! And he says I want a woman! I asked him don't you have a wife? He said: I need many! I went to the officer to get my divorce signed, instead he said I should not get divorced and instead get married again without divorce, illegally. Because he said without a husband it will be hard to find a job. He was right, but I didn't have money to pay him . . .

These things make you age faster . . . you get depressed . . . you have a lot of stress and it damages you. Perhaps there is a means to get out of this . . .

In Western countries, prostitutes have welfare and governmental insurance. They get medical checkups and so forth. Here we don't have a right to exist . . . Why? We are workers too, you know. . .

A second woman forced to sell her body tells him:

The men who come for my services are all kinds: ranging from bazaari [shop-keepers], students, doctors, old, young, illiterate . . . Basically anyone who has money to buy a woman for some time. Most of them treat us really badly . . . Because they give us money, they think they have the right to do anything with us . . . and we tolerate it.

Today in our society no one is financially secure. I can't pay my rent . . . You tell me what should I do? If I don't sell my body tonight, I don't have money tomorrow . . . In a society where there is no job, no security, and no rights, what can a person do? You go to the streets and you're always afraid that Islamic guards might arrest you for any reason; a wisp of hair showing from your *hejab*, a faint lipstick, anything goes . . .

If I was living in a society where I could work and support myself independent of anyone, I would have never gone after selling my body. Then maybe I would have had a physical need to be with someone, and I could choose . . . I would have been able to live with my feelings, as I wished . . . with joy . . . But in this situation, the government has made men the buyers and people like me the sellers . . .

Moslem was distraught because none of the American networks wanted to buy the film. They didn't want to destabilise Khatami's regime! Moslem himself is a child of the Revolution. Without it he would never have become a film-maker. He comes from a very poor family. His father is a muezzin and Moslem's upbringing was ultra-religious. Now he hates religion, and with a passion that even I can't reproduce. Moslem refused to fight in the war against Iraq. He was arrested. This experience transformed him:

It was 1978–9 when I started a little newspaper stand on the corner of a crowded street in Sangsar. Every week I would get books and newspapers of political groups and sell them in the newspaper stand. After a while it became a spot for interested youth to discuss the political situation.

One night the Islamic guards which called themselves 'Hezbollah' attacked the newspaper stand and burned the place. I took the burned books and put them in front of the stand every day for a week. Then they arrested me and took me to the prison.

The prison was a hard but good experience for me. It was in the prison that I felt I am reaching a stage of intellectual maturity. I was resisting and I enjoyed my sense of strength. I felt that I saved my life from the corrupted world of clergies and this is a price I was paying for it. I was proud of it. After one year in prison, they told me that I would be released on the condition that I sign papers stating that I will participate in Friday sermons and religious activities. I refused to sign. They kept me in the prison for one more year.

When I was released from the prison, my birthplace seemed too small for me. I felt suffocated in there. So I came to Tehran. I worked in the mornings and went to the 'Free' university at nights. [Free university is a private university with high tuition.]

In the early Eighties, I was not interested in cinema. My inner thoughts and struggles would not allow me to pay attention to cinema or have any long-term plan. I kept thinking that I can never adapt to the situation in Iran. The whole social and political atmosphere bothered me seriously.

After the war ended [1989], the government made a law that required people to change their old birth certificates into new ones. I knew that if I went to change my birth certificate, I would have to give up my fake documents. It would become clear that I was a drafted soldier who did not go to war. On the other hand the cost of university was very high. So I decided to do my military service. After I came back, I looked for a job and accidentally I found a film magazine that was looking for a reporter. I took the job. Even though I tried to interview the non-governmental film-makers and literary figures, I knew well that if I write anything – even if critical – the regime would still be able to take the credit by saying that they allow criticism and therefore they are democratic! Cinema was in total control of the state and film-makers were bound by the limitations of the system.

If I interviewed film-makers such as Mehrjooyi, Makhmalbaf or Kiarostami, it would ultimately benefit the political system. But I told myself that I would allow the regime to take such advantage of me temporarily . . . I thought my work in the media would serve as a cover for my own projects, which were to document the hideous crimes of the political regime itself. I knew that I would not be able to make the kind of films I really want to make due to the censorship regulations. Any scenario that I would write would have never got the permission of the Islamic censorship office. I knew that my time and energy would get wasted. So I decided to make eight documentaries secretly. I filmed my footage in the period between 1994 and 1998 and I smuggled it out of Iran. Due to financial problems I've only been able to finish editing two of my films. One is *Close Up, Long Shot* and the other is *Shamloo, the Poet of Liberty*.

The first film is about the life of Hossein Sabzian, who was the main character of Kiarostami's drama-documentary called *Close Up*. The latter is the story of a guy who tries to present himself as Makhmalbaf, whom he resembles physically, to a family. The family buy his story and try to sponsor one of his movies, thinking he is the famous Makhmalbaf. He lives with the family for four days and ultimately the family realise that he is making the whole thing up. They get him arrested. A few years after Kiarostami's film, I went to visit Sabzian. He loves cinema. His wife and children get frustrated with him and finally leave him. Today, he lives in a village on the outskirts of Tehran and has come to the conclusion that his love for cinema has resulted in nothing but misery. In my film he says: 'People like me get destroyed in societies like the one we live in. We can never present ourselves. There are two types of dead: flat and walking. We are the walking dead!'[105]

We could find stories like this and worse in every Muslim country. One thing more and then I'll stop. There is a big difference between the Muslims

---

105 Moslem Mansouri did not speak English or Urdu and I did not speak Farsi. We communicated through an Iranian exile of Jewish origin, Elham Ghetaynchi. I am extremely grateful to her for translating the extracts from the transcripts and the interview.

of the diaspora . . . those whose parents migrated to the Western lands . . . and those who still live in the House of Islam. The latter are far more critical because religion is not crucial to their identity. It's taken for granted that they are Muslims.

In Europe and North America things are different. Here an official multiculturalism has stressed difference at the expense of all else. Its rise correlates with a decline in radical politics as such. 'Culture' and 'religion' are softer, euphemistic substitutes for socio-economic inequality – as if diversity, rather than hierarchy, were the central issue in North American or European society today. I have spoken to Muslims from the Maghreb (France), from Anatolia (Germany); from Pakistan and Bangladesh (Britain), from everywhere (United States) and a South Asian sprinkling in Scandinavia. Why is it, I often ask myself, that so many are like you? They have become much more orthodox and rigid than the robust and vigorous peasants of Kashmir and the Punjab, who I used to know so well. The British prime minister is a great believer in single-faith schools. The American president ends each speech with 'God Save America'. Osama starts and ends each TV interview by praising Allah. All three have the right to do so, just as I have the right to remain committed to most of the values of the Enlightenment. The Enlightenment attacked religion – Christianity, mainly – for two reasons: that it was a set of ideological delusions, and that it was a system of institutional oppression, with immense powers of persecution and intolerance. Why, then, should I abstain from religious criticism?

Why should we abandon either of these legacies today? Who would imagine that religions have become less of an illusion since the days of Holbach or Gibbon? I have never liked relativism or special pleading. What I want to know is why there is never a single Muslim name when the Nobel Prizes for Physics and Chemistry are announced each year. Are intelligence, talent and inspiration absent from Muslim genes? They never were in the past. What explains the *rigor mortis*?

Sweet irony: did you know that the only Muslim to win the Nobel Prize for Physics was someone I knew? A Pakistani citizen, Professor Abdus Salam. Alas, he was a member of the Ahmadi sect which had been deprived of its status as Muslims. While he was a Muslim when he got the prize, a few years later he was informed by the law that he was not. He used to joke with a sad expression that although he was not a Muslim in Pakistan, he was still one in India, in Europe and East Africa.

I don't want you to misunderstand me. My aversion to religion is by no means confined to Islam alone. And nor do I ignore, as this book demonstrates, the role which religious ideologies have played in the past in order to move the world forward. It was the ideological clashes between two rival interpretations of Christianity – the Protestant Reformation versus the Catholic Counter-Reformation – that led to volcanic explosions in Europe. Here was an example of razor-sharp intellectual debates fuelled by theological passions, leading to a civil war, followed by a revolution. The sixteenth-century Dutch revolt against Spanish occupation was triggered off by an assault on sacred images in the name of confessional correctness. The introduction of a new prayer book in Scotland was one of the causes of the seventeenth-century Puritan Revolution in England, the refusal to tolerate Catholicism sparked off its successor in 1688. The intellectual ferment did not cease and a century later the ideas of the Enlightenment stoked the furnaces of revolutionary France. The Church of England and the Vatican now combined to contest the new threat, but ideas of popular sovereignty and republics were too strong to be easily obliterated.

I can almost hear your question. What has all this got to do with us? A great deal, my friend. Western Europe had been fired by theological passions, but these were now being transcended. Modernity was on the horizon. This was a dynamic that the culture and economy of the Ottoman Empire could never mimic. The Sunni–Shia divide had come too soon and congealed into rival dogmas. Dissent had, by this time, been virtually wiped out in Islam. The Sultan, flanked by his religious scholars, ruled a state-Empire that was going to wither away and die. If this was already the case in the eighteenth century, how much truer it is today. Perhaps the only way in which Muslims will discover this is through their own experiences, like Iran.

The rise of religion is partially explained by the lack of any other alternative to the universal regime of neo-liberalism. Here you will discover that as long as Islamist governments open their countries to global penetration, they will be permitted to do what they want in the socio-political realm. The American Empire used Islam before and it can do so again. Here lies the challenge. We are in desperate need of an Islamic Reformation that sweeps away the crazed conservatism and backwardness of the fundamentalists but, more than that, opens up the world of Islam to new ideas which are seen to be more advanced than what is currently on offer from the West. This would necessitate a rigid separation of state and mosque; the dissolution of the clergy; the assertion by Muslim intellectuals of their right to interpret the texts that are the collective property of Islamic culture as a whole; the freedom to think freely and rationally and the freedom of imagination. Unless we move in this direction we will be doomed to re-living old battles, and thinking not of a richer and humane future, but of how we can move from the present to the past. It is an unacceptable vision.

I've let my pen run away with me and preached my heresies for too long. I doubt that I will change, but I hope you will.

PART V

Epilogue: The Road to Bali

Strangers came from the West . . . they wished to make profits from the productiveness of the soil and commanded the native to devote part of his labours and time to the growth of . . . products which would yield a greater margin of gain in the European markets. To make the lower man do this, a very simple policy sufficed. He obeys his chiefs, and so it was only necessary to win over those chiefs by promising them part of the profit, and . . . the scheme succeeded completely.

Multatuli (Eduard Douwes Dekker), 1820–1887, *Max Havelaar*

In such times too the rage for politics roared along like a tidal wave, out of control. Each person felt as though she, he could not be truly alive without being political, without debating political questions. In truth, it was as though they could stay alive even without rice. Even schoolteachers, who had all along lived 'neutrally', were infected by the rage for politics – and, so far as they were able, they influenced their pupils with the politics to which they had attached themselves. Each struggled to claim new members for his party. And schools proved to be fertile battlefields for their struggles. Politics! Politics! No different from rice under the Japanese Occupation.

Pramoedya Ananta Toer (1925–), *Dia Jang Menjerah*
(She Who Gave Up) in *Tjerita dari Blora* (Tales of Blora),
1952 (trans. Benedict Anderson)

Usually the corpses were no longer recognisable as human. Headless. Stomachs torn open. The smell was unimaginable. To make sure they didn't sink, the carcasses were deliberately tied to, or impaled upon, bamboo stakes. And the departure of the corpses from the Kediri region down the Brantas achieved its golden age when bodies were stacked together on rafts over which the PKI [Indonesian Communist party] banner grandly flew. . . . Once the purge of Communist elements got under way, clients stopped coming for sexual satisfaction. The reason: most clients – and prostitutes – were too frightened, for, hanging up in front of the whorehouses, there were a lot of male Communist genitals – like bananas hung out for sale.

Pripit Rochijat Kartawidjaja (1949–),
'Am I PKI or non-PKI?', *Indonesia*, 40 (October 1985)

The West's best news for years in Asia.

Time (on the Indonesian massacres), 15 July 1966

23

A small town in Java

The year is 1960. Pakistan is experiencing the third year of its first military dictatorship. It is early evening. We've biked four or five miles from the university and now, with the bikes leaning safely against the trunk of an old tree, we are waiting for the foreign guest. I've dragged three very grumpy friends to the Upper Mall in Lahore, near a bridge by the old canal, and we take turns to hold a large placard that reads WELCOME ANTI-IMPERIALIST SOEKARNO, making sure that there are never more than three of us together at the same time. Section 144 of the colonial penal code, forbidding gatherings of more than three persons, is in force and we don't want to be arrested before we've welcomed the Indonesian leader.

The morning newspapers had informed us that our homegrown pro-imperialist field marshal would accompany Soekarno from Lahore airport to Government House. Hence our presence and the message on the placard. But Soekarno is late. Very late. The sun set over an hour ago. It's getting chilly and we're tired. The street is virtually empty, which is difficult to imagine today. Should we retire to a café or a kebab-house? I veto the suggestion. My friends groan, cursing themselves, Soekarno and me in Lahori Punjabi, with the phrase 'torn arsehole' punctuating constant crude references to the genitals of various members of all our families. Suddenly there is a roar of motorbikes and the uniformed outriders come into vision, followed by the presidential limousine. As the car slows down near the bridge, we hold up our placard underneath the streetlights and cheer. The Indonesian leader smiles and waves back at us. It has to be us because, apart from the plain-clothes cops dressed in their pristine white *shalwar*/shirt suits and trying desperately to appear normal, no other bystanders are present. Soekarno is not, alas, accompanied by the field marshal as we had hoped but by the nawab of Kalabagh, a feudal brute who doubles up as the provincial governor (and who has recently imposed a ban on my speaking in public), and Zulfiqar Ali Bhutto, the cabinet minister representing the military regime. Bhutto is still serving the dictatorship. Well known for his seignorial appetites, we joke that this is probably the reason he has been selected to welcome the Indonesian leader in Dhaka (then the capital of East Pakistan) and fly back with him to the power-centres in West Pakistan.[106] Our mission accomplished, we grab our bikes and make for home.

Why the need to welcome Soekarno in person? Apart from demonstrating contempt for the uniformed despot governing Pakistan, there were other reasons. Soekarno was the political leader who had organised and hosted a conference of newly independent African and Asian states in February 1955, the first attempt to create a non-aligned movement that could collectively resist the demands imposed on individual post-colonial states by imperialisms old and new. Bandung was selected as the venue and afterwards the 'Bandung spirit' was often invoked by countries that had recently won their freedom. Where in Allah's name was Bandung? After much map searching I found it in an old Oxford atlas. It was just a small town in Java.

Together with Nasser of Egypt, Nehru of India, Chou-en-Lai from China and Pham van Duong from North Vietnam, the Indonesian leader had agreed to promote a form of national-cosmopolitanism, the *Panch Shila* ('Five Principles'), as the basis of international relations in the post-colonial world: mutual respect for each other's territorial integrity and sovereignty, mutual non-aggression, mutual non-interference in each other's internal affairs, equality and mutual benefit, peaceful co-existence. There was also a modest token of Western displeasure at the gathering: some intelligence agency had blown up a plane carrying delegates from Vietnam.

Pakistan, too, was present at the conference – as Washington's Trojan

---

106 Later I discovered that this was indeed the case and that the arrival of the plane had been delayed on Bhutto's orders. The foreign guest was in coital mode and no interruptions were permitted.

donkey. Subsequently when the Non-Aligned Movement began to meet, Pakistan and other members of pro-Western security pacts were automatically excluded. This exclusion angered some of us. Pakistan's wretched, venal politicians had sold their souls and the country in return for US military and economic aid. Soekarno's visit was an opportunity to demonstrate our displeasure with the local satrap.

And there was another reason. In the clandestine quiz we sometimes organised in the university canteen to shock the less political of our peers, a much-favoured double-barrelled question was posed thus: 'Which is the largest Muslim country in the world? Answer: Indonesia. Which is the largest communist party outside the communist world? Answer: the PKI – the Communist Party of Indonesia.' This became a source of real pride. If there could be a large radical party in Indonesia, why not in Pakistan? Whatever the reason it had nothing to do with Islam or its culture. In Pakistan, the communists had been banned in 1952 and all other parties in 1958. Soekarno's tolerance of the left was reason enough to see him as a positive figure, even though some veterans from an older generation of Lahore leftists did not share this view. They were deeply suspicious. After all, had he not collaborated with the Japanese? And a ferocious argument would commence, pitting radical nationalist against communist. Surely, if Soekarno had used the Japanese, he had done so to mobilise a national anti-Dutch consciousness in Java. Was that any more reprehensible than the decision of the Indian communists to cease all opposition to the British empire during the Second World War, after Hitler's attack on the Soviet Union? To each his own. And the tea-house debate would continue with neither side admitting defeat. It would require the intervention of a much-respected chain-smoking poet, who listened in silence, to effect a compromise. We would agree that, regardless of his past, Soekarno, in his present incarnation, undoubtedly belonged to the 'anti-imperialist camp'.

Other questions arose. How had this huge archipelago, stretching for over three thousand miles along the Equator, produced such a strong nationalism? I began to search for books that would answer this question, but there were none in my father's study and the entry in an old edition of the encyclopaedia was unhappily out of date. What I did learn that year was that Indonesia was not just Java and Sumatra, but a collection of over ten thousand islands. Most were uninhabited and well over 50 per cent of the population lived on Java, the most fertile island of the entire archipelago. Fertile in every sense of the word.

Our house was filled with hundreds, probably thousands, of English-language editions published in the 1950s by the Foreign Languages Publishing House in Moscow. They used to arrive in large parcels and, despite their uninspired social-realist jacket designs, were prominently displayed on the shelves. Though they were regularly dusted after every summer storm, the covers faded rapidly and the chemical interaction of cheap Soviet paper with the summer heat of Lahore produced a musty smell that I have not encountered elsewhere. It became an indelible part of my youth – as delicious as a *madeleine*. And a few months after Soekarno's visit, I stumbled across a collection of essays by a Russian belletrist, *The Golden Rose* by Konstantin Paustovsky, his reflections on world literature.

It was while reading Paustovsky that I came across the name of Multatuli, the *nom de plume* of the Dutch novelist Eduard Douwes Dekker. Paustovsky compared his work to the paintings of Vincent Van Gogh. 'A man will go through hell's fire,' wrote the Russian, and 'will perform miracles to follow his inner urge.' He described Dekker's privileged social background, his glittering university career, his appointment as an imperial civil servant in Java and how this experience transformed his personality and his life. Paustovsky had obviously been impressed by the self-image of the Dutchman and did not know (how could he?) that Dekker was a notorious fantasist who told a lot of lies about his social origins and education; he wanted to be a good aristocrat, but if this had been his real social background he would not have accepted a colonial posting. What is undoubtedly the case is that the young Dutchman was disgusted by the workings of colonialism: economic exploitation and brutality. Even so he wanted to be the protector of the native, rather than his equal. He made no effort to conceal his contempt for Dutch generals and the viceregal establishment. His alienation was expressed in public and he openly befriended the Javanese. He was sacked and sent home in disgrace. Back in Holland, he was elected as a member of the Dutch parliament and used his position as a platform to denounce the iniquities of colonial rule. His speeches were mocked, his petitions ignored and he began to be treated like a person who has lost his mental balance.

Reviled by the real world, he turned to writing novels under a pen name – Multatuli ('long-suffering' in Latin). *Max Havelaar* was the first and is still regarded as one of the most scathing literary denunciations of the colonial order. Paustovsky insists that the second novel, *Love Letters*, was even more powerful and self-assured, but Dekker was now an outcast, expelled from the world that had produced him. He became poverty-stricken and left Holland, and was unable to find a publisher anywhere. Later, some Dutch publishers offered to buy his manuscripts. He was delighted, but they forced him to relinquish all rights to his work. He agreed. All he wanted was to see his work in print. He assumed it was pure venality. He could not imagine that the manuscripts had been bought for the opposite reason, in order to suppress them so that Dutch merchants could sleep easily in their beds. But this was Paustovsky's invention. Perhaps he had been misinformed or perhaps he wanted to demonstrate his anti-imperialist credentials to the editors of the Foreign Languages Publishing House. Whatever his reasons, the reality was that *Max Havelaar* was a sensation, almost immediately translated in London and Paris; and, more importantly, Dekker's modernist prose style was hailed as the foundation of modern Dutch literature. Much of the book is a hilarious, scornful satire on Dutch greed in Amsterdam and corruption and violence in the East Indies. Dekker became a celebrity, but was notoriously incapable with money, and became a spendthrift and an addictive gambler. Hence the occasional poverty.

Slowly, some of the pieces of the archipelagic puzzle began to come together. Each national movement bears the mark of its imperialist maker. Dutch misrule provoked the nationalism that educated Soekarno's generation. Mahatma Gandhi was a product of the British empire. Ho Chi Minh was formed in the crucible of French Indo-China. Prior to the Second World War, more European lives were lost in Indonesia than in Indo-China or South Asia. During the three years (1811–15) that the British ruled the country, the governor, Sir Stamford Raffles, wrote of the Javanese that 'ever since the arrival of the Europeans, they have neglected no opportunity of attempting to regain their independence'.

Prince Diponegoro of Jogjakarta led the first major anti-colonial uprising – the Java War of 1825–30. Like the 1857 anti-British uprising in India, it was a blind, instinctive rebellion by the old rulers angered by the organised disintegration of the old order. Diponegoro was a senior prince, but not the sultan, whom he despised. He was an intelligent man, given to mysticism. When he was tricked into being captured he was exiled to the northern tip of Sulawesi, where he died. He wrote a long, interesting memoir in which he says that he intended to 'conquer' Java.

In Java, the colonial order upset the rulers without pleasing the peasants. When Diponegoro raised the banner of revolt, the peasants rallied behind him. The Javanese became adept in guerrilla warfare and were not easily subdued. The Europeans lost 8,000 lives, but native casualties were much higher: 200,000 Javanese perished, the majority from disease and starvation. The only way General de Kock could win was by destroying whole villages and depriving the population of food. The total loss of life was vastly greater than during the 1857 anti-British uprising in India. The entire nineteenth century, barring six or seven years, witnessed regular peasant uprisings against Dutch rule. It took the colonial authorities over three decades to subjugate the Sumatran state of Aceh and even then their control was never absolute.

During the Second World War a Far-Eastern rival drove the Dutch out of Java. In Indo-China a Vichyite regime began to collaborate with Japan. How would Asian nationalists react to an Asian imperialism, which claimed to support local nationalism against their European oppressors? The communists led the Vietnamese nationalist movement. After the Soviet entry into the war, the Japanese and Vichy France were the enemy and Ho Chi Minh's resistance organisation continued the struggle.

In Java, the nationalists saw the expulsion of the Dutch as a big opportunity and initially collaborated with the Japanese. The Indian nationalist movement was deeply divided on the issue and, had a Japanese expeditionary force invaded India, there is little doubt that a sizeable wing of the national movement would have clambered aboard its tanks to drive out the British. On the eve of the Japanese invasion, the Dutch governor of East Java, van der Plas, gave about 20,000 guilders, a considerable sum, to Amir Sjarifuddin, an extremely decent left-liberal Christian, asking him to build an underground with the money. Amir went looking for the scattered remnants of the Communist Party and enrolled some of them. When the Japanese arrived, they got the Dutch archives and secret police informers and rolled up the underground in a few weeks. Almost all (perhaps thirty people) were executed. Amir was saved by Soekarno's intervention, but had a 'bad war' in Japanese prisons, where he was tortured. There was no real anti-Japanese movement till the last month of the war, and it was confined to the educated elite of Jakarta. Popular anti-Japanese resentment was widespread, however, and after mid-August many Japanese were murdered.

In August 1945, after the defeat of Japan, France and Holland believed that it was their right to recover their colonial possessions in Vietnam and Indonesia, but they had reckoned without the local population. The leadership, however, was extremely nervous. Soekarno and Hatta were afraid the allies would arrive immediately and arrest them as collaborators, so refused at first to declare independence. Impatient youths then kidnapped them and took them to the small town of Rengasdengklok, about an hour by car from Jakarta. Thanks to the mediation of Rear-Admiral Maeda, an enlightened naval officer assigned to liaise between navy-controlled East Indonesia and army-controlled Java, a deal was worked out whereby Soekarno and Hatta would be released and returned to Java, the army would pretend not to know what was going on, and a timid, two-sentence Declaration of Independence would be drawn up in Maeda's house. It was anything but heroic.

Since the French and the Dutch had no troops in the area, the British were given the task (under the terms of the Allied agreement signed in Potsdam in July 1945) of receiving the Japanese surrender in these territories, and ruling them until troops from France and Holland were ready to resume their traditional responsibilities. Soekarno declared independence on 17 August 1945 and Ho Chi Minh a few weeks later on 2 September.

It was only in September that Lord Mountbatten, the British commander in South-East Asia, was in a position to send troops to Vietnam and Indonesia, and even then he had to borrow them from the Indian Army. Some 20,000 troops from the 20th Indian Division began arriving at Saigon on 6 September, under the command of General Douglas Gracey. 'I was welcomed on arrival by the Vietminh,' Gracey later boasted, 'and I promptly kicked them out.'

Ho Chi Minh's failure to confront the British was not a tactical decision based on local conditions. It was the result of the link with Moscow. Stalin had no qualms in betraying either the revolution or his own comrades, but he was careful not to offend his bourgeois allies – regardless of whether it was Hitler, Churchill or Roosevelt – unless it became necessary. Naturally, the West had no such inhibitions and ditched Stalin without a second thought. In 1945, Stalin did not want any communist party to contest the Dutch, British or the French empires. As a communist, Ho Chi Minh accepted Moscow's discipline in public, while privately pursuing a more autonomous course. Ho was a wily bird, who had attended the Versailles Conference in 1919 and been around the communist movement since the 1920s. He was already quietly dealing with the Americans in the person of Archimedes Patti, who arranged for supplies to be dropped to Ho, and also lobbied for US recognition of Ho.[107] Not exactly what Stalinist discipline had in mind, but the US, like Stalin, could not accept a nationalism that was independent. Soekarno did not need to pirouette in the same fashion. He defended the national interests of the archipelago.

On 22 September 1945, with British connivance, French troops arrived and seized all public buildings. In a shocked response, the Vietminh organised a general strike and erected barricades, but British forces eventually regained control of the city, after shelling certain areas and rearming a number of Japanese troops held in their care and protection. Some forty British and Indian troops were killed, and over a hundred wounded, before the British withdrew in January 1946, to be replaced by a substantial French force. The result of all this was a long war which ended only in 1975. By that time the Vietnamese had fought three imperialist powers and defeated two of them: Japan, France and the United States.

The British-led force from the Indian Army did not arrive off Java until 29 September 1945. Soekarno's supporters greeted them with banners proclaiming 'Indonesia for the Indonesians'. The British occupied a number of coastal towns, Jakarta, Demarang and Malang, but encountered considerable resistance from Soekarno's forces. Once again the British were obliged to rearm Japanese troops, for use against the local inhabitants.

The British met with a serious reverse in Surabaya, the second largest town in Java and its main industrial and commercial centre. Some 4,000 British troops had arrived here on 25 October 1945. Their commander, Brigadier Mallaby, ordered the Indonesians to disarm and surrender the city. Three days later, an Indonesian force of more than 20,000 attacked his troops. Mallaby was killed, along with 200 of his men.

---

107 K. Damodaran, a communist leader from Kerala, met Ho in the late 1950s and asked him why communism had won in Vietnam and not in India. 'In India', replied Ho, 'you had Gandhi. Here I was Gandhi.' See 'Memoirs of an Indian Communist', *New Left Review* I, 93, September–October 1975, pp. 35–59.

The British immediately sent reinforcements into Surabaya, demanding an Indonesian surrender on 9 November. Receiving no reply, two cruisers and three destroyers began shelling the city on the following day, while RAF fighter-bombers dropped 1,500lb bombs on Indonesian positions. Eventually, after three days of street fighting, the city fell to the British. British and Indian casualties at Surubaya were estimated at more than 900 killed and wounded, while Indonesian casualties were over 10,000. Fighting continued in Java into 1946, with Indonesian forces being driven out of Bandung by the British in March. Dutch troops now began replacing the British, who finally withdrew in November 1946. Total British and Indian casualties in the Indonesian campaign were 620 killed and 1,447 wounded, with another 327 missing. Over 1,000 Japanese troops were killed fighting alongside the British. Indonesian casualties in this post-war war are estimated at 20,000 dead. These facts help to explain the Indonesian hatred of the British and the subsequent confrontation over Malaya.

There is little doubt that Mountbatten and the British high command were taken aback by the fierce Indonesian resistance. Or that this had an impact on ordinary British and Indian soldiers and seamen. They had won the anti-fascist war in Europe in alliance with the Soviet Union. Now they were being asked to crush nationalist revolutions in alliance with the hated Japanese. The war had radicalised soldiers and sailors and many of them now felt that the colonial wars were unjust. The victims, too, never forgot the fact that it was a British Labour government that had despatched troops and commandeered the Japanese to crush nationalist revolutions in Asia.[108]

For most of the Second World War, Holland itself, like France, had been under German occupation. This had not quenched the desire of the Dutch or French ruling elites to reoccupy their old colonies. They saw no connection between the Dutch/French anti-fascist resistance and the

---

108 John Newsinger has described how the solidarity movement spread to Australia causing real problems for the British empire:

> While the fighting continued merchant seamen – mainly Indians and Indonesians but including some British – went on strike, refusing to carry troops and munitions to Indonesia. Their action supported by the Australian trade union movement and Australian dockers blacked any ships sailing for Indonesia, eventually tying up over 500 vessels.

Indonesian or Vietnamese *maquis*. They were separate worlds. The racism once used to justify slavery had been smoothly transferred to justify the imperial reoccupation of Vietnam and Indonesia. Unlike Washington, the men in London, Paris and Amsterdam did not realise that the old empires were finished. The reconquest was merely the beginning of their death-agony. All this would soon be replaced with a new brand of imperialism: American.

In one remarkable episode Indian seamen flown in to break the strike were addressed by the Duke of Gloucester, the King's brother, who commended their loyalty. The interpreter translated this as a ringing call to defy the imperialists and join the strike . . . which they promptly did! Collections for the strike were even held on British warships in Australian ports. So damaging was this display of solidarity that Mountbatten himself travelled to Sydney to unsuccessfully plead with the trade unions to call the blacking off. ('The empire strikes back', *Socialist Review*, no. 189, September 1995.)

24

Islam on the Equator

The trade winds that first blew Islam eastwards to the coasts of India and China appear to have completely bypassed the archipelago. The followers of the Prophet arrived late on the islands of Sumatra and Java and without any trace of sand on their sandals. The early history is vague and contradictory. The first Muslim tombs in northern Sumatra only date back to the thirteenth century and there is no convincing evidence to suggest sizeable Muslim settlements before that time.

According to the Arab geographer al-Masudi, however, the first Muslim migration to the region was from ninth-century China. A peasant uprising in South China during the reign of the T'ang Emperor Hi-Tsung (878–889) led to a pogrom of the dominant merchant-traders community in Khanfu (Canton). Between 120,000 and 200,000 Muslims were massacred. Many survivors fled and reached the Malayan coast and some crossed the straits to the islands. There is no concrete evidence to prove where they landed and where they ended up, though the massacres of Chinese Muslims have been documented.

Purist Muslims everywhere like to think of their ancestors as either being descended from or being converted by the purest of the pure: the Arabs who founded the religion. This is rarely the case. As recently as the 1960s a row broke out in Indonesia when Professor Slametmuljana published a book arguing quite plausibly that the nine founding fathers (Wali) of missionary Islam were mostly Chinese.

Later there were migrations from coastal Gujarat in western India, a natural outcome of the Gujarati monopoly of the Moluccan spice trade, and from the Malabar coast. This was the route followed by Ibn Battuta, the celebrated fourteenth-century travel writer. Like modern practitioners of the genre, he sometimes allowed his imagination to overwhelm his powers of observation, but the description of a Sultanate on the coast of 'Jawa (Sumatra)' rings true, even if its exact geography is difficult to locate:

> We saw the island when we were still half a day's journey from it. It is verdant and fertile; the commonest trees there are the coco-palm, areca, clove, Indian aloe, jack-tree, mango, *jamun*, sweet orange and camphor cane. The commerce of its inhabitants is carried on with pieces of tin and native Chinese gold, unsmelted. The majority of aromatic plants which grow there are in the districts occupied by infidels. . .[109]

Ibn Battuta is welcomed to the island by the amir Dawlasa and together they ride into the town of Sumutra, 'a large and beautiful city encompassed by a wooden wall with wooden towers'. He describes the court in a city still packed with infidels. They had bought peace by agreeing to pay the *jizya* – a poll tax Islam imposed on unbelievers. It would take Islam another three hundred years to win over the bulk of the population of Java and Sumatra, but it inserted itself gently, as Buddhism and Hinduism had done several centuries earlier.

It was South Asian Sufi mystics and Muslim traders from the Coromandel coast and Gujarat who began to win converts and, as in the case of Kashmir, it was the conversion of a ruler that won over his subjects as well. Islam's capacity to adjust its doctrinal beliefs to meet the needs of the indigenous population had been effective in China, Africa, Persia and South Asia. It is also the main explanation for its rapid spread throughout the archipelago. Some Muslim sultans of Java were often elevated to sainthood after their deaths and their tombs became an important site of worship for believers, without provoking clerical fury. This was not dissimilar to the worship of Sufi saints in the Punjab or Persia or Anatolia. The reaction of orthodox believers was sometimes severe, but their numbers were few, and far from snuffing out the old traditions they were always in danger of drowning in them.

---

109 Ibn Battuta, *Travels in Asia and Africa, 1325–1354* (trans. H.A.R. Gibb), London 1929, pp. 272–81.

Prior to the arrival of Buddhism and its successor, Hinduism, the indigenous populations had (as in the Americas and elsewhere) believed in a world controlled by spirits. According to native traditions these beings inhabited forests and rivers and seas and mountains. Their anger explained natural disasters. Goodwill could be bought through sacrifices and ill-will neutralised by wearing charms and amulets and investing shamans with magical powers. Superstitions became a part of everyday life.[110] Since it was widely believed that many spirits spoke through women, they were assigned an important role in religious rituals and hence in the local power structure. This could also explain the emergence of transvestite cults: men dressing as women for reasons political and cultural rather than sexual. Buddhism and Hinduism had assimilated many of these superstitions and the Sufi variant of Islam continued to tolerate these practices.

Sufi philosophy often explained Allah's permanent presence in nature and in the everyday life of human beings. That is why a collective worship was not essential. Each believer could discover Allah in his/her own special way. Ibn Arabi (1165–1240), one of the great mystical philosophers of Islam, developed the doctrine of the Unity of Being, a pre-Spinozist belief in the creator being visible in different aspects of nature and the human spirit, and the possibility of a perfect man, in whom all the attributes of the divine being were present. The mysticism suited the Ottoman sultans at a time when they were busy in non-mystical activities such as militarily expanding their empire. Sultan Selim I flouted orthodoxy by ordering the rebuilding of Ibn Arabi's mausoleum in Damascus. Some of Ibn Arabi's followers took his argument to the extreme, arguing that real knowledge of Allah only became possible when men and women reached the pinnacle of ecstasy, which could be both sexual and non-physical. A version of this (where alcohol substituted for the joys of union) was preached in western Sumatra by Hamzah Fansuri in the second half of the sixteenth century:

---

110 It is curious, for instance, how sneezing denotes impending misfortune in numerous cultures. Christians immediately bless a person who's sneezed, Jews say 'Good health', Muslims offer thanks to Allah for his mercy.

His radiance is a blazing glow
In all of us
It is He who is the cup and the *arak*
Do not look for him far away, child.

This was both reassuring and helpful, as was the Sufi insistence on a teacher–disciple relationship within their different orders. The semi-worship of the holy teacher was appreciated in a culture which had already experienced centuries of Hindu and Buddhist dominance. Sufi philosophy was undoubtedly much simplified in the process of transmission, but the essence was preserved in the most noticeable aspect of this mysticism: it preached total independence from sectarian religious groups and all orthodox interpretations of the Koran. It abhorred ritual. Many mystics argued that orthodox believers had to be hypocrites because they sealed off their faith from their own daily practices in the material world. A Sufi by contrast insisted that the creator only dwelt in the inner realm of spirit and thus sought to break with and shame the outer world of matter. He refused to accept an Allah who was only on the outside.

Sufi teachers often explained mystical ideas to native adherents in a language that deployed familiar points of reference as in this example from Java: 'It is said that human sight may be compared to coconut milk, which in the long run will become oil; to an unripe banana, which gradually grows half-ripe . . . gradually human sight is perfected by the lord so that there is no doubt that the eye will behold the essence.'

For the large majority of believers, apart from the discipline of new rituals, Islam simplified their existence. The spirits did not need to be placated by sacrifices or the worship of a whole network of gods and goddesses, but through worship of Allah and his Prophet. This dynamic duo provided a safe guard against all forms of evil.

Many of the old superstitions, however, refused to die. To this day in many coastal villages, fishermen offer a token sacrifice to the spirits of the sea before they embark on a journey. And other superstitions persist as well. In *The Girl from the Coast*, an affecting novel based on the life of his maternal grandmother in the late nineteenth century, one of Toer's characters, a disabled tambourine man, is behaving oddly:

'Look at him; he's acting crazier than before,' a man remarked. 'How'd he get that way?'

'Cursed from birth is what I heard,' the first man answered. 'When his mother was pregnant with him, she pulled the legs off a live crab – which is why he can't use his arms and legs for work.'[111]

The one Muslim custom that did require a total breach with the past and forced a change in everyday life was the taboo on eating swine. This had to be and was publicly observed by all Muslims, regardless of whether they were mystics or orthodox believers, though in hard times it is possible that pig and wild boar was eaten (as it was by Muslim peasants in South Asia), usually after dark and under the pretence that it was really a small buffalo or a calf.

From Sumatra and Java, Islam leap-frogged to Borneo and other neighbouring islands, finally establishing an important bridgehead which became the Sultanate of Sulu and Mindanao in the Philippines. The first wave of Islam achieved success through a combination of trade, conversion of local rulers, intermarriage and, occasionally, conquest. The principal early rivals of Islam were its old enemies from the Iberian Peninsula. The crucial intervention came in the form of de Albuquerque's conquest of Malacca in 1511, which gave the Portuguese control of the Asian maritime trade. Some decades later, the Spanish arrived in the Philippines and drove the Muslims out of today's Manila, and eventually confined them to the Mindanao–Sulu zone. Both Iberian states managed substantial conversions to Catholicism, while the eastern tip of Java remained Hindu-Buddhist until the eighteenth century. There are still remote mountain areas in East and West Java which are not Muslim.

The Muslim merchants who took Sulawesi (Celebes), one of nature's most exquisitely sculpted islands, established a naval sultanate on the southwest coast of the island in the early years of the seventeenth century: the kingdom of Macassar. But the lateness of Islam in this region coincided with the expansion of European mercantile capitalism. C.M.H. Clark, an Australian historian, has described how the Muslim navy of Macassar took

---

111 Pramoedya Ananta Toer, *The Girl from the Coast* (trans. Willem Samuels), New York 2002. The manuscripts of the other two novels of the planned trilogy were confiscated and destroyed by Suharto's soldiers.

Islam 'to the frontiers of civilization, from which if they had pushed further . . . they would have moved into New Guinea and from there across to
the north coasts of Australia. They had begun to do this just when the
coming of the European ended the spread of Islam.'[112] It may have ended
any sensational spread of the religion, but it continues to grow and migrations have provided Australia itself with a sizeable Muslim community.

It was, of course, ironic that the European who came in the sixteenth
century was usually a Portuguese or a Spanish captain, fresh from the
reconquest of the Iberian peninsula and only too keen to wipe out 'the
Moors' elsewhere in the world. Both Vasco de Gama and Afonso de
Albuquerque justified their piracy in the archipelago as a crusade against
Islam. When de Albuquerque occupied Malacca in 1511 he began a tradition of banditry that would be loyally maintained for the next three
centuries by the European colonists who followed in his tracks:

> he captured and looted all Muslim vessels he encountered; he demanded that the
> Sultan of Malacca let him build a Portuguese fort; when he built the fort he
> destroyed Muslim graves for building materials; and he summarily executed the
> leading Javanese trader. This and subsequent Portuguese behaviour made St
> Francis Xavier say that their knowledge was restricted to the conjugation of the
> verb *rapio* (to steal), in which they showed 'amazing capacity for inventing new
> tenses and participles'. Not surprisingly, they could get no local support for their
> ambitions in the spice island.[113]

The Protestants from Holland proved more successful. They were less
brutal than the Portuguese and the rivalry between the two led to a rise in
prices and helped disarm local suspicions. The Dutch East India Company
soon established its control in Java, but it never seriously attempted
Christianisation, which would have been expensive and would have interfered with its usually friendly relations with Muslim rulers. Commercial

---

112 C.M.H. Clark, *A History of Australia, volume 1,* Melbourne 1962. In 1803, European missionaries in Arnhem Land in northern Australia reported encounters with sailors from a Macassar
fleet, who claimed that their ancestors had been visiting the northern coast for centuries and had
brought steel, pottery and tobacco for the native population. Not being fully 'civilised' themselves
they confined their activities to trade instead of wiping out the natives.

113 Bruce Grant, *Indonesia,* Melbourne 1964.

interests overpowered missionary lusts. Besides, the European religious wars were underway, and Protestant pastors were quite few in number, divided by sect, and badly needed in Europe. There were few conversions to Christianity until the Dutch state took over from the defunct East India Company in the early nineteenth century, a pattern not dissimilar to what happened in India.

The Dutch East India Company, like its British namesake, was among the early pioneers of the first capitalist globalisation. Unlike today's corporations, the old companies did not have automatic support from the Dutch and English states. But their charters gave them the right to create, fund and supply their own armies, which they did. Dutch rule in the archipelago was brutally enforced. Superior technology enabled them to rule the islands, which they did with the help of the traditional ruling classes in Java, but their hold was never as firm as that of their British co-imperialists in India.

The belated arrival of Islam had affected how the religion was perceived and practised. The American anthropologist Clifford Geertz divided Javanese Islam into two basic categories. The *abangan* believed in a relaxed, syncretic version, which accepts the Prophet and the Book, but without abandoning the rituals, habits and traditions of previous centuries and other religions. The *santri* is more rigid in his beliefs, refusing to accept the demarcation line between divine truth and reason, between unquestioning obedience and intellectual tolerance. 'The otherness, awfulness and majesty of God,' writes Geertz, and 'the intense moralism, the rigorous concern with doctrine, and the intolerant exclusivism which are so much a part of Islam are very foreign to the traditional outlook of the Javanese.'[114]

This is undoubtedly the case, but while accepting the specificity of indigenous Javanese traditions, it is difficult not to detect the same pattern here as in other parts of the Islamic world. As I have attempted to demonstrate in this book, every culture penetrated by Islam has produced similar divisions and from the earliest times. In the Arab peninsula itself as well as the Maghreb, West Africa and South Asia, one can uncover local variants of

---

114 Clifford Geertz, *The Religion of Java,* Chicago 1960.

abangan and *santri*: in each case it is versions of the latter who find it difficult to co-exist with fellow co-religionists and who argue incessantly on the interpretation of texts and laws. Nor is 'intolerant exclusivism' a vice confined to Islam. It exists within Judaism, Christianity and, of late, Hinduism, examples of which can be sighted any day in Israel, the United States and India.

Dutch rule in Indonesia was more thorough and more oppressive and, as a result, less effective than that of its British counterpart in India. A quarter of a million Dutch settlers moved to the conquered islands (a slightly higher figure than the total British presence in India over two hundred years) where they recreated their own community, complete with the Dutch Reformed Church, which could never establish a total hegemony. Other Protestant churches and sects multiplied throughout the colony. But the high settlement figure established by the Dutch censuses of the 1920s and 1930s is somewhat misleading. From early times Dutch (Protestant!) colonial law refused to recognise any intermediate categories of person between native and white – unlike their Iberian Catholic cousins, who invented the *mestizo*. According to Dutch law, if a white man who fathered a native woman's child acknowledged the offspring these were registered as white. If he did not (and most did not) then they became natives – hence the large number of brown-skinned whites and blue-eyed natives. A majority of the 250,000 whites were actually Eurasians.

The Dutch settlement was considered vital to the control of a colony whose resources determined the economic status of the Orange motherland. It was cash that cemented the Hollanders to their possessions in the East, and Amsterdam's dependence on its colony was far greater than that of any other European power. Without Java, the Dutch would have become little more than a cold flatland on the edge of the North Sea. The tulips could not have compensated for the loss of the archipelago. With it they were the world's third most profitable colonial power. Prior to the Second World War, the Dutch East Indies supplied 90 per cent of the world's quinine, 86 per cent of its pepper, 37 per cent of its rubber, 19 per cent of its tea as well as sugar, coffee, oil, kapok, coconut-palm products, etc. Their desperation to return after the Japanese defeat had nothing to do with sentiment or psychology or civilization or culture or democracy. It was cold-blooded economics that stoked their lust for the islands. Many

Anglo-centric historians have stressed the peculiarly instrumentalist aspects of Dutch rule. Colonial culture was exceptionally barren. The experience produced no literature worth the name. No equivalent of Kipling or Flaubert or Conrad or Maugham ever emerged. Dutch gin was a poor substitute for the lack of a literature. This is not the case. It is simply that Dutch is not a politically important language. Dutch and Indonesian scholars might argue that Couperus and Multatuli are better than Kipling, or that Albers and Springer are way above Maugham. Springer's haunting novel *Bandung, Bandung* still has the power to bring tears to sensitive eyes.

C.M.H. Clark stressed the contrast with the Iberians:

> The Portuguese Catholics spoke of infinite merit: the Dutch Calvinists spoke of uncommonly large profit. There was something sensuous and elemental in their (Portuguese) discussion of the uses to which they would put the spices from the Moluccas. They wanted pepper for food and for a physic, ginger because it made a man go more easily to the stool . . . cloves because they strengthened the liver, the mouth and the heart, furthered digestion . . . preserved sight, and four drams being drunk with milk, procured lust.

What Professor Clark failed to note was that the bulk of the Portuguese were relatively recent converts to Catholicism. Their appreciation of the merits of certain spices was a direct inheritance from the herbalists and physicians of Islam, whose scholarly treatises on sexuality and medicine left a permanent mark on Iberian culture, which the Inquisition could suppress but not extinguish. Dutch Protestantism, by contrast, had been sealed off by history from the world of a thousand and one nights. It is true that Rembrandtian Holland was full of wild sex, but punishment soon followed in the shape of Calvinism. By the time the Hollanders had consolidated their occupation of Muslim lands it was too late for the benefit of Dutch culture as a whole.[115]

---

115 The Dutch came as conquerors and an official Puritanism was the dominant ideology, which did have an impact on those natives who underwent a Dutch education and, consequently, became ultra-defensive on sexuality under Islam. But the majority was untouched by this until after independence. Despite the religiosity of the mullahs, deeply subversive epic poems with an encyclopaedic flavour were written and orally transmitted (often in fragments) throughout the islands.

In a startling essay, 'Professional Dreams', Benedict Anderson discusses the two classics *Serat Centhini* and *Suluk Gatholoco* which demonstrate better than anything else the clash between

There is evidence to suggest that some individual Dutchmen profited from their new location, abandoned the Puritan ethic and learnt to soar above their limited sexual horizons in the company of Javanese instructors of both sexes, but any generalisation in this regard would be foolish. A lot of the sex in the Indies was straightforwardly sordid. In the late 1930s there was a massive witch-hunt against homosexuals, in which many high officials and great scholars were involved and which was on a scale that had no equivalent in the history of the British or French empires, let alone the Ottomans.

In the economic realm, the Dutch used Chinese traders as their favoured middlemen (just as the Jews were used as intermediaries by the nobles and counts of eastern and central Europe so that they avoided direct contact with tenants and serfs), while relying on the native aristocracy to preserve every-day law and order. Most of the rulers were *fainéants* and feeble collaborators. It took a rebellion led by a dissident prince to create real problems in the nineteenth century. Meanwhile, as more troops trundled eastwards, more commodities travelled westwards and with them came the profits so eagerly awaited by the Mynheers in Amsterdam.

How long could this last? How would the native population react to three hundred years of colonial oppression? What instruments were available to them? Interestingly, a serious attempt was made by a prominent mixed-race would-be political leader to found a party similar to the Indian National Congress (whose founder was a liberal Englishman) and possibly inspired by that example. The idea emanated from Eduard F. E. Douwes Dekker, the great-nephew of the great Multatuli. He founded the Indian Party in 1912 as a multi-racial organisation with the declared aim of handing the islands

---

official and unofficial cultures. The sexual insolence of the poetry, its casual references to male homosexuality, aroused the wrath of Dutch scholars who found such work 'disgusting'. They must have found it threatening too, since the two works in question brought to the forefront what Victorians in Britain and Holland dreamt about endlessly but also repressed. The Centhini playfully uncovers the hypocrisy of orthodox believers. Anderson writes of the 'spendthrift relationship between religion and sexuality of the Centhini as exemplified by the episode where Cebolang, after a sleepless night of fellatio and mutual masturbation with two santri teenagers, nonchalantly rises to lead the pesantren's early prayers.' Benedict Anderson, *The Spectre of Comparisons*, London and New York 2000, pp. 105–30.

over to those 'who make their home there'. The new party opposed direct rule from Amsterdam and demanded independence and racial equality. It was a plea for dominion status, but with an important difference. Unlike Australia and New Zealand, the local Dutch, Eurasians and native Javanese and Sumatrans would all have the same rights. It would be a multi-racial and not a white dominion. The colonial administration refused to tolerate any such suggestion. The party was banned and its leaders expelled from Java.

The refusal of the colonial authorities to tolerate a secular, multi-racial, constitutionalist party created an enormous vacuum. It soon became obvious that this could not be filled by well-meaning but ineffective organisations such as Budi Utomo ('noble endeavour'), organised by Javanese students in Batavia in 1910 with the aim of social and educational modernisation of the islands accompanied by a plea for a more enlightened colonial administration. The group was directed to service the needs of the tiny Javanese middle class rather than the peasants and plantation workers who comprised a large majority of the population.

Relief came from a most unusual quarter: a Muslim traders' organisation, Sarekat Islam ('Islamic league'), which had been formed by Javanese *batik* merchants in 1909 to protect Indonesians against Chinese traders. In 1870, colonial policy became officially 'liberal' in the old sense of the word. Till then even the Dutch could not go to the colony without a special passport. Restrictions were now lifted and almost anyone could enter the East Indies. Chinese fleeing the chaos of post-Taiping China sought refuge here. They spoke only Chinese and had little interest in the native population beyond buy and sell. But even they were bound by the old institutions of the pass system and the residential system, which forbade anyone the Dutch decided was Chinese from living outside designated ghettos in the towns, and from travelling freely. These laws started to crumble after 1905, and were gone by 1918. Then the real flood began, which included a large number of 'Chinese', so described by colonial law, who knew nothing of the Chinese language but were thoroughly acculturated into local diets, customs and languages. This was why the hitherto protected *batik* merchants went into a panic.

In 1912, Tjokroaminoto, a Surabaya businessman, became the chairman of the Sarekat Islam and expanded the organisation by calling for a struggle against Christian missionary activities. These did not pose any serious problems, but it was a thinly disguised attempt to mobilise against the Dutch presence. From a distance, Lenin astutely described the new development as the birth of a mass nationalist politics linked to Islam and the emergence of a native capitalist intelligentsia. It took the Dutch slightly longer (about ten years) to reach the same conclusion.

From 1912–1922 the Sarekat Islam experienced a phenomenal growth. Both *santri* and *abangan* joined its ranks, in this way announcing the birth of a united green-tinged national organisation that was prepared for sacrifices in the struggle against the Dutch. During the same period, the more purist elements among the *santri* set up the Muhammidiyah, a modernist Islamic society with a self-denying ordinance: it was explicitly non-political and would limit itself to education and social-welfare projects. Its founder, Hadji Dahlan, was a follower of the Cairene reformer Abduh and a progressive Muslim. He organised Muslim women, created schools for them, encouraged boy-scout groups and football teams, a curriculum and approach completely alien to the schools of the *pesantaren*. The organisation was widely respected even by non-Muslims, and in recent years some of its members have argued in favour of a complete separation of religion from politics, a de facto secularism.

A young man of means from Java or Sumatra would sometimes seek relief from Dutch colonialism by disappearing to the Hijaz to perform the *hajj* in Mecca. Some did not return. Those who did embraced the anticolonial cause, but their Muslim rhetoric was often little more than nationalism disguised in religious garb. With hindsight, it is tempting to look back at the first pilgrims to Mecca and see them as the forebears or harbingers of post-1965 political Islam, but the temptation should be avoided for such a view is ahistorical. The fact is that in their desire to combat and defeat the Dutch, the more politically conscious sectors of the population were prepared to look everywhere and anywhere. Moreover the *hajj* had been going on for centuries, and the Dutch did not dare to block it, though they spied on it from a consular post in Jiddah. Orientations depended on the times – *hadjis* in the 1820s brought

Wahhabism, in the 1850s new forms of Sufi mysticism, in the 1890s modernism à la Abduh and Al-Afghani.

Early nationalists and, later, many communists sought to mediate between piety and rationalism, mysticism and science, by an imagined compartmentalisation of the human mind. A frontal assault on religion was deemed inopportune. But then, as now, they knew full well that it was the relationship of real forces – temporal power and not religion – that determined the shape of the world. All alliances had to be constructed in this light. As a result, the real pole of attraction was not Mecca or even Ottoman Istanbul (in which many hopes had been expended over many years, but which had not provided much concrete help), but Tokyo. The developments in Meiji Japan had been noted as far afield as Istanbul. And now the combination of an Ottoman warship arriving in Singapore in 1890, en route to Japan, kindled local enthusiasms. The European trade in African slaves had necessitated the use of racism. Subsequently this became a crucial plank in the ideological scaffolding of European imperialism. The victims responded by creating a counter-world-view. As the *Ertogrul* lay docked in Singapore, excited nationalists asked each other if this could be the beginning of a Turco-Japanese alliance against the white European empires?

The Japanese victory over the Tsarist navy in 1905 was greeted with enthusiasm in the colonial world and created the basis for the 1905 'dress-rehearsal' in Russia. For many this became the model of a resurgent Asia and numerous nationalist intellectuals in the colonies viewed the Rising Sun as a potential ally. In Bengal as well as Java, news of the rise of Japan percolated through to the countryside. The traditional culture of the archipelago provided a mystical twist: rumours began to circulate of 'a great ship that would sail through the clouds with a Japanese army that would overthrow the Dutch'. An even more fantastical hope expressed by *al-Imam*, a Muslim journal published in Singapore, was that Japan, needing to convert to one of the universal religions in order to compete in the modern world, might choose Islam. Why? Because Islam alone guaranteed racial equality, whereas Christianity, as the religion of the empires, would never treat the Japanese as equals and for that reason, the paper noted, 'it would not surprise the reader . . . if we say that a Muslim Japan would become the leader of all the people east of Bab-al Mandab [the gateway to the Red Sea]'.[116] Even when it became clear that the Crescent and Star could not replace the Rising Sun, the kingdom of Japan remained a source of inspiration for Asian nationalism.[117] But other winds began to blow as well.

In 1914, the Dutch Marxist Henrik Sneevliet initiated the Indies Social Democratic Association. It consisted of a handful of Marxists, including Tan Malaka and Semaun, who later became the founders of the Indonesian Communist Party (PKI). Prior to that they had entered the Sarekat Islam in order to do 'mass work'. The victory of the Russian Revolution provided a counter to both Japan and an indiscriminating nationalism. The followers of Tan Malaka and his comrades now began to agitate openly within the ranks of the Sarekat Islam for a more explicit revolutionary–nationalist orientation. A delegation from the organisation attended the Conference of the Toilers of the East in Baku in 1920. It was here, with hundreds of delegates from the Muslim world, that Grigorii Zinoviev, then president of the Communist International, became over-emotional and called on the Muslim world to launch a jihad against all empires. The applause included guns being fired in the air.

In 1921 the communist faction in Sarekat Islam, which included some who had performed the *hajj* in Mecca, demanded a turn to revolution at the annual conference. The mood can be judged from the fact that even the most moderate response (from Agus Salim) stressed repeatedly, if inaccurately, that Muhammad had preached socialism twelve hundred years before Marx. Salim had denounced 'the *doppelganger* soul of the PKI' and defended the 'pure soul of Sarekat Islam'. But the 'impure' PKI had almost smothered the souls of the 'pure'. What else could have produced the remarkable personality of Mohammed Misbach (1876–1926) or the 'Red Hadji' ('Hadji'

---

116 For this and other related information see Michael Francis Laffan, *Islamic Nationhood and Colonial Indonesia*, London and New York 2003, pp. 160–65.

117 When, after the First World War, the victors founded the League of Nations, Japan (then an ally) suggested the League's Charter should outlaw racism. The very thought outraged the United States and Britain and it was promptly vetoed.

indicated he had made the pilgrimage to Mecca), as he became known. Attempts in different parts of the world to create political organisations that blended Islam and communism had failed miserably. But occasionally the endeavour produced individuals in whose person the fusion was achieved: Hadji Misbach was one such person. He played an important part in the anti-colonial struggle and was exiled to Irian together with PKI prisoners in the late 1920s.[118]

After the organisation split, a majority of its members went with the radicals. Sarekat Islam maintained a presence, but it was no longer a mass organisation and after some years it faded away. The more orthodox members were to find homes in the modernist Islamist organisations; a few defected to the Nahdlatul Ulema (NU), which was founded in 1926 as an orthodox response to modernist Islam and was ultra-critical of the ulama's syncretic and Sufi practices.

Astonishingly, tropical Islam had given birth to what later became the largest communist party outside China and Russia. The PKI grew. It organised trades unions, led strikes and established a network of publications. Then, like other communist parties, it accepted Moscow's dictat, but on the rare occasions it was offered useful advice from the Soviet capital it chose to ignore it. In 1927, Moscow warned *against* a premature uprising in Java,

---

118 Reading about Misbach reminded me of Maulana Bhashani. A religious peasant leader in East Bengal, he had worked closely with communists in the 1930s and 1940s and adopted much of their rhetoric. He had visited Beijing and met Mao and Chou in the early Sixties. Unlike Misbach, the Bengali Maulana was easily flattered and the Chinese persuaded him to cease opposing the Ayub dictatorship. He told me all this when we went on a weeklong walk through the Bengali countryside in 1969. By that time he had become critical of Chinese policies and asked if I could become his 'political secretary', an offer I regretfully declined. Later a colleague and admirer of his told me that Bhashani had won his following amongst the peasants through preaching militancy and the Koran. He had told the peasants that he was fluent in Arabic. One day a visiting Egyptian scholar called on him in his village. Peasant supporters surrounded Bhashani, as usual. The Egyptian conversed in Arabic but appeared puzzled by the Maulana's responses. Bhashani pleaded another engagement and cut the discussion short. After he left the scholar turned to a Bengali professor who had accompanied him and asked: 'Can you explain why every time I asked him something he replied by quoting verses from the Koran?' It was then that Dhaka's intellectuals realised that the Red Maulana couldn't speak Arabic and had learnt the Koran by rote like many others. This meant that he had no idea what the Book meant.

when local conditions were clearly unripe. The PKI ignored the warning and unleashed an anti-colonial insurrection. The people were not ready and the PKI easily isolated. The notable thing is that the two provinces where the rebellion was most dynamic, Banten and West Sumatra, were among the most strongly Muslim!

Dutch revenge was characteristically vicious. Several hundred communists and sympathisers were shot dead. Thirteen thousand Indonesians were detained and six thousand communists were imprisoned or deported. In prison, the PKI leaders resolutely refused to accept that they had done anything wrong. They took violently against Tan Malaka, the Comintern representative, for opposing the revolutionary uprising. This issue remained hot until 1965.

But a colonial situation cannot keep a people down for too long. A new generation soon came to the fore – the famous generation of '45, which had either experienced or participated in the defeats of Japan and Holland. It was a confident, mocking generation, full of hope and audacious. All this was reflected in the poetry of the period, one of whose leading exponents, Chairil Anwar, a self-educated bohemian rationalist and linguist, captured the spirit of the era. Anwar was only twenty-seven when he died, felled by a deadly trio – typhus, tuberculosis and syphilis – which had attacked him simultaneously. He had no time for religion. His legacy included a short poem entitled *Heaven:*

Like my mother, and my grandmother too,
Plus seven generations before them,
I also seek admission to heaven,
Which the Jamiah Islam and the Muhammidiyah say has rivers of milk
And thousands of houris all over.

But there's a contemplative voice inside me,
Stubbornly mocking: Can you ever
Get dry after soaking in the blue sea,
After the sly temptations waiting in every port?
Anyway, who can say for sure
That there really are houris there
With voices as rich and husky as Nina's, with eyes that flirt like Jati's?

25

A tropical gulag

Every night, for over eight years, a prisoner on Buru Island in Indonesia fought against cruelty, disease and creeping insanity by telling stories to his fellow political outlaws. It kept hope alive in them. As they listened to him, the prisoners momentarily forgot where they were or who had sentenced them to years of suffering. The storyteller was Pramoedya Ananta Toer, a leading intellectual of the Indonesian left and a brilliant writer of fiction. Arrested after the military coup in Jakarta in 1965, he spent twelve years in the hell that was Buru Island – a tropical version of the Siberian gulag. Over three thousand and one nights Pram forced himself and the other captives to concentrate on another world where fiction painlessly blended with history.

It was not his first prison journey and this led him to compare present-day conditions with the colonial past. There was no room for doubt. Conditions were qualitatively worse than they had been almost two decades ago when from 1947 to 1949 he was imprisoned in Bukitduri. Then he had been actively engaged in the revolutionary struggle against the Dutch after the Second World War. The Dutch, unlike their post-colonial mimics, had not deprived him of writing implements and it was in Bukitduri that he wrote his first novel, *The Fugitive,* a 170-page masterpiece superior in composition and content to the fiction of Albert Camus, with whom Western critics sometimes compared him.

Suharto's dictatorship had imprisoned him without cause or justification. They did not like his ideas; they wanted to stop his brain from working, to take his voice away from him. He was Indonesia's most distinguished novelist, known in the academic world of the United States and elsewhere. They dared not execute him, but hoped that the conditions in which he was kept would take care of the problem, just as they had for Mussolini in fascist Italy when he ordered that Antonio Gramsci should not be executed, but that 'his brain must be stopped from working'. There were times when Pram himself believed he would never leave the *tapol* archipelago alive.

In *The Mute's Soliloquy* – an affecting account of his years in prison – he describes, in spare, contained prose, the institutionalised brutality of the new order. The old cargo vessel on which he and 800 prisoners are being transported to Buru reminds him of the 'coolies on Captain Bontekoe's ship, the kidnapped Chinese on Michener's ship bound for Hawaii . . . the four million Africans loaded onto British and American ships for transport across the Atlantic'. In extreme moments during the colonial period, the threatened and insecure Dutch administrators, aware of the Javanese obsession with cleanliness, used to hurl faeces at the natives in order to humiliate and debase them. The new order's prison ship went one better. The prisoners' hold was adjacent to the latrine and during stormy weather the two locations became inseparable. The prisoners were regularly mistreated and starved so that only the fittest would survive. Toer describes a desperate menu:

> Imagine a diet of gutter rats, the mouldy outgrowth on papaya trees and banana plants, and leeches, skewered on palm-leaf ribs prior to eating. Even J.P., one of our most well-educated prisoners, found himself reduced to eating *cicak*, though he always broke off the lizard's toe pads first. He'd become quite an expert at catching them. After amputating the lizard's toes, he would squeeze the unfortunate creature between his thumb and forefinger, shove it to the back of his throat, and swallow it whole. The man's will to defend himself against hunger was a victory in itself.

And all the while the regime sent in preachers and Islamist journalists to inspect the minds of the inmates and urge them to become believers. Despite their desolation and helplessness, few prisoners moved in that direction:

> I have no doubt that this year, just as in previous years, at the beginning of the fasting month my mates and I will be treated to a lecture by a religious official specially brought in from the free world, on the importance of fasting and controlling one's hunger and desires. Imagine the humor of that!

After fifteen years in his country's prisons, a campaign by Amnesty and other groups in the West helped to secure Pram's release, but it was conditional: he was under house arrest for a while, but for much longer under city arrest. He could not be reported about in the press, his books were banned, indeed still are formally, though the law is no longer enforced. But his time was his own and he could write again.

The allegories he had tried out on the political prisoners during desperate times on Buru became a much-acclaimed quartet of novels known as Minke's Story or the Buru Quartet. The first of them, *This Earth of Mankind*, was published in 1980, topped the bestseller list for ten months and was soon followed by its successor, *Child of All Nations*. This too became a bestseller. What is curious is that these books were actually published before they were banned, and afterwards sold on the black market. This was how thousands of Indonesian citizens welcomed their most celebrated dissident back to literary life. The novels – part social-realist, part historical – were set in the colonial period. Inspiration was provided by the legendary figure of Tirto Adhi Suryo, the father of Indonesian nationalist journalism. For most Indonesian readers, forced by the political climate to stifle their own thoughts, the scale and depth of the works produced a dramatic effect. Toer was writing about the past, but much of what he wrote resonated with the present. He posed an implicit question: Was Suharto and the new order a continuation of the colonial regime?[119]

When the books were banned in 1981 one of the publishers was imprisoned for three months. The 'second imperialists' of the new order explained the ban by accusing Toer of 'spreading Marxist-Leninist ideas', but because

---

119 The Nobel Prize Committee in Stockholm was well aware both of the quality of Toer's work and the appalling conditions he was suffering in prison at the time. But nothing moved these old men with blocked minds and hardened hearts, not even a plea from the *Washington Post Book World*. They were veterans of the cultural cold war and its double standards. Rewarding Boris Pasternak and Alexander Solzhenitsyn had all been part of their life's work, but acknowledging the gifts of an Indonesian writer, whose library and notebooks were burnt by the uniformed hoodlums of General Suharto – the founders of a new order backed by the West till the very end – was beyond their capacity. They could, of course, argue that the prize had been denied on literary merits. Pasternak was awarded the prize not for his brilliant poetry but for a second-rate novel, banned by a philistine Soviet bureaucracy. The ban won him the prize. Toer was on the wrong side.

of his 'literary dexterity' it was difficult to provide concrete examples of the crime. Perhaps what worried them was the casualness of an exchange between two colonial police officers in *House of Glass*, a conversation of the sort that probably took place regularly in many government offices during the Suharto period:

> In his textbook English he said: 'You have always tried to behave like a responsible and rational being. You seem to want to try not to act in a colonial way. I can sense that you are beginning to get fed up and sick of this colonial prison. I can understand the conflict that you must be suffering inside.'
> 'Thank you, Meneer. Perhaps that is also the reason why you prefer America?'
> 'You are not very wrong there, Meneer.'
> 'But there is oppression too in America', I added.
> 'It is not so much that there is oppression, I think. There is freedom to oppress, yes, that's true. But there is also the freedom not to be oppressed. Here there is only the freedom to oppress. There is no freedom not to be oppressed.'
> Who would have guessed that he could talk like that? Someone so close to His Excellency the Governor-General?

How had post–independence Indonesia reached the stage where its military rulers outdid the Dutch in repression? Why had a people who had fought so bravely against the Dutch, the Japanese and then the Dutch again, accepted the insolence, greed, rapine and slaughter imposed by their own army? Why had they accepted exactions that accelerated their own wretchedness? They had no choice. There were a defeated people. Some had placed their trust in Soekarno, some in Allah and others still in D.N. Aidit and the PKI. Since Allah was not readily available and his followers on the island divided into different organisations, the poor in town and country (and not they alone) depended on the combined forces of nationalism and communism to protect them and satisfy their needs.

If the first half of the twentieth century was an epoch of wars and revolutions, the second half was characterised by the rise of nationalism, the extinction of the European empires and the cold and hot wars fought by the United States against the Soviet Union and China, and later with China against the Soviet Union. It was a complex world, typified by contradictions on every level: political, economic and ideological. Above all, it was a world where people still believed that change was possible. On every continent there were political organisations seeking to make the revolution by an overthrow of the existing order. Cuba's victory both inspired and limited the process elsewhere in Latin America: the enemy had become ultra-vigilant.

The Chinese triumph of 1949, the Vietnamese victories of 1945 and 1954, and one could add the Huk rebellion in the Philippines, the communist insurgency in Malaya, the defeat of the Dutch in Java, created a new relationship of forces in Asia. To prevent the Korean peninsula from following the Chinese path required a vicious three-year war, which the United States fought under the UN banner. To hold back a communist triumph in Vietnam meant the US occupation of South Vietnam and a fifteen-year war which the United States lost – the first real defeat in its history if one doesn't count the burning of the White House as well as the rest of Washington DC by the British in 1812.

While all this was going on, and the United States and the Soviet Union were engaged in a permanent defence of their own interests, a space emerged for newly independent states – India, Egypt, Algeria, Indonesia, Tanzania – to play both sides against each other and preserve their independence. For a number of nationalist leaders it became the *sine qua non* of their anti-imperialism that they built their own equivalents of the ruling communist parties in Moscow and Beijing and repressed all unruly opposition. The degree of such repression varied, depending on local conditions and native traditions.

In Indonesia, after a stormy interlude that included a serious PKI-supported insurrection against the nationalist regime in Madiun in 1948, Soekarno thought it prudent to draw the PKI into an alliance to govern the country. His own position appeared unchallengeable and he assumed that the PKI inside the united front (NASAKOM) would disarm them politically while permitting him to use PKI strength in the country to keep sections of the army under control. It was a typical Bonapartist calculation and might have worked had it not been for the events of September 1965.

Washington was alarmed by the alliance, and alerted its surrogates in Indonesia. It was already fighting a war in Vietnam and was genuinely worried by the possibility of a PKI take-over after Soekarno's death. In 1962, the United States suffered its first setback in Vietnam, when communist guerrillas attacked and destroyed a superior contingent of US and South Vietnamese troops near the village of Ap Bac. The triumph was hailed in both the Soviet and Chinese press as a sign of Washington's vulnerability. In Indonesia, too, both the nationalist and communist press reported this and related developments in Indo-China. A polarisation began to take place within the upper echelons of the armed services of Indonesia.

To add to the confusion there was a de facto break between China and the Soviet Union. On the face of it the Chinese adopted a more militant position, attacking the Soviet communists for 'peaceful co-existence' with the United States. Communist parties split along pro-Soviet and pro-Chinese lines or attempted to remain neutral, as did the Cubans, Koreans and the Vietnamese.

The PKI leaders opted for China and D.N. Aidit became a regular visitor to China, welcomed with the honours usually reserved for a head of state. The irony is that while the PKI supported China in international affairs, its domestic policy was actually Khrushchevite, very cautious, very reformist and approved by Beijing because it enjoyed friendly relations with Soekarno's Indonesia. They had no desire to topple the regime. The PKI leaders, too, were aware that the party had suffered badly after the insurrections of 1927 and 1948. Their own needs coincided with those of Beijing and in the convoluted argot of the period, Aidit explained that 'the Indonesian revolution is at the present stage bourgeois-democratic in character and not socialist or proletarian', and that the task of the PKI was 'to struggle to conquer its leadership'. What this meant, he informed the School of Advanced Studies of the Central Committee of the Chinese Communist Party on 2 September 1963, was that

> The alliance with the national bourgeoisie has also been realised. The national bourgeoisie starts to return to the side of revolution. . . . We have now collaborated with the Indonesian bourgeoisie for nearly ten years, and the revolutionary forces have continually developed rather than grown fewer during this time, whereas the reactionary forces have experienced failure after failure.[120]

If Aidit had been the editor of a Marxist review these delusions would have been quickly forgotten, bypassed by history, but this was not the case

---

120 D.N. Aidit, *The Indonesian Revolution and the Immediate Tasks of the Indonesian Communist Party*, Beijing 1965.

because in one important respect his assessment was deadly accurate. The legitimacy enjoyed by the Indonesian communists had led to a phenomenal increase in membership and influence. Aidit was addressing the Chinese Central Committee as the leader of the largest organised political party in Indonesia and the largest communist party outside the communist world. The PKI had 3 million members and more than 10 million sympathisers grouped in mass organisations of various sorts including trades unions. It had an impressive network of journals, whose influence stretched far beyond the PKI. Aidit, Lukman and other PKI veterans could be forgiven for basking in the new-found respectability brought about by the deal done with Soekarno. They had all served spells in prison. They had lost leaders and activists during the resistance to the Dutch, the Japanese and the Mark One Soekarno regime. Now they felt close to power and aware that their presence had enabled the Soekarno government to push through actual laws, the first on agrarian reform, and the other on crop-sharing, in 1960–1. It was when bureaucrats, *hadjis*, and the military steadily blocked the implementation of these laws that the PKI undertook to force them through from below via so-called 'unilateral actions'. The response from the reactionaries was so fierce (rural activists implementing the reforms were systematically murdered) that Aidit had to call off the campaign.

Some of Aidit's dispositions must have been made on the assumption that time was on his side. The PKI leader was banking on biological inevitability, which would, sooner or later, remove Bung Karno from the scene. Then it would be their turn, the time for real change. Other PKI leaders were less sanguine, knowing full well that it was Soekarno's protection that had enabled them to survive and grow. How would they manage after he died? They appeared to have forgotten the elementary laws of revolution, and, unforgivably, fostered illusions that led their supporters to underestimate the enemy. Far from preparing a revolution, as was later alleged, the PKI was totally unprepared for the turn that events took and, for that reason, had failed to arm its supporters politically (let alone in any other way) for any confrontation with the state. In Marxist terms they were guilty of original sin. They had overestimated an individual (Soekarno), and underestimated the power and autonomy of an institution that underpinned the state: the army.

Unlike its Pakistani or Indian counterparts, the Indonesian Army was not a pure, 100 per cent colonial construct. It reflected the different colonial and nationalist traditions of the archipelago. PETA, the 'auxiliary' army formed by the Japanese in 1943 on Java and Bali, provided a large bulk of the officer corps of the 1945 revolution (up to 80 per cent); another 10 per cent were from the mercenary Dutch colonial military; and a crucial 5 per cent came from a special military academy set up on Java in 1940 after Holland had been occupied by the Nazis. Thus the officer corps included nationalists of the '45 generation but were led by men who had fought with the Dutch against the nationalists (Generals Nasution and Suharto), a layer that had collaborated actively with the Japanese in the Motherland Defence Force (Suharto again) and, most importantly, an influential group that included both and was trained in the United States. Training in the US began sometime in 1954 – the height of the Cold War – and the hundreds if not thousands later sent were all veterans of the nationalist revolution.

Another dissimilarity with its South Asian counterparts was that the chain of command had often been broken: the story of 1945–65 is full of mutinies, attempted coups, war-lordism, regional rebellions, all led by veterans of the revolution. There was an unstated military philosophy that regarded most civilian politicians (excluding Soekarno who was admired by most officers as the founding father of the new republic) as corrupt and debased. The Council of Generals was uniformly hostile to Soekarno's friendship with Beijing and his alliance with the PKI. Some of this was nationalist hostility, a residue of the popular anti-Chineseism that characterised the colonial period. But mainly it was Cold War anti-communism. It was hardly a secret that most of the generals were keen to clip the testicles of the PKI. Most, but not all. There was a typical Asian irony: General Parman, head of military intelligence, who was killed on 1 October 1965 and whose hobby was children's electric trains, was the younger brother of Ir. Sakirman, a member of the PKI's Politburo.

On 30 September 1965, a group led by colonels and majors set up a clandestine Revolutionary Council, which authorised an attempt to push through a 'pre-emptive coup'. Their chairman, Lieutenant-Colonel Untung, claimed that the military high command, grouped in the Council of Generals, and backed by the CIA, was preparing a coup to topple Soekarno, destroy the left-wing parties and impose a military dictatorship. In a lightning move, Untung's commandos captured six leading generals.

Untung commanded a battalion in the presidential guard, the Tjakrabirawa regiment. Three of the generals were killed while being arrested because they resisted with gunfire of their own. The other three were executed at the Halim air-force base, exactly by who it is still unclear, but certainly by men in uniform, and possibly air-force personnel. When Benedict Anderson spoke recently with Sergeant-Major Bungkus, who was on one of the strike teams, he was told that orders were to arrest but not kill the generals, and that 'his general' had surrendered without any blood being shed. At the air base he handed him over to some other units, whose identity he was not sure of.[121]

Both Soekarno and the PKI denied all foreknowledge. Those who argued that Untung's attempt to seize power was a deliberate provocation designed to bring about the destruction of both Soekarno and the PKI were dismissed as fantasists, but subsequent revelations from the CIA made it clear that both it and British intelligence were heavily involved in the affair. It was alleged that Suharto (regarded at the time as non-ideological) had been informed of the plans but had done nothing to deter the plotters. His informant was said to be Colonel A. Latief, a member of the Revolutionary Council, who was arrested but never permitted to testify. Astonishingly, Latief was not executed, probably because he was a close friend of the Suharto family, especially Mrs Suharto. He was bayoneted and shot while he was being arrested, but did not die. And he spent thirteen years in prison, where he was kept in appalling conditions, but survived to tell his story. In his memoirs, published after Suharto's fall, he insists that Suharto had been fully briefed beforehand by Latief himself of the planned coup. If this is so it means that the future dictator did not warn the other generals, allowed them to die, then used 30 September to wipe out the left and remove Soekarno from power.[122]

There is little doubt that the main beneficiaries of 30 September (as of 11 September 2001) were the very people the events had been designed to weaken. All the available evidence now suggests that Untung and his colleagues were either working for or, what is more likely, were duped by US and British intelligence agencies into killing senior generals, who while hostile to

---

121 I am grateful to Benedict Anderson for communicating this information to me.
122 Benedict Anderson, 'Petrus Dadi Ratu', *New Left Review II*, 3, May–June 2000.

the PKI were not prepared to topple Soekarno. As in Chile some years later, the CIA decided to remove any obstinate generals not prepared to topple Salvador Allende and that is why General Schneider had to be despatched. Suharto and Pinochet were brothers in blood, fed by the same masters, fêted by the same media pundits and honoured by Nixon, Reagan and Mrs Thatcher.

There were several oddities about 30 September 1965. Untung explicitly rejected the support of the crowd and did not call for street mobilisations, which was strange if the aim was to protect Soekarno. Even weirder was one of Untung's first public proclamations: he announced the demotion of all officers above him in rank to his own rank. People below him in rank who supported him would get promotions. It is difficult to imagine a policy more likely to have solidified all the senior officers against him. Was this pure stupidity or had Central Intelligence Castings chosen well?

Several months after the Indonesian massacres, James Reston was to write admiringly of the new order in an article headlined 'A Gleam of Light in Asia' and admitted that

> Washington is being careful not to claim any credit for this change in the sixth most populous and one of the richest nations in the world, but this does not mean that Washington had nothing to do with it. There was a great deal more contact between the anti-Communist forces in that country and at least one very high official in Washington before and during the Indonesian massacre than is generally realised.[123]

The movement behind 30 September remains a partial mystery, but what is clear is that it was cleverly manipulated. Earlier that year the British ambassador, Sir Andrew Gilchrist, had sent a message home which contained an interesting sentence: 'I have never concealed from you my belief that a little shooting in Indonesia would be an essential preliminary to effective change.' Two years earlier a CIA memorandum dated 1962 stated calmly that President Kennedy and British Prime Minister Harold Macmillan had 'agreed to liquidate President Soekarno, depending on the situation and available opportunities'.[124]

---

123 *The New York Times*, 19 June 1966.
124 Mark Curtis, 'Democratic Genocide', *The Ecologist*, Vol. 26, No. 5, September–October 1996.

Whatever the political weaknesses of the PKI leadership, one can confidently assert that if Aidit and Lukman had been the masterminds behind
Untung it would not have been such a half-baked affair. The PKI would
have prepared insurrections in Java, Bali and Sumatra, and they would have
armed their supporters instead of watching passively while they were slaughtered like sacrificial lambs before a religious festival.[125]

General Suharto, in charge of the Strategic Reserve Command,
mobilised the army and within twenty-four hours had the situation under
control. From the very first week, the army insisted that the events of 30
September had been planned and executed by the PKI. No serious evidence
was provided and D.N. Aidit was arrested in a village where he had been
hiding and executed. The testimony, obtained under torture, of Njono, a
senior trades unionist and PKI leader, was mottled with contradictions.[126]
Njono, too, was executed. Suharto and his military colleagues then ordered
the killings of other PKI leaders and embarked on a generalised pogrom of
the Indonesian left. Throughout the archipelago, Islamist vigilantes, in many
cases the young volunteers of the youth wing of the Nahdlatul Ulema
(NU), were unleashed in a jihad against the 'red devils'. From October 1965
till January 1966 Indonesia was engulfed in a bloodbath, with the worst
killings taking place in Hindu Bali. A 'little shooting' had indeed taken
place, brutalising the country's culture and opening up a gigantic vacuum in
its political life. In almost every region, the Army had incited the massacres.

The bulk of the media in the United States and Australia were not too
bothered by the massacres. Why should they be given that their side was
reaping the benefits? By contrast, the CIA made no attempt to conceal, at
least not from itself, the scale of what had taken place. A classified document
revealed the following:

In terms of numbers killed, the anti-PKI massacres in Indonesia rank as one of the
worst mass murders of the twentieth century, along with the Soviet purges of the
1930s, the Nazi mass murders during the Second World War, and the Maoist
bloodbath of the early 1950s. In this regard, the Indonesian coup is certainly one

---

125 See Benedict R. Anderson and Ruth T. McVey, *A Preliminary Analysis of the October 1,
1965, Coup in Indonesia,* New York 1971.
126 Ibid.

of the most significant events of the twentieth century, far more significant than many other events that have received much greater publicity.[127]

Despite certain absences – the civilian casualties in Hiroshima, Nagasaki and Korea of 1945–53 were equally horrific – the assessment was accurate except in one important regard. The agency was far too modest about its own role in the affair. In 1958 a Rumanian émigré, Guy J. Pauker – CIA consultant, Rand Corporation, National Security Council adviser and Berkeley academic – had suggested strengthening the Indonesian Army by using it as a conduit for economic as well as military aid. He described the officers as men with 'above-average qualities of leadership, patriotism and commitment to moral values', who could be trusted sooner, rather than later, to 'strike, sweep their house clean, and rededicate themselves to higher purposes'. Pauker, who died in 2002, was described to me recently by another US academic in the field as 'a real bastard and a shrewd opportunist'. His advice was certainly taken seriously and the three witches of the American Empire – Pentagon, CIA, DIA – counselled General Suharto to be bold, bloody and resolute.[128]

'I probably have a lot of blood on my hands, but that's not all bad. There's a time when you have to strike hard at a decisive moment.' With these words, Robert J. Martens, formerly a 'political officer' in the US embassy in Indonesia, told freelance journalist Kathy Kadane how US diplomats and CIA officers provided up to 5,000 names to Indonesian army death squads in 1965, and checked them off as they were killed or captured.[129]

The consequences of the uninterrupted repression of the Indonesian left affected the country politically, economically and psychologically. Prior to 1965, the political culture of Indonesia had been vibrant. Even after

---

127 Central Intelligence Agency, Directorate of Intelligence, 'Intelligence Report: Indonesia 1965, the coup that backfired', Washington, 1968. Quoted in Adam Schwarz, *A Nation in Waiting*, Sydney 1999.

128 P.D. Scott, 'America and the Overthrow of Soekarno, 1965–67', in Malcolm Caldwell (Ed.), *Ten Years of Military Terror in Indonesia*, Nottingham 1975.

129 Kadane's article was reprinted in the *San Francisco Examiner* (20 May 1990) and the *Washington Post* (21 May 1990), but the *New York Times* rode in to the rescue with an officially inspired damage-control riposte by a Mr Michael Wines (12 July 1990) and, as so often is the case, the story died.

Soekarno dissolved parliament, debates and discussions never stopped. The new order banned politics except those of the official variety. And economics? An apposite answer is provided in Pramoedya Ananta Toer's prison notebooks:

> By 1965, when Soekarno was toppled, a strongly competitive force emerged – multinational capital – which saw in Indonesia a source of raw materials, cheap labour and a large market. This is the lever that prized Soekarno from his position. The great *Brahmin*, who had dreamed of an Indonesia with political sovereignty, economic independence, and cultural integrity was unable to hold back the forces of multinational capital.[130]

And nor was the PKI. Multinational capital had swooped down on Java like a hungry eagle. Suharto and the new-order crowd were happy to live off its droppings. But the high-rise buildings that soon littered the Jakarta skyline could not overcome the deep trauma that the country was suffering. The ghosts of murdered communists, the political prisoners, the families who survived, the very few exiles who managed to escape abroad, the self-atomised intellectuals who felt guilty for being alive, the guilty ones who had killed, all contributed to heightening the escapist fantasies of a new order underwritten by Western capitalism and local fear and which Benedict Anderson was later to baptise as the Dry-Rot Order.[131]

The exarch's family and its immediate circle grew richer by the day. The political cleansing of 1965–66 had created the basis for an institutionalised de-politicisation of the country. Politics were strictly controlled and the citizens

---

130 Pramoedya Ananta Toer, *The Mute's Soliloquy: A Memoir*, New York 1999.

131 Benedict Anderson, the historian of their country most respected by non-official Indonesians, was banned from entering Indonesia in 1973. His professorship at Cornell did not help to open any doors. His writings displeased Suharto's backers in Washington and it was not in US interests to demand his entry. Anderson returned to Jakarta in 1999 and received an emotional welcome. His books and essays had become amongst the most treasured *samizdats* during the Dry-Rot Order. The flame that had been extinguished in Indonesia kept burning in Cornell. Anderson, too, must have been overcome by the reception awarded to him. His public lecture was delivered in near-perfect *Behasa*; its emotional charge, authority and sheer brilliance reminded his audience of the intellectual losses they had suffered over the last three decades. An English translation, 'Indonesian Nationalism Today and in the Future', was published in *New Left Review* I, 238, May–June 1999.

were frightened. Suharto was regularly 're-elected' by large majorities. The *New York Times* recorded no serious complaints. Most dissenters were in prison and only on rare occasions were their words reported in the press. The following exchange on Buru Island in 1978 between a Jakarta hack and Pramoedya Ananta Toer was instructive, if not typical of the period. The desire to seal off politics from culture was almost Anglo-Saxon in its desperation:

> Journalist: Do you still believe that literature cannot be separated from politics?
> Pram: Just as politics cannot be separated from life, life cannot be separated from politics. People who consider themselves to be non-political are no different; they've already been assimilated with the current political views – they just don't feel it any more. This is normal. Throughout history, almost all literary works have been political. People must broaden their understanding and accept the fact that politics, *not* political parties, is tied in with anything and everything that is related to power. As long as man is a social animal, he will participate in political activity . . . look at the Javanese literary classics: don't they support the power structure of their time? What I'm saying is that a political work can also be a literary work.
> Journalist: But isn't politics dirty?
> Pram: There is dirty politics and there is clean politics.
> Journalist: What do you have to say about your ten years of detention?
> Pram: It's not ten years; it's going on thirteen. I view this period of almost thirteen years as one consequence of the nation-building process.
> Journalist: And your own feelings? Your personal feelings?
> Pram: They're not important. As an individual I'm not important in this process.
> Journalist: What if Indonesian society doesn't want to accept you back? What would you think about that?
> Pram: Easy – I've always been willing to leave. As Amir Pasaribu once said, 'It is better to be a foreigner in a foreign land than a stranger in one's own land.'

As long as Washington remained satisfied, Suharto's power was practically unlimited. And as long as Washington was satisfied so were London, Bonn and Canberra. The massacre of a million Indonesians had already revealed that the sensitivities of Western politicians and media pundits were dulled to the point of atrophy. They all understood the need for a 'little shooting'. What Suharto did afterwards could only be an anti-climax. A country closed to its own people was always open to foreign capital. Suharto prided himself on the fact that he and not Soekarno had brought this prosperity to the archipelago.

Everything was now under his control: politics, economics and the military. An official Islamist party was sponsored by the state and, some years later, Suharto, who had initially shown little interest in religion, began to flaunt his own Islam. This turn pleased neither the NU nor the Muhammidiyah. Neither wanted to see its duopoly hold over religion broken by the state. The NU became oppositional. Having helped to wipe out the PKI, the NU leaders had assumed that they and they alone could fill the vacuum. They had begun to preach the virtues of patience. Now they realised that Suharto had betrayed their illusions.

In 1975, the Indonesian Army was sent to invade and occupy East Timor, a former Portuguese colony about to become fully independent. It had never been claimed by the Dutch or by their nationalist successors in Jakarta. But in 1974 a democratic revolution had erupted in Portugal. It toppled the decrepit dictatorship in Lisbon. One of its causes had been the liberation movements in Angola, Mozambique and Guinea, which had affected the young Portuguese officers and soldiers. The captains and majors who had taken power were determined to free the colonies, first in Africa and later in the archipelago. A radical–nationalist liberation movement, Fretilin, had begun a struggle in East Timor and it was obvious that it commanded the support of a majority of East Timorese. But the United States had recently suffered a severe blow with the Vietnamese triumph in Saigon. The last thing it wanted was a 'communist' victory in East Timor. Suharto and his generals became the willing instruments of an imperial strategy. More blood would flow.

One-third of the population of the island died as a result of massacres, torture, imprisonment and starvation. In Washington and Canberra, the politicians said little. The atrocities in East Timor were carried out under the command of officers whose hands still bore marks of the murders committed earlier: the congealed blood of up to a million of their own people. This time, too, much Islamist rhetoric was used to justify the slaughter of Christians in Indonesia while in East Timor, the Catholic hierarchy was told that the invasion had been necessary to rid the island of the 'communists' who led Fretlin.[132]

---

132 The stench and violence that accompanied the 'Dry Rot' invasion of East Timor were recounted in a remarkable fictional reconstruction by the Anglo-Chinese writer Timothy Mo, in his novel *The Redundancy of Courage*, London and New York 1992.

And with Western support, Suharto and his gang, once again, got away with mass murder. Washington and London had no complaints. In those days humanity was never invoked when defending Western interests. And this support remained solid till the very end. But the day came when the crowds began to assemble in the streets again and the Indonesian generals and their backers in Washington were faced with a choice. Were they prepared to massacre another million in order to keep a corrupt leader and his venal family in power? No, they weren't. The Cold War was over. China was now a dynamic capitalist state. Few spots disfigured the sun of US hegemony. Washington could afford to be generous. Suharto was allowed to fall. And Australia was asked to send troops to East Timor under the UN flag to control the blood-lust of the Indonesian militias. The defeat in East Timor made the military more inclined to assert its strength at home. The old well had been poisoned. Those who followed him could not challenge or reverse his legacy. They, too, had blood on their hands. The physical elimination of the PKI had left a gigantic vacuum in the country. After 1965, the Islamists had assumed they would become part of the Dry-Rot Order and govern in a partnership with Suharto, just as the PKI had done with Soekarno. Now their time had come.

Abdulrahman Wahid was the leader of the NU – the Islamist party whose semi-autonomous youth league, Ansor, had hurled its members into vigorous battle against the communists and wiped out thousands of the 'red vermin'. Many of the killers eventually went mad, unable to live with the knowledge of what they had done. More importantly, the expected political reward never came. Suharto was temperamentally unsuited to share spoils of any sort. The NU became estranged. Violence, once embedded inside an organisation, is difficult to uproot. It is, after all, a skill and it can be sold or used against newer enemies or on behalf of the spivs and racketeers produced by Dry-Rot or in the name of confessional terror. Thugs taught to kill by the state are rarely unemployed for long.

After Suharto's departure, the real alternatives were limited. Wahid became president and while in office he urged an end to the legal ban on Marxism and publicly apologised for the role of NU Muslims in 1965; not much perhaps, but no other political leader did even this. Wahid's disastrous presidency, however, cost him most of his credibility. In the 1999 elections his party came in third, behind the odious figure of Akbar Tandjung, a wily hack of Suharto's Golkar – the ruling non-party party of the Dry-Rot period. In spite of having been convicted of massive fraud, and having his appeal rejected, he still refuses to quit his positions as head of Golkar and Speaker of Parliament. Who would rule the country? Who else but Soekarno's daughter? Over the last few decades Asia has witnessed a remarkable recurrence: a populist male politician is assassinated, executed or removed from power and years later the people remember him by electing his wife or daughter to high office or waiting in its anteroom. Asia has had more women leaders than any other continent: Mrs Bandaranaike (Sri Lanka), Benazir Bhutto (Pakistan), Hasina Waheed, Khaleda Zia (Bangladesh), Aung Sun Ky (Burma) and now the inappropriately named Megawati, in Indonesia.

She, too, had expressed no regrets for murders carried out by right-wing nationalist gangs from her party (PNI/PDI) among leftists of the same party as well as the PKI, especially in Bali in 1965–66. Later, she had defended the occupation of East Timor. If one used Multatuli's injunction of the colonial period – that a key function of a human being is to be human – as a criterion, then it would have to be admitted that there were few politicians in post-Suharto Indonesia who could be regarded as human beings. Certainly not these two enfeebled leftovers that would now run the country, for the first year in tandem. But it was the same army in the background, the same criminal breed of senior officers, the same brutalised and debased soldiery, and once again it was waging war against its own people in Aceh and West Papua.

In these conditions the rise of extremist religious organisations was hardly a surprise. The Darul Islam was one such group, accused of involvement in attacks on non-Muslims. Another was the Jamiyah Islamiyah (the Party of Islam), a tiny organisation compared to the NU or the Muhammidiyah.

26

An island made secure

Bali has long been under the sway of Hinduism. What makes it unique is that it remains so today: the only island in the archipelago to resist the appeal of the Koran and the only one where Hindus remain an overwhelming majority. Over the centuries it became a refuge and a fortress. Not long after the Ottomans took Constantinople, the Hindu empire based in Jogjakarta fell and its ruling family, together with the entire court and its apparatus, including Brahmin priests and scholars, musicians and dancers, poets and singers, fled to Bali. This new layer increased the density of Brahmins in an already caste-infested island. Contrary to the popular image, the Balinese were the tough islanders, the Gurkhas of the archipelago. A few of the Balinese settlers in Java may have converted to Islam, but the island itself remained immune. Why? The argument that its culture had evolved to such a degree that any other explanation of the cosmos was unacceptable does not ring true. After all, Java was not so different and the same applied to the interior of pre-Islamic Sumatra. So what explains Balinese exceptionalism? It was the usual combination of geography, demography, politics and commerce, added to the undoubted military prowess of the Balinese. Elsewhere in the region, the triumphs of Islam had been achieved without violence. The Balinese resistance, too, might have been worn down if the Europeans had not arrived.

In a remarkable study of the island, Geoffrey Robinson has demonstrated how the Dutch colonial administration, extremely worried by the rise of communist and nationalist currents in the 1920s, embarked on a process of social and cultural engineering in Bali.[133] In the name of 'tradition' it restored and buttressed the power of the old rulers and the priests and backed the creation of new cultural and religious practices as a dam to protect the powerful upper castes. The object was to maximise the collection of revenue and minimise the possibilities of resistance by a systematic Dutch–Brahmin collaboration to preserve political order. The consequences were unsurprising: mass poverty, landlessness, resentment and coercion.

The Dutch presence became a vital buffer, deliberately preserving the cultural/religious status quo. The Balinese rajas were not averse to non-Balinese Muslim settlements, provided they did not infringe the rules and restrictions of caste and custom. A number of Muslim villages in the north co-existed with the Hindu majority.

The Japanese occupation instituted a different form of patronage: they encouraged the lower castes and the nationalist-minded youth. These dividing lines affected the island society and partially determined political alliances until 1965, when the island was bathed in blood. By that time the PKI had become the second largest force on the island and politics were completely polarised. The land reforms had created a class divide. The religious lobby (Muslims, Christians, Hindu-Balinese) joined forces to insist that institutional religious land-holdings be exempted from the laws: a United Front of Jesuits/Mullahs/Brahmins. This had unexpected and sinister consequences. Rich landowning *ulama* and *hadjis*, under pressure from the PKI, seem often to have 'donated' their extra land to *wakaf* (Islamic charitable foundations to which every Believer must contribute) belonging to local mosques and *madrasas*, and then got themselves appointed to the governing boards of these *wakaf*. The institutional land-holdings of the famous *madrasa* at Gontor (in those days almost the only one which insisted on everyday use of Arabic) had increased ten times over the 1962–65 period. While it was easy for the left to attack particularly wealthy *hadjis* or *ulama*, it was much more difficult to criticise these religious institutions without seeming to be obsessively hostile to religion. The Muslim masses would come to the defence of mosques and schools in a way they would not have done for particular *ulama* or *hadjis*. In this way religion and land conflicts became completely intertwined.

---

133 Geoffrey Robinson, *The Dark Side of Paradise: Political Violence in Bali*, Cornell 1995.

And two years before the massacres there was a natural disaster: Gunung Agung, the volcanic mountain that dominates the island, erupted violently and the lava rolled over 25,000 people. The Hindu priests and the mullahs saw in this act the gods/Allah expressing their displeasure at man's impudence in trying to change the natural order of life on earth. And many Balinese saw in it a bad omen.

The 1965 mass murders in Bali were not simply a result of confessional rage; other motives were fury over land reform and sharecropping laws, complex clan loyalties, class conflict. A special correspondent of the *Frankfurter Allgemeine Zeitung* wrote of bodies lying on roads or heaped in pits, rivers red with blood, half-burned villages with fearful peasants cowering in the shells of their huts. He described the hysteria and fear that had led some Hindu people suspected of being communists to join the rampaging soldiers and Islamist volunteers and kill alleged PKI supporters themselves in order to prove that they were 'not PKI'. Hindu priests, worried by the socially disruptive effects of the PKI's local policies, supported the troops. They named names, took soldiers to secret locations and defended the killings as sacrifices needed to appease the spirits angered by PKI sacrileges. Over a period of six months, up to a million people were butchered, probably more. In Bali alone the death toll was over 150,000. Robinson argues that a key line of conflict went back to the revolution; many of those who joined the PKI in the 1950s were anti–Dutch nationalists in the 1940s; their rivals in the PNI (later Megawati's PDIP) were collaborators.

By the end of December 1965, over 70,000 names had been erased from the police register; more than 100,000 PKI members had been *diamankan* or 'made secure', while over 40,000 were waiting to be executed. Not satisfied at the pace of the killings, Suharto despatched a favourite thug, Sarwo Edhie, with a strong troop of commandos to bring the affair to a rapid conclusion. He did. By the end of January 1966, the whole island had been thoroughly cleansed and 'made secure'. The populations of over a dozen Balinese villages had been sliced in half over a three-month period. No protests were registered by Washington or Canberra. Intelligence chiefs here and in London were no doubt congratulating themselves on a job well done. Elsewhere there was silence. But Peter Dale Scott – the Canadian diplomat-turned-scholar-poet – warned of the spread of the 'killer wind' in 'Coming to Jakarta: A Poem About Terror'.

But none of us experienced
    that pervasive smell of death
    those impassable rivers

clogged with corpses
    Robert Lowell is that why
    even you a pacifist

had so little to say about it?
    Or you gentle reader
    let us examine carefully

the good reasons
    you and I
    don't enjoy reading this

Like the time
    in the steep Engadine
    we saw the silent avalanche

fall away from the mountain
    hair and eyebrows
    the first to feel

the murmurations
    of the spreading
    killer wind

A feature of the killings is that they took place overwhelmingly in rural areas. Cities were the safest place to be. Most likely there you would go to jail, probably be tortured, but you wouldn't be murdered. This helps explain why the NU's Ansor played so big a part, since the NU is the party of syncretic traditionalist Islam, which is strongest in the villages of Java. It also explains why the modernists, mostly urban, had a much smaller role, though it is from this stream that the present-day extremists derive as offshoots. And a killer breeze came back to Bali with a vengeance.

The men accused of having organised the bombing of two bars in Bali on 12 October 2002, which killed 183 people (of whom 53 were Australians), belonged to a local Islamist organisation, but contrary to the rhetoric of the Cheney–Bush–Rumsfeld junta in Washington, no serious links to al-Qaida have been discovered. Despite heavy pressure from Washington and Canberra, the tough-minded Balinese police chief heading the inquiry, General Mangku Pastika, initially refused to accept that there is a definite al-Qaida connection. Reporting from the region, Benedict Anderson has said: 'Travelling in Indonesia in the aftermath of the October 12th Bali bombing, it was striking to find that never, in private conversation, and only rarely in the public press, did anyone accept the Washington doctrine that the outrage was the work of a worldwide conspiracy, directed by al-Qaida.'[134]

This did not stop the Western media from insisting that it was al-Qaida, with CNN.com citing 'FBI documents' as its 'proof'. More such proof came from another source. 'That is a vast, vast array of islands,' Brigadier General John Rosa, deputy director for operations of the US Joint Staff, has said. 'Are there easy places to hide there? You betcha.' If this were true, would not al-Qaida be slightly reluctant to do anything that drew attention to the fact? After all, their principal leader, Osama bin Laden, is still on the 'Wanted: Dead or Alive' list of the FBI and every other agency.

Since the fall of Suharto, there has been little coverage of Indonesia in the Western media. The tragedy of dead, white lives brought the country to the fore once again, but the superficial character of what was published was painful, if not surprising. The fact is that since 1998, many Indonesians have been experiencing a degree of violence reminiscent of 1965 and the invasion of East Timor. Christian and Muslim extremists have reduced the Moluccan city of Ambon to a shell: memories of Beirut, Grozny and Ramallah. In Borneo there have been clashes between the native Dayaks and Madurese immigrants with the former supported by sections of the army. A virtual civil war is taking place in the Sumatran province of Aceh, which has exacted a heavy price in loss of lives (several thousand) and property. Different factions within the army have been heavily involved in funding, training and arming some of the private armies that are currently wreaking havoc in different parts of the country. The Indonesian army itself has, over the years, perfected its ability to torture and kill and has been busy practising

---

134 Unpublished speech given in Bangkok, December 2002.

its atrocities in Western Papua against a tiny liberation organisation which seeks to protect its country from the marauding multinationals. But piracy and gangsterism is not confined to Indonesia alone. In this context, the bombings in Bali are not a complete puzzle. They fit perfectly into the local context.

On 25 November 2002, the Australian daily *The Age* published an article by Matthew Moore under the headline 'Al Quaeda links with Bali bombing strengthens'. In Indonesia, the police chief General Pastika remained contemptuous of these and similar reports. He had the men. They belong to the Djemaah Islamiya (DI Party of Islam), which models itself on Pakistan's Jamaat-e-Islami (JI). The DI's leading cleric, Abu Bakr Ba'asyir was inspired by the JI's founder, Maulana Maududi. But while the JI in Pakistan carefully distinguishes itself from the country's hard-core terrorist groups, its Indonesian copy is far less discriminating. Its members have confessed to bombing churches and other acts of terror. It is perfectly possible that they might have had some informal meetings with operatives linked to al-Qaida. The most recent information from the Indonesian authorities has named a local cleric, Hanbali, wanted for various offences, as the person who provided the cash for the Bali bombing. Where did he get the money? As usual in the murky world of violence and counter-violence, nothing is yet clear.

Indonesia has long been awash with confessional violence involving all the religions in the region. It is perfectly possible that the DI bombs were part of a local campaign against the consumption of alcohol or the use of Bali for sex-tourism or a hundred other similar reasons. What has been really affected is the economy of the island: over half of Bali's revenue is tourist generated. There are cheap bed-and-breakfast places and five-star hotels charging US$3000 a room, offering private pools for each guest, and welcoming aging jet-setters like Mick Jagger and Barbra Streisand. The tourist image of the island as a haven for peace, which was never true, has now been shattered in full public view. The motives of the bombers remain a mystery, but no evidence so far indicates any desire to punish Australia.

While asylum-seekers rioted in their concentration camps to protest against their living conditions, the Australian elite wallowed in self-pity, its leaders only too keen to impress on the rest of the world that this was a down-under 9/11. But the attempt failed. For the rest of the world it was a 72-hour wonder (a day longer than if it had happened in Kenya or Pakistan or Nigeria or Sudan), and it disappeared off the US networks soon after. How could Australia's right-wing prime minister, John Howard, have imagined that his country could ever compete in the sympathy stakes with the great Empire? 'For the rest of Australian history,' he said,

> 12 October 2002 will be counted as day on which evil struck, with indiscriminate and indescribable savagery, young innocent Australians who were engaging in an understandable period of relaxation and whose innocence was palpable and whose death and unjury we join the rest of the Australian community in marking and mourning today.
>
> In many respects the word terrorism is too antiseptic an expression to describe what happened. It is too technical and too formal. What happened was barbaric brutal mass murder without justification.

In Indonesia itself, the event was put into a different perspective. It was a small tragedy in an archipelago that had experienced the worst mass murder since the Judeocide of the Second World War. And not a single official in Australia had denounced what took place in 1965. The kangaroos had come home to roost.

Did anyone in Canberra ever ask how Indonesia had come to this pass? The pretence that Australian innocence had somehow been violated became a generalised theme in that country's media and political discourse. Innocence? Australia has been involved in every major conflict of the last century. Its citizens have been used as fodder to defend the British empire (First and Second World Wars) and the American Empire (Korea, Vietnam, Afghanistan and, no doubt, Iraq). Was Australia innocent of the massacres committed in Indonesia in 1965–6? Was it innocent when it went along with the Indonesian occupation of East Timor even as Australian journalists reporting the brutalities were being captured and killed by Suharto's and Kissinger's soldiers? The political elite that rules Australia likes to bask in its old identity, but the country itself has changed beyond recognition over the last twenty-five years. It's the rulers who have been left behind.

Meanwhile in Indonesia everything is now deregulated. The country was and remains loyal to the economics dictated by the international institutions. The cumulative result of the policies pushed through over the last three decades can now be inspected closely. What we see is disintegrating social, economic and cultural structures: the edifice of Soekarno's Indonesia has been deliberately and consciously dynamited. The future is uncertain. New tragedies lurk on all the big islands. A far, far cry from the dreams of early nationalism. Under questioning from a hostile Western journalist in the mid-Sixties, Soekarno had shouted:

> I'll tell you what I have to be proud about. In twenty years I have made this country of 7,000 islands, from Sabang to Merauke, stretching wider than the United States of America, composed of people of different heritage, speaking different tongues with varying demands and needs, into ONE NATION! They are all Indonesians now. They all speak one language. They think like I do – as an Indonesian. They feel as I do – as Indonesians who will never permit colonialism and imperialism to invade our shores again in whatever form they take. Is that not something to be proud of? . . . Don't you understand that there is more to this life than becoming rich? People like you can only think of success in terms of material things. Economics is all you think of. . .[135]

How true.

---

135 Quoted in Tarzie Vittachi, *The Fall of Sukarno*, London 1967.

Appendix

On the Israeli–Arab war

Isaac Deutscher★

As an introduction, could you sum up your general view of the Israeli–Arab war?
The war and the 'miracle' of Israel's victory have, in my view, solved none
the problems that confront Israel and the Arab states. They have, on the
contrary, aggravated all the old issues and created new, more dangerous
ones. They have not increased Israel's security, but rendered it more vul-
nerable than it had been. I am convinced that the latest, all-too-easy
triumph of Israeli arms will be seen one day, in a not very remote future, to
have been a disaster in the first instance for Israel itself.

Let us consider the international background of the events. We have to
relate this war to the worldwide power struggle and ideological conflicts
which form its context. In these last years American imperialism, and the
forces associated with it and supported by it, have been engaged in a tremendous political, ideological, economic and military offensive over a vast area
of Asia and Africa; while the forces opposed to them, the Soviet Union in
the first instance, have barely held their ground or have been in retreat. This
trend emerges from a long series of occurrences: the Ghanaian upheaval, in
which Nkrumah's government was overthrown; the growth of reaction

★ Isaac Deutscher was interviewed by Alexander Cockburn, Tom Wengraf and Peter Wollen
for *New Left Review*, 20 June 1967

in various Afro-Asian countries; the bloody triumph of anti-communism in Indonesia, which was a huge victory for counter-revolution in Asia; the escalation of the American war in Vietnam; and the 'marginal' right-wing military coup in Greece. The Arab–Israeli war was not an isolated affair; it belongs to this category of events. The counter-trend has manifested itself in revolutionary ferment in various parts of India, the radicalisation of the political mood in Arab countries, the effective struggle of the National Front of Liberation in Vietnam; and the worldwide growth of opposition to American intervention. The advance of American imperialism and of Afro-Asian counter-revolution has not gone unopposed, but its success everywhere outside Vietnam has been evident.

In the Middle East the American forward push has been of relatively recent date. During the Suez war, the United States still adopted an 'anti-colonialist' stance. It acted, in seeming accord with the Soviet Union, to bring about the British and French withdrawal. The logic of American policy was still the same as in the late 1940s, when the state of Israel was in the making. As long as the American ruling class was interested primarily in squeezing out the old colonial powers from Africa and Asia, the White House was a mainstay of 'anti-colonialism'. But having contributed to the debacle of the old empires, the United States took fright at the 'power vacuum' that might be filled by native revolutionary forces or the Soviet Union or a combination of both. Yankee anti-colonialism faded out, and America 'stepped in'. In the Middle East this happened during the period between the Suez crisis and the last Israeli war. The American landings in Lebanon in 1958 were designed to stem a high tide of revolution in that area, especially in Iraq. Since then the United States, no doubt relying to some extent on Soviet 'moderation', has avoided open and direct military involvement in the Middle East and maintained a posture of detachment. This does not make the American presence any less real.

How would you situate Israel's policy in this perspective?
The Israelis have, of course, acted on their own motives, and not merely to suit the convenience of American policy. That the great mass of Israelis believe themselves to be menaced by Arab hostility need not be doubted. That some 'bloodthirsty' Arab declarations about 'wiping Israel off the map' made Israeli flesh creep is evident. Haunted by the memories of the Jewish

tragedy in Europe, the Israelis feel isolated and encircled by the 'teeming' millions of a hostile Arab world. Nothing was easier for their own propagandists, aided by Arab verbal threats, than to play up the fear of another 'final solution' threatening the Jews, this time in Asia. Conjuring up Biblical myths and all the ancient religious–national symbols of Jewish history, the propagandists whipped up that frenzy of belligerence, arrogance and fanaticism of which the Israelis gave such startling displays as they rushed to Sinai and the Wailing Wall and to Jordan and the walls of Jericho. Behind the frenzy and arrogance there lay Israel's suppressed sense of guilt towards the Arabs, the feeling that the Arabs would never forget or forgive the blows Israel had inflicted on them: the seizure of their land, the fate of a million or more refugees, and repeated military defeats and humiliations. Driven half-mad by fear of Arab revenge, the Israelis have, in their overwhelming majority, accepted the 'doctrine' behind their government's policy, the 'doctrine' that holds that Israel's security lies in periodic warfare which every few years must reduce the Arab states to impotence.

Yet whatever their own motives and fears, the Israelis are not independent agents. The factors of Israel's dependence were to some extent 'built in' in its history over two decades. All Israeli governments have staked Israel's existence on the 'Western orientation'. This alone would have sufficed to turn Israel into a Western outpost in the Middle East, and so to involve it in the great conflict between imperialism (or neo-colonialism) and the Arab peoples struggling for their emancipation. Other factors have been at play as well. Israel's economy has depended for its tenuous balance and growth on foreign Zionist financial aid, especially on American donations. These donations have been a curse in disguise for the new state. They have enabled the government to manage its balance of payments in a way in which no country in the world can do without engaging in any trade with its neighbours. It has distorted Israel's economic structure by encouraging the growth of a large, unproductive sector and a standard of living which is not related to the country's own productivity and earnings. Israel has in effect lived well above its means. Over many years nearly half of Israel's food was imported from the West. As the American administration exempts from taxation the earnings and profits earmarked as donations for Israel, Washington has held its hand on the purses on which Israel's economy depends. Washington could at any time hit Israel by refusing the tax exemption (even though this would lose it the Jewish vote in elections). The threat of such a sanction, never uttered but always present, and occasionally hinted at, has been enough to align Israeli policy firmly with the United States.

Years ago, when I visited Israel, a high Israeli official listed to me the factories that they could not build because of American objections – among them steel mills and plants producing agricultural machinery. On the other hand, there was a list of virtually useless factories turning out fantastic amounts of plastic kitchen utensils, toys, etc. Nor could any Israeli administration ever feel free to consider seriously Israel's vital, long-term need for trade and close economic ties with its Arab neighbours or for improving economic relations with the USSR and Eastern Europe.

Economic dependence has affected Israel's domestic policy and 'cultural atmosphere' in other ways as well. The American donor is the most important foreign investor operating in the Holy Land. A wealthy American Jew, a 'worldly businessman' among his gentile associates and friends in New York, Philadelphia or Detroit, he is at heart proud to be a member of the Chosen People, and in Israel exercises his influence in favour of religious obscurantism and reaction. A fervent believer in free enterprise, he views with a hostile eye even the mild 'socialism' of the Histradrut and the Kibbutzim, and has done his bit in taming it. Above all, he has helped the rabbis to maintain their stranglehold on legislation and much of the education; and so to keep alive the spirit of racial-talmudic exclusiveness and superiority. All this has fed and inflamed the antagonism towards the Arabs.

The Cold War imparted great momentum to the reactionary trends and exacerbated the Arab–Jewish conflict. Israel was firmly committed to anti-communism. True, Stalin's policy in his last years, outbreaks of anti-semitism in the USSR, anti-Jewish *motifs* in the trials of Slansky, Rajk and Kostov, and Soviet encouragement of even the most irrational forms of Arab nationalism, all bore their share of responsibility for Israel's attitude. Yet it should not be forgotten that Stalin had been Israel's godfather; that it was with Czechoslovak munitions, supplied on Stalin's orders, that the Jews had fought the British occupation army – and the Arabs – in 1947–48; and that the Soviet envoy was the first to vote for the recognition of the state of Israel by the United Nations. It may be argued that Stalin's change of attitude towards Israel was itself a reaction to Israel's alignment with the West. And in the post-Stalin era the Israeli governments have persisted in this alignment.

Irreconcilable hostility to Arab aspirations for emancipation from the West thus became *the* axiom of Israeli policy. Hence Israel's role in 1956, in the Suez war. Israel's Social Democratic ministers, no less than Western colonialists, have embraced a *raison d'état* which sees its highest wisdom in keeping the Arabs backward and divided and playing their reactionary Hashemite and other feudal elements against the republican, national-revolutionary forces. Early this year, when it seemed that a republican uprising or coup might overthrow King Hussein, Mr Eshkol's government made no bones about it that in case of a 'Nasserite coup' in Amman, Israeli troops would march into Jordan. And the prelude to the events of last June was provided by Israel's adoption of a menacing attitude towards Syria's new regime which it denounced as 'Nasserite' or even 'ultra-Nasserite' (for Syria's government appeared to be a shade more anti-imperialist and radical than Egypt's).

Did Israel, in fact, plan to attack Syria some time in May, as Soviet Intelligence Services believed and as Moscow warned Nasser? We do not know. It was as a result of this warning, and with Soviet encouragement, that Nasser ordered mobilisation and concentration of troops on the Sinai frontier. If Israel had such a plan, Nasser's move may have delayed the attack on Syria by a few weeks. If Israel had no such plan, its behaviour gave to its anti-Syrian threats the kind of plausibility that Arab threats had in Israeli eyes. In any case, Israel's rulers were quite confident that their aggressiveness *vis-à-vis* either Syria or Egypt would meet with Western sympathy and bring them reward. This calculation underlay their decision to strike the pre-emptive blow on June 5th. They were absolutely sure of American, and to some extent British, moral, political and economic support. They knew that no matter how far they went in attacking the Arabs, they could count on American diplomatic protection or, at the very least, on American official indulgence. And they were not mistaken. The White House and the Pentagon could not fail to appreciate men who for their own reasons, were out to put down the Arab enemies of American neo-colonialism. General Dayan acted as a kind of Marshal Ky for the Middle East and appeared to be doing his job with startling speed, efficiency and ruthlessness. He was, and is, a much cheaper and far less embarrassing ally than Ky.

Could we now turn to the Arab side of the picture, and their behaviour on the eve of the crisis?

The Arab behaviour, especially Nasser's divided mind and hesitation on the eve of hostilities, present indeed a striking contrast to Israel's determination and uninhibited aggressiveness. Having, with Soviet encouragement, moved his troops to the Sinai frontier, and even put his Russian-made missiles in position, Nasser then, without consulting Moscow, proclaimed the blockade of the Straits of Tiran. This was a provocative move, though practically of very limited significance. The Western powers did not consider it important enough to try and 'test' the blockade. It provided Nasser with a prestige gain and enabled him to claim that he had wrested from Israel the last fruit of their 1956 victory. (Before the Suez war Israeli ships could not pass these Straits.) The Israelis played up the blockade as a mortal danger to their economy, which it was not; and they replied by mobilising their forces and moving them to the frontiers.

Soviet propaganda still continued to encourage the Arabs in public. However a conference of Middle Eastern Communist Parties held in May (its resolutions were summarised in *Pravda*) was strangely reticent about the crisis and allusively critical of Nasser. What was more important were curious diplomatic manoeuvres behind the scenes. On May 26th, in the dead of night (at 2.30 a.m.) the Soviet ambassador woke up Nasser to give him a grave warning that the Egyptian army must not be the first to open fire. Nasser complied. The compliance was so thorough that he not only refrained from starting hostilities, but took no precautions whatsoever against the possibility of an Israeli attack: he left his airfields undefended and his planes grounded and uncamouflaged. He did not even bother to mine the Tiran Straits or to place a few guns on their shores (as the Israelis found out to their surprise when they came there).

All this suggests hopeless bungling on Nasser's part and on the part of the Egyptian Command. But the real bunglers sat in the Kremlin. Brezhnev's and Kosygin's behaviour during these events was reminiscent of Khrushchev's during the Cuban crisis, though it was even more muddle-headed. The pattern was the same. In the first phase there was needless provocation of the other side and a reckless move towards the 'brink'; in the next sudden panic and a hasty retreat; and then followed frantic attempts to save face and cover up the traces. Having excited Arab fears, encouraged them to risky moves, promised to stand by them, and having brought out their own naval units into the Mediterranean to counter the moves of the American Sixth Fleet, the Russians then tied Nasser hand and foot.

Why did they do it? As the tension was mounting, the 'hot line' between the Kremlin and the White House went into action. The two superpowers agreed to avoid direct intervention and to curb the parties to the conflict. If the Americans went through the motions of curbing the Israelis, they must have done it so perfunctorily, or with so many winks that the Israelis felt, in fact, encouraged to go ahead with their plan for the pre-emptive blow. (We have, at any rate, not heard of the American ambassador waking up the Israeli prime minister to warn him that the Israelis must not be the first to open fire.) The Soviet curb on Nasser was heavy, rude, and effective. Even so, Nasser's failure to take elementary military precautions remains something of a puzzle. Did the Soviet ambassador in the course of his nocturnal visit tell Nasser that Moscow was sure that the Israelis would not strike first? Had Washington given Moscow such an assurance? And was Moscow so gullible as to take it at face value and act on it? It seems almost incredible that this should have been so. But only some such version of the events can account for Nasser's inactivity and for Moscow's stunned surprise at the outbreak of hostilities.

Behind all this bungling there loomed the central contradiction of Soviet policy. On the one hand the Soviet leaders see in the preservation of the international status quo, including the social status quo, the essential condition of their national security and of 'peaceful coexistence'. They are therefore anxious to keep at a 'safe distance' from storm centres of class conflict in the world and to avoid dangerous foreign entanglements. On the other hand, they cannot, for ideological and power-political reasons, avoid altogether dangerous entanglements. They cannot quite keep at a safe distance when American neo-colonialism clashed directly or indirectly with its Afro-Asian and Latin-American enemies, who look to Moscow as their friend and protector. In normal times this contradiction is only latent, Moscow works for détente and rapprochement with the USA; and it cautiously aids and arms its Afro-Asian or Cuban friends. But sooner or later the moment of crisis comes and the contradiction explodes in Moscow's face. Soviet policy must then choose between its allies and protégés working against the status quo, and its own commitment to the status quo. When the choice is pressing and ineluctable, it opts for the status quo.

The dilemma is real and in the nuclear age dangerous enough. But it confronts the USA as well, for the USA is just as much interested as is the USSR in avoiding world war and nuclear conflict. This, however, limits its freedom of action and of political–ideological offensive far less than it restricts Soviet freedom. Washington is far less afraid of the possibility that some move by one of its protégés, or its own military intervention might lead to a direct confrontation of the superpowers. After the Cuban crisis and the war in Vietnam, the Arab–Israeli war has once again sharply illuminated the difference.

One critical problem is obviously whether the Israelis have ever had any chance of establishing normal or merely tolerable relations with the Arabs? Did they ever have any option at all? To what extent was the last war the outcome of a long chain of irreversible events?

Yes, to some extent, the present situation has been determined by the whole course of Arab–Israeli relations since the Second World War and even since the First. Yet I believe that some options were open to the Israelis. Allow me to quote to you a parable with the help of which I once tried to present this problem to an Israeli audience:

A man once jumped from the top floor of a burning house in which many members of his family had already perished. He managed to save his life; but as he was falling to the ground, he hit a person standing down below and broke that person's legs and arms. The jumping man had no choice; yet to the man with the broken limbs he was the cause of his misfortune. If both behaved rationally, they would not become enemies. The man who escaped from the blazing house, having recovered, would have tried to help and console the other sufferer; and the latter might have realised that he was the victim of circumstances over which neither of them had control. But look what happens when these people behave irrationally. The injured man blames the other for his misery and swears to make him pay for it. The other one, afraid of the crippled man's revenge, insults him, kicks him and beats him up whenever they meet. The kicked man again swears revenge and is again punched and punished. The bitter enmity, so whimsical at first, hardens and comes to overshadow the whole existence of both men and to poison their minds.

You will, I am sure, recognise yourselves (I said to my Israeli audience), the Israeli remnants of European Jewry, in the man who jumped from the blazing house. The other character represents, of course, the Palestine Arabs, more than a million of them, who have lost their lands and their homes. They are resentful; they gaze from across the frontiers on their old native places; they raid you stealthily, and swear revenge. You punch and kick them mercilessly; you have shown that you know how to do it. But what is the sense of it? And what is the prospect?

The responsibility for the tragedy of European Jews, for Auschwitz, Majdanek, and the slaughters in the ghetto, rests entirely on our Western bourgeois 'civilisation', of which Nazism was the legitimate, even though degenerate, offspring. Yet it was the Arabs who were made to pay the price for the crimes the West committed towards the Jews. They are still made to pay it, for the 'guilty conscience' of the West is, of course, pro-Israeli and anti-Arab. And how easily Israel has allowed itself to be bribed and fooled by the false 'conscience money'.

A rational relationship between Israelis and Arabs might have been possible if Israel had at least attempted to establish it, if the man who jumped from the burning house had tried to make friends with the innocent victim of his descent and compensate him. This did not happen. Israel never even recognised the Arab grievance. From the outset Zionism worked towards the creation of a purely Jewish state and was glad to rid the country of its Arab inhabitants. No Israeli government has ever seriously looked for any opportunity to remove or assuage the grievance. They refused even to consider the fate of the huge mass of refugees unless the Arab states first recognised Israel, unless, that is, the Arabs surrendered politically before starting negotiations. Perhaps this might still be excused as bargaining tactics. The disastrous aggravation of Arab–Israeli relations was brought about by the Suez war, when Israel unashamedly acted as the spearhead of the old bankrupt European imperialisms in their last common stand in the Middle East, in their last attempt to maintain their grip on Egypt. The Israelis did not have to align themselves with the shareholders of the Suez Canal Company. The pros and cons were clear; there was no question of any mixture of rights and wrongs on either side. The Israelis put themselves totally in the wrong, morally and politically.

On the face of it, the Arab–Israeli conflict is only a clash of two rival nationalisms, each moving within the vicious circle of its self-righteous and inflated ambitions. From the viewpoint of an abstract internationalism nothing would be easier than to dismiss both as equally worthless and reactionary. However, such a view would ignore the social and political realities of the situation. The nationalism of the people in semi-colonial or colonial countries, fighting for their independence must not be put on the same moral–political level as the nationalism of conquerors and oppressors. The former has its historic justification and progressive aspect which the latter has not. Clearly, Arab nationalism, unlike the Israeli, still belongs to the former category.

Yet, even the nationalism of the exploited and oppressed should not be viewed uncritically, for there are various phases in its development. In one phase the progressive aspirations prevail; in another reactionary tendencies come to the surface. From the moment when independence is won or nearly won, nationalism tends to shed its revolutionary aspect altogether and turns into a retrograde ideology. We have seen this happening in India, Indonesia, Israel, and to some extent even in China. And even in the revolutionary phase each nationalism has its streak of irrationality, an inclination to exclusiveness, national egoism and racism. Arab nationalism despite all its historic merits and progressive functions, also contains such ingredients.

The June crisis has revealed some of the basic weaknesses of Arab political thought and action: the lack of political strategy; a proneness to emotional self-intoxication; and an excessive reliance on nationalist demagogy. These weaknesses were among the decisive causes of the Arab defeat. By indulging in threats of the destruction of Israel and even of extermination – and how empty these threats were has been amply demonstrated by the Arabs' utter military unpreparedness – some of Egypt's and Jordan's propagandists provided plenty of grist to Israeli chauvinism, and enabled Israel's government to work up the mass of its people into the paroxysm of fear and ferocious aggressiveness which then burst upon Arab heads.

It is a truism that war is a continuation of policy. The six days' war has shown up the relative immaturity of the present Arab regimes. The Israelis owe their triumph not merely to the pre-emptive blow, but also to a more modern economic, political and military organisation. To some extent the war drew a balance on the decade of Arab development since the Suez war and has revealed its grave inadequacies. The modernisation of the socio-economic structures of Egypt and the other Arab states and of Arab political

thinking has proceeded far more slowly than people inclined to idealise the
present Arab regimes have assumed.

The persisting backwardness is, of course, rooted in socio-economic
conditions. But ideology and methods of organisation are in themselves
factors of weakness. I have in mind the single-party system, the cult of
Nasserism, and the absence of free discussion. All this has greatly hampered
the political education of the masses and the work of socialist enlightenment.
The negative results have made themselves felt on various levels. When
major decisions of policy depend on a more or less autocratic Leader, there
is in normal times no genuine popular participation in the political
processes, no vigilant and active consciousness, no initiative from below.
This has had many consequences, even military ones. The Israeli pre-emptive blow, delivered with conventional weapons, would not have had such
devastating impact if Egypt's armed forces had been accustomed to rely on
the initiative of individual officers and soldiers. Local commanders would
then have taken the elementary defensive precautions without waiting for
orders from above. Military inefficiency reflected here a wider and deeper,
social-political weakness. The military–bureaucratic methods of Nasserism
hamper also the political integration of the Arab movement of liberation.
Nationalist demagogy flourishes only all too easily; but it is no substitute for
a real impulse to national unity and for a real mobilisation of popular forces
against the divisive, feudal and reactionary elements. We have seen how,
during the emergency, excessive reliance on a single Leader made the fate of
the Arab states dependent in fact on Great Power intervention and accidents
of diplomatic manoeuvre.

*To return to Israel, what use is it going to make of victory? How do the Israelis visu-
alise their further role in that part of the world?*
Paradoxically and grotesquely, the Israelis appear now in the role of the
Prussians of the Middle East. They have now won three wars against their
Arab neighbours. Just so did the Prussians a century ago defeat all their
neighbours within a few years, the Danes, the Austrians and the French. The
succession of victories bred in them an absolute confidence in their own efficiency, a blind reliance on the force of their arms, chauvinistic arrogance, and
contempt for other peoples. I fear that a similar degeneration – for degeneration it is – may be taking place in the political character of Israel. Yet as the

Prussia of the Middle East, Israel can be only a feeble parody of the original. The Prussians were at least able to use their victories for uniting in their Reich all German-speaking peoples living outside the Austro-Hungarian Empire. Germany's neighbours were divided among themselves by interest, history, religion and language. Bismarck, Wilhelm II and Hitler could play them off against one another. The Israelis are surrounded by Arabs only. Attempts to play the Arab states against one another are bound to fail in the end. The Arabs were at loggerheads with one another in 1948, when Israel waged its first war; they were far less divided in 1956, during Israel's second war; and they formed a common front in 1967. They may prove far more firmly united in any future confrontation with Israel.

The Germans have summed up their own experience in the bitter phrase: '*Man kann sich totsiegen!*' 'You can rush yourself victoriously into your grave.' This is what the Israelis have been doing. They have bitten off much more than they can swallow. In the conquered territories and in Israel there are now nearly a million and five hundred thousand Arabs, well over 40 per cent of the total population. Will the Israelis expel this mass of Arabs in order to hold 'securely' the conquered lands ? This would create a new refugee problem, more dangerous and larger than the old one. Will they give up the conquered territories? No, say most of their leaders. Ben Gurion, the evil spirit of Israeli chauvinism, urges the creation of an 'Arab Palestinian State' on the Jordan, that would be an Israeli Protectorate. Can Israel expect that the Arabs will accept such a Protectorate ? That they will not fight it tooth and nail ? None of the Israeli parties is prepared even to contemplate a binational Arab–Israeli state. Meanwhile great numbers of Arabs have been 'induced' to leave their homes on the Jordan, and the treatment of those who have stayed behind is far worse than that of the Arab minority in Israel that was kept under martial law for 19 years. Yes, this victory is worse for Israel than a defeat. Far from giving Israel a higher degree of security, it has rendered it much more insecure. If Arab revenge and extermination is what the Israelis feared, they have behaved as if they were bent on turning a bogey into an actual menace.

Did Israel's victory bring any real gain to the United States? Has it furthered the American ideological offensive in Afro-Asia?
There was a moment, at the ceasefire, when it looked as if Egypt's defeat led to Nasser's downfall and to the undoing of the policy associated with his

name. If that had happened, the Middle East would have almost certainly been brought back into the Western sphere of influence. Egypt might have become another Ghana or Indonesia. This did not happen however. The Arab masses who came out in the streets and squares of Cairo, Damascus and Beirut to demand that Nasser should stay in office, prevented it happening. This was one of those rare historic popular impulses that redress or upset a political balance within a few moments. This time, in the hour of defeat, the initiative from below worked with immediate impact. There are only very few cases in history when a people stood in this way by a defeated leader. The situation is, of course, still fluid. Reactionary influences will go on working within the Arab states to achieve something like a Ghanaian or Indonesian coup. But for the time being neo-colonialism has been denied the fruit of Israel's 'victory'.

Moscow's influence and prestige have, as a result of these events, suffered a grave reverse. Is this a permanent loss or a temporary one? And is it likely to have an effect on political alignments in Moscow?
'The Russians have let us down!' was the bitter cry that came from Cairo, Damascus and Beirut in June. And when the Arabs saw the Soviet delegate at the United Nations voting, in unison with the Americans, for a ceasefire to which no condition for a withdrawal of the Israeli troops was attached, they felt utterly betrayed. 'The Soviet Union will now sink to the rank of a second- or fourth-rate power,' Nasser was reported to have told the Soviet ambassador. The events appeared to justify the Chinese accusation of Soviet collusion with the United States. The debacle aroused an alarm in Eastern Europe as well. 'If the Soviet Union could let down Egypt like this, may it not also let us down when we are once again confronted by German aggression?', the Poles and the Czechs wondered. The Yugoslavs, too, were outraged. Tito, Gomulka and other leaders rushed to Moscow to demand an explanation and a rescue operation for the Arabs. This was all the more remarkable as the demand came from the 'moderates' and the 'revisionists' who normally stand for 'peaceful coexistence' and rapprochement with the USA. It was they who now spoke of Soviet 'collusion with American imperialism'.

The Soviet leaders had to do something. The fact that the intervention of the Arab masses had saved the Nasser regime unexpectedly provided

Moscow with fresh scope for manoeuvre. After the great letdown, the Soviet leaders again came to the fore as the friends and protectors of the Arab states. A few spectacular gestures, breaking off diplomatic relations with Israel, and speeches at the United Nations cost them little. Even the White House showed 'understanding' for their 'predicament' and for the 'tactical necessity' which presently brought Kosygin to the United Nations Assembly.

However, something more than gestures was required to restore the Soviet position. The Arabs demanded that the Soviet Union should at once help them to rebuild their military strength, the strength they had lost through compliance with Soviet advice. They asked for new planes, new tanks, new guns, new stocks of munitions. But apart from the cost this involved – the value of the military equipment lost by Egypt alone is put at a billion pounds – the reconstitution of the Arab armed forces carries, from Moscow's viewpoint, major political risks. The Arabs refuse to negotiate with Israel; they may well afford to leave Israel to choke on its victory. Rearmament is Cairo's top priority. Israel has taught the Egyptians a lesson: next time the Egyptian air force may strike the pre-emptive blow. And Moscow has had to decide whether it will supply the weapons for the blow.

Moscow cannot favour the idea of such an Arab retaliation, but neither can it refuse to rearm Egypt. Yet Arab rearmament will almost certainly tempt Israel to interrupt the process and strike another pre-emptive blow, in which case the Soviet Union would once again be faced with the dilemma which has worsted it in May and June. If Egypt were to strike first, the United States would almost certainly intervene. Its Sixth Fleet would not look on from the Mediterranean if the Israeli air force were knocked out and the Arabs were about to march into Jerusalem or Tel Aviv. If the USSR again kept out of the conflict, it would irretrievably destroy its international power position.

A week after the ceasefire the Soviet Chief of Staff was in Cairo; and Soviet advisers and experts crowded the hotels there, beginning to work on the reconstitution of Egypt's armed forces. Yet Moscow cannot face with equanimity the prospect of an Arab–Israeli competition in pre-emptive blows and its wider implications. Probably the Soviet experts in Cairo were making haste slowly, while Soviet diplomacy tried to 'win the peace' for the Arabs after it had lost them the war. But even the most clever playing for time cannot solve the central issue of Soviet policy. How much longer can the Soviet Union adapt itself to the American forward push? How far can it retreat before the American economic-political and military offensives across the Afro-Asian area? Not for nothing did *Krasnaya Zvezda* already in June suggest that the current Soviet conception of peaceful coexistence might be in need of some revision. The military, and not they alone, fear that Soviet retreats are increasing the dynamic of the American forward push; and that if this goes on a direct Soviet–American clash may become inevitable. If Brezhnev and Kosygin do not manage to cope with this issue, changes in leadership are quite possible. The Cuban and Vietnamese crises contributed to Khrushchev's downfall. The full consequences of the Middle Eastern crisis have yet to unfold.

What solutions do you see to this situation? Can the Arab–Israeli conflict still be resolved in any rational manner?
I do not believe that it can be so resolved by military means. To be sure, no one can deny the Arab states the right to reconstitute their armed forces to some extent. But what they need far more urgently is a social and political strategy and new methods in their struggle for emancipation. This cannot be a purely negative strategy dominated by the anti-Israeli obsession. They may refuse to parley with Israel as long as Israel has not given up its conquests. They will necessarily resist the occupation regime on the Jordan and in the Gaza strip. But this need not mean a renewal of war.

The strategy that can yield the Arabs far greater gain than those that can be obtained in any Holy War or through a pre-emptive blow, a strategy that would bring them real victory, a civilised victory, must be centred on the imperative and urgent need for an intensive modernisation of the structure of the Arab economy and of Arab politics and on the need for a genuine integration of Arab national life, which is still broken up by the old, inherited and imperialist-sponsored frontiers and divisions. These aims can be promoted only if the revolutionary and socialist tendencies in Arab politics are strengthened and developed.

Finally, Arab nationalism will be incomparably more effective as a liberating force if it is disciplined and rationalised by an element of internationalism that will enable the Arabs to approach the problem of Israel more realistically than hitherto. They cannot go on denying Israel's right to exist and indulging in bloodthirsty rhetoric. Economic growth, industrialisation, education, more efficient organisation and more sober policies are bound to give the Arabs what sheer numbers and anti-Israeli fury have not been able to give them, namely an actual preponderance which should almost automatically reduce Israel to its modest proportions and its proper role in the Middle East.

This is, of course, not a short-term programme. Yet its realisation need not take too much time; and there is no shorter way to emancipation. The short cuts of demagogy, revenge and war have proved disastrous enough. Meanwhile, Arab policy should be based on direct appeal to the Israeli people over the heads of the Israeli government, on an appeal to the workers and the *kibbutzim*. The latter should be freed from their fears by clear assurances and pledges that Israel's legitimate interests are respected and that Israel may even be welcome as a member of a future Middle Eastern Federation. This would cause the orgy of Israeli chauvinism to subside and would stimulate opposition to Eshkol's and Dayan's policy of conquest and domination. The capacity of Israeli workers to respond to such an appeal should not be underrated.

More independence from the Great Power game is also necessary. That game has distorted the social-political development of the Middle East. I have shown how much American influence has done to give Israel's policy its present repulsive and reactionary character. But Russian influence has also done something to warp Arab minds by feeding them with arid slogans, and encouraging demagogy, while Moscow's egoism and opportunism have fostered disillusionment and cynicism. If Middle East policy continues to be merely a plaything of the Great Powers, the prospect will be bleak indeed. Neither Jews nor Arabs will be able to break out of their vicious spirals. This is what we, of the Left, should be telling both the Arabs and the Jews as clearly and bluntly as we can.

The crisis clearly caught the Left by surprise and found it disoriented and divided, both here and in France, and, it seems, in the United States as well. In the States fears have bee expressed that the division over Israel might even split the movement against the war in Vietnam.

Yes, the confusion has been undeniable and widespread.I shall not speak here of such 'friends of Israel' as Messrs Mollet and his company, who like Lord Avon and Selwyn Lloyd, saw in this war a continuation of the Suez campaign and their revenge for their discomfiture in 1956. Nor shall I waste words on the right-wing Zionist lobby in the Labour Party. But even on the 'extreme Left' of that party men like Sidney Silverman behaved in a way as if designed to illustrate someone's saying: 'Scratch a Jewish left-winger and you find only a Zionist.'

But the confusion showed itself even further on the Left and affected people with an otherwise unimpeachable record of struggle against imperialism. A French writer known for his courageous stand against the wars in Algeria and Vietnam this time called for solidarity with Israel, declaring that if Israel's survival demanded American intervention, he would favour it and even raise the cry '*Vive le Président Johnson*'. Didn't it occur to him how incongruous it was to cry '*A bas Johnson!*' in Vietnam and '*Vive!*' in Israel? Jean-Paul Sartre also called, though with reservations, for solidarity with Israel, but then spoke frankly of the confusion in his own mind and its reasons. During the Second World War, he said, as a member of the Resistance he learned to look upon the Jew as upon a brother to be defended in all circumstances. During the Algerian war the Arabs were his brothers, and he stood by them. The present conflict was therefore for him a fratricidal struggle in which he was unable to exercise cool judgment and was overwhelmed by conflicting emotions.

Still, we must exercise our judgment and must not allow it to be clouded by emotions and memories, however deep or haunting. We should not allow even invocations of Auschwitz to blackmail us into supporting the wrong cause. I am speaking as a Marxist of Jewish origin, whose next-of-kin perished in Auschwitz and whose relatives live in Israel. To justify or condone Israel's wars against the Arabs is to render Israel a very bad service indeed and to harm its own long-term interest. Israel's security, let me repeat, was not enhanced by the wars of 1956 and 1967; it was undermined and compromised. The 'friends of Israel' have in fact abetted Israel in a ruinous course.

They have also, willy-nilly, abetted the reactionary mood that took hold of Israel during the crisis. It was only with disgust that I could watch on television the scenes from Israel in those days; the displays of the conquerors' pride and brutality; the outbursts of chauvinism; and the wild celebrations of the inglorious triumph, all contrasting sharply with the pictures of Arab suffering and desolation, the treks of Jordanian refugees and the bodies of Egyptian soldiers killed by thirst in the desert. I looked at the medieval figures of the rabbis and *khassidim* jumping with joy at the Wailing Wall; and I felt how the ghosts of Talmudic obscurantism – and I know these only too well – crowded in on the country, and how the reactionary atmosphere had grown dense and stifling. Then came the many interviews with General Dayan, the hero and saviour, with the political mind of a regimental sergeant-major, ranting about annexations and venting a raucous callousness about the fate of the Arabs in the conquered areas. ('What do they matter to me?' 'As far as I am concerned, they may stay or they may go.') Already wrapped in a phoney military legend – the legend is phoney for Dayan neither planned nor conducted the six days' campaign – he cut a rather sinister figure, suggesting the candidate to the dictator's post: the hint was conveyed that if the civilian parties get too 'soft' on the Arabs this new Joshua, this mini-de Gaulle, will teach them a lesson, himself take power, and raise Israel's 'glory' even higher. And behind Dayan there was Begin, minister and leader of the extreme right-wing Zionists, who had long claimed even Trans-Jordania as part of 'historic' Israel. A reactionary war inevitably breeds the heroes, the moods and the consequences in which its character and aims are faithfully mirrored.

On a deeper historical level the Jewish tragedy finds in Israel a dismal sequel. Israel's leaders exploit in self-justification, and over-exploit Auschwitz and Treblinka; but their actions mock the real meaning of the Jewish tragedy.

European Jews paid a horrible price for the role they had played in past ages, and not of their own choosing, as representatives of a market economy, of 'money', among peoples living in a natural, money-less, agricultural economy. They were the conspicuous carriers of early capitalism, traders and money lenders, in pre-capitalist society. As modern capitalism developed, their role in it, though still conspicuous, became less than secondary. In Eastern Europe the bulk of the Jewish people consisted of poverty-stricken artisans, small traders, proletarians, semi-proletarians and outright paupers. But the image of the rich Jewish merchant and usurer (the descendant also of Christ's crucifiers) lived on in Gentile folklore and remained engraved on the popular mind, stirring distrust and fear. The Nazis seized this image, magnified it to colossal dimensions, and constantly held it before the eyes of the masses.

August Bebel once said that antisemitism is the 'socialism of the fools'. There was plenty of that kind of 'socialism' about, and all too little of the genuine socialism, in the era of the Great Slump, and of the mass unemployment and mass despair of the 1930s. The European working classes were unable to overthrow the bourgeois order; but the hatred of capitalism was intense and widespread enough to force an outlet for itself and focus on a scapegoat. Among the lower middle classes, the lumpen-bourgeoisie, and the lumpenproletariat a frustrated anti-capitalism merged with fear of communism and neurotic xenophobia. These moods fed on crumbs of a mouldering historic reality which Nazism used to the utmost. The impact of Nazi Jew-baiting was so powerful in part because the image of the Jew as the alien and vicious 'blood-sucker' was to all too many people still an actuality. This accounted also for the relative indifference and the passivity with which so many non-Germans viewed the slaughter of the Jews. The socialism of the fools gleefully watched Shylock led to the gas chamber.

Israel promised not merely to give the survivors of the European-Jewish communities a 'National Home' but also to free them from the fatal stigma. This was the message of the *kibbutzim*, the Histadruth, and even of Zionism at large. The Jews were to cease to be unproductive elements, shopkeepers, economic and cultural interlopers, carriers of capitalism. They were to settle in 'their own land' as 'productive workers'.

Yet they now appear in the Middle East once again in the invidious role of agents not so much of their own, relatively feeble, capitalism, but of powerful Western vested interests and as protégés of neo-colonialism. This is how the Arab world sees them, not without reason. Once again they arouse bitter emotions and hatreds in their neighbours, in all those who have ever been or still are victims of imperialism What a fate it is for the Jewish people to be made to appear in this role! As agents of early capitalism they were still pioneers of progress in feudal society; as agents of the late, over-ripe, imperialist capitalism of our days, their role is altogether lamentable; and they are placed once again in the position of potential scapegoats. Is Jewish history to come full circle in such a way? This may well be the outcome of Israel's 'victories'; and of this Israel's real friends must warn it.

The Arabs, on the other hand, need to be put on guard against the socialism or the anti-imperialism of the fools. We trust that they will not succumb to it; and that they will learn from their defeat and recover to lay the foundations of a truly progressive, a socialist Middle East.

Index